ST. IRENAEUS OF LYONS

Against the Heresies

Ancient Christian Writers

THE WORKS OF THE FATHERS IN TRANSLATION

No. 72

ST. IRENAEUS OF LYONS: AGAINST THE HERESIES

Books 4 and 5

TRANSLATED AND ANNOTATED
BY
DOMINIC UNGER, OFM CAP,

WITH AN INTRODUCTION AND FURTHER REVISIONS
BY
SCOTT D. MORINGIELLO

THE NEWMAN PRESS
New York / Mahwah, NJ

Caseside design by Lynn Else
Book design by Lynn Else

Library of Congress Control Number: 2023938914

ISBN 978-0-8091-0626-4 (hardcover)
ISBN 978-1-58768-564-4 (e-book)

Published by The Newman Press
an imprint of Paulist Press
997 Macarthur Boulevard
Mahwah, New Jersey 07430

www.paulistpress.com

PRINTED AND BOUND IN THE UNITED STATES OF AMERICA

CONTENTS

LIST OF ABBREVIATIONS

A	Arundel codes
ACW	Ancient Christian Writers (New York/Mahwah, NJ)
Aldama, *Maria*	J. A. de Aldama, *Maria en la patrística siglos I y II* (Madrid, 1970)
ANF	Ante-Nicene Fathers (Buffalo, NY–New York, NY)
Bacq	Phillipe Bacq, *De l'ancienne à la nouvelle Alliance selon S. Irénée: unité du livre IV de l'Adversus haereses* (Paris, 1978)
BVK	Bibliothek der Kirchenväter (Kempten and Munich: J. Kösel, 1911–30)
Daniélou	J. Daniélou, "La typologie millenariste de la semaine dans le Christianisme primitif," VC 2 (1949): 1–16.
DSp	Dictionnaire de la spiritualité (Paris, 1937–)
FS	Franciscan Studies (St. Bonaventure, NY [n.s. 1945–])
González	J. I. González Faus, *Carne di Dios.* Significado salvador de la Encarnación en la teología de san Ireneo (Barcelona, 1969)
Grabe	The edition of the *Adversus haereses* by Joannes Ernestus Grabe (Oxford, 1702)
Harvey	W.W. Harvey (editor) *Sancti Irenaei episcopi Lugdunensis Libros quinque adversus haereses : textu graeco in locis nonnullis locupletate, versione latina cum codicubus claromontano ac arundeliano denuo collata, praemissa de placitis gnosticorum prolusione, fragmenta necnon graece, syriace, armeniace, commentatione perpetua et indicibus variis* (Cambridge, 1857)
Houssiau	A. Houssiau, *La Christologie de saint Irénée* (Louvain-Gembloux, 1955)

Joppich	G. Joppich, *Salus carnis. Eine Untersuchung in der Theologie des hl. Irenäus von Lyon* (Münsterschwarzacher Studien 1 [1964])
Jossa	G. Jossa, *Regno di Dio e Chiesa: Richerche sulla concezione escatologica ed ecclesiologica dell' "Adversus haereses" di Ireneo di Lione* (Naples, 1970)
Jossua	J. P. Jossua, *Le salut. Incarnation ou Mystére Pascal chez les Péres de l'Eglise, de S. Irénée á S. Leon le Grand* (Paris, 1968)
Lawson	J. Lawson, *The Biblical Theology of St. Irenaeus* (London, 1948)
Massuet	R. Massuet, *"Tou" en hagiois patros hēmōn Eirēnaiu episkopu Lugdunu kai martyros elenchu kai anatropēs tēspseudonymu gnōseōs biblia pente = Sancti Irenaei episcopi Lugdunensis et martyris detectionis et eversionis falso cognominatae agnitionis, seu contra haereses libri quinque : post Francisci Feuardentii et Joannis Ernesti Grabii recensionem castigati denuo ad mss. codices Romanos, Gallicanos et Anglicanos, necnon ad antiquiores editiones, et a multis, quibus scatebant, mendis expurgati; aucti novisfragmentis; observationibus ac notis copiosissimisque glossariis et indicubus illustrati et locupletati; quibus omnibuspraemittuntur, ejusque vitae ac ges orum historia discutitur* (Paris, 1857)
ME	*Maria et ecclesia. Acta Congressus Mariologici-Mariani in civitate Lourdes anno 1958 celebrati* (Rome, 1959)
Orbe	A. Orbe, *Teología de San Ireneo,: Comentario al libro 5 del Adversus Haereses.* 3 vols. Biblioteca de Autores Cristianos (Madrid, 1985-88)
Orbe, *Antrop.*	A. Orbe, *Antropología di S. Ireneo* (Madrid, 1969)
Orbe, *Greg.*	A. Orbe, "Ipse tuum calcabit caput (S. Ireneo y Gen. 3.15)," *Gregorianum* 52 (1971): 95–149; 215–69
Proof	St. Irenaeus, *Proof of the Apostolic Preaching* (ACW 16, 1952) tr. by J. P. Smith
RSR	Recherches de Science Religieuse
Stieren	The edition of the *Adversus haereses* by A. Stieren (Liepzig: T. O. Weigel, 1848–53)
Unger, FS	D. J. Unger, "Christ's Role in the Universe according to St. Irenaeus," *FS* 5 (1945): 3–20; 114–137

Unger, ME	D. J. Unger, "Sancti Irenaei, Lugdunensis Episcopi, doctrina de Maria Virgine Matre, socia Iesu Christi Filii sui ad opus recapitulationis," *ME* 4 (1959): 67–140
VC	*Vigiliae Christianae* (Amsterdam, 1947–)
Wingren	G. Wingren, *Man and the Incarnation, A Study in the Biblical Theology of Irenaeus*, tr. by R. Mackenzie (Philadelphia, 1959)

INTRODUCTION

Before a gathering of the Irenaeus Joint Orthodox-Catholic Working Group in the fall of 2021, Pope Francis announced his intention to declare St. Irenaeus of Lyons a Doctor of the Church with the title Doctor Unitatis, the Doctor of Unity. Recalling that Irenaeus's name contains the word *peace*, Pope Francis noted that Christian peace "reconciles" and "brings together in unity."[1] Francis's predecessor, Pope Benedict XVI, said in a weekly catechesis on the Fathers of the Church that Irenaeus emerged as "the first great theologian who created systematic theology; he himself speaks of the system of theology, that is of the internal coherence of all faith."[2] We can bring together the words of Popes Francis and Benedict. Thanks to Irenaeus, Christians can see the coherence and unity of their faith and how their faith unifies them with God and with one another. Irenaeus bridges another divide. These two popes remind us that Irenaeus is not simply an author whose works appeal to scholars of early Christianity. As Pope Benedict XVI notes, Irenaeus taught that there is "no superior Christianity for intellectuals." Instead, Irenaeus's vision stands for all Christians in all ages. "The faith publicly confessed by the Church is the common faith of all."[3] As such, the works of Irenaeus should be available to all—scholars and laypeople alike.

With this in mind, we are pleased to present this volume, which completes the translation of Irenaeus's magnum opus *Adversus Haereses*—Against the Heresies. Paulist Press published volume 1 of *Adversus Haereses* in 1992. This was translated and annotated by Dominic Unger, OFM Cap, with further revisions by John Dillon. Volumes 2 and 3 were published in 2012. Both were based on the work of Fr. Unger, whose untimely death meant that he could not complete the project. John Dillon revised volume 2 and Michael Slusser introduced it. Irenaeus Steenberg wrote the introduction for and revised the notes and translation of volume 3.[4] In this volume, I have updated Fr. Unger's work. Since he wrote, there has been particular emphasis in the scholarship on how Irenaeus has structured his arguments in *Adversus Haereses* and his deep theological, philosophical, and rhetorical sophistication.[5]

Scholars of early Christianity have come to understand that Irenaeus was not simply, or even primarily, a heresiologist. He is first and foremost an interpreter of the Scriptures who sought to explain the truth of Christianity by offering a comprehensive interpretation of the unifying message of the Christian Scriptures. He also makes an argument about what constitutes the Scriptures. He is the first voice of early Christianity to view the entire Christian drama, which is recounted in the old and new covenants and the continuing life of the Church. His contributions to the history of Christian theology are numerous, and in this introduction, I want to highlight four that bear directly on Books 4 and 5 of *Adversus Haereses.* These four are (1) the rule of faith, (2) *oikonomia,* (3) *anakephalaiosis,* and (4) the *homo vivens.* In order to fill out the picture of these themes, I also need to discuss the role of Scripture in Irenaeus, his cultural context, and his use of the word *gnostic.*

The Faith

Scholars often associate Irenaeus with the "rule of faith" or the "rule of truth." Irenaeus, however, does not use the term "rule of faith." Instead, he refers to "the faith."[6] He discusses this numerous times in *Adversus Haereses,* most importantly in Book 1, chapters 9–10 and chapter 22.[7] If you were to ask someone today what *faith* means, you'd likely get an answer about a private belief that does not rely on and might well be opposed to reason or evidence. Faith in this sense would likely be connected to feeling. Whatever the merits of this definition, it has little to do with Christianity and certainly nothing to do with Irenaeus. For Irenaeus, the faith is a threefold statement about God and God's relationship with creation. Irenaeus writes that the Church received from the apostles and their disciples "the faith in one God the Father Almighty...in one Jesus Christ, the Son of God, who was enfleshed for our salvation, and in one Holy Spirit" (1.10.1). Through the Prophets, the Holy Spirit "preached the Economies, the coming, the birth from a Virgin, the passion, the resurrection from the dead, and the bodily ascension into heaven of the beloved Son, Christ Jesus our Lord" (1.10.1). The Prophets declared, furthermore, that Christ will come "from heaven in the glory of the Father to recapitulate all things and to raise up all flesh of the whole human race" (1.10.1). We can say, then, that for Irenaeus, there are three points to the faith. The first is in the Father, Son, and Holy Spirit. The second is in the work of the Spirit in the old and new covenants. The third is in the redemptive work of Christ. You will notice there that the faith as Irenaeus states it provides an outline of the Scriptures. But it does more than this. By offering this outline, the faith provides a key to understand scriptural passages. The faith reminds the reader of Scripture that one and the same God creates and saves, that one and the same God works in the old and new covenants, that one and the same God is the God and Father of Jesus Christ, who is both God and man.

The faith of the Church provides a rule for understanding the Scriptures. But Irenaeus also discusses the faiths—and the rules—of his various opponents. He describes what they believe, how those beliefs influence the way they interpret the Scriptures, and ultimately how those beliefs are incoherent on their own terms. The first two books of *Adversus Haereses* lay out and refute his opponents' rules. Books 3, 4, and 5 lay out, describe, and are shaped by the rule that comes from the apostles. In Book 3, Irenaeus establishes the role the Church plays in proclaiming the faith in one God the Father, one Jesus Christ, and one Holy Spirit. Book 3 is thus an explication of the first point of the faith. In Book 4, Irenaeus shows how Christ fulfills the prophecies of the old covenant, how the old and new covenants form one *oikonomia* of God's salvation. We can align Book 4 with the second point of the faith. Likewise, we can align Book 5 with the third point of the faith. In Book 5, Irenaeus focuses on Christ's interpretation of Scripture an on Christ's just judgment. Thus, we can see how the faith shapes both the Scriptures *and* Irenaeus's argument about the Scriptures in *Adversus Haereses.*

Scripture in Irenaeus

For Irenaeus, the books that belong in the Scriptures are the books that conform to the rule of faith. In other words, the faith precedes the Scriptures, even as the faith provides the interpretative key to understanding the Scriptures. To be sure, Irenaeus did not have a physical Bible in the way we envision one today. Irenaeus would have read the Greek translation of the Hebrew Bible known as the Septuagint. He would have had a collection of writings that have come to be part of the New Testament.[8] The exact relationship between the books of the old covenant (in the Septuagint) and the writings of the new covenant (the gospels, epistles, and so forth) was part of a continuing debate. And a large part of that debate was what books belonged in the new covenant.

The fact that today people (with important exceptions) now think of the Bible as a single book that begins with Genesis and ends with Revelation shows that Irenaeus won the argument with his opponents on this point.[9] Not only do people think of Genesis and Revelation as belonging between the same covers, but they also believe that these books are part of the same story. Another way to say this is to say that, for Irenaeus, the Scriptures—the old and new covenants—form one economy (*oikonomia*) of God's creation and salvation. In order to say more about this, let us turn to Irenaeus's cultural context.

Irenaeus's Cultural Context

Like all of us, Irenaeus's education and cultural background deeply influenced how he understood Christianity. After all, he was not only a leader of a Christian community, but he was also an educated member of society. We should not find it surprising, then, that Irenaeus borrows terms from his cultural context to write about Christianity. We have already discussed the rule of faith. The word that gets translated into English as "rule" is the Greek word *kanon.* This word has specific philosophical and rhetorical connotations in Greek.[10] Today we use *canon* to describe a list of "approved" books. Besides *kanon,* Irenaeus borrows two words from that tradition and uses them to great effect in his theological treatise. These two words—*oikonomia* and *anakephalaiosis*—have both rhetorical and scriptural valences, and both are essential for understanding Irenaeus's argument in Books 4 and 5.

A passage from the Letter to the Ephesians can show us how Irenaeus would have been comfortable using "rhetorical" terms in his theological argument. In the first chapter of that epistle, we read: "In all wisdom and insight, he has made known to us the mystery of his will in accord with his favor that he set forth in him as a *plan* for the fulness of time, *to sum up* all things in Christ, in heaven and on earth" (Eph 1:8–10). The word for "plan" here is *oikonomia* and the world for "sum up" is *anakephalaiosis.* Thus, Irenaeus finds these rhetorical terms in Paul. For the rhetor, *oikonomia* is the arrangement of the speech after he has decided what points he will discuss. The word itself means the management of a household. In this sense the economy of God can be understood as God's rule over and care for creation.[11] The history of salvation is God's ordered *oikonomia,* the management of God's household. Christ, as the Word of God, is the speech through which God recapitulates all of creation, as the Word tells the history of the people of Israel. Irenaeus shows that the entire Scripture, from Genesis to Revelation, makes up the economy of God's creation and salvation. He also shows how Christ stands at the center of this economy. This is Irenaeus's task in Book 4. When the Scriptures are interpreted properly, they reveal that the Prophets spoke of Christ, and so the God of the old covenant is the same God and Father of Jesus Christ.

If we reread Ephesians 1:8–10 rhetorically and theologically, we can see that Christ is the *anakephalaiosis* of God's economy of salvation. The *anakephalaiosis* or *recapitulatio* is the final moment in a speech. The orator's task is to make clear the stakes of the decision before his audience. This is Irenaeus's task in Book 5. The stakes are nothing less than the salvation that comes through a life of faith that understands oneself as part of God's economy of salvation. If one follows the apostolic rule of faith, one becomes fully alive. We see this in the most famous line of *Adversus Haereses.*

Homo vivens

Adversus Haereses ultimately presents two visions of Scripture: the apostolic and the diabolical. The apostolic vision comes from the apostles and is carried on by Irenaeus. It presents the Scriptures as they ought to be interpreted. The diabolical vision comes from the rules of Irenaeus's opponents. Irenaeus underlines this comparison when he discusses Christ's temptation in Book 5, chapter 20. I use the word *vision* here purposely. The theme of vision is important for Irenaeus. It is a theme found both in the Scriptures he interprets and in the rhetorical tradition in which he was schooled.[12] Irenaeus's text paints a picture of what choices lay before his readers and what the consequences of those choices are. Ultimately, Irenaeus seeks to reveal the vision of God's economy of salvation that is recapitulated by Christ.

Any discussion of Books 4 and 5 ought to include something about Irenaeus's most famous dictum, *homo vivens gloria dei,* the living human being is the glory of God.[13] Part of the reason the line is so famous is that it seems to be able to apply to any number of contexts. But Irenaeus provides context for what he means immediately following. He writes, *vita hominis visio Dei*—the life of the human being is the vision of God. The question, then, is what the vision of God means. Irenaeus knows full well that God can be seen in Christ, but

Irenaeus's understanding of vision is broader than that. For Irenaeus, in order to behold the vision of God, one must understand properly the picture found in the Scriptures. In Book 4, Irenaeus argues that the old and new covenants refer to Christ and in Book 5, he shows the ramifications of the choice one makes in following that interpretation or not. Once one partakes of this vision, he is truly a living human being and the glory of God. The only proper response to beholding this vision is to praise God. Irenaeus wants to unify all people—make all people *homines viventes*—in the praise of God who created and saved them.

Thus, the *homo vivens* is the one to whom God has manifested the Word. And this human being can see God only because he has understood that the Scriptures recount the economy of God's salvation. Indeed, such an understanding *is* seeing God, which is simply another way to talk about human salvation. The story found in the economy of salvation is the story of preparing for the Lord's arrival. It is ultimately the story of understanding oneself in light of the economy of salvation. Irenaeus hopes to persuade his audience that God's economy—proclaimed in the law and the Prophets, lived in and through Christ, and taught by the apostles—makes them fully alive.

Overview of Books 4 and 5

With all of this in mind, let us turn to a general overview of both books. Remember that these books follow the outline of the faith as Irenaeus explains it. The first part of the faith is the belief in one Father, one Son, and one Holy Spirit. In chapters 1 through 19 of Book 4, Irenaeus shows how Jesus only speaks of one God and Father who was present in the old covenant and the new. The second part of the faith is the work of the Holy Spirit in the economy of salvation. In chapters 20 through 35 Irenaeus demonstrates how the old covenant prophesies the new. The third part of the faith is the redemptive work of Christ. In chapters 36 through 41, Irenaeus discusses Christ's parables and how they relate to judgment.[14] By showing the unity of the old and new covenants through the words of Christ, Irenaeus argues that the God of both covenants is one and the same. By showing how the old covenant prophesies the new, Irenaeus proves through the interpretation of Scripture the unity of God's *oikonomia* of creation and salvation. The parables Irenaeus discusses deal with the salvation of human beings. By showing how these parables ought to be understood in light of the old covenant, Irenaeus both recapitulates his argument about the unity of the Scriptures and reiterates how Christ himself recapitulates all things through his interpretation of the Scriptures.

We can divide Irenaeus's discussion in Book 5 into three major parts.[15] These parts also mirror the three major moments of the faith. In chapters 1 through 14, he focuses on an exegesis of Paul that proves the resurrection of the flesh. These chapters demonstrate the power and unity of God. In chapters 15 through 24, he shows how the unity of God the Creator and God the Father of Jesus Christ is shown in the life of Christ. In these chapters Irenaeus shows the unity of the God of the old and new covenants by explaining how Christ interprets the words of the Prophets in his life and teaching. In chapters 25 through 36, he shows how the unity of God the Creator and God the Father of Jesus Christ is portrayed through an exegesis of the Scriptures concerning the end times. These latter chapters, then, focus on Christ's work of recapitulation. In Book 5, Irenaeus wants to present as clearly as he can the choice that faces the reader of Scripture. Either the reader will follow the apostolic rule of faith that Irenaeus follows or the rules of Irenaeus's opponents. If the reader of Scripture does follow the interpretation based on the apostolic rule of faith, he will surely be the *homo vivens* who participates in the vision of God.

Gnosticism

Thus far in this introduction, I have consistently referred to "Irenaeus's opponents." I have not referred to "Gnostics" or "Gnosticism." I should spend a bit of time discussing why. Traditionally, Irenaeus's opponents were collectively known as the "Gnostics," who believed in a set of doctrines loosely called "Gnosticism." Gnosticism, so it seemed, taught that the creator god was different from the God and Father of Jesus Christ. Gnostics held that the material creation was bad, and that Jesus offered saving knowledge that led to freedom from the body and from creation as a whole. Only certain elect people could fully understand this teaching.

As thumbnail sketches go, this one is fine, and it certainly points to some beliefs that certain teachers held. We should note, though, that Irenaeus is quite careful to note which teachers and which teaching he is opposing at various points in his treatise. He rarely uses the word *gnostic*.[16] Instead, he refers to Ptolemy, Valentinus, Marcion, and a host of other specific teachers. Throughout the text, and especially in Books 1 and 2, Irenaeus lays out specific teaching and distinguishes it from other teaching. A careful reading of Irenaeus would show that he does not indulge in the sorts of generalizations some might claim he does. But I follow the tide of scholarship that largely avoids "Gnostic" and "Gnosticism" altogether.[17] I have modified Fr. Unger's notes to change "Gnostics" to "Irenaeus's opponents."

ST. IRENAEUS OF LYONS AGAINST THE HERESIES

Book 4[1]

Section 1

UNITY OF OLD AND NEW COVENANTS THROUGH WORDS OF CHRIST

PREFACE

1. My dear friend, we are sending you, as we promised, this fourth book of the work entitled THE EXPOSÉ AND REFUTATION OF THE FALSE KNOWLEDGE.[2] In it we shall confirm by the Lord's discourses what we have already said.[3] Then you, too, as you requested, will receive from us the means, from every source, for confounding the heretics, and when you have completely beaten them back, you will not allow them to continue longer in the "profundity"[4] of error or to drown in the sea of ignorance; rather, you will turn them back to the harbor of Truth and make them receive their salvation.[5]

2. Whoever wishes to convert them must, however, carefully know their systems.[6] Surely, it is not possible for one to heal those who are ill if one is ignorant of the ailment of the one who is ill. Wherefore those who lived before us, and were indeed better than we, were nevertheless not able satisfactorily to refute the followers of Valentinus, because they did not know their system, which we very carefully handed down to you in the First Book.[7] There, too, we have shown that their doctrine is a summary of all heretics. For that reason, in the Second Book,[8] we have used them as a mirror for the entire refutation, because whoever disproves these heretics as he ought disproves all who are evil-minded; and whoever refutes these refutes all heresy.

3. Really, their system is the most blasphemous of all, since they assert that the Creator and Maker who, as we have shown, is the one God, was emitted from the fall or degeneracy. Moreover, they blaspheme against Our Lord, too, cutting off and dividing Jesus from Christ, and Christ from Savior, and Savior, in turn, from Word, and Word from Only-begotten.[9] And just as they asserted that Maker was produced from Degeneracy, so they taught too that Christ and Spirit were produced for the sake of the Degeneracy, and that Savior is the fruit of the Aeons that were emitted from Degeneracy.[10] The result is that there is nothing among them that is not blasphemous. So, in the preceding Book we have shown what the doctrine of the apostles is in

regard to all these points. They not only did not hold anything of the kind—they who *from the beginning were eyewitnesses and ministers of the word* of Truth.[11] On the contrary, since through the Spirit they foresaw those who would mislead the more simple-minded,[12] they announced in advance that we should flee from such doctrines.[13]

4. Indeed, *as the serpent deceived Eve,*[14] promising her what he did not have, so these men, too, offer greater knowledge and unspeakable mysteries and promise a reception, as they assert, with the Fullness, but plunge them to death, since they make those who believe in them rebel from him who created them. Even at that time the rebel angel, by means of the serpent, brought about the disobedience of men and then thought he was hidden from the Lord. For that reason, God gave him the same shape and name.[15] Now, however, since these are the last times, evil is spread among men, which makes them not only apostates but also blasphemers of the Fashioner by means of many machinations, that is, through all the heretics who have been mentioned. All these, though they start out from different regions and teach different doctrines, agree in the same intention of blasphemy, by teaching blasphemy against God our Creator and Nourisher, and by denying salvation to man. Thus they inflict on men a deadly wound.

Humanity is, however, a mixture of soul and flesh who has been formed according to God's likeness[16] and fashioned by his hands, that is, by the Son and the Holy Spirit, to whom he also said, *Let us make man.*[17] So the intention of the one [the Devil] who envies our life[18] is to make men disbelieve their salvation, and to become blasphemers against God the Fashioner. For whatever all the heretics have said with the greatest solemnity ultimately comes to this: that they blaspheme the Maker and deny salvation to God's handiwork, that is, to flesh, on account of which God's Son made the entire Economy,[19] as we have shown in many ways. We have also made clear that no other is called God by the Scriptures except the Father of all, and the Son, and those who possess the adoption.[20]

Chapter 1
Proof That Our Lord Knew Only One God and Father

1. This, then, is certain and constant: No other God and Lord was announced by the Spirit in his own name than the God who has

dominion over all things together with his Word.[1] This is also certain and constant: those who believe in the one and true God and in Christ Jesus the Son of God receive the Spirit of adoption. Likewise, the apostles themselves did not call anyone else God or name anyone else Lord.[2] Even more so, Our Lord, who commanded us to confess no one as Father except the one who is in heaven,[3] who is the one God and the one Father, did not call anyone else Lord. Consequently, what these circumventors and most perverse sophists assert is manifestly shown to be false. They assert, namely, that what they thought up is in reality God and Father, but by name,[4] inasmuch as he has dominion over creation, as these perverse mythologists assert,[5] thinking up ideas against God as they do. Passing over the doctrine of Christ and of themselves divining false doctrines, they dispute against God's entire economy. For they assert that their Aeons are called gods and fathers, and lords, and even heavens, while their mother they call both earth and Jerusalem and give her many other names.[6]

2. Now, to whom is it not evident that if the Lord had known many fathers and gods, he would not have commanded his disciples to acknowledge one God and to call this same one alone Father? On the contrary, he distinguished[7] those who are gods only by name from him who is truly God, so that they might not mistake his doctrine, nor understand the one in place of the other. If he had commanded us to call one Father and God, whereas he himself would at times confess other fathers and gods in the same sense, he would appear to command one thing to his disciples while he himself would do something else. But such [manner of action] is not the part of a good teacher but of one who deceives and is envious. The apostles, too, according to these men, are shown to be transgressors of the rule, if this one is not the only God and Father, as we have demonstrated. And so Jesus, since he commanded one to be called Father, would be for them the author and teacher of transgression by imposing on them the necessity of confessing the Creator as his Father, as has been demonstrated.

Chapter 2

What Is Meant By: "I Praise You, Father, Lord of Heaven and Earth"?

1. Now, Moses made a summary of the whole Law, which he had received from the Creator. He spoke thus:[1] *Give ear, O heavens, and I*

will speak; and let the earth hear the words of my mouth. David said his help was from the Lord.[2] *My help comes from the Lord, who made heaven and earth.* Isaiah, too, confessed that words come from the God who made heaven and earth and rules over them:[3] *Hear, O heavens, and give ear, O earth; for the Lord has spoken.* And again,[4] *Thus says God the Lord who created the heavens and stretched them out, who spread forth the earth, and what comes from it; who gives breath to the people upon it and spirit to those who walk in it.*

2. Again, Our Lord Jesus Christ professes the same one as his Father when he says,[5] *I praise you, Father, Lord of heaven and earth.* What Father do these most perverse sophists of Pandora wish us to understand? Is it Profundity, whom they invented of themselves; or their mother, or Only-begotten? Or is it the god whom the Marcionites or the rest thought up? He really is not God, as we have shown in many ways. Or, as is true, is it the Maker of heaven and earth, whom also the Prophets preached, whom Christ, too, professes as his Father, whom in turn the Law announces when it says,[6] *Hear, O Israel: The Lord our God is one God.*

3. That the writings of Moses speak of Christ, he himself told the Jews, as John has recorded in the Gospel:[7] *If you believed Moses, you would believe me also, for he wrote of me. But if you do not believe his writings, neither will you believe my words.* He pointed out very clearly that the writings of Moses are his words. If, therefore, the words of Moses are his, without doubt, as we have demonstrated, those of the rest of the Prophets are his too. The Lord himself showed that Abraham said to the rich man concerning all those who were still alive,[8] *If they do not hear Moses and the Prophets, neither will they believe if someone should rise from the dead.*

4. Now, it is not a fable that is told us about a poor man and a rich man. No, he has taught us, first, that no one should indulge in pleasures; nor should one be a slave to his lusts and forget God by spending the time in worldly entertainments and in many banquets. *For there was a certain rich man,* he said,[9] *who was clothed in purple and fine linen and who feasted sumptuously every day.* Of such the Spirit, too, spoke through Isaiah:[10] *They drink wine to the accompaniment of harps and timbrels, lyres and flutes, but they do not regard the deeds of the Lord or see the works of his hands.* Lest we too, therefore, should incur the same punishment as these men, the Lord shows us their end, and at the same time he points out that if they were obedient to Moses and the Prophets, they would believe in him whom these had announced, God's Son,

who rose from the dead and bestows life on us. He shows, too, that all things, that is, Abraham and Moses and the Prophets, even *Christ* himself *who rose from the dead,*[11] are from one substance. In him even many who are of the circumcision believe, who listen to both Moses and the Prophets preaching the coming of God's Son. But these scoffingly assert that those men [of the Old Testament] are of another substance; neither do they acknowledge *the firstborn of the dead.*[12] They understand two distinct beings: Christ, who remained impassible, and Jesus, who suffered.[13]

5. Certainly, they do not receive from the Father the power to know the Son, nor do they learn of the Father from the Son, who clearly and without parables teaches about him who is truly God.[14] *Do not swear at all,* he said,[15] *either by heaven, for it is the throne of God, or by the earth, for it is his footstool, or by Jerusalem, for it is the city of the great King.* Surely, these things are said openly of the Maker, just as Isaiah said,[16] *Heaven is my throne and the earth is my footstool.* Besides this God there is no other. For then he would not be called God or great King by the Lord, because no one can be compared with or extolled about above such a one. To be sure, anyone who has someone superior to himself and is under someone's power can be called neither God nor great King.[17]

6. Nor can they assert that these words were spoken ironically, since they are convicted by the very words, which were spoken truthfully. He who spoke was Truth itself, and truly did he vindicate his house, casting out of it the money changers, who engaged in buying and selling. He said to them,[18] *It is written: my house shall be called a house of prayer; but you have made it a den of thieves.* Now, if he preached another God, what justification did he have to do and say this and to vindicate his house? [He did it] in order to show up the transgressors of his Father's Law. He did not bring an accusation against the house, nor did he rebuke the Law, which he *came to fulfill,*[19] but he did accuse those who did not make good use of the house and who transgressed the Law. And so [he accused] the Scribes and the Pharisees who since the days of the Law began to condemn God and did not receive his Word, that is, did not believe in Christ. Of them Isaiah said,[20] *The princes are rebels and companions of thieves. They love bribes and run after gifts. They do not defend the fatherless, and they do not attend to the widows' cause.* Jeremiah speaks in the same strain:[21] *They who rule my people know me not; they are senseless and stupid children, they are skilled in doing evil, but how to do good they know not.*

7. On the other hand, as many as feared God and were anxious about his Law ran to meet Christ and were all saved. He said to the disciples,[22] *Go rather to the lost sheep of the house of Israel.* Of the Samaritans, when the Lord sojourned among them for two days, it is said,[23] *Many more believed because of his word. They said to the woman, "It is no longer because of your words that we believe, for we have heard for ourselves and we know that this is indeed the Savior of the world."* Paul, too, said,[24] *And so all Israel will be saved.* Moreover, he called the Law our tutor toward Christ Jesus.[25] And so they did not ascribe the infidelity of certain ones to the Law, for the Law did not forbid them to believe in God's Son, but it even admonished them, saying[26] that men can be saved from the ancient wound of the serpent[27] in no other way except they believe in him who, in the likeness of sinful flesh,[28] is *exalted from the earth* on the tree of witness and *draws all things to* himself,[29] and *gives life* to the dead.[30]

Chapter 3

The True God Cannot Change or Cease.

1. These wicked men assert that if the heavens are God's throne and the earth is his footstool, since it is said that the heavens and the earth will pass away,[1] then when these things pass away, this God, too, who is enthroned on them, must pass away, and so he is not the God who is above all things. Now, first, they do not know what is meant by heaven as a throne and earth as a footstool, for they do not know what God is. They think that he sits down as men do and is contained within bounds but does not himself contain.[2] They are also ignorant of what is meant by the passing away of heaven and earth. Paul, however, was not ignorant of that. *For the form of this world is passing away,*[3] he said. David solves their question. In Psalm 101 he says that when this form passes away,[4] not only does God continue but also his servants. He put it thus:[5] *Of old you did lay the foundation of the earth, O Lord, and the heavens are the works of thy hands. They will perish, but you endure; they will all wear out like a garment. You change them like raiment, and they pass away; but you are the same, and your years have no end. The children of your servants shall dwell secure; their posterity shall be established forever.*[6] He clearly points out what things pass away and who it is that continues always, God together with his servants. Isaiah has similar words:[7] *Lift up your eyes to the heavens, and look at the earth beneath; for the heavens will vanish like*

smoke, the earth will wear out like a garment, and they who dwell in it will die in like manner; but my salvation will be forever, and my justice will not cease.

Chapter 4
The Destruction of Jerusalem, Ordered by God, Did Not Diminish Him.

1. Furthermore, they dare to say about the Lord and about Jerusalem that if it were the city of the great King,[1] it would not be forsaken.[2] The case would be similar were one to say, if straw is God's creation, it would never be forsaken by the grain; and the twigs of a vine, if they have been made by God, would never be cut off if devoid of clusters. Now these things are not primarily for their own sakes, but for the sake of the fruit that grows on them, and they are forsaken when this has ripened and has been removed, and those that can no longer be used for producing fruit are removed entirely.[3] The case of Jerusalem is similar. She bore in herself the yoke of servitude;[4] by it, man, who before was not submissive to God when death reigned,[5] was tamed, and having been tamed was made fit for liberty.[6] But when the fruit of liberty had arrived, it grew to maturity and was harvested and stored in the granary, and those who were able to produce fruit were carried away from her [Jerusalem] and disseminated over the entire world.[7] In reference to this Isaiah says,[8] *The sons of Jacob shall bud, and Israel shall blossom, and the entire earth shall be filled with its fruit.* For after the fruit had been disseminated over the entire earth, she who once produced such fruit was rightly forsaken and removed completely. It was Christ *according to the flesh*[9] who was produced from her as fruit, and the apostles too. But now she is no longer of any use for producing fruit. For whatever has a beginning in time must also have an end in time.

2. Since, then, the Law began with Moses, it was logical for it to cease with John, because Christ had come for its fulfillment.[10] That is why[11] *the Law and the prophets were with them until John.* Likewise, since Jerusalem began with David having fulfilled the time, it was necessary that its legislation come to an end when the new covenant was revealed. For God does all things with measure and order, and with him nothing is unmeasured, since nothing is unplanned.[12] The one spoke well who said that the unmeasurable Father was measured in the Son; for the Son is the measure of the Father, since he even comprehends him.[13]

But Isaiah says that their [Jerusalem's and the Law's] dispensation was temporal,[14] *And the daughter of Zion is left like a booth in a vineyard, and like a lodge in a cucumber field.* But when will these things be forsaken? Will it not be when the fruit is taken away and the leaves alone are left, which can no longer produce fruit?

3. Why do we speak of Jerusalem, since *the form of the* entire *world* must *pass away,*[15] when the time of its passing away comes, so that the fruit might be gathered into the granary, but the straw that was left be burned? *For behold, the day comes burning like an oven, and all the sinners and the evil-doers will be stubble; the day that comes shall burn them up.*[16] Now, John the Baptist points out who this Lord is that brings on such a day, when he says of Christ,[17] *He will baptize you with the Holy Spirit and with fire. His winnowing fork is in his hand, and he will clear his threshing floor and gather his wheat into the granary: but the chaff he will burn with unquenchable fire.* So it is not one who produces the wheat and another the straw, but one and the same; and he judges them, that is, separates them. Now the wheat and the straw are inanimate and irrational and were made such by nature. Man, however, is rational, and by virtue of this he is like God;[18] he was made free in his will and master of himself, and so has within himself the principle of sometimes becoming wheat, but sometimes straw. So he will be justly condemned, since, though he was made rational, he lost true reason, and living irrationally he opposed God's justice, giving himself up to every worldly spirit and serving all lusts, just as the prophet said:[19] *Man when he was in honor did not understand; he has been compared to senseless beasts, and made like to them.*

Chapter 5
The Law and the Prophets Proclaimed Only One God; Him, Too, Christ Acknowledged as His Father.

1. God, therefore, is one and the same, who rolls up the heavens as a book[1] and renews the face of the earth.[2] It is he who made temporal things for the sake of man, so that he might grow to maturity in them and produce the fruit of immortality.[3] It is he who because of his kindness bestows, in addition, the eternal things,[4] *that in the coming ages he might show the unsearchable riches of his kindness.* It is he who was preached by the Law and the Prophets. It is he whom Christ

acknowledged to be his Father. He is, moreover, the Maker; he is the God who is above all things, as Isaiah said,[5] *I am witness, says the Lord God, and the servant whom I have chosen, that you may know and believe and understand that I myself am. Before me there was no other God, and after me there will be none. I am the Lord, and there is no savior besides me. I have declared and have saved.* And again,[6] *I am God, the first and I will be for ever.* He does not say this ambiguously or proudly or by way of boasting. But, because it was impossible to learn about God without God, he teaches people to know God through his Word.[7] So, to those who are ignorant of these things and therefore think they have discovered another Father, one can rightly say,[8] *you are wrong because you know neither the Scriptures nor the power of God.*

2. In truth, Our Lord and Teacher, in the answer he gave to the Sadducees who say there is no resurrection, thus dishonoring God and discrediting the Law, both proved there is a resurrection and revealed God. *You are wrong,* he said to them,[9] *because you know neither the Scriptures nor the power of God. And as for the resurrection of the dead,* he continued, *have you not read what was said by God, I am the God of Abraham, and the God of Isaac, and the God of Jacob?* And he added, *he is not the God of the dead but of the living, for all men live for him.* By these words he certainly made it clear that he who spoke from the bush to Moses and manifested that he is the God of the Fathers,[10] he is *the God of the living.* Really, who is *the God of the living* unless he who is [truly] God and above whom there is no other God? Him also the Prophet Daniel announced, when King Cyrus of the Persians asked for him,[11] *Why do you not worship Bal?* by saying, *Because I do not revere man made idols, but the living God who created heaven and earth, and has dominion over all flesh.* And again he said,[12] *I worship the Lord my God, for he is the living God.*

The one, therefore, who was worshipped by the Prophets as the living God, *he is the God of the living.* It is his Lord, too, who spoke to Moses and who refuted the Sadducees and who bestowed the gift of the resurrection, pointing out both things to those who are blind, that is, the resurrection and God. For if *he is the God not of the dead but of the living,* yet was called the God of the Fathers who were sleeping, undoubtedly they *are Living for God* and have not perished, since *they are children of the resurrection.*[13] Now, Our Lord himself is the resurrection, as he said,[14] *I am the resurrection and the life.* But the Fathers are his children; for it was said by the Prophet,[15] *In place of your fathers your sons were born.* So Christ himself, together with the Father, is *the God of the living,* who spoke to Moses and who also was manifested to the Fathers.[16]

3. While teaching this very doctrine, he said to the Jews,[17] *Your father Abraham rejoiced that he was to see my day; he saw it and was glad.* Why? *Abraham believed God, and it was reckoned to him as righteousness.*[18] First, because he is the *Maker of heaven and earth, the only God;*[19]second, because he will make his [Abraham's] descendants like the stars of heaven.[20] This is what Paul says,[21] *Like lights in the world.* Rightly, then, leaving behind all his earthly kin, he followed the Word of God. he travelled as a pilgrim with the Word that he might dwell as a citizen with the Word.[22]

4. Rightly, moreover, did the apostles, who descended from Abraham, leave behind the boat and their father and follow the Word of God.[23] Rightly do we too, since we receive the same faith that Abraham had, take up our cross as Isaac did the wood and follow him.[24] For in Abraham man learned his first lesson and became accustomed to follow the Word of God. Abraham by virtue of his faith carried out the precept of the Word of God and readily offered his only-begotten and beloved son as a sacrifice to God, so that God in turn might have the good pleasure of offering his beloved and Only-begotten Son for his [Abraham's] entire offspring as a sacrifice for our redemption.[25]

5. Since, therefore, Abraham was a prophet and saw in the Spirit the day of the Lord's coming and the economy of his passion, through whom[26] he himself and all who believe in God, just as he believed, will be saved, he rejoiced exceedingly. The Lord, then, was not unknown to Abraham, since he desired to see his days. Nor was the Father of the Lord, for he (Abraham) learned from the Word of the Lord, and he believed in him. For this reason it was also reckoned to him by the Lord as justice. For it is faith in God that justifies man, and for this reason he [Abraham] said, *I lift up my hand to God the Most High, Maker of heaven and earth.*[27] But the evil-minded try to overthrow all these things, because of one saying which was not understood correctly by them.[28]

Chapter 6

What Is the Meaning of "No One Knows the Father Except the Son," and on What Occasions Did the Son Reveal the Father?

1. To explain, when the Lord manifested himself to the disciples as the Word who makes known the Father and rebuked the Jews who

thought that they possessed God, though they even set aside the Word through whom God is known, he said,[1] *No one knows the Son except the Father, nor does anyone know the Father except the Son, and any one to whom the Son chooses to reveal.* Both Matthew and Luke wrote the same thing, and Mark did too.[2] John passed up this passage. Now these men[3] who wish to be wiser than the apostles write it thus, *No one knew the Father except the Son, nor the Son except the Father, and any one to whom the Son chooses to reveal*; namely, they interpret it as if the true God had not been known by anyone before our Lord's coming.[4] They assert, too, that the God who was heralded by the Prophets is not the Father of Christ.

2. Now, if Christ began to exist only when he came as man, and if [only] from the time of Tiberius Caesar the Father had been mindful of providing for men, and if it were shown that his Word was not always with his handiwork, not even then was it necessary to preach another god but to investigate the reasons for so great carelessness and neglect. For there should be no such question, one that would grow to such proportions as even to change God and destroy our faith in the Maker who nourishes us by means of his creation. For just as we direct our faith toward the Son, so too we ought to have a firm and unchangeable love toward the Father. Well does Justin say in his book *Against Marcion*:[5] "I would not have believed the Lord himself, if he had announced any other than our Maker and Creator and Nourisher. But since the Only-begotten Son came to us from the one God who made this world and fashioned us, and contains and administers all things—thus recapitulating in himself his own handiwork—my faith towards him is firm, and my love toward the Father is unchangeable, since God grants us both."

3. For neither can anyone know the Father, unless through the Word of God, that is, unless the Son reveals; nor the Son, unless through the good pleasure of the Father. But the Son fulfills the good pleasure of the Father;[6] for the Father does the sending, but the Son is sent and comes. The Word of the Father himself, on the one hand, knows the Father who, as far as we are concerned, is invisible; and since he is ineffable, the Son declares him to us.[7] On the other hand, the Father alone knows his Word. That both of these are so, the Lord revealed to us. For this reason the Son reveals the knowledge of the Father by the manifestation of himself, because the manifestation of the Son is the knowledge of the Father, since all things are manifested by the Word. In order, therefore, that we might know that the Son

who came is the one who brings the knowledge of the Father to those who believe in him, he said to the disciples:[8] *No one knows the Son except the Father, nor the Father except the Son, and to whomever the Son reveals.* Thereby he taught himself and the Father what he is,[9] that we might not accept any other Father except the one who is revealed by the Son.

4. But this (Father) is the Maker of heaven and earth, as is shown from his [the Lord's] words; he is not a false Father who was thought up by Marcion or Valentinus or Basilides or Carpocrates or Simon, or the rest of the falsely called Gnostics.[10] To be sure, none of these was God's Son, but Christ Jesus Our Lord is, against whom they level their contrary teaching by daring to preach an unknown God. But they ought to hear it said against themselves: How is he unknown if he is known by them? For whatever is known by even a few is not unknown! The Lord, however, did not say that the Father and the Son could not be known at all; for then his coming would have been useless. For why did he come hither? Was it perhaps to tell us, "Don't look for God, he is unknown; you will not find him," as the disciples of Valentinus falsely assert that Christ said to their Aeons?[11] But what a vain assertion! The Lord taught us that no one can know God unless God teaches him; that is, without God, God cannot be known; on the other hand, [the Lord taught] that it is the Father's will that God should be known. For those to whom the Son reveals him know him.[12]

5. For this purpose the Father revealed the Son, that through him he [Father] might be manifested to all and might receive into imperishability and eternal rest the just who believe in him. Now, to believe in him is to do his will. But he will justly shut up in the darkness those who do not believe and so shun his light and of their own accord choose the darkness.[13] The Father, therefore, has revealed himself to all by making his Word visible to all; and, in turn, the Word, since he may be seen by all, has shown the Father and the Son to all. And so the just judgment of God will be upon all who in like manner saw but did not believe in like manner.

6. It is by creation itself that the Word reveals God the Creator; and by the world, the Lord and Maker of the world; and by the handiwork, the Artificer who fashioned it;[14] and by the Son, the Father who begot the Son. All speak of these things in the same manner, but all do not believe them in the same manner. The Word, moreover, announced himself and the Father in like manner through the Law and the Prophets, and all the people heard in like manner; but not all believed in like manner. Besides, through the Word himself, when he

had become visible and tangible, the Father was manifested, although all did not in like manner believe in him; but all saw the Father in the Son.[15] For the Father is whatever is invisible of the Son, while the Son is whatever is visible of the Father.[16] For this reason, when he was present, all addressed him as Christ and named him God. Why, even the demons, on seeing the Son, said,[17] *We know who you are, Holy One of God.* The Devil, too, when he saw him and tempted him, said,[18] *If you are the Son of God.* So, all saw and spoke of the Son and of the Father, but not all believed.

7. Indeed, it was necessary that Truth should receive testimony from all and be a judgment for salvation for believers but for condemnation for disbelievers, that all might be judged justly. [It was necessary,] moreover, that faith in the Father and the Son be witnessed to by all,[19] that is, be strengthened by all by receiving testimony from all—from those of the household [of the faith] because they are friends, and from foreigners[20] because they are enemies. Really, the true and incontrovertible test is that which bears the seals of testimony from even the enemies.[21] For they had been convinced of the present matter by a clear vision of him, both testifying to him and pointing him out. Later, however, they broke out into enmity and made accusations and held that their own testimony is not true.

There was, therefore, not one who was known and another who said, *No one knows the Father*, but one and the same, to whom the Father has made all things subject.[22] And he receives testimony from all, that he is truly man and truly God from the Father, from the Spirit, from the angels, from creation itself, from men, from the rebel spirits, from the demons, even from the Enemy, and last of all from death itself.[23] The Son, however, administering all things for the Father,[24] works from the beginning even to the end. Without him no one can know God. For the Son is the knowledge of the Father, but the knowledge of the Son is in the Father, and it has been revealed through the Son.[25] For this reason the Lord said,[26] *No one knows the Son except the Father; nor does anyone know the Father except the Son, and anyone to whom the Son may reveal.* "May reveal" was not said only for the future, as if the Word began to manifest the Father then when he was born of Mary; it was meant in general for all time. For the Son, being present with his handiwork from the beginning, reveals the Father to all to whom the Father wills and when he wills and how he wills. And so *in all things and through all things* there is *one God the Father,*[27] and one Word, and one Spirit, and one salvation for all who believe in him.

Chapter 7
How Abraham Was Taught by the Word

1. Hence, Abraham, too, having known through the Word the Father *who made heaven and earth,*[1] acknowledged him to be God. When he had learned by the apparition that God's Son would become Man among men, through whose coming his posterity would become *as the stars of heaven,*[2] he longed *to see that day,* so that he too might embrace Christ; and when *he saw* him by means of the Spirit of prophecy, *he was glad.*[3] For this reason, Simeon, too, who was a descendant of his, brought the joy of the Patriarch to a climax and said:[4] *Lord, now let your servant depart in peace, according to your word; for my eyes have seen your salvation, which you have prepared in the presence of all peoples, a light for revelation to the Gentiles, and for glory to the people Israel.* Even angels announced great joy to the shepherds who were keeping watch.[5] Mary, moreover, said:[6] *My soul magnifies the Lord, and my spirit rejoices in God my Savior.* Thus Abraham's exultation descended upon those of his posterity who were awaiting Christ and saw him and believed in him.[7] But the exultation was reciprocal; it returned from the children to Abraham, who had longed to see the day of Christ's coming. Well, then, did Our Lord testify in his regard. *Your Father Abraham rejoiced,* he said,[8] *that he might see my day, he saw it and was glad.*

2. He said this not only because of Abraham, but to show that all who from the beginning had knowledge of God and prophesied Christ's coming received the revelation from the Son himself. This Son in these last times became visible and touchable[9] and spoke with the human race, so that from the stones he might raise up children to Abraham and might fulfill the promise that God had made to him [Abraham], and might make his posterity *as the stars of heaven.*[10] John the Baptist said as much,[11] *For God is able from these stones to raise up children to Abraham.* Jesus did that when he drew us away from the religion of stones[12] and transferred us from the hard and unfruitful ideas,[13] and established in us a faith like Abraham's. Paul likewise testified, saying that we are Abraham's children by virtue of the similarity of faith and the promise of the inheritance.[14]

3. So there is one and the same God who called Abraham and gave him the promise.[15] And he is the Maker who through Christ prepares *the lights of the world,*[16] those believers from among the Gentiles. He says,[17] *You are the light of the world;* that is, you are stars of heaven. Rightly, therefore, have we shown that this One is known by no one

except the Son, and by those to whomever the Son may reveal. Now the Son reveals to all those by whom the Father wills to be known; so neither does anyone know God without the Father's good pleasure, nor without the Son's administration. For this reason, the Lord said to the disciples,[18] *I am the way, and the truth, and the life; no one comes to the Father, but by me. If you had known me, you would have known the Father also; henceforth you know him and you have seen him.* From those passages it is evident that he [God] is known through the Son, that is, through the Word.

4. Consequently, the Jews apostatized from God by not receiving his Word but thinking they can know the Father by himself without the Word, that is, without the Son. They were ignorant of the One who spoke in human form to Abraham[19] and who also said to Moses,[20] *I have seen the affliction of my people in Egypt and I have come down to deliver them.* These things, in fact, the Son, who is the Word of God, performed from the beginning in advance, and the Father did not need the angels for making the creation and fashioning man, for whose sake even the creation was made. Nor was he in need of any service for giving form to the things that have been made, and for ordering man's affairs.[21] No, he had a rich and ineffable service, because his Offspring and his Pattern,[22] that is, the Son and the Spirit, the Word and the Wisdom,[23] minister to him in all his affairs—they whom all the angels serve and to whom they are subject.[24] So those are foolish who because of the saying, *No one knows the Father except the Son,* introduce another, an unknown Father.

Chapter 8
How Christ Fulfilled the Promise God Made to Abraham

1. Foolish, too, are both Marcion and his disciples for excluding Abraham from the inheritance,[1] to whom the Spirit by many prophets and now also by Paul gave testimony that he *believed God, and it was reckoned to him as righteousness.*[2] The Lord in turn bore witness to him; first by raising up children from the stones, and then by making his posterity *as the stars of heaven.*[3] He said,[4] *And men will come from east and west, from north and south to sit at table with Abraham, Isaac, and Jacob in the kingdom of heaven.* Again, he said to the Jews,[5] *When you see Abraham and*

Isaac and Jacob and all the prophets in the kingdom of God, and you yourselves thrust out. So it is evident that those who deny salvation to Abraham, and fashion another god besides the one who made the promise to him, are outside God's kingdom and are disinherited from imperishability, because they set God as naught and blaspheme him who through Christ Jesus brought into the kingdom of heaven Abraham and his posterity, which is the Church, to which, through Christ Jesus, are given both the adoption and the inheritance promised to Abraham.[6]

2. As a matter of fact, the Lord vindicated Abraham's posterity and loosed it from bondage and called it to salvation. By way of example, he made clear in the case of the woman whom he healed and said to those who do not have a faith like Abraham's,[7] *You hypocrites! Does not each one of you on the sabbath untie his ox or his ass, and lead it away to water? And ought not this woman, a daughter of Abraham whom Satan bound for eighteen years, be loosed from this bond on the Sabbath day?* So it is evident that those who believed in him as Abraham did, he loosed and gave life, though he did nothing contrary to the Law by healing on the sabbath.

Really, the Law did not forbid people to be healed on the sabbath. It was even wont to circumcise[8] them on that day,[9] and ordered the priests to perform functions on behalf of the people. Why, it did not forbid even the healing of mute animals. [The pool] Siloam, too, often effected cures on the sabbath days;[10] for that reason many sat around it on the sabbath days. The Law, indeed, commanded them to abstain from servile work, that is, from all avarice, which is aroused by business and by other worldly practices.[11] On the other hand, it exhorted them to engage in deeds of the soul, which are carried out by the mind and by good words for the benefit of neighbors. For this reason, the Lord rebuked those who unjustly reproached him for healing on the sabbath. The fact is, he did *not break the Law but fulfilled it*[12] by performing the works of the High Priest,[13] namely, by appeasing God on behalf of men, and cleansing lepers, healing the sick, and himself dying that man who had been exiled[14] might leave the condemnation and fearlessly return to his inheritance.[15]

3. Nor did the Law forbid those who were hungry to take food that was on hand on the sabbaths. It did, however, forbid reaping and gathering into the granary. And so the Lord said to those who blamed the disciples when *they plucked the ears of grain and ate:*[16] *Have you not read what David did when he was hungry, he and those who were with him? How they entered the house of God, and took and ate the bread of the Presence,*

which it is not lawful for any but the priests to eat, and also gave it to those with him? Thus he excused his disciples by the words of the Law, and pointed out that it was licit for the priests to act freely. Now David was recognized by God as a priest,[17] even though Saul persecuted him. For all the just possess a priestly rank.[18] All the apostles of the Lord are priests who here below do not inherit fields or houses but always serve the altar and God. Of these Moses, too, spoke in Deuteronomy when blessing Levi,[19] *Who said of his father and of his mother, "I regard them not"; he disowned his brothers and ignored his children. For he observed thy precepts, and kept thy covenant.* But who are they who have left father and mother and have bidden farewell to all neighbors for the sake of the Word of God and his covenant, except the disciples of the Lord? Again, Moses says of them,[20] *They shall have no inheritance. For the Lord himself shall be their inheritance.* And again,[21] *The Levitical priests, that is, all the tribe of Levi, shall have no portion or inheritance with Israel, the offerings to the Lord are their inheritance, these they shall eat.* As so Paul on his part says,[22] *Not that I seek the gift, but I seek the fruit.* He means, since the Lord's disciples possessed the Levitical inheritance, it was lawful for them when hungry to take food from the grains; *for the laborer deserves his food.*[23] Likewise, *the priests profaned the sabbath in the temple, and still were not blameworthy.*[24] And why were they not blameworthy? Because while they were in the temple they did not perform worldly functions, but those of the Lord. Thus they fulfilled the Law. They did not transgress it; as, for example, the one who of his own accord brought dry wood into the camps of God and was justly stoned.[25] *Every tree therefore that does not bear good fruit is cut down and thrown into the fire.*[26] And,[27] *If anyone destroys God's temple, God will destroy him.*

Chapter 9
Both Covenants Have Only One Author and One Purpose.

1. All things,[1] therefore, are from one and the same substance, namely, from one and the same God, as the Lord for his part said to the disciples,[2] *therefore, every scribe who has been trained for the kingdom of heaven is like a householder who brings out of his treasure what is new and what is old.* He did not teach that one God brought out the old things and another the new; but he was one and the same. For the Lord is the

householder who has dominion over the Father's entire home, giving a suitable law to the slaves and those uninstructed;[3] but to the free men and those justified through faith he gives suitable precepts, and to the children he opens up the inheritance.[4] Now it was his disciples whom he called scribes and teachers of the kingdom of heaven. Of them, too, he said,[5] *Therefore I send you wise men and scribes and teachers, some of whom you will kill and persecute from town to town.* Thus, then, the new and the old that are brought out from the storeroom, he, without contradicting himself, calls the two covenants. The old covenant he shows to be the previous Law; the new, the mode of life that is according to the Gospel.

Of this David said,[6] *O sing to the Lord a new song.* And Isaiah,[7] *Sing to the Lord a new song. The beginning is his. Let them give glory to his name from the top of the earth; let them declare his powers in the coastlands.* And Jeremiah says,[8] *Behold I will make a new covenant not like the covenant which I made with your fathers on mount Horeb.* But one and the same householder made both covenants, the Word of God, Our Lord Jesus Christ who spoke with both Abraham and Moses, who restored liberty to us in the newness and made the grace which is from himself abound.[9]

2. *Something greater than the temple is here,* he said.[10] But "greater" and "less" are not said about things that have nothing in common and are of opposite natures and mutually repugnant, but of things that are of the same substance and have something in common but differ only in quantity and size. For example, water from water, light from light, and grace from grace. So the law that was given for liberty is greater than that which was given for servitude.[11] It is therefore diffused not on one nation but in the whole world. One and the same Lord, however, who is greater than the temple and greater than Solomon and greater than Jonah,[12] gives gifts to man, namely, his own presence and the resurrection from the dead. But he does not change God, nor proclaim another Father, but one and the same who always has more gifts to measure out to those of his household; and who gives more and greater gifts in the measure in which their love toward him grows. The Lord said as much to his disciples,[13] *You shall see greater things than these.* Paul, too, said,[14] *Not that I have already obtained this, or am already justified, or am already perfect.* For[15] *we know in part and we prophesy in part; but when the perfect comes, the imperfect will pass away.*

So when what is perfect will come, we shall not see a different Father but the same one whom we now long to see; *Blessed are the pure in heart for they shall see God.*[16] Nor shall we await a different Christ and

Son of God from the one who was born of the Virgin Mary, who suffered, in whom we believe, and whom we love. What Isaiah said is to the point,[17] *And they will say in that day: Lo, this is our God; we have waited for him, and we have rejoiced in our salvation.* Peter, too, wrote in his letter,[18] *without having seen him you love him; though you do not now see him you believe in him and rejoice with unutterable joy.* Nor shall we receive a different Holy Spirit from the one who is with us, and who *cries out, Abba, Father.*[19] In these [Divine Persons] we shall receive the increase and make progress so that we shall no longer enjoy God's blessings through a mirror and by means of enigmas, but face-to-face.[20] Thus, though even now we receive something greater than the temple or than Solomon, namely, the presence of God's Son; nevertheless, we have not learned of another God besides the Maker and Creator of all things, who has been manifested to us from the beginning; nor another Christ, God's Son, besides the one heralded by the Prophets.

3. Since the new covenant was known and announced by the Prophets, he too was heralded who would make it according to the Father's good pleasure.[21] He was manifested to men just as God willed, in order that by believing in him they might always make progress, and might through the covenants make progress toward the perfection of salvation.[22] For there is one salvation and one God, but the precepts that fashion man are many, and not a few the steps that lead man to God. It is lawful for an earthly and temporal king who is but a man sometimes to give greater advancements to his subjects. Now, should that not be permitted to God, since he is the same and always wills to bestow greater grace on the human race, and continuously to honor with many gifts those who please him?

If it would be an advancement to think up another god besides the one who was announced from the beginning, and to think up a third one besides this second one who is thought to have been found, then it will be the same kind of advancement to go from the third one to a fourth, and from this to another. Now, if such a thinking considers itself always making progress, it would never come to a standstill in one God.[23] Truly, when he has been expelled by the one who exists and has turned his back on him, he will seek forever, but never find God.[24] On the contrary, it will always swim in the depth of incomprehensibility,[25] unless he converts through repentance, and having returned whence he had been expelled, he confesses and believes the one God the Father to be the Creator who was announced by the Law and the Prophets and was testified to by Christ.

This Christ said to those who accused his disciples of not keeping the tradition:[26] *Why do you transgress the commandments of God for the sake of your tradition? For God commanded: "Honor your father and your mother"; and "He who speaks evil of father and mother, let him surely die."* A second time he said, *so, for the sake of your tradition you have made void the word of God.* Most clearly does Christ confess as Father and God him who said in the Law,[27] *Honor your father and your mother that it may be well with you.* For the truthful God professed that the precept of the Law was the word of God, and called no one else God except his Father.

Chapter 10

The Same God Inspired the Old and the New Testaments. The Old Foretold the Son's Coming and His Passion.

1. Well, then, does John, too, recall that the Lord said to the Jews,[1] *You search the Scriptures, because you think that in them you have eternal life; and it is they that bear witness to me, yet you refuse to come to me that you may have life.* How, therefore, could the Scriptures testify to him unless they were of one and the same Father, instructing people in advance[2] about his Son's coming and announcing in advance the salvation which is from him?[3] *For if you believed in Moses, you would believe in me also, for he wrote of me.* [This is true] in the sense that God's Son was implanted everywhere in the Scriptures.[4] At one time he speaks with Abraham when about to eat with him,[5] at another time with Noah, giving him the measurements [for the ark];[6] at another time, he is looking for Adam;[7] at another time he punishes the Sodomites;[8] then, too, he appears to Jacob and directs him on his journey;[9] next he speaks with Moses from the bush.[10] One cannot count the number of times that God's Son is manifested by Moses. He was not ignorant of the day of his passion and announced this in advance typically, when speaking of the Pasch. Indeed, on the very same [day] that was foretold by Moses so long before, the Lord suffered and so fulfilled the Pasch.[11] He described not only the day but also the place and the end of the times and the sign of the setting sun. He said,[12] *You may not offer the Passover sacrifice (Pascha) within any of your towns, which the Lord your God gives you: but in the space which the Lord your God will choose, to make*

his name dwell in it; there you shall offer the Passover sacrifice (Pascha) in the evening at the going down of the sun.

2. His coming, too, he had already manifested when he said,[13] *The scepter shall not depart from Judah, nor the mace from between his feet until he to whom (the scepter) belongs comes; and he is the hope of the peoples. Binding his foal to the vine, and his ass's colt to the choice vine. He will wash his garments in wine, and his vesture in the blood of the grapes. His eyes will be joyful from wine, and his teeth whiter than milk.* Let those, then, who are rumored as examining everything inquire at what time the ruler and leader ceased in Judah, and who is the hope of the peoples, and who the vine, and who his colt and what his garment, and which the eyes, and what the wine. Let them examine all statements and they will find that no other than Our Lord Jesus was announced. For this reason Moses rebuked the people for being ungrateful. He said,[14] *Do you thus requite the Lord, you foolish and senseless people?* Again, he pointed out that the Word who created and made them in the beginning is shown hanging on a tree, in these last times, redeeming us and giving us life, yet they do not believe in him. For he said,[15] *Your life shall hang before you and you shall not trust your life*; and again,[16] *Is not he your father, who created you, and made you, and established you?*

Chapter 11

In the Old Testament There Was Development in Revelation through the Word.

1. The Lord has made it clear that it was not only the Prophets, but also many righteous men who through the Spirit foreknew his coming and prayed that they might reach the time when they would see their Lord face-to-face and hear his discourses. To the disciples he said,[1] *Many prophets and righteous men longed to see what you see, and did not see it, and to hear what you hear, and did not hear it.* How, then, did they long both to hear and to see unless they had foreknowledge of his future coming? And how could they foreknow that unless they had received the foreknowledge from him? And how do the Scriptures testify concerning him unless all things have always been revealed through the Word by one and the same God and manifested to those who believe? For at one time he speaks with his handiwork, at another time he gives the Law, at another time he reproves, at still another

time he exhorts, and finally he frees the slave and adopts him as son, and at the proper time bestows the inheritance of imperishability for the perfection of man.[2] Indeed he fashioned him that he might grow and flourish, as Scripture says,[3] *Be fruitful and multiply.*

2. Further, God differs from man in this, that God makes, but man is made. And he who makes is always the same, but he who is made must receive a beginning and a middle, a growing and maturing.[4] God, again, gives benefits; man receives benefits. God is perfect in every respect, being equal and similar to himself, since he is all light and all mind and all substance and the fount of all good.[5] But man makes progress toward God and receives an increase. In fact, just as God is always the same, so man is found in God[6] and always makes progress toward God. For neither does God ever cease bestowing gifts on man and enriching him, nor does man cease receiving gifts and being enriched by God. Really, man who is grateful to him who made him is the receptacle of his goodness and the product of his glory; on the contrary, the ungrateful man and one who spurns the Fashioner and is not subject to his Word is the receptacle of his just judgment. He [Word] has promised to give a greater amount to those who always bear fruit and who, having the Lord's silver piece, multiply it. He said,[7] *Well done, good and faithful servant; you have been faithful over a little, I will set you over much; enter into the joy of your master.* By this the Lord himself promised the greater amount.

3. So then, just as the Lord promised to those who at present bear fruit to give them the greater amount, according to the gift of his grace but not according to a change of knowledge,[8] since the Lord remains the same, and the same Father is revealed; in like manner, through his coming, one and the same Lord bestows a greater gift of grace on those who come later than on those who lived under the old covenant. In fact, those, too, heard, through the servants, that the King would come, and so rejoiced moderately, in keeping with their hope that he would come. Those, however, who saw him present, and have won freedom and are in possession of his gift, have the greater grace and the more abundant joy, since they rejoice over the King's presence,[9] as also David says,[10] *But my soul shall rejoice in the Lord, and shall be delighted in his salvation.* For this reason, too, when he entered Jerusalem, all who were along the way, who, like David, had a strong desire in their soul,[11] recognized their King, spread their garments for him, and decorated the street with green branches, and cried out with great joy and exultation:[12] *Hosanna to the Son of David! Blessed is*

he who comes in the name of the Lord! Hosanna in the highest! But there were the envious and wicked stewards who circumvented their inferiors and dominated those who had changeable minds,[13] and so wished that their King had not come. They said to him,[14] *Did you not hear what these are saying?* The Lord gave this answer, *Yes, have you never read, "Out of the mouth of babes and sucklings you have brought perfect praise?"* Thus he showed that what had been predicted of God's Son by David was fulfilled in himself; namely, he pointed out that those men did not know the power of Scripture or the economy of God,[15] and that he who was announced by the Prophets is Christ, whose name is praised in all the earth, since he *brings perfect praise out of the mouth of babes and sucklings for his Father. That is why his majesty is elevated above the heavens.*[16]

4. If, therefore, the same one, Our Lord Jesus Christ, is present who was heralded by the Prophets, and if his coming bestows the fuller grace and the greater gift on those who accepted him, it is evident that the Father, too, is the same one who was proclaimed by the Prophets, and that the Son at his coming did not bring the knowledge of another Father but of the same one who was heralded from the beginning. From him, too, the Son brought liberty for those who rightfully and readily and wholeheartedly serve him. On the contrary, there are the scoffers and those who are not submissive to God but for the sake of praise from men observe outward purifications—which were handed down as types of future things, as if the Law sketched some shadow and delineated the eternal by the temporal, the heavenly by the earthly[17]—they imagined that they observed more than was prescribed, as though they were more diligent than God himself,[18] whereas within they were full of hypocrisy and of covetousness, and of every malice.[19] For those he brought eternal perdition, cutting them off from life.

Chapter 12

The Agreement of the Laws in the Old and the New Covenants Proves the Identity of God in Both.

1. In point of fact, the tradition of the elders, which they pretended to observe as part of the Law, was contrary to the Law given by Moses. On this account Isaiah, too, said,[1] *Your dealers mix the wine with water.* Thus he showed that the elders mixed with God's severe

precept the watered-down tradition, that is, they set up a spurious law, one contrary to the Law.[2] This the Lord made clear when he said to them,[3] *Why do you transgress the commandment of God because of your tradition?*[4] But they not only set at naught God's Law by transgression, mixing wine with water; they also set up, in opposition to it, their law, which even now is called Pharisaical.[5] In it they remove some precepts but add others, and others still they interpret as they please. These precepts their teachers especially employ.[6] Since they wished to defend them as traditions, they refused to submit to God's Law, which instructs them about Christ's coming.[7] Why, they blamed the Lord when he healed on the Sabbath, which, as we have said, the Law did not forbid. Really, they themselves, in a certain sense, heal on the Sabbath by circumcising on the Sabbath.[8] But they did not rebuke themselves for transgressing God's precept by the tradition and the Pharisaical law mentioned, and for not keeping the precept[9] of the Law, that is, the love for God.[10]

2. The Lord taught us that that is the first and greatest commandment, and that the next is the one toward our neighbor, when he said that the entire Law and the Prophets depend on these commandments.[11] He himself did not bring a greater commandment than this; no, he renewed this very one, ordering his disciples to love God with their whole heart and others as themselves. Now if he had descended from some other father, he would never have adopted from the Law the first and greatest commandment, but would certainly have striven by every means to refer this greater commandment to the perfect Father, and not use the one given by the God of the Law.[12] Paul, moreover, said,[13] *Love is the fulfilling of the Law*; and that, when all things have been abolished, *faith, hope and love abide, but that the greatest of these is love*;[14] and that knowledge without love toward God is worthless, so are also the knowledge of mysteries and faith and prophecy—all are, without love, meaningless and futile,[15] whereas love perfects the perfect man; and that the man who loves God is perfect in this world and in the future. In truth, we will never cease to love God; rather, the more we will see him, so much the more will we love him.[16]

3. So, just as in the Law and in the Gospel the first and the greatest commandment is to love the Lord God from our whole heart, and after that, one similar to it, to love one's neighbor as oneself, so the Author of the Law and of the Gospel is shown to be one and the same. To be sure, since the commandments of the perfect life are the same in both covenants, they manifest the same Lord who prescribed

particular precepts suitable to each covenant, but for the more excellent commandments, even the best, without which one cannot be saved, he ordered the same ones in both [covenants].

4. Now, the Lord does not confound (this God) by showing that the Law is from another God, when he says as follows to the crowds and the disciples whom he used to teach:[17] *The Scribes and the Pharisees sit on Moses' seat; so practice and observe all things whatever they tell you; but not what they do; for they preach but do not practice. They bind heavy sacks and lay them on men's shoulders; but they themselves will not move them with their finger.* So he did not blame the Law given by Moses, which he exhorted to be kept, while Jerusalem was still intact. But he did rebuke those who, though they proclaim the words of the Law, are devoid of love,[18] and for this reason were unjust toward God and their neighbor. As Isaiah said,[19] *This people honors me with their lips, while their hearts are far from me. In vain do they worship me, teaching doctrines and precepts of men.* The Law given by Moses he did not call "precepts of men" but the traditions that the priests themselves fabricated and that they defended, and so set at naught God's Law and were, in consequence, not subject to his Word. In fact, that is what Paul said concerning them,[20] *Being ignorant of the righteousness that comes from God, and seeking to establish their own righteousness, they did not submit to God's righteousness. For Christ is the end of the Law, that everyone who has faith may be justified.* And how is Christ the end of the Law if he is not also its beginning? For he who brought on the end is the same one who wrought the beginning. He it is who says to Moses,[21] *I have seen the affliction of my people who are in Egypt, and I am come down to deliver them.* So the Word of God was accustomed from the beginning to ascend and descend for the sake of the salvation of those who were ill.

5. That the Law taught man in advance that he must follow Christ, he himself made clear to the one who asked him what he must do to inherit eternal life. He answered,[22] *If you would enter life, keep the commandments.* And when he asked,[23] *Which?* Our Lord said, *You shall not commit adultery; you shall not kill; you shall not steal; you shall not bear false witness; honor your father and mother; and you shall love your neighbor as yourself.* Thus to those who wish to follow him, he proposed the commandments as steps for entering life. He addressed these points to one, but he meant them for all. The man, however, said,[24] *All these I have observed.* But perhaps he had not, since it would not have been said to him, *Keep the commandments.* So the Lord, exposing his avarice, said to him,[25] *If you would be perfect, go, sell your possessions, and divide*

them among the poor and come, follow me. To them, then, who would do this, he promised the portion of the apostles. He did not announce to those who would follow him a God the Father different from the one who had been announced from the beginning by the Law, nor another Son, nor mother, the Intention of the Aeon that was in suffering and in degeneracy, nor the Fullness of thirty Aeons, which was shown to be empty and unstable, nor a fable that was invented by other heretics.[26] No, he taught them to keep the commandments that God ordered from the beginning, and to do away with their former avarice by good works, and to follow Christ. Zacchaeus made it clear that one does away with the past avarice when one divides his possessions among the poor. He said,[27] *Behold, one half of my possessions I give to the poor; and if I have defrauded anyone of anything, I restore it fourfold.*

CHAPTER 13
CHRIST REMOVED THE BONDAGE OF THE OLD LAW, WITHOUT ABROGATING ITS NATURAL PRECEPTS, TO FREE MEN FOR SERVING GOD AS CHILDREN.

1. The Lord did not abrogate the natural precepts of the Law by which man was justified <and> that those who were justified by faith and pleased God observed also before the giving of the Law.[1] Rather, he set an example for it and fulfilled it. One can show this from his own words:[2] *For it was said to men of old, he said, "You shall not commit adultery." But I say to you that every one who looks at a woman lustfully has already committed adultery with her in his heart.* And again,[3] *It was said, "You shall not kill!" But I say to you that everyone who is angry with his brother without cause, shall be liable to judgment.* And,[4] *It was said, "You shall not swear falsely." But I say to you, Do not swear at all; But let your speech be, "Yes, yes; No, no!"* And many other such statements. Now, all these statements do not contain an opposition to or an abrogation of the past [commandments], as the followers of Marcion loudly shout, but a fulfillment and an amplification, as Christ himself said,[5] *Unless your righteousness exceeds that of the scribes and Pharisees, you will never enter the kingdom of heaven.* What was this "exceeds"? First, not merely to believe in the Father, but also in the Son who was already revealed; for he is the one who leads man into communion and union with God. Second, not merely to talk, but also to do. These men were wont to talk but did nothing.[6] And not merely

to abstain from wicked works, but also from the desire of them. Now, he was not teaching these things as opposed to the Law but as fulfilling the Law, and as implanting in us the justification of the Law. It would have been contrary to the Law, if he had commanded his disciples to do what the Law had forbidden. To command them not only not to abstain from the works forbidden by the Law but also from the desire of them is not opposed to it, as we have said. Nor is it the part of one who abrogates the Law, but of one who fulfills and extends it.

2. For the Law, set up as it was for slaves, instructed the soul by corporeal means[7] that were extrinsic to the soul, and as if by a chain drew it on to obedience of the commandments, so that man might learn to serve God.[8] The Word, however, freed the soul and taught that through it the body must be cleansed willingly.[9] When this happened, it was necessary to take off the bonds of servitude to which man had already become accustomed and to follow God without bonds; moreover, to extend the laws of liberty and to increase submissiveness to the King, so that no one should turn back and appear unworthy of him who freed him. Now reverence and obedience toward the householder is the same for servants as for children; but the children have greater confidence, because the energy of liberty is greater and more glorious than the obedience rendered in servitude.

3. For this reason, too, instead of, *You shall not commit adultery*, the Lord commanded us not to have lustful desires; and instead of *You shall not kill*, not even to get angry,[10] and instead of giving tithes, to give all things to the poor;[11] and to love not merely the neighbors but also the enemies;[12] and not merely to be generous givers and benefactors, he says, but also to forgive gratuitously those who take away what belongs to us. And[13] *from him who takes away your cloak do not withhold your coat as well, and of him who takes away your goods, do not ask them again. And as you wish that men would do to you, do so to them.* The effect should be that we should not be saddened as those who are unwilling to be robbed, but may rejoice as those who give willingly, rather bestowing a favor upon neighbors than constrained by need. *And if any one, he says,*[14] *forces you to go one mile, go with him two.* For so you do not follow as a slave but may lead as a free man and offer yourself as helpful and useful to your neighbor in all things, not having regard to their evil, but perfecting your goodness, making yourself like to the Father, who[15] *makes his sun rise on the evil and the good, and sends rain on the just and the unjust.*

Now all these laws, as we have said, are not the part of one who abrogates the Law, but of one who fulfills and extends it among us. That is as if one would say that the greater energy of liberty has implanted in us a fuller submissiveness and affection for the liberator. To be sure, he did not free us in order that we might depart from him—for no one who is set outside the reach of the Lord's goods can acquire for himself the nourishment of salvation—but that we might love him more, having obtained more grace. And the more we love him, the greater the glory we will receive from him when we are always in the Father's presence.

4. Since, therefore, all the natural precepts are common to us and to them [of the Old Law], they had in those the beginning and origin, but in us they have growth and the extension. To assent to God and follow his Word, and to love him above all things, and one's neighbor as oneself—man is man's neighbor[16]—and to abstain from all evil activity, and whatever other [precepts] are common to both [covenants], manifest one and the same God. And this is Our Lord, the Word of God, who first drew the servants to God, but afterward freed those who were submissive to him, as he himself tells his disciple:[17] *No longer do I call you servants, for the servant does not know what his master is doing. But I have called you friends, for all that I have heard from my Father I have made known to you.* Now when he says, *No longer do I call you servants,* he very clearly points out that he is the one who first established for men the servitude toward God through the Law and afterward granted them liberty. When he says, *for the servant does not know what the master is doing,* he manifests by his coming the ignorance of the slave people. When he calls his disciples God's *friends,* he clearly shows that he is the Word of God whom also Abraham, having become *God's friend,*[18] followed willingly, not with bonds, in the generosity of his faith. But the Word of God did not acquire the friendship with Abraham because of a need [on his part],[19] perfect as he was from the beginning; rather, inasmuch as he is good, he gave eternal life to Abraham, because God's friendship bestows imperishability on those who strive for it.[20]

Chapter 14
God, Who Has No Need of Man, Graciously Bestows His Favors on Him.

1. Neither,[1] therefore, did God in the beginning form Adam as if he were in need, but that he might have someone on whom to

confer his benefits. Certainly, not only before Adam's time but even before the entire creation, the Word was wont to glorify his Father, remaining in him; he in turn was glorified by the Father, as he tells us,[2] *Father, glorify thou me with the glory which I had with thee before the world was made.* Nor did he command us to follow him because he needed our service, but to grant us salvation. To follow the Savior means to partake of salvation. To follow the Light means to receive light; those, however, who are in the light do not themselves enlighten the light <and make it resplendent> but are enlightened and made resplendent by it.[3] They bestow nothing upon it, but they receive the benefit of being enlightened by the light. Just so the service toward God bestows nothing upon God, nor does God need human service; on the contrary, he grants life, imperishability, and eternal glory to those who follow and serve him. He bestows a benefit on those who serve him, precisely because they serve him; and on those who follow him, precisely because they follow him. He, however, receives no benefit from them, for he is rich, perfect, without any need. God, nevertheless, demands service of men,[4] in order that, since he is good and merciful, he might bestow a benefit on those who persevere in his service. For, as God is in want of nothing, so man is in need of fellowship with God. Really, man's glory is this: to persevere and remain in God's service. For this reason, the Lord said to the disciples,[5] *You did not choose me, but I chose you.* He pointed out that they have not glorified him by following him, but they are glorified by him because they follow God's Son. And again,[6] *I desire that they also, whom thou hast given me may be with me where I am, to behold my glory.* He was not boasting vainly about this, but he wished to share his glory with his disciples. Of that Isaiah said,[7] *I will bring your offspring from the east; and from the west I will gather you; I will say to the north, "Bring here"; and to the south, "Do not hold back"; bring my sons from afar, and my daughters from the end of the earth, everyone who is called by my name. For my glory I have created and formed and made him.* [He said] this, because *wherever the body is, there the eagles will be gathered together.*[8] Thus we share in the glory of the Lord, who fashioned us and prepared us that as long as we are with him we might share in his glory.

2. In like manner, in the beginning God fashioned man with a view to giving gifts; next he chose the Patriarchs with a view to their salvation; then he formed the people in advance, teaching the uneducated people to follow God; then he prepared the Prophets

on the earth, thus accustoming man to carry his Spirit and to have communion with God.[9] He himself has need of no one. However, he bestows communion on those who have need of him. And as an architect he sketches the work of salvation for those who pleased him. By himself he furnishes guidance to those who did not see him in Egypt, while for those who became unruly in the desert he laid down a very apt law. To those who entered the good land, he gave a worthy inheritance. For those who converted to the Father he killed *a fatted calf* and put on *the best robe.*[10] So by many ways he brought the human race into harmony for the symphony of salvation.[11] With this in view, John says in the Apocalypse,[12] *And his voice was like the sound of many waters.* Really, the waters of God's spirit are many,[13] because the Father is rich and bountiful.[14] In addition, the Word passed through all those ways and bestowed without envy a benefit on those who were subject to him, writing for each creature an appropriate and apt law.

3. In the same manner, he decreed for the people by law the making of the tabernacle, the building of the temple, the election of the Levites, the sacrifices and the offerings, the purifications,[15] and all the rest of the ministry. He has no need of any of these things, since he is always full of all good things, of every odor of sweetness, having in himself all the perfumes of sweet-smelling odors, even before Moses existed. Moreover, he instructed his people who easily turned to the idols, teaching them in advance by many callings that they persevere in serving God. Thus he called the people by the things of secondary importance to things of primary importance, that is, by types to realities; by temporal things to eternal things; by bodily things to spiritual things; by earthly to heavenly, as was said to Moses,[16] *Make it after the pattern, which was shown you on the mountain.* Because for forty days he learned to hold fast God's words and the heavenly patterns, and the spiritual images and the types of things to come. Paul said as much,[17] *They drank from the rock that followed them, and the rock was Christ.* Again, having spoken of the things in the Law, he continued,[18] *Now all these things happened to them as a type, but they were written for our instruction; upon whom the end of the ages has come.* So it was through types that they learned to fear God and to persevere in his service.[19]

CHAPTER 15
THE PURPOSE OF THE NATURAL AND OF THE MOSAIC LAWS

1. So then, the Law was both a training for them and a prophecy about future things.[1] To explain, at first God admonished them by the natural precepts that he had given and implanted in men from the Beginning; that is, by the Decalogue.—If any one does not observe it, he does not have salvation.—He demanded nothing more of them. As Moses said in Deuteronomy,[2] *These words the Lord spoke to all your assembly at the mountain, and he added no more. And he wrote them upon two tables of stone, and gave them to me, in order that those who wished to follow him might observe the commandments.*

However, when they had turned to making a calf, and with their minds returned to Egypt, desiring to be slaves in place of free men, they received the rest of the servitude suitable to their desire, which did not cut them off from God but did subdue them by the yoke of servitude. That is what Ezekiel the Prophet said when giving the reasons for making such a law:[3] *and their eyes were set on the desire of their heart. Moreover, I gave them statutes that were not good, and ordinances by which they could not have life.* And Luke wrote that Stephen,[4] the first of the deacons chosen by the apostles and the first to be put to death on account of testimony to Christ, spoke as follows about Moses:[5] *He received living oracles to give to us. But your fathers refused to obey him, but thrust him aside, and in their hearts they turned to Egypt, saying to Aaron, "Make for us gods to go before us; as for this Moses who led us out from the land of Egypt, we do not know what has become of him." And they made a calf in those days and offered sacrifice to the idol and rejoiced in the works of their hands. But God turned and gave them over to worship the host of heaven, as it is written in the book of the Prophets: "Did you offer to me slain beasts and sacrifices, for forty years in the wilderness, O house of Israel? And you took up the tent of Moloch, and the star of the god of Rephan, the figures which you made to worship."* He points out plainly that such a law, which was not given by another God but by the same God, was suitable to their servitude. Wherefore, Moses says in Exodus,[6] *And I will send an angel before you; but I will not go up among you for you are a stiff-necked people.*

2. But that is not all. The Lord revealed that certain commandments were given to them by Moses because of their hardness of heart, and because they refused to be submissive:[7] *Why then did Moses*

command one to give a certificate of divorce, and to put her away? He said to them, "For the hardness of your heart, he permitted these things but from the beginning it was not so." He thus excused Moses as *a faithful servant,*[8] and he professed the one God who made man and woman in the beginning, but he rebuked them for being stubborn and for not being submissive. Because of this they received from Moses the commandment of divorce suitable to their stubbornness.

But why say these things about the old covenant, when even in the new covenant the apostles are found to do the same thing for the reason mentioned? Paul says directly,[9] *It is I who say these things, not the Lord*; and again,[10] *But I say this by way of concession, not of command; and* again,[11] *Now concerning virgins I have no commandment of the Lord, but I give my opinion, as one who by the Lord's mercy is trustworthy*. Moreover, in another place he says,[12] *Lest Satan tempt you through lack of self-control.* If, therefore, even in the new covenant the apostles are found making concessions by certain precepts because of the lack of self-control of some, lest such persons become stubborn and despair of salvation completely and become apostates from God, we must not wonder if also in the old covenant the same God wished to have something similar for the benefit of the people, leading them on by the ordinances mentioned, that they might swallow the saving hook of the Decalogue and be held fast by it,[13] and might not return to idolatry, nor become apostates from God, but might learn to love him with all their hearts.

Now if any one, because of the disobedience of the Israelites and because of those who have been lost, should assert that the Law is weak, he will find that in our own calling, *many are called but few are chosen;*[14] and that some are wolves inwardly but outwardly they are clothed with sheep skins.[15] [They will also find] that God has always guarded both the free will and autonomy in man, and his admonitions, so that those who do not obey him would be justly judged precisely because they had not obeyed him; and that those who do obey him and believe in him would be crowned with imperishability.[16]

Chapter 16

Justification Was Never Effected by Circumcision. Christ Did Not Abrogate the Decalogue.

1. From Scripture itself, moreover, we learn that circumcision was not given by God to effect perfection of holiness, but as a sign that the race of Abraham might continue to be recognized, as we learn from Scripture itself, which says,[1] *God said to Abraham, "Every male among you shall be circumcised. You shall circumcise in the flesh of your foreskin, and it shall be a sign of the covenant between me and you."* The Prophet Ezekiel said the same about the sabbaths,[2] *I gave them also my sabbaths, as a sign between me and them, that they might know that I the Lord sanctify them.* And in Exodus God said to Moses,[3] *You shall keep my sabbath, for this is a sign between me and you throughout your generations.* So these things were given as signs. But the signs were not without symbolic meaning, that is, without significance or useless, since they were given by a wise artist. Now, circumcision according to the flesh looked forward to circumcision according to the spirit. *For,* as the Apostle says,[4] *we have been circumcised with a circumcision made without hands.* And the Prophet said,[5] *Circumcise the hardness of your heart.*

The sabbaths, however, taught that the service toward God was to last through the whole day.[6] *For we were regarded,* the Apostle Paul says,[7] *all the day long as sheep to be slaughtered*; that is, we have been consecrated, and we are in the service of our faith all the time and persevere in it; and we abstain from all avarice,[8] neither acquiring nor possessing treasures on earth.[9] [The sabbath] was pointed out as God's rest from the things that had been made, that is, the kingdom[10] in which man who perseveres in serving God will rest and partake of God's table.

2. Further, that man was not justified by these things, but that they were given as signs for the people is shown by the fact that Abraham, without circumcision and without the observance of the sabbaths, *believed in God and it was reckoned to him as righteousness, and he was called the friend of God.*[11] Lot, too, without having been circumcised was led out of Sodom and obtained salvation from God.[12] Noah, likewise, who was pleasing to God, was not circumcised, still he received the measurements [of the ark] for the world of the second race [of men].[13] Enoch, too, being pleasing to God without circumcision, functioned as ambassador to the angels, though he was a man, and *was*

transferred [to heaven] and is preserved until now as a witness of God's just judgment, because the angels who had transgressed fell to earth as a punishment, but the man who was pleasing [to God] was transferred to salvation.[14] Moreover, all the rest of the multitude of the righteous before Abraham, and of the Patriarchs who lived before Moses, were justified without the things mentioned and without the Law of Moses, Moses himself said this to the people in Deuteronomy,[15] *The Lord our God made a covenant with us in Horeb. Not with your fathers did he make the covenant but with you.*

3. Why, then, did the Lord not make a covenant for the Patriarchs? Because the Law is not laid down for the just.[16] Now, the just Patriarchs had the power of the Decalogue written in their hearts and souls; namely, they loved God who made them and abstained from injustice toward their neighbors. Consequently, it was not necessary for them to be admonished by corrective written [laws], because they had within themselves the justice of the Law.[17] But when, in Egypt, this justice and the love for God had gone into oblivion and became extinct, God, because of his great benevolence toward men, necessarily revealed himself with a living voice and led the people out of Egypt with power,[18] so that man might again become God's disciple and follower. And he afflicted the disobedient that they might not contemn him who created them, and he nourished them with manna that they might receive the spiritual food, as Moses says in Deuteronomy,[19] *He fed you with manna, which your fathers did not know, that you might know that man does not live by bread alone but by every thing of God that proceeds out of his mouth.* It also commanded love toward God and insisted on justice toward one's neighbor, so that man might not be unjust to and unworthy of God. God prepared man by the Decalogue for friendship with himself and for concord with his neighbor. These things were useful for man, but God was in need of nothing from man.

4. It is for this reason that Scripture says,[20] *These words the Lord spoke to all the assembly of the sons of Israel at the mountain, and he added no more.* For as we have said, he needed nothing from them. Then, too, Moses said,[21] *And now Israel, what does the Lord your God require of you but to fear the Lord your God, to walk in all his ways, to love him, and to serve the Lord your God, with all your heart and with all your soul?* Now these things made man glorious, supplying what was wanting to him, namely, God's friendship. But they profited God nothing. God, really, did not need man's love. But God's glory was lacking to man,[22] which he could not acquire in any other way than by obedience to God. And so Moses

again said to them,[23] *Choose life, that you and your descendants may live, loving the Lord your God, obeying his voice, and cleaving to him; for that means life to you, and length of days.* For the sake of preparing man for that life, the Lord by himself spoke the words of the Decalogue to all alike.[24] And so they equally remain among us, having been extended and strengthened, but not abolished, by his coming in the flesh.[25]

5. But the commandments for servitude were given separately to the people by Moses. They were suitable for their disciplining, as Moses himself said,[26] *And the Lord commanded me at that time to teach you the statutes and ordinances.* So these commandments that had been given to them for servitude and [were given] as a sign, he abrogated by the new covenant. But the commandments that are the natural and free and general laws of all people he strengthened. Moreover, by adoption he generously gave to men without envy, to know God the Father and to love him with his whole heart, and to follow his Word without deviating, not only by abstaining from evil actions, but also from desiring them.[27] But he also strengthened the fear, for the children must fear more than the servants, and must have greater love toward their Father.[28] For this reason the Lord said,[29] *On the day of judgment men will give an account for every careless word*; and,[30] *Everyone who looks at a woman lustfully has already committed adultery with her in his heart*; and,[31] *Everyone who is angry with his brother without cause shall be liable to judgment.* This he said that we might know that we will give an account to God not only of our deeds as servants, but also of our words and thoughts, as those who have received the power of liberty, in which man is tested all the more about whether he will reverence and fear and love the Lord.[32] Peter, too, said,[33] *without using your freedom as a pretext for evil,* but for testing and manifesting the faith.[34]

Chapter 17

God Did Not Ordain the Levitical Ministry for His Own Benefit.

1. Moreover, the Prophets most fully indicate that God did not need their ministry, but for their sake commanded some observances in the Law. Again, the Lord manifestly taught that God does not need the offering of men, but he [ordained] them on account of man who makes the offering, as we will show. For when Samuel saw them

neglect justice and abstain from the love of God, and they thought that God ought to be appeased by sacrifices and the rest of the typical observances, he spoke to them as follows:[1] *God does not desire burnt offerings and sacrifices, but he desires that his voice be obeyed. Behold, a good ear is better than sacrifice, and to hearken is better than the fat of rams.* David on his part said,[2] *Sacrifices and offerings you did not desire; but you have given me an open ear. Burnt offering and sin offering you have not required.*[3] Thus he taught them that God desires obedience which will save them, rather than sacrifices and burnt offerings, which are of no value to them for justice.[4] At the same time he prophesied the new covenant. But more clearly still he speaks about these things in Psalm Fifty,[5] *For if you had desired sacrifice I would indeed have given it; were I to give a burnt offering you would not be appeased. A sacrifice to God is a broken spirit; a broken and contrite heart the Lord will not despise.* That God does not have need of anything, he expressed in the preceding Psalm:[6] *I will accept no bull from your house, nor he-goat from your folds. For every beast of the forest is mine; the cattle on the hills, and the oxen. I know all the birds of the air; and the beauty of the field is mine. If I were hungry, I would not tell you for the world and all that is in it is mine. Do I eat the flesh of bulls, or drink the blood of goats?*

Then lest someone think that he repudiated these things because he was angry, he continues by way of giving counsel to him:[7] *Offer to God a sacrifice of praise, and pay your vows to the Most High, and call upon me in the day of trouble, I will deliver you, and you shall glorify me.* By this he repudiated the things by which sinners thought God was appeased and he shows that he has need of nothing. He does, however, exhort and advises about the things by which man is justified and draws near to God.

Isaiah makes the same statement:[8] *To what purpose do you offer me the multitude of your sacrifices? says the Lord.* And when he had repudiated the burnt offerings, sacrifices, offerings, as well as the new moons, feast days, the sabbaths, the festivals, and the rest of the services accompanying these observances, he continued exhorting them about the things that pertain to salvation:[9] *Wash yourselves, make yourselves clean, remove the evil of your doings from before my eyes. Cease to do evil, learn to do good, seek justice, save the oppressed, defend the fatherless, plead for the widow; and then come, let us reason together, says the Lord.*

2. He did not repudiate their sacrifices as an angry man would; no, he had pity on their blindness and suggested the true sacrifice, by the offering of which they would appease God, that they might receive life from him. As is said elsewhere,[10] *A broken heart is a sacrifice to God. A*

heart that glorifies its Maker is a sweet fragrance to God. For, if because of his anger he had repudiated their sacrifices, as if they were unworthy of receiving his mercy, he would certainly not admonish these same ones about the things through which they could be saved. But because God is merciful, he does not cut them off from his good counsel. In point of fact, it was through Jeremiah that he said,[11] *To what purpose do you bring me frankincense from Sheba, the sweet cane from a distant land? Your burnt offerings and sacrifices do not please me.* He continued,[12] *Hear the word of the Lord, all you men of Judah. Thus says the Lord, the God of Israel: "Amend your ways and your doings, and I will let you dwell in this place. Do not trust in deceptive words—because in no way will these be of profit to you—saying: 'The temple of the Lord, the temple of the Lord.'"*

3. Again, in order to point out that he led them out of Egypt, not that they might offer sacrifice to him but that they might forget the idolatry of the Egyptians and hearken to the voice of the Lord, which was for them salvation and glory, he spoke as follows through the same Jeremiah,[13] *Thus says the Lord: Add your burnt offerings to your sacrifices, and eat the flesh. For in the day that I brought them out of Egypt I did not speak to your fathers, or command them concerning burnt offerings and sacrifices. But this command I gave them, saying, "Obey my voice, and I will be your God, and you will be my people, and walk in all my ways that I command you, that it may be well with you." But they did not obey or incline [their ear], but walked in the counsels of their evil heart, and went backward and not forward.* And again, he said through the same Prophet,[14] *But let him who glories glory in this, that he understands and knows me, that I am the Lord who practices kindness, justice, and judgment in the earth.* He added, *for in these things I delight, says the Lord,* not in sacrifices, or burnt offerings or oblations.

For, the people did not possess these things from the beginning, but as a consequence, and for the reason mentioned. In regard to this Isaiah again says:[15] *You have not* [brought] *me sheep for your burnt offerings, or honored me with sacrifices. You have not ministered to me with sacrifices; nor wearied me with frankincense. You have not brought me sweet cane with money; nor have I desired the fat of your sacrifices; but you have stood before me with your sins, and with your iniquities. But,* he asked,[16] *to whom shall I look but to him that is humble and quiet, and trembled at my words? Fats*[17] *and fat flesh will not take away from you your crimes. For,*[18] *this is the fast that I have chosen, says the Lord. Loose all the bonds of wickedness; undo the thongs of violent dealings, let the oppressed go free, and break every yoke. Gladly share your bread with the hungry, and bring the homeless stranger into your house. If you see someone naked, cover him, and despise not those of the household of your descendants. Then shall your light break forth like the dawn, and your healing shall spring up, and righteousness shall go before you, and the glory of the Lord shall be your rear guard, and while you are yet speaking I shall answer you, "Here I am."*

Zachariah, too, in the Twelve Prophets, pointed out to them God's will when he said,[19] *Thus says the Lord of hosts. Render true judgment, show kindness and mercy each to his brother, do not oppress the widow, the fatherless, the sojourner, or the poor; and let none of you recall evil against his brother in your heart.* And again,[20] *These are the things that you shall do: Speak the truth to one another; render in your gates judgments that are peaceful. Do not recall evil in your heart against your brother, and love no false oath; for all these I hate, says the Lord.*

David likewise says,[21] *What man is there who desires life, and covets good days? Keep your tongue from evil and your lips from speaking deceit. Depart from evil, and do good: seek peace, and pursue it.*

4. From all these things it is evident that God did not demand from them sacrifices and burnt offerings but faith and obedience and justice for the sake of their salvation. For example, in the Prophet Hosea, God taught them his will when he said,[22] *I desire steadfast love and not sacrifice,* the knowledge of God rather than burnt offerings. Our Lord, too, gave them the same admonition. He said,[23] *If you had known what this means, "I desire mercy and not sacrifice," you would not have condemned the guiltless.* By this he testifies to the Prophets that they preached the truth but accuses these [the hearers] of being foolish through their own fault.

5. Again, while giving advice to his disciples to offer to God the first fruits[24] of his creatures—not as if he were in need,[25] but that they might not be unfruitful or displeasing—*he took bread, a creature of his, and gave thanks, saying This is my body. And in like manner, the chalice, which comes from the creation of which we are a part, he acknowledged to be his blood, and he taught that it is the new oblation of the new Covenant.*[26] This oblation the Church received from the apostles and offers in the whole world to God, who gives us nourishment, the first fruits of his own gifts in the new covenant.[27] Malachi pointed this out beforehand in the Twelve Prophets as follows:[28] *I have no pleasure in you, says the Lord Almighty, and I will not accept an offering from your hand. For from the rising of the sun to its setting my name is glorified among the nations, and in every place incense is offered to my name and a pure offering; for my name is great among the nations, says the Lord Almighty.* Thus he pointed out in the plainest manner, that the first people stopped making oblation to

God, but that *a sacrifice is offered in every place,* and that *a pure* one; and that his *name is glorified among the nations.*

6. Now, what other name is there that is glorified among the nations, except that of Our Lord, by whom the Father is glorified, and man is glorified?[29] And since it [the name] belongs to his own Son, and was made by him [the Father],[30] he calls it his own. By way of illustration, if some king would paint an image of his son, rightly would he call that his own image for two reasons; namely, because it is the image of his own son, and because he made it. So also, the name of Jesus Christ, which is glorified in the Church throughout the world, the Father confesses to be his own, both because it is the name of his Son, and because he wrote it and gave it for the salvation of men.[31] Since, therefore, the Son's name belongs to the Father, too, and since the Church makes an oblation <in every place> to God Almighty[32] through Jesus Christ, well did Malachi say, in regard to both points, *And in every place incense is offered to my name, and a pure offering.*[33] Now, John tells us in the Apocalypse that the incense is the prayers of the saints.[34]

CHAPTER 18
ONLY THE PURE SACRIFICE OF THE CHURCH PLEASES GOD.

1. The oblation of the Church, then, which the Lord taught must be offered in the entire world, was reckoned by God a pure offering, and it was acceptable to him. Not that he has need of an offering from us, but because he who makes an offering is himself glorified by that offering if his gift is accepted. For by a gift to a king both honor and affection are shown. Such a gift Our Lord wished us to offer in all simplicity and innocence, and so he proclaimed,[1] *And so if you are offering your gift at the altar, and there remember that your brother has something against you, leave your gift there before the altar and go; first be reconciled to your brother, and then come and offer your gift.* So it is necessary to offer to God the first fruits of his creation, as also Moses said,[2] *You shall not appear before the Lord your God empty-handed,* so that in the very things in which man was unpleasing, in these he was reckoned as pleasing to him, and receives honor from him.[3]

2. Oblations, therefore, as a class were not rejected, for there were oblations there [Old Testament], and there are oblations here [New Testament]; there were sacrifices in the People [Israel], and there are sacrifices in the Church.[4] Only the kind has been changed, since, of course, it is no longer offered by servants, but by freemen. The Lord, to be sure, is one and the same, but there was a peculiar character for the servants' oblation, and there is a peculiar character for the freemen's so that the sign of liberty might be shown also by the oblations. For with God nothing is purposeless, or without meaning.[5] On that account these [the Jews] dedicated their tithes; but those who received liberty dedicate all their goods to the Lord's services, giving gladly and freely the lesser as holding hope for greater things.[6] Here the widow, poor as she is, deposits her entire living into God's treasury.[7]

3. For example, in the beginning God *had regard for* the gifts of Abel, because he offered them with simplicity and justice; for the sacrifice of Cain, however, *he had no regard*, because Cain's heart was divided through jealousy and wickedness against his brother.[8] God noted that when he exposed his hidden thoughts,[9] *Have you not sinned if you do offer rightly, but do not divide rightly? Calm yourself*, because God is not appeased by sacrifice. For if one would attempt to make an offering purely and rightly and lawfully, however only according to outward appearances, but within his soul would not rightly share fellowship with his friend and would not fear God, he would not deceive God by the sacrifice that was offered rightly by outward appearance while having sin within.[10] Nor would such a sacrifice profit him anything; rather, what is profitable is the giving up of evil that has been conceived within, lest this [evil], through the simulated action, but more through the sin, make man a killer of himself.[11] With this in view the Lord said,[12] *Woe to you scribes and Pharisees, hypocrites! for you are like whitewashed tombs, outwardly the tomb appears to be beautiful, but within it is full of dead men's bones and of all uncleanness. So you also outwardly appear righteous to men, but within you are full of hypocrisy and iniquity.* To explain, though they were considered as offering rightly according to external appearances, still within themselves they had jealousy like Cain's, for which reason they killed the just one[13] and transgress the advice of the Lord, just as Cain did.[14] For he said, *Calm yourself*, but he did not come to an agreement. What is calming oneself except to stop from intended attack?

In a similar strain Christ said,[15] *You blind Pharisees, first cleanse the inside of the cup and of the plate, that the outside also may be clean.* But they did not listen. But Jeremiah said,[16] *But your eyes and your heart are not good, but are set upon dishonest gain, and upon shedding innocent blood, and upon oppression, and upon homicide.* Isaiah too,[17] *You carry out a plan but not mine; and you made a league, but not by my spirit.* Therefore in order that their inner will and intention, having been brought to light, may show that God is without fault and does not work evil (he is the kind who reveals the secrets but does not work evil) when Cain would not calm himself, he said to him,[18] *Its [sin's] desire is for you, but you must master it.* To Pilate he spoke in like manner,[19] *You would have no power over me, unless it had been given you from above.* God always grants to one who is just that, having been tested by the things he suffers and endures, he may be received; but that the evildoer, having been condemned for what he did, may be expelled. Therefore, sacrifices do not sanctify man, for God does not need sacrifices; but the intention,[20] when pure, of the one who offers, sanctifies the sacrifice and assures that God will accept it as from a friend. But[21] the sinner who kills an ox for me is like one who kills a dog.

4. Since, therefore, the Church offers with simplicity, rightly has her gift been regarded by God as a pure sacrifice. On this point Paul wrote to the Philippians,[22] *I am filled, having received from Epaphroditus the gifts you sent, a fragrant offering, a sacrifice acceptable and pleasing to God.* For it is necessary that we make an offering to God and be found pleasing in every respect to God the Maker, offering up the firstfruits of his creatures with a pure intention, sincere faith, firm hope, and fervent love. And this pure oblation the Church alone offers to the maker; she offers of his creation, with thanksgiving.[23]

The Jews, on the contrary, no longer make an offering, for their hands are full of blood[24] because they did not accept the Word through whom [the offering] is offered to God.[25] But neither do all the assemblies of the heretics make an offering. Some, by asserting that there is another Father besides the Maker, show him to be covetous of what is not his own, and desirous of it, when they offer the things that belong to our creation. On the other hand, those who assert that our creation was made from degeneracy, ignorance, and suffering, sin against their Father when they offer him the fruits of ignorance, suffering, and degeneracy; they rather heap insult on him than offer him thanks. But how are they consistent in holding that the bread over which thanks was offered is the body of their Lord and that the chalice is his blood, if they do not hold that he is the Son of the Creator of the world, namely, his Word, through whom the trees fructify and the springs overflow, and *the earth produces first the blade, then the ear, and finally the full wheat in the ear*?[26]

5. How, moreover, can they assert that the flesh that is nourished by the Lord's body and blood will perish and will not receive life?[27] So let them either change their opinion or abstain from offering the things mentioned. Contrariwise, our doctrine is in harmony with the Eucharist, and the Eucharist in turn confirms our doctrine.[28] For we offer to God the things that are his own, while we proclaim harmoniously the communion and union of the flesh and the spirit.[29] To explain, just as the bread, which is from the earth, when it receives the invocation of God, is no longer common bread, but the Eucharist,[30] consisting of two things, the earthly and the heavenly,[31] so also our bodies, when they receive the Eucharist, are no longer perishable, since they possess the hope of the resurrection.

6. We make an offering to him not as if he were in need, but to give thanks[32] for the gift[33] and to sanctify the creature. For in proportion as God does not need our things, we have need of making an offering of something to God. As Solomon said,[34] *He who is kind to the poor lends to the Lord.* For the God who has need of nothing, takes to himself our good actions in order to bestow on us his goods in reward. This is what Our Lord said,[35] *Come, O Blessed of my Father, inherit the kingdom prepared for you from the foundation of the world; for I was hungry and you gave me food; I was thirsty, and you gave me drink; I was a stranger, and you welcomed me; I was naked and you clothed me, I was sick and you visited me, I was in prison and you came to me.* Therefore, just as he does not need these things and still wills that they be done for our sake lest we be unfruitful, so the same Word gave to the people the commandment of making offerings, though he did not need them, that the people might learn to serve God. In the same way, he wills that we offer the gift at the altar frequently without intermission.[36] There is, therefore, an altar in heaven:[37] for to that place our prayers and our offerings are directed; there is a temple too: as John says in the Apocalypse:[38] *And God's temple was opened.* And there is a tent. He said,[39] *Behold, the tent of God, in which he will dwell with men.*

Chapter 19

Earthly Things Are Types of Heavenly, but the Heavenly Are Not Types of the Earthly, Much Less Is God the Type of an Unknown God.

1. The people received the gifts and offerings and all the sacrifices as types, as was shown to Moses on the Mount by the one and same God whose name is at present glorified in the Church among all the nations.[1] Now it is fitting that the earthly things that have been arranged on our behalf should be types of the heavenly realities, which were, nevertheless, made by the same God. Really, in no other way could he make a likeness of spiritual things. On the other hand, to assert that the supercelestial and spiritual realities that, as far as we are concerned, are invisible and ineffable, are types of still other heavenly things and of another Fullness, and that God is the image of another Father, is to join up with those who stray from the Truth and who are absolutely foolish and stupid. In fact, those [heretics] are forced, as we have very often shown, always to think up types of types and images of images, and never to bring their mind to a standstill in the one and true God. Really, their thoughts have risen above God, having in their hearts surpassed the Master himself. Though in imagination they have elevated themselves above him and surpassed him, still in reality they have strayed from the true God.

2. Rightly may one say to such, even as the Word suggests:[2] "To what extent do you extol your thoughts above God, you imprudently proud people? You have heard that *the heavens were marked off with a span.*[3] Tell me the dimensions, and relate to me the innumerable cubits, explain to me the fullness, *the breadth, the length and the height,* the beginning and the end of the circumference, which man's heart does not understand or comprehend. The heavenly treasures are truly great. God cannot be measured in his heart, and he who grasps the earth in the hollow of his hand cannot be comprehended in his mind.[4] Who will see the dimension of his right hand? Who will know his finger? Or who will understand his hand which measures the immense spaces, which by its own dimension stretches over the dimensions of the heavens, and which grasps in its palm the earth with the abysses, which contains within itself the breadth and length and depth below, and the height above, of the entire creation, [namely] whatever is seen, and heard and understood, and what is invisible?[5] And for this

reason,[6] he is the God who is *far above all rule and authority and power and dominion, and above every name that is named,*[7] of all things that were made and created. He it is who fills the heavens[8] and looks into the depths.[9] He is also with each one of us; for it says,[10] *I am a God at hand, and not a God afar off. Can a man hide himself in secret places so that I cannot see him?* For his hand grasps all things. It is his hand that enlightens the heavens; it enlightens also the things under heaven; and *it searches the minds and the hearts*[11] and is present in hidden and secret parts of ourselves, yet it nourishes and conserves us visibly."

3. Now, if man does not comprehend the fullness and the greatness of his hand, how can anyone understand or know so great a God in his heart? Yet, as if they had already measured him and seen through and through him and had completely explored him, they imagine there is above him another Fullness of Aeons and another Father, though they do not look upward toward heavenly things but descend into the deep Profundity of foolishness! Really, they assert that their Father extends to the border of the things outside the Fullness but that Demiurge does not reach up to the Fullness. Thus they hold that neither of them is perfect and comprehends all things. For to the former will be lacking the entire created world that is outside the Fullness; the latter [will lack] the created world that is within the Fullness. And so neither will be the God of all things. Now it is manifest to all that no one can declare the greatness of God from the things made by him. And everyone whose wisdom is worthy of God will acknowledge that his greatness lacks nothing, but comprehends all things and reaches even to us, and is with us.

Section 2

HOW THE OLD COVENANT PROPHESIES THE NEW

Chapter 20

God Formed the World through His Word and Spirit. To Us in This World He Is Invisible, but Not Unknown.

1. It is, therefore, not possible to know God according to his greatness, because it is impossible for the Father to be measured. However, according to his love [it is possible].[1] For it is that love which leads us to God through the Word. By obeying him we always learn that he is so great a God, and that it is he who through himself created and adorned and contains all things.[2] Now, "all things" includes us and this world of ours. And so we too, together with all things the world contains, were made by him. Of this Scripture speaks,[3] *And God formed man, taking dust from the ground, and breathed into his nostrils the breath of life.* And so the angels did not create or fashion us; nor could the angels have made an image of God; nor could anyone else besides the Word of God;[4] nor could a Power far distant from the Father of all things. Really, God had no need of these things to make the things that he had decreed beforehand with himself, as if he did not have his hands. Surely, the Word and the Wisdom, the Son and the Spirit, were always present with him. Through these and in these he created all things freely and autonomously. It was these he addressed when he said,[5] *Let us make man to our image and likeness.* He himself took from himself the substance of the creatures, and the exemplar of the things made, and the shape of the ornaments in the world.[6]

2. Correctly, then, has the writing expressed itself that says,[7] "First of all believe that there is one God, who established all things and adorned them, having created all things out of nothing that they might have existence. He comprehends all things but is comprehended by no one." Correctly, too, did Malachi in the Prophets say,[8] *Has not one God created us? Have we not all one Father?* In keeping with that, the Apostle, too, says,[9] *One God and Father who is above all, and in us all.* Likewise, the Lord, on his part, says,[10] *All things have been delivered to me by my Father,* clearly by him who made all things. Surely, he did not give him another's possessions, but his own.[11] Now in "all things" *nothing* has been *left out,*[12] and so he is *judge of the living and the dead.*[13] *For he has the key of David,*[14] *he opens and no one shall shut, he shuts and no one shall open.* For *no one* else,[15] *in heaven or on the earth or under the earth was able to open the scroll of his Father, or to look into it,* except *the Lamb who had*

been slain, and who *ransomed* us by his *blood.* From the God who made all things by his Word and adorned them by his wisdom he received the power over all things when *the Word became flesh,*[16] in order that he who, as the Word of God, has sovereign power in the heavens might have sovereign power also on earth,[17] as *a holy Man,*[18] who *committed no sin; no guile was found on his lips;* and in order that he might have sovereign power over the things under the earth, having himself been made *The Firstborn of the dead;*[19] in order, too, that all things might see their King,[20] as we have already said; and that the Father's light might fall upon the flesh of Our Lord, and might from his resplendent flesh come into us; and thus man, having been clothed with the Father's light,[21] might arrive at imperishability.[22]

3. We have shown by many arguments that the Word, that is, the Son, was always with the Father.[23] Now, that Wisdom, who is the Spirit, was with him before all creation,[24] he tells us through Solomon:[25] *God by wisdom founded the earth; by understanding he established the heavens; by wisdom the deeps broke forth, and the clouds drop down the dew.* And again:[26] *The Lord created me the beginning of his ways for his works, and before the ages he made me; in the beginning before he made the earth, before he made the depths; and before the springs of waters had sprung up, before the mountains were established; moreover, before all the hills, I was brought forth.* And again:[27] *When he established heaven, I was there with him, and when he established the fountains of the deep, when he fortified the foundations of the earth, I was beside him shaping up [all things]. I was his delight; every day I rejoiced in his presence always, when he rejoiced in his finished world, and delighted in the sons of men.*

4. There is, therefore, one God who created and shaped up all things through his Word and Wisdom. But he is the Creator who in turn gave this world to the human race. By reason of his greatness he is unknown to all his creatures—for no one has probed his depths, neither the ancients who have gone to rest, nor the people living now—but by reason of his love he is always known through him by whom he made all things.[28] Now, this is his Word, Our Lord Jesus Christ, who in these last times was made man among men, that he might join the end to the beginning, that is, man to God. Therefore, the Prophets, having received the gift of prophecy from the same Word, foretold his coming in the flesh, by which the mingling and communion of God and man was wrought according to the Father's good pleasure. The Word of God proclaimed from the beginning that God would be seen by men;[29] that he would converse with them upon earth, and speak

with them, and be present with his handiwork,[30] saving it, and allowing himself to be received by it, and freeing *us from the hand of all who hate us,*[31]—namely, from every spirit of transgression—and causing us *to serve him in holiness and righteousness all our days,*[32] in order that man might embrace God's Spirit and enter into the Father's glory.

5. The Prophets pointed out these things in prophecy, but not in the sense that some [heretics] assert, namely, that, since the Father of all things is invisible, the God who was seen by the Prophets was a different one. Such an assertion is made by men who are totally ignorant of what prophecy is. In truth, prophecy is the prediction of future things; that is, the pointing out beforehand of things that will happen later.[33] The Prophets, then, pointed out beforehand that God would be seen by men; as also the Lord said,[34] *Blessed are the pure of heart, for they shall see God.* Yet, in respect to his greatness and ineffable glory, no one shall see God and live,[35] for the Father is incomprehensible.

On the other hand, in keeping with [his] love and kindness and omnipotence, he grants to those who love him this: to see God, which also the Prophets foretold.[36] For *things that are impossible with men, are possible with God.*[37] For man, of himself, cannot see God. But when he wills, he can be seen by men; namely, by whom he wills, when he wills, and in what manner he wills, because God is all-powerful. He was seen in the past by prophecy through the Spirit; he is seen at present by adoption through the Son; he will be seen as Father in the kingdom of heaven.[38] In this, the Spirit prepares man for God's Son, then the Son leads man to the Father, finally, the Father bestows imperishability for eternal life, which comes to everyone by the fact that he sees God.[39]

To illustrate, those who see the light are within the light and partake of its splendor; so those who see God are within God and partake of his splendor. But this splendor gives them life. And for this reason, he who cannot be received and comprehended and seen offers himself so he can be seen and comprehended and received by men, in order that he might give life to those who receive and see him through faith.[40] For, just as his greatness is unsearchable, so his goodness, because of which he is seen and bestows life on those who see him, is ineffable. For to live without life is impossible; but the support of life comes from participating in God; participating in God, however, is to know God and to enjoy his goodness.

6. Men, therefore, will see God in order that they may live, having been made immortal by the vision and having attained even unto God. As we have said,[41] the Prophets manifested by types that God would be

seen by men who bear his Spirit and always wait for his coming. Moses spoke of this in Deuteronomy,[42] *In that day we shall see God speaking with men, and yet man will live.* In fact, some of them saw the prophetic Spirit and his workings that were poured out for all kinds of charisms. Others saw the Lord's coming and the economy, which existed from the beginning, by which he fulfilled *the will* of his Father, both *as it is in heaven* and as it is *on earth.*[43] Still others saw the Father's glories fitted, according to the times, to both who at that time saw and heard, and who would hear in the future. That is how God was manifested; for through all these things the Father is revealed: the Spirit works and the Son ministers and the Father approves, and so man is perfected unto salvation. This is expressed through the Prophet Hosea:[44] *It was I who multiplied visions,* he says, *and through the Prophets gave parables.* And the Apostle explained the same thing when he said:[45] *Now there are varieties of gifts, but the same Spirit; and there are varieties of service, but the same Lord; and there are varieties of working, but the same God, who inspires all things in all. To each is given the manifestation of the Spirit for the common good.* But since he who *works all things in all* is God, he is in his nature and greatness invisible and ineffable to his creatures, but by no means unknown—for all things learn through his Word that there is one God the Father, who contains all things, and gives existence to all, as the Lord said:[46] *No one has ever seen God; except the Only-begotten God,*[47] *who is in the bosom of the Father, he has made him known.*

7. So the Father's Son reveals him from the beginning, since, of course, he is with the Father from the beginning. He consistently and harmoniously and in a timely manner showed the human race prophetic visions and diversity of graces and his own ministrations and the Father's glorification, so as to be useful.[48] For where consistency is, there too is harmony; and where harmony, there too timeliness; and where timeliness, there too is usefulness. For this reason the Word was made the Dispenser of the Father's glory for the usefulness of men for whose sake he made such great economies by which he showed God to men and presented man to God. He guarded the invisibility of the Father, lest man become a despiser of God, and that he might always possess something toward which he might make progress. On the other hand, he showed God to men as visible by means of many economies, lest man, defecting from God entirely, would cease to exist. For living man is the glory of God, while the vision of God is the life of a man. To be sure, if the revelation of God through the creation bestows

life on all who live on earth, much more does the manifestation of the Father through the Word bestow life on those who see God.[49]

8. Since, therefore, God's Spirit pointed out future things through the Prophets, preparing and fitting us beforehand, so that we might be subject to God; and since man was supposed to see God through the good pleasure of the Holy Spirit, it was necessary that those through whom the future was foretold would themselves see the God whom they predicted men would see.[50] The purpose of this was that "God" and "God's Son" and "the Son and the Father" might not only be spoken of prophetically, but might be seen by all the members who had been sanctified and instructed in the things of God, that man might be prepared and disciplined beforehand[51] to apply himself to the glory that would later be revealed to those who love God. For the Prophets prophesied not only by word but also by vision, conduct, and the actions that they performed, according as the Spirit would suggest.[52] In keeping with this, therefore, they saw the invisible God, as Isaiah said:[53] *With my eyes I have seen the King, the Lord of Hosts.* They signified that man saw God with his eyes and heard his voice. According to this, then, they saw also God's Son as Man conversing with men, and while they prophesied of him who was to come, they spoke of him who was not yet present, and they announced the impassible as passible; and he who was then in heaven, they affirmed had descended into *the dust of death.*[54] And of the rest of the economies of the recapitulation, some they saw by means of visions; some they preached by word; some they pointed out symbolically by action. The things that were to be seen, they saw visibly; the things that were to be heard, they preached by word; the things that were to be acted out, they carried out by action. Yet all things they announced prophetically. Consequently, to the people who had transgressed the Law, Moses said that God was fire when he threatened that a day of fire would be brought upon them by God. But to those who had the fear of God, he said:[55] *The Lord God, merciful and slow to anger and abounding in steadfast love and faithfulness, keeping justice and steadfast love for thousands, forgiving iniquities and transgressions and sins.*

9. And the Word spoke with Moses, appearing before him just as one speaks with his friend.[56] But Moses longed to see openly him who spoke with him. So he was told:[57] *You shall stand on the top of the rock, and I will cover you with my hand. And while my glory passes by you shall see my back, but my face shall not be seen. For man shall not see my face and live.* Thus he pointed out two things: that it is impossible for man to

see God; and that man will see God in these last times through God's wisdom, on the top of the rock, that is, on his coming as Man. And for this reason, [the Lord] conversed with him face-to-face on the top of the mountain, with Elijah assisting, as the Gospel relates.[58] Thus, in the end, he fulfilled the pristine promise.

10. So the Prophets did not see God's very face openly but the economies and mysteries by which man would see God. So was it told to Elijah:[59] *Go forth, tomorrow, and stand before the Lord. And behold, the Lord will pass by, and behold a great and strong wind rent the mountains, and broke in pieces the rocks before the Lord, but the Lord was not in the wind; and after the wind an earthquake, but the Lord was not in the earthquake; and after the earthquake a fire, but the Lord was not in the fire; and after the fire a voice of a gentle air.* By such ways the Prophets too, who were very indignant because of the people's transgressions and because of the killing of the Prophets, were taught to act more gently; and the Lord's coming, which would come after the Law given by Moses, was pointed out—[a coming] that would be gentle and tranquil, in which he neither *broke the bruised reed, nor quenched the dimly burning flax.*[60] The gentle and peaceful rest of his kingdom was, likewise, manifested. For after the wind that makes the mountains crumble, and after the earthquake, and after the fire, tranquil and peaceful times of his kingdom are coming. Then God's Spirit gives life to man with all tranquility and lets him grow.[61]

Through Ezekiel, moreover, it was made still clearer that the Prophets saw God's economies partly, but they did not see God himself perfectly.[62] For when this [Prophet] had seen *the appearance of God* and the cherubim and the wheels, and when he had related the mystery of the entire movement, and when he had seen *the likeness of a throne* above them, and on the throne *a likeness as of a man's appearance,* and the things that were on his loins as the appearance of amber; and when he had manifested the things below as the appearance of fire and all the rest of the vision of the throne,[63] he added,[64] *This was the appearance of the likeness of the glory of the Lord,* lest anyone should think that he saw God perfectly in these things.

11. If neither Moses, therefore, nor Elijah, nor Ezekiel, all of whom saw many things of the heavenly regions, saw God, but saw the likeness of God's glory and the prophecies of the future things, it is evident that the Father is invisible. Of him the Lord, too, said,[65] *No one has ever seen God.* But his Word, just as he willed and for the benefit of those who saw, revealed the Father's glory and unfolded the

economies. This, too, the Lord said,[66] *The Only-begotten God who is in the bosom of the Father, he has made him known.* And so the Revealer of the Father, the Word himself, being rich and bountiful, was not seen by those who saw him in one type, or in one feature, but according to the purposes of his economies.[67] So it was written in Daniel. At one time he was seen by the company of Hananiah, Azariah, and Mishael, assisting them in the fiery furnace and in the oven and saving them from the fire.[68] He says,[69] *The appearance of the fourth is like a son of God.* At another time[70] [he was seen] as *a stone cut out of the mountain by no human hands,* smiting the temporal kingdoms and winnowing them, and he himself fills the earth. Again,[71] this same one is seen *like a Son of Man coming with the clouds of heaven,* and *coming to the Ancient of Days,* and accepting from him universal *dominion and glory and kingdom. And his dominion is an everlasting dominion, and his kingdom shall not be destroyed.*[72]

John, too, the Lord's disciple, saw, in the Apocalypse, the priestly and glorious coming of his reign.[73] *Then I turned to see the voice that was speaking to me, and on turning I saw seven golden lampstands, and in the midst of the lampstands One like a son of man, clothed with a long robe, and with a golden girdle round his breast. His head and his hair were white as wool, white as snow; his eyes were like a flame of fire, his feet were like bronze refined in a furnace, and his voice like the sound of many waters; in his right hand he held seven stars; from his mouth issued a sharp two-edged sword, and his face was like the sun shining in full strength.* Now, among these things he points out first the glory from the Father, as the head, and the priestly feature, as the long robes;—for this reason Moses vested the high priest according to this type[74]—second, the end [of the world] as the bronze refined in the fire, which denotes the firmness of faith and perseverance in prayers on account of the refining fire that will come at the end of time.[75] John could not endure the vision, for he says,[76] *I fell at his feet as though dead.* Thus was fulfilled the Scripture text,[77] *No one shall see God and live.* And when the Lord had revived him [John] and reminded him that he is the one in whose bosom he had reclined at the Supper and asked who it is that would betray him,[78] he said,[79] *I am the first and the last, and the living one; I died, and behold I am alive for evermore, and I have the keys of Death and Hades.* After this he saw the same Lord in a second vision. He said,[80] *Between the throne and the four living creatures and among the elders, I saw a Lamb standing as though it had been slain, with seven horns and with seven eyes, which are the seven spirits of God sent out into all the earth.* Again, he said of the Lamb:[81] *Then I saw heaven opened; and behold, a white horse! He who sat upon it is called Faithful and True, and in righteousness he judges and makes war. His eyes are like a flame of fire, and on his head are many diadems; and he has a name inscribed which no one knows but himself. He is clad in a robe dipped in blood, and the name by which he is called is "The Rod of God." And the armies of heaven, arrayed in fine linen, white and pure, followed him on white horses. From his mouth issues a sharp sword with which to smite the nations; and he will rule them with a rod of iron; he will tread the wine press of fury of the wrath of God the Almighty. On his robe and on his thigh was inscribed "King of Kings and Lord of Lords."* Thus the Word of God always possessed something resembling sketches of things to be done by himself, and he showed to men something resembling a form of the Father's economies, teaching us about the things of God.

12. He was seen,[82] however, by the Prophets not only through visions that were seen and sermons that were preached in advance, but also in actions, that he might prefigure and show forth in advance future things. On this account the Prophet Hosea took *a wife of harlotry,* thus prophesying by action that *the land will forsake the Lord by great harlotry.*[83] This means those men who are on earth; yet from among such men it will please God to take the Church, which is to be sanctified by union with his Son, just as she [Hosea's wife] was sanctified by union with the Prophet. That is why Paul said,[84] *The unbelieving wife is consecrated through her believing husband.*[85] Moreover, the Prophet named his children[86] *Not-pitied* and *Not-a-people,* in order that, as the Apostle explained,[87] *He who was Not-a-people might become a people*; and *she who was Not-pitied might obtain mercy; and in the very place where it was said. Not-a-people, there they will be called "sons of the living God."*[88] What had been done typically by action by the Prophet, the Apostle shows has truly been done by Christ in the Church.

Another example: Moses took an Ethiopian woman as wife, thus making her an Israelite,[89] showing in advance that the wild olive is inserted in the tame olive[90] and will partake of its richness. For, when Christ was born according to the flesh, he had to be sought out by [his] people to be killed, but to be freed in Egypt, that is, among the Gentiles, and to sanctify those who were infants there, whence he also formed for himself a Church. (For, Egypt was from the beginning Gentile, as was also Ethiopia.) On this account the nuptials of the Word were manifested by the nuptials of Moses; and by the Ethiopian spouse was manifested the Church, which is from among the Gentiles.[91] Those who detract, accuse, and ridicule her shall not be clean. Indeed, they will be lepers and shall be cast out of the camp of the righteous.[92]

Still another example. The harlot Rahab, though she condemned herself as a Gentile, guilty of all sins, welcomed three spies—namely, the Father and the Son with the Holy Spirit—who were spying on the entire land, and hid them in her house. When the entire city in which she lived had fallen to ruins, at the sound of the seven trumpets, the harlot Rahab together with her whole house was saved by faith in the scarlet sign.[93] The Lord referred to this when he said to those who did not admit his coming, namely, the Pharisees, and who nullify the sign of the scarlet, which was the Passover, the redemption, and the departure of the people from Egypt,[94] *The tax collectors and the harlots go into the kingdom of heaven before you.*

Chapter 21

The Patriarchs, Especially Abraham, Prefigured Our Faith by Their Words and Actions.

1. The fact that our faith was prefigured also in Abraham, since he was the Patriarch of our faith and, so to say, the prophet of our faith, the Apostle has taught quite fully in his *Letter to the Galatians:*[1] *Does he who supplies the Spirit to you and works miracles among you, do so by works of the Law, or by learning with faith? Thus Abraham "believed God, and it was reckoned to him as righteousness." So you see that it is men of faith who are the sons of Abraham. And the Scripture, foreseeing that God would justify the Gentiles by faith, preached the gospel beforehand to Abraham, "In you shall all the nations be blessed."* So then, those who are men of faith are *blessed with Abraham who had faith.* For this reason he called him not only the prophet of faith but also the father of those among the Gentiles who believe in Christ Jesus, because his faith and ours is one and the same. He, because of God's promise, believed in the future things as if they had already taken place. We, likewise, because of God's promise, view through faith the inheritance that is in the kingdom.[2]

2. Isaac's story, too, is not without its typical significance. In the *Letter to the Romans* the Apostle says:[3] *also when Rebecca had conceived by one man, our forefather Isaac,* she received an answer from the Word, *in order that God's purpose of election might continue, not because of works, but because of his call.* She was told:[4] *Two people are conceived by you, and two*

nations are in your womb; one people shall overcome the other, and the older shall serve the younger. From this it is evident that not only the actions of the Patriarchs but also Rebecca's childbirth was a prophecy about the two people: that one is the greater and the other the less; that one will be in servitude but the other free. Still, both are of one and the same father. Our God and theirs is one and the same, who *knows what is hidden, who is aware of all things before they come to be.*[5] That is why he said,[6] *Jacob I loved, but Esau I hated.*

3. Now, if anyone examines Jacob's deeds, he will find that they are not aimless, but full of meaning. First, in his birth, the way he caught hold of his brother's heel and so was called Jacob, that is, Supplanter[7]—one who holds and is himself not held, one who binds the feet but is himself not bound, one who wrestles and wins, one who holds with his hand the heel, that is victory. The Lord, the type of whose birth Jacob prefigured, was born to fulfill this. Of him John said in the Apocalypse,[8] *He went out conquering, and to conquer.* Second, he received the rights of the firstborn when his brother despised them.[9] In like manner, the younger people [Gentiles] received the Firstborn of all, Christ,[10] when the older people rejected him, saying,[11] *We have no king but Caesar.* Again, the entire blessing is in Christ. For this reason the latter people snatched away from the Father the blessings of the former people, as Jacob took away the blessing from Esau.

That is why the one brother endured the ploys and persecutions of the other, just as the Church suffers the same things at the hands of the Jews. The twelve tribes, the race of Israel, were born in a foreign land,[12] since Christ also would be in a foreign land generating the twelve-pillared foundation of the Church.[13] Various sheep accrued to Jacob as his reward;[14] Christ's reward, too, are the people who come together from the various and diverse nations into the one cohort of faith. So the Father promised, saying,[15] *Ask of me and I will make the nations your inheritance, and the ends of the earth your heritage.*

Since Jacob became the Lord's prophet by the multitude of his sons,[16] it was by all means necessary that he bear sons by the two sisters, even as Christ did by the two laws of the one and same Father. In the same way, even by the handmaids, thereby indicating that Christ should raise up sons of God from the freemen and the slaves according to the flesh,[17] bestowing on all the gifts of the Spirit who gives us life.[18] But he did all things for the sake of the younger sister with the beautiful eyes,[19] who prefigured the Church, on account of whom Christ suffered.[20] In those days, through his Patriarchs and

Prophets he prefigured and announced beforehand the future things, exercising in advance his role in God's economies, accustoming his inheritance to obey God, to be on a pilgrimage in the world, to follow his Word, and to prefigure future things. Certainly, with God there is nothing aimless or without significance.

Chapter 22
Christ Is the Savior of All.

1. In the last times, *when the fullness of time came* for freedom,[1] the Word himself *washed away the filth of the daughters of Zion*[2] by washing the feet of his disciples.[3] For this is the end of the human race, which is heir to God:[4] that, just as in the beginning through the first men, all of us were reduced to servitude by the debt of death, so in the end, through the last men, all who were disciples from the beginning, having been cleansed and washed from the things of death, might come to the life of God.[5] For, he who washed the feet of the disciples sanctified the entire body and brought them to cleanliness. Wherefore he served food to them while they were reclining in the earth, to whom he came to minister life. As Jeremiah says:[6] "The Lord, the Holy One of Israel, has remembered his dead, who slept in the land of burial, and he descended to them that he might preach to them his saving good news, for saving them." For this reason, too, were the eyes of the disciples heavy when Christ began his passion; and when the Lord found them sleeping, the first time he left them alone, indicating God's patience in regard to men who were slumbering; but when he came the second time, he woke them, and got them up,[7] indicating that his passion is the awakening of the sleeping disciples, on account of whom *he also had descended into the lower parts of the earth*,[8] to see with his own eyes those of his creation who had not fully achieved. Of these he said to the disciples,[9] *Many prophets and righteous men longed to see and hear what you see and hear.*

2. Surely, Christ came not only on account of those who in the times of Tiberius Caesar believed in him. Nor only on account of those who are living at present did the Father exercise his providence, but on account of absolutely all people from the beginning who, according to their power, each in their own generation, both feared and loved God and practiced righteousness and piety toward their neighbors[10] and longed to see Christ and to hear his voice. For this reason,

in his second coming all such will be roused from sleep and raised up before the rest who will be judged,[11] and he will establish them in his kingdom. Really, it is one God who directed the Patriarchs in their affairs and who[12] *justified the circumcised on the ground of their faith and the uncircumcised because of their faith.* For, just as we were prefigured in the first [men] and announced beforehand, so they in turn find their finished form in us,[13] that is, in the Church, and they receive the reward for their labors.

Chapter 23
The Prophets Made the Work of the Apostles Lighter.

1. On this account the Lord said to the disciples:[1] *Well, I tell you, lift up your eyes, and see how the fields are already white for harvest. He who reaps receives wages and gathers fruit for eternal life, so that sower and reaper may rejoice together. For here the saying holds true, "One sows and another reaps!" I sent you to reap that for which you did not labor, others have labored and you have entered into their labor.* Who then, are they who have labored and have ministered to God's economies? It is evident that it was the Patriarchs and the Prophets, who also prefigured our faith and spread throughout the world the coming of God's Son, who and what he would be, in order that the men who would come later and have the fear of the Lord would readily accept the coming of Christ, having been instructed by the Scriptures.[2] This is why, when Joseph realized that Mary was pregnant and thought of dismissing her secretly, the angel said to him in a dream:[3] *Do not fear to take Mary your wife, for that which is conceived in her is of the Holy Spirit; she will bear a son, and you shall call his name Jesus, for he will save his people from their sins.* He [the angel] continues by way of convincing him:[4] *Now all this took place to fulfill what the Lord spoke by the prophet, saying,*[5] *Behold the Virgin shall conceive and bear a son, and his name shall be called Emmanuel.* Thus he convinced him through the Prophet's words and excused Mary, showing that she is the same one who was announced beforehand by Isaiah as *the Virgin* who would *bear Emmanuel.* Wherefore, when Joseph was convinced beyond doubt, he both took Mary and joyfully offered service in all the rest of the rearing of Christ: the undertaking of the journey even to Egypt, the returning from there, and the migration to

Nazareth.[6] Finally, those who were ignorant of the Scriptures, of God's promise and of the economy of Christ,[7] called him the father of the Child.[8] On this account the Lord himself read the prophecies of Isaiah at Capernaum:[9] *The Spirit of the Lord is upon me, because he has anointed me to bring good tidings to the poor; he has sent me, to heal the broken-hearted, to proclaim release to the captives, and sight to the blind.* He showed that he himself was announced beforehand by the Prophet Isaiah. He said,[10] *Today this Scripture has been fulfilled in your hearing.*

2. On this account, too, when Philip had found the eunuch of the Queen of the Ethiopians reading the following from Scripture:[11] *As a sheep led to slaughter or as a lamb before its shearer is dumb, so he opens not his mouth,* in his humiliation justice was denied him. The Prophet reviewed for him all the rest about his passion and his coming in the flesh and how he was dishonored by unbelievers. Thus he easily persuaded him to believe in him, that he is Christ Jesus who was crucified under Pontius Pilate and suffered all that the Prophet had predicted, and that he is God's Son who gives eternal life to men.[12] And as soon as he had baptized him, he departed. For there was nothing wanting to him who had been catechized in advance by the Prophets.[13] He was not ignorant of God the Father, nor of the economy of his dealing with men, but only of the coming of God's Son. When he knew him in a brief space of time, he continued his journey joyfully, to become in Ethiopia the herald of Christ's coming. Wherefore, Philip did not expend much effort on him, because he was prepared in the fear of God by the Prophets in advance. Moreover, on this account, the apostles, too, when gathering together the sheep of the house of Israel that had been lost,[14] addressing them from the Scriptures, showed them that this Jesus crucified is the Christ, the Son of the living God,[15] and they persuaded a large multitude who had the fear of God. And on one day there were baptized three and four and five thousand.[16]

Chapter 24

Catechizing the Gentiles Was Harder Than Catechizing the Jews.

1. For this reason, Paul, on his part, since he was the Apostle of the Gentiles, said,[1] *I worked harder than any of them.* For the catechizing of the former was easy, since they had the proofs from the Scriptures,

and those who used to listen to Moses and the Prophets[2] also easily accepted *the Firstborn of the dead*[3] and *the Author of the life* of God,[4] who destroyed Amalech because of the extension of hands[5] and revived man from the bite of the serpent by faith in himself.[6]

As we have shown in the preceding book,[7] the Apostle was accustomed to catechize the Gentiles to forsake the superstition of idolatry and to worship one God, the Creator of heaven and earth and the maker of the entire creation; moreover, that the Word was this God's Son, through whom he created all things, and that he became man among men in the last epoch of the world, and refashioned the human race[8] but destroyed and conquered man's Enemy, and gave to his handiwork victory against the Adversary. But although those who were of the circumcision did not keep God's words, because they held them in contempt, they, nevertheless, had been instructed in advance not to commit adultery or fornication, not to steal or cheat, and that whatever is done to the detriment of one's neighbor is evil and hateful to God.[9] Wherefore they easily consented to abstain from these, because they had learned them in advance.

2. It was necessary, however, that the Gentiles learn precisely this that such actions are evil, destructive, useless, and harmful to those who do them. He, therefore, who had received the apostolate of the Gentiles *worked harder than* those who preached God's Son among the circumcised. For the Scriptures that the Lord approved and fulfilled by coming just as he had been announced beforehand helped them. But in that case [of the Gentiles] it was a kind of strange teaching and a new doctrine that the gods of the Gentiles were no gods at all but idols of the demons; that there is one God *who is above all rule and authority and dominion, and above every name that is named*;[10] and that his Word, which is by nature invisible, was made visible among men and descended *unto death, even death on a cross*;[11] and that those who believe in him would become imperishable and impassible, and would receive the kingdom of heaven. These things were preached to the Gentiles without the Scriptures; so, those who preached among the Gentiles *worked harder*. Then, too, the faith of the Gentiles, who followed the Word of God without the instruction of the Scriptures, is shown to be more generous.

Chapter 25
Both Covenants, Which Were Prefigured by Abraham and Tamar, Have One and the Same God.

1. Thus, then, it behooved Abraham to have sons, namely, such as God *raised up from stones*,[1] and attached them to him who was the prince and the herald of faith.[2] He had received the covenant of the circumcision, though he was uncircumcised, after justification through faith,[3] that both covenants would be prefigured in him, and so he would become the father of all those who follow the Word of God[4] and are on pilgrimage in this world, that is, the [father] of the believers from among the circumcised and of those among the uncircumcised. A parallel case is had in Christ *the chief cornerstone*,[5] *upholding the universe*[6] and gathering into one faith of Abraham those from both covenants who are fit for God's edifice. But the faith without circumcision, inasmuch as it united the end to the beginning, has become the first and the last. To explain, it was in Abraham before circumcision, and in the other righteous who pleased God, as we have shown; again, in the last times it appeared in the human race through the Lord's coming; circumcision, however, and the Law of the works held sway in the intermediate time.[7]

2. This is shown by types also in many other cases; for instance, already by Tamar the daughter-in-law of Judah.[8] For, when she had conceived twins, one put out his hand first. When the midwife thought that he was the firstborn, she tied a scarlet sign on his hand; but when that had been done and he had drawn back his hand, his brother Phares came out first, and after him Zara with the scarlet sign. Thus the Scripture clearly manifests the people with the scarlet sign, that is, the faith without circumcision, which was shown in advance in the Patriarchs, then was withdrawn, so his brother might be born; next he who was in second place was born first, and was recognized by the scarlet sign which was on him, that is the passion of the Righteous One. This was first prefigured in Abel and then represented by the Prophets but was fulfilled in the last times in God's Son.

3. It was proper that certain things should be announced beforehand by the Patriarchs in a fatherly manner, and that others should be prefigured by the Prophets in a legal manner,[9] while still others should be given form according to the pattern of Christ by those who

have received the adoption. All things, nevertheless, are manifested in the One God. For, even though Abraham was one man, he prefigured in himself two covenants, in which some have sown and others have reaped:[10] *For here the saying holds true, says Scripture, "One sows and another reaps."* But there is one God who gives to both whatever is suitable: to the sower the seed, and to the reaper the bread to eat.[11] Just as there is one *who plants* and another *who waters,* but one God *who gives the growth.*[12] Now the Patriarchs and the Prophets sowed the word about Christ; but the Church did the reaping, that is, she got the fruit. For this reason, those [Patriarchs and Prophets] also pray that they might have a dwelling in her, as Jeremiah says,[13] *Who will give me in the wilderness a last lodging place?* Then both *the sower and the reaper may rejoice together*[14] in the kingdom of Christ, who is present to all with whom God was pleased from the beginning, and granted that his Word be present with them.

Chapter 26

Christ Is the Treasure Hidden in the Scriptures. The Church Is the Interpreter of the Scriptures.

1. If anyone, therefore, reads the Scriptures attentively, he will find in them a discourse about Christ and the symbolic meanings about the new calling.[1] To illustrate, he is *the treasure hidden in the field,* that is, in this world; for *the field is the world,*[2] but he *has been hidden* in the Scriptures, since he was pointed out by types and parables that, humanly speaking, could not be understood before the things prophesied would be fulfilled,[3] namely, the Lord's coming. And for the same reason the Prophet Daniel said,[4] *Shut up the words and seal the book until the time of the end, until many learn, and knowledge will increase. At that time when the shattering will be accomplished, many will understand all these things.* Jeremiah, likewise, said,[5] *In the latter days they shall understand.* For every prophecy, before it is fulfilled, is an enigma and contradiction for men. But when the time has come and what was prophesied has taken place, then the prophecy can be given a clear explanation. For this reason, even at present when the Law is read by the Jews, it is like a fable; for they do not have the explanation of all the things pertaining to the coming of God's Son in human nature. Contrariwise,

when it is read by Christians, it is a *treasure hidden in the field*[6] but disclosed and explained by Christ's cross. It enriches man's understanding, shows forth God's wisdom, manifests his economies relative to man, delineates Christ's kingdom in advance, announces beforehand that the man who loves God makes so much progress that he will also see God and hear his voice and be glorified by hearing his voice, to the extent that the rest cannot look upon his glorious face. That is what was spoken by Daniel:[7] *Those who are wise shall shine like the brightness of the firmament, and among the many righteous like stars for ever and ever.* It is, therefore, just as we have shown, if one reads the Scriptures. For the Lord discoursed with the disciples after the resurrection from the dead. He showed from the Scriptures that[8] *the Christ should suffer and thus enter* into his glory, and that forgiveness of sins *should be preached in the whole world.* And that disciple[9] *who brings out of his treasure what is new and what is old* will be perfect and like the householder.

2. One must, therefore, obey the presbyters of the Church, those, namely, who, as we have shown,[10] possess the succession from the apostles. Together with the succession of the episcopate, they have received the certain charism of the Truth[11] according to the Father's good pleasure. On the other hand, one ought to hold in suspicion the rest who depart from the original succession and assemble in any manner whatever,[12] and to consider them heretics, and evil-minded, or schismatics and puffed up and pleasing themselves, or again as hypocrites, acting so for the sake of gain, or out of vainglory. Now, all of these have fallen away from the Truth. And as heretics, bringing strange fire, that is, strange doctrines, to God's altar, they will be burned by heavenly fire, as Nadab and Abihu.[13] Those, however, who rise up against the Truth and exhort others against God's Church remain in hell, swallowed up by a chasm in the earth, as those who were with Korah, Dathan, and Abiram.[14] But those who rend and separate the unity of the Church receive the same punishment as did Jeroboam.[15]

3. Now, those who were believed by many to be presbyters, but who are slaves of their own lusts and do not put the fear of God in first place in their hearts, but who heap contumely on others and are puffed up with the pride of priority seating,[16] and do evil things in secret, and say,[17] *No one sees us,* are reproved by the Word, who does not judge according to appearance or regard the face, but looks into the heart.[18] They will hear the words that were prophesied by Daniel:[19] *You Offspring of Canaan, and not of Judah, beauty has seduced you, and lust has perverted your heart, You who are grown old in evil days, now your past*

sins have come out, making unjust judgments, condemning the innocent, but letting the guilty go free, whereas the Lord said, "The innocent and just you shall not kill." Our Lord also said in regard to them,[20] *But if that wicked servant says to himself, "My master is delayed," and begins to beat his men-servants and maid-servants and eats and drinks and gets drunk, the master of that servant will come on a day when he does not know and in an hour he does not expect, and will cut him off and make him share the lot of the unfaithful.*

4. So it is our obligation to keep away from all such presbyters and, contrariwise, to adhere to those who, as we have said, guard the doctrine of the apostles[21] and who together with those of the priestly rank offer sound doctrine and blameless conduct for the formation and correction of the rest. By way of example, Moses, to whom so great leadership was entrusted, relying on a good conscience, justified himself before God when he said,[22] *I have not taken anything of theirs out of covetousness; and I have not harmed one of them.* Another example, after Samuel had been judge of the people many years, and was leader of Israel without pride, in the end he justified himself. He said:[23] *I have lived with you from my youth until this day. Testify against me before the Lord and before his anointed, if I have taken any of your ox or ass, if I have domineered over anyone, or oppressed anyone, or if I have taken a bribe at anyone's hand, or sandals. Testify against me, and I will restore it to you; And the people said to him: You have not domineered over any of us, or oppressed us, or taken anything from any man's hand.* Then he bore witness to the Lord and said: *The Lord is my witness against you, and his anointed is witness this day, that you have not found anything in my hand. And they said, he is witness.* Still another example, the Apostle Paul, though he had a clear conscience, said to the Corinthians:[24] *We at least are not, like so many, adulterating God's word, but as men of sincerity, as commissioned by God, in the sight of God we speak in Christ. We have wronged no one, we have corrupted no one, we have taken advantage of no one.*

5. Such are the presbyters that the Church nourishes. Of them the Prophet also said,[25] *And I will give peace to your taskmasters and to your overseers righteousness.* The Lord, too, said of them:[26] *Who is the faithful and wise steward, whom his master has set over his household, to give them their food at the proper time? Blessed is that servant whom his master when he comes will find so doing.* Paul teaches us where to find such presbyters when he says,[27] *God has appointed in the Church, first Apostles, second Prophets, third teachers.* So one must learn the Truth from there where the Lord's charisms have been placed, with whom, namely, there is the apostolic succession of the Church, and the sound and irreproachable

mode of living and the unadulterated and imperishable doctrine.[28] For these guard also our faith in one God who made all things, and they increase the love toward God's Son, who made so many economies for our sake. They also expound the Scriptures without danger to us, neither blaspheming God nor dishonoring the Patriarchs, nor holding the Prophets in contempt.

Chapter 27
Every Sin Will Be Punished According to the Degree of Guilt.

1. For instance, I have heard from a certain Presbyter, who has heard it from the apostles, whom he had also seen, as also from their disciples,[1] that a deserving punishment [as is clear] from the Scriptures was dealt out to the ancients for acting without the Spirit's counsel. For, since God is not a respecter of persons,[2] he dealt out a suitable punishment for things not done according to his will. For example, when David suffered the persecution from Saul on account of justice, and fled from King Saul and did not take revenge on his enemy,[3] he was really singing of Christ's coming and instructing the Gentiles with wisdom, and doing all things according to the Spirit's counsel, and was pleasing to God. But when, because of his lust, he took Bathsheba, Uriah's wife, to himself, Scripture said of him,[4] *But the thing which David had done displeased the Lord.* And the Prophet Nathan was sent to him to manifest his sin to him, that he, by passing sentence on himself and condemning himself, might obtain mercy and forgiveness from Christ:[5] *For the Lord sent Nathan to David, and he said to him, "There were two men in a certain city, the one rich and the other poor. The rich man had very many flocks and herds; but the poor man had nothing but one little ewe lamb, which he had brought up, and it grew up with him and with his children; it used to eat of his morsel and drink from his cup, and it was like a daughter to him. Now, there came a traveler to the rich man, and he was unwilling to take one of his own flock or herd to prepare for the wayfarer, who had come to him, but he took the poor man's lamb, and prepared it for the man that was come to him. Then David's anger was greatly kindled against the man; and he said to Nathan, "As the Lord lives, the man that has done this deserves to die, and he shall restore the lamb fourfold, because he did this thing, and because he had no pity on the poor man." And Nathan said to him, "You are the man who did*

this." Then he continues with the rest: He upbraids him, enumerates the benefits of God toward him and that he had angered the Lord by his deed. For such deeds do not please God; on the contrary, great anger hangs over his house. At this David was moved to compunction and said, *"I have sinned against the Lord,"* and he sang the Psalm of Confession.[6] And he awaited the Lord's coming, who would wash and cleanse man held bound by sin.

The same is true of Solomon, while he continued to judge rightly and asked for wisdom,[7] and when he built the type of the true temple,[8] and when he told of the glories of God[9] and announced the peace that would come to the Gentiles,[10] and foreshadowed Christ's reign, and spoke three thousand canticles in praise of God,[11] and when he gave a natural explanation of God's wisdom in creation in regard to all the trees, and all the plants, and all the birds, quadrupeds and fishes,[12] and said,[13] *Will God indeed dwell with men on earth? Behold the heavens cannot contain him.* Also when he pleased God, and all men admired him, and all the kings of the earth sought his favor, that they might listen to his wisdom which God had given him.[14] The Queen of the South came to him from the ends of the earth to learn the wisdom that he possessed.[15] The Lord, too, said[16] that she would rise in judgment against the generation of those who hear his words but do not believe in him, and would condemn them, because she was submissive to the wisdom announced by God's servant, whereas these despise the wisdom offered by God's Son; for Solomon was a servant, but Christ was God's Son and Solomon's Lord. So while Solomon served God blamelessly and ministered to his economies, then he was praised. But when he took wives from all the Gentiles and permitted idols to be erected in Israel, Scripture says of him:[17] *Now King Solomon loved women, and took to himself foreign women. For when Solomon was old his heart was not wholly true to the Lord his God, for the foreign women turned away his heart after other gods. So Solomon did what was evil in the sight of the Lord, as David his father. And the Lord was angry with Solomon, because his heart was not wholly true to the Lord, like the heart of David his father.* Scripture strongly rebuked him, as the Presbyter said, *so that no human being might boast in the presence of God.*[18]

2. For this reason, too, the Lord descended into the regions below the earth, to proclaim the good news of his coming also to them and that remission of sins existed for those who believe in him.[19] Now all those who hoped in him believed in him, that is, the just and the Patriarchs and the Prophets who foretold his coming and ministered

to his economies. He forgave their sins as well as ours, and so we may not impute the sins to them without showing contempt for God's grace. For just as they did not impute to us our uncontrolled deeds that we did before Christ was manifested in us, so it is not right for us to impute the sins to those who sinned before Christ's coming. For[20] *all men fell short of the glory of God*; they are, however, not justified by themselves, but through the Lord's coming if they direct their attention toward his light. However, their deeds *were written down for our instruction*,[21] that we might know, first, that our God and theirs is one and the same who is not pleased with sins, even if they are committed by people in high standing; and, second, that we should abstain from evil.

In fact, if those men of old, who surpassed us in gifts but for whose sake God's Son had not yet suffered, were disgraced so much because they sinned in some manner and catered to the lusts of the flesh, what will not those suffer who are living now who despised the Lord's coming and catered to their pleasures? For the former the Lord's death was healing and forgiveness of sins, but for those who now sin, Christ[22] *will never die again, death no longer has dominion over him*; but *the Son will come in the glory* of the Father[23] to demand with interest from his stewards the money which he has entrusted to them; and from those to whom he had given the most, he will demand the most.[24] And so we must not, as that Presbyter said, be proud or reprove the ancients, but we must fear lest after having had the knowledge of Christ, we should do something unpleasing to God and should no longer receive forgiveness of our sins, but should be excluded from his kingdom.[25] With this in mind Paul said,[26] *For if he did not spare the natural branches, neither will he spare you, you who though a wild olive shoot, were grafted to the richness of the olive tree, and have become a sharer in its richness.*

3. In the same way, you will see that the transgressions of the common people were described, not for the sake of the transgressors of that time but for our instruction, and that we might know that there is one God against whom they sinned, and against whom certain ones sin at present who claim to believe in him. The Apostle brings this out very clearly in his *Letter to the Corinthians.* He says,[27] *For I would not have you ignorant that our fathers were all under the cloud, and all passed through the sea, and all were baptized into Moses, in the cloud and in the sea, and all ate the same spiritual food and all drank the same spiritual drink. For they drank from the spiritual rock which followed them, and the rock was Christ. Nevertheless with most of them God was not pleased, for "they were overthrown*

in the wilderness." Now these things are a type for us, not to desire evil as some desired. Do not be idolators as some of them were; as it is written, "The people sat down to eat and drink and rose up to dance." We must not indulge in immorality, as some of them indulged in immorality, and twenty-three thousand fell in a single day. We must not put Christ to the test, as some of them put him to the test, and were destroyed by the serpent; or grumble, as some of them grumbled, and were destroyed by the Destroyer. Now all these things happened to them as a type, but they were written down for our instruction, upon whom the end of the ages has come. Therefore, let anyone who thinks that he stands take heed lest he fall.

4. So the Apostle demonstrates without doubt and without contradiction that there is one and the same God who judged the sins of the past and who seeks out the sins of the present. And since he pointed out the reason for putting these things in writing, all these men are found to be uninstructed and audacious and even imprudent who, because of the transgression of the men of old and because of the disobedience of many of them, assert that the God of these men was the Creator of the world, and that he was made in degeneracy, but that there is another Father who was handed down by Christ, and this is the one whom each one of them thought up. They did not understand that just as in those days God *was not pleased with most of them* who sinned,[28] so now *many are called, but few are chosen,*[29] and that just as then the unrighteous and the idolators and the immoral lost their lives,[30] so it is now. For the Lord announced that[31] such *are cast into eternal fire.* The Apostle, too, said,[32] *Or do you not know that the unrighteous will not inherit the kingdom of God? Do not be deceived; neither the immoral nor idolators, nor adulterers, nor the homosexuals, nor Sodomites, nor thieves, nor the greedy, nor drunkards, nor the revilers, nor the robbers, will inherit the kingdom of God.* That he is not saying this of those who are outside, but to us, lest we be cast outside the kingdom of God if we do such things, he continues,[33] *And such were some of you. But you were washed, you were sanctified in the name of the Lord Jesus Christ, and in the Spirit of God.* And just as then those who did evil and destroyed others were condemned and cast out, so now, the eye that scandalizes is dug out, and the foot and hand [are cut off], lest the rest of the body perish in like manner.[34] And we have a commandment,[35] *If a brother is guilty of immorality or greed, or is an idolater or reviler, drunkard or robber—do not even eat with him.* Again the Apostle says,[36] *Let no one deceive you with empty words, for it is because of these things that the wrath of God comes upon the sons of disobedience. Therefore do not associate with them.* And as then also

the rest who approved them and associated with them, shared in the condemnation of sinners, so now[37] *a little leaven ferments the whole lump.* And as then God's anger came down upon the unrighteous, so now in like manner, as the Apostle says,[38] *The wrath of God is revealed from heaven against all ungodliness and wickedness of men who by their wickedness suppress the truth of God.* And as then God's vengeance came upon the Egyptians who unjustly punished Israel,[39] so now too, as the Lord says,[40] *And will God not avenge his elect, who cry to him day and night? I tell you, he will vindicate them speedily.* Also the Apostle preaches in the same way in the Letter to the Thessalonians:[41] *Since God deems it just to repay with affliction those who afflict you, and to grant rest with us to you who are afflicted when the Lord Jesus is revealed, who will come from heaven with his mighty angel in flaming fire, inflicting vengeance on those who do not know God, and upon those who do not obey the gospel of our Lord Jesus. They shall suffer the punishment of eternal destruction, coming from the face of the Lord*[42] *and from the glory of his might, when he comes on that day to be glorified in his saints, and to be marveled at in all who have believed in him.*

Chapter 28

Men Who Look Only to Christ's Mercy and Forget about His Justice Are Foolish.

1. In the past as well as in the present, therefore, there is the same justice of God that vindicates God—in the past in type and for a time and with moderation; in the present in reality and perpetually and more severely. For the fire is eternal and *the wrath of God that will be revealed from heaven coming from the Lord's face*[1] inflicts greater punishment on those who fall into it. David said as much,[2] *But the face of the Lord is against evildoers, to cut off the remembrance of them from the earth.*

Hence, the Presbyter showed that those are very foolish who, from the things that happened to the men of old who did not obey God, attempt to introduce another Father; and who, contrariwise, oppose all the things the Lord in his mercy had done for saving those who received him at his coming,[3] but who are silent about his judgment and all things that will come upon those who heard his words yet did not act accordingly,[4] and that[5] *it would have been better* for them *if they had never been born,* and that[6] *it shall be more tolerable on that day of judgment for Sodom and Gomorrah than for that City* (Jerusalem), which did not receive the word of his disciples.

2. As a matter of fact, just as in the new covenant the faith that men have toward God was increased by receiving God's Son in addition, so that man might become partakers of God, in like manner was the diligence too of our mode of living increased, since we are commanded to abstain not only from evil deeds, but also from evil thoughts themselves and *idle words* and *silly talk and levity.*[7] Similarly, the punishment of those who do not believe in the Word of God, and hold his coming in contempt, and turn their backs upon him, has been increased; for it is no longer temporal but has been made eternal.[8] Truly, to whomever the Lord says,[9] *Depart from me, you cursed, into the eternal fire,* will be damned forever; and to whomever he says,[10] *Come, O blessed of my Father, inherit the kingdom prepared for you forever,* these will always receive the kingdom and will make progress in it, since there is one and the same God the Father and his Word, who always assists the human race with many economies and performs many things. He has from the beginning been saving those who are being saved, namely, those who love God and follow the Word of God, in keeping with their generation. And he has been condemning those who are being condemned, namely, who forget God and are blasphemers and transgressors of his doctrine.

3. The very heretics whom we have mentioned before have gone mad,[11] because they hold the Lord blameworthy—him whom they claim to believe. In fact, the very things that they note about God, namely, that in times past he condemned the unbelievers and smote the Egyptians but saved the obedient, these same things will recur in the case of the Lord, who will condemn eternally those whom he condemns, and will forgive eternally those whom he forgives.[12] He will be found, according to their own words, to have been made the occasion of the greatest sin for those who laid hands on him and *who pierced him.*[13] For if he had not come in that manner, certainly they would not have become the murderers of their Lord; and if he had not sent the Prophets to them, certainly they would not have killed them.[14] The same [is true of] the apostles. So, to those who accuse us and say, "If the Egyptians had not been afflicted with the plagues and had not been drowned in the sea when persecuting Israel, God could not have saved his people," we shall retort, "Then, if the Jews had not become murderers of their Lord (which deprived them of eternal life), and had not killed the apostles and persecuted the Church,[15] and if thus

they would not have fallen into the depths of [God's] wrath, we could not have been saved. As a fact, just as those of old received salvation through the blindness of the Egyptians, so now we, through blindness of the Jews. As the death of their Lord is damnation for those who crucified him and did not believe in his coming, so it is salvation for those who believe in him."[16]

In explanation, the Apostle writes in his Second Letter to the Corinthians,[17] *For we are the aroma of Christ to God, among those who are being saved and those who are perishing, to one a fragrance from death to death, but to the other a fragrance from life to life.* Therefore, for whom is it a fragrance from death to death if not to the ones who do not believe and who are not submissive to the Word of God? Who, on the other hand, are the ones who even in the past handed themselves over to death? They were the ones who do not believe and who are not submissive to God. Again, who are the ones who have been saved and have received the inheritance? They are the ones who believed in God and guarded the love toward him, as for example, Caleb, the son of Jephunneh, and Joshua, the son of Nun,[18] and the innocent boys who <did not speak against God and who> had no consciousness of evil.[19] Who are, however, the ones who are saved at present and who receive eternal life? Are they not the ones who love God and who believe in his promises, and who have become infants with respect to evil?[20]

Chapter 29
God Is Not the Author of Sin.

1. But these men object that God *hardened the heart* of Pharaoh and of his servants.[1] Now, those who make that accusation do not read in the Gospel where *the disciples said to the Lord,*[2] *Why do you speak to them in parables? the Lord answered: Because to you it has been given to know the secrets of the kingdom of heaven, but to them I speak in parables, because seeing they do not see, and hearing they do not hear; that with them is fulfilled the prophecy of Isaiah who says, "Harden the heart of this people, and make their ears dull, and blind their eyes." But blessed are your eyes which see what you see, and your ears which hear what you hear.* Surely one and the same God, on the one hand, blinds those who do not believe and who set him at naught,[3] just as the sun, his creature, affects those who because of a defect of the eyes cannot look at its light.[4] He grants, on

the other hand, a fuller and greater illumination of the mind to those who believe him and follow him.

In keeping with this discourse, the Apostle in turn writes in his Second Letter to the Corinthians,[5] *In their case, the god of this world has blinded the minds of the unbelievers, to keep them from seeing the light of the gospel of the glory of Christ.* Again to the Romans,[6] *And since they did not see fit to acknowledge God, God gave them up to a base mind and to improper conduct.* But in his Second Letter to the Thessalonians, when speaking of the Antichrist, he clearly asserts,[7] *Therefore God sends upon them a strong delusion to make them believe what is false, so that all may be condemned who did not believe the truth, but had pleasure in unrighteousness.*

2. If at the present time, then, since God knows all things in advance, he hands over to their unbelief all whom he knows to be unbelievers, and turns his face from such and leaves them in the darkness that they chose for themselves, what is there unusual if in the past he handed over to their unbelief Pharaoh and his associates who would never believe? That is what the Word said to Moses from the bush:[8] *But I know that Pharaoh the King of Egypt will not let you go unless compelled by a mighty hand.* Now, in the sense that the Lord spoke in parables and blinded Israel so that seeing they might not see, because he knew their unbelief, in the same sense he also *hardened the heart* of Pharaoh, that he might not see that it is God's finger[9] that leads the people, and might not believe, but might be precipitated into the sea of unbelief, thinking that their departure was through acts of magic, and that the Red Sea did not offer passage to the people through God's power, but that it happened that way naturally.

Chapter 30
God Did Not Direct the Jews to Despoil the Egyptians.

1. Those, however, who make an objection and accusation because the people, when about to leave, at God's command, took from the Egyptians[1] vessels of all kinds and clothes and walked off with them, and from these things built the tabernacle in the wilderness,—these convict themselves as ignorant of God's decrees and economies, as the Presbyter said. For, if God had not consented to this typical journey, namely, in the faith in which we are established, by which we

departed from the class of the Gentiles, no one would be able to be saved. We are all heirs to either a small or a great possession that we have acquired from the *mammon of iniquity.*[2] Really, whence the houses we live in, the clothes we wear, and the vessels we use, and the rest of the needs of our daily life, if not from the things that we acquired by avarice, while we were Gentiles, or that we received from Gentile parents, relatives, or friends, who got them through avarice? Not to speak of the fact that even now in the state of faith we acquire possessions. For who does not sell without wanting to make profit from him who buys? And who does not buy without wanting to derive something beneficial from him who sells? And who carries on a trade without doing so precisely to gain a livelihood? And what about the faithful who are *in the royal palace,*[3] do they not possess the vessels that belong to Caesar, and does not each of them give, according to his means, to those who have nothing? The Egyptians were debtors to Israel not only in respect to property but also in respect to life, on account of the previous kindness of the Patriarch Joseph. Now, in what way are the Gentiles our debtors, from whom we receive both profit and benefits? Whatever they acquire with effort, these we who are in the faith make use of without effort.

2. Up to that time the people served the Egyptians in the worst kind of slavery. Scripture tells us:[4] *When the Egyptians oppressed the sons of Israel, and made their lives bitter with hard service, in mortar and brick, and in all kinds of work in the fields, in all the works in which they violently oppressed them,* they built for them fortified cities[5] and labored much and, over many years, increased their possessions; and that they did under every kind of slavery, since the Egyptians were not only ungrateful toward them but wished to destroy them all. What injustice, then, was committed if out of the many things they took a few; and if they left as poor people, taking only a small reward for their great service, though, if they had not served them, they could have had great possessions and could have left as a rich people?

By way of illustration, suppose a free man had been carried away by violence by another, and had served him many years and had increased his [lord's] possessions, then when finally he gets some little support, he thinks of taking a small portion of his [lord's] property, and on leaving takes only a few things from those acquired by his many labors and from the large possessions acquired, and is then accused of acting unjustly. No, it is the one who reduced him to slavery who will appear to be the unjust judge. Of the same ilk are those who blame the people for taking for themselves a few things from the many and who do not blame those who render no thanks for the service of the Fathers, and who even reduced them to the severest slavery and acquired a very great gain from them, and who assert that the Israelites acted unjustly for taking from their labors uncoined gold and silver in a few vessels, as we have said; who, on the contrary, assert that they themselves act justly—let us tell the truth even though it seems ridiculous to some—when they carry in their belts coined gold and silver and brass with Caesar's inscription on it, which they got from the labors of others.

3. If we make a comparison between them and us, who seems to have obtained the goods in the more just way? Was it the people who descended from the Egyptians, who were debtors in every respect; or was it we who descended from the Romans and the other nations who owed nothing to us?[6] Why, even the world owes its peace to them, so that we can travel and sail without fear where we will.[7] Against these, therefore, the word of the Lord is apropos. He said,[8] *You hypocrites, first take the log out of your own eye, and then you will see clearly to take the speck out of your brother's eye.*

To explain, if the one who makes such accusations against you and boasts that by his "knowledge" he is separated from the group of the Nations, and that he has in his possession no goods obtained from others but is literally naked and goes about in bare feet and lives in the mountains without house, as some animal that feeds on plants, he deserves pardon for not knowing anything about our way of life. If, on the contrary, he shares in all the things that are said to belong to others, and criticizes the fact that they are a type, he shows himself most unjust, and he twists this sort of accusation against himself.[9] For he will be found to carry about the possessions of others and desire the things that are not his. It was for this reason that the Lord said,[10] *Judge not that you may not be judged. For with the judgment you pronounce, you will be judged.* Not that we should not correct others, or that we should consent to their evil deeds; but that we do not judge God's economies unjustly, since he justly planned all of them in types. It was because he knew that we would distribute our goods that we got from another that he said,[11] *He who has two coats, let him share with him who has none; and he who has food, let him do likewise.* And,[12] *For I was hungry and you gave me food, I was naked and you clothed me.* And,[13] *But when you give alms, do not let your left hand know what your right hand is doing.*

We are, in fact, justified by doing good with the rest of our goods, in a sense, buying back our own goods from others' goods. But I say "from other's goods" not as if the world were not God's but because we possess these gifts as received from others, just like these [Israelites] from the Egyptians, who knew not God. And by these very things we set up within ourselves God's tent; for God dwells within those who do good to others. To the point is what the Lord said,[14] *Make friends for yourselves by means of the mammon of unrighteousness, so that when you have been evicted, they may receive you into the eternal dwellings.* For whatever we acquired from injustice while we were Gentiles, these things, after we believed, we converted to good use for the Lord and are thereby justified.

4. So these things were necessarily acted out beforehand in type, and according to them was built God's tent. They received them justly as we have shown; we were manifested in them in advance, we who would serve God by means of others' goods. In point of fact, the entire exodus of the people from Egypt [was set] by God as a type and an image of the exodus of the Church that would take place from the Gentiles. And for this reason he led her from there into his inheritance, which not Moses, God's servant, but Jesus, God's Son, will give as inheritance. Now if one will give more careful attention to what was said by the Prophets about the end, and what John, the Lord's disciple, saw in the Apocalypse, he will find that the Gentiles everywhere are to receive the same plagues that Egypt did then in particular.[15]

Chapter 31

One Should Not Condemn as Crimes What Scripture Did Not Condemn.

1. When relating such things about the ancients, the Presbyter was wont to refresh us and say: "We ought not to rebuke the Patriarchs and the Prophets with the sins with which Scripture rebukes them, or to become like Ham who ridiculed his father's shame, and so fell under a curse.[1] Rather, we should give thanks to God for them, because by the Lord's coming the sins were forgiven them; for he said that they give thanks and rejoice in our salvation. On the other hand, in regard to sins, which Scripture relates simply and does not reprove, we ought not to make any accusations, since we are not more diligent

than God, and we cannot *be above the Master*;[2] rather we must seek their type. For nothing of the things set down in Scripture without being condemned is purposeless."[3]

An example is Lot, who led his daughters out of Sodom, who [later] were with child by their father; he had left his wife at the boundary *as a pillar of salt* until this present day.[4] For, Lot did not get the knowledge and idea of such an act from his own will or carnal desire, yet he fulfilled a type. As Scripture says,[5] *And that night the firstborn went in, and lay with her father, and Lot did not know when she lay down and when she arose*; and of the younger the same is said, *And he did not know when she lay down with him, or when she arose.* So since the man was unaware of the matter, and was not satisfying lust, an economy was being fulfilled, by which the two daughters, namely, the two assemblies [Jews and Gentiles], were pointed out as having children from one and the same father without carnal lust. Nor was there any other who could have given them the "seed" and the fruit of children, as was written,[6] *And the firstborn said to the younger, "Our father is old, and there is not a man left on earth to come in to us after the manner of all the earth. Come, let us make our father drunk with wine, and we will lie with him, that we may raise up offspring from our father."*

2. Thus, in their simplicity and innocence these daughters spoke in that way, because they thought that all men had perished, just as the Sodomites had, and that God's wrath had descended on the entire earth. And so they are excusable, since they thought they alone, with their father, were left for the conservation of the human race, and for that reason they circumvented their father.[7] By their words it was pointed out that there was no other than our Father who could give the power of bearing children to the elder and the younger Assemblies.

The Father of the human race is the Word of God, as Moses points out when he says,[8] *Is not he your Father, who created you, and made you and established you?* So when did he pour out on the human race this "seed," that is, the Spirit of forgiveness of sins by whom we are given life? Was it not when he was wont to eat with men and to drink wine on the earth? For it says,[9] *The Son of Man came eating and drinking*; also when, while reclining, he slumbered and fell asleep, as he says through David,[10] *I lay down and have taken a sleep.* That he did this while associating with us in this life, he says again,[11] *And my sleep was pleasant to me.* All this was pointed out through Lot, because the "seed" of the Father of all, namely, the Spirit of God, by whom all things were made, was commingled and united with flesh, namely, with his handiwork;

and by this comingling and union the two Assemblies bear living children from their Father for the living God.

3. And while this was taking place, his wife remained in Sodom. She was no longer perishable flesh but remained a statue of salt always. By means of those natural things, customary among men, she manifested that the Church, which is *the salt of the earth,*[12] was left within the boundaries of the earth, enduring the conditions of men. And while members are always taken away from her, she continues entire as the statue of salt, that is, *the bulwark of the faith,*[13] giving strength to the children and sending them on to the Father.

Chapter 32
One God Was the Author of Both Covenants.

1. The Presbyter, a disciple of the Apostle, discoursed along this line, too, showing that both covenants were from one and the same God. To be sure, there is no other God besides the one who made and fashioned us. Neither is there any basis for the thesis of those who assert that this world of ours was made by the angels, or by some other power, or by some other god. Indeed, once a person forsakes the Creator of all things and concedes that this creation of ours was made by someone else or through someone else,[1] he must necessarily fall into multiple inconsistencies and many contradictions for which he can give no defense, neither plausible nor true. That is why those who introduce other doctrines hide from us their notion about God, knowing the unstable and futile nature of their doctrine, and fearing lest they be vanquished and their salvation would be endangered.[2]

On the contrary, if one believes[3] in the one God who also made all things through his Word, as Moses said,[4] *God said, "Let there be light," and there was light*; and as we read in the Gospel,[5] *All things were made through him, and without him was made not anything*; and also in the Apostle Paul,[6] *One Lord, one faith, one baptism, one God and Father, who is above all and through all and in all,*—such a one[7] will first of all *hold fast the Head, from whom the whole body, being closely joined and knit together through every joint for the functioning in due measure of every single part, makes for the growth of the body, for the building up of itself in love.*[8] From then on, every word will be consistent for him,[9] if he also reads the Scriptures carefully, together with the presbyters of the Church, with whom is the apostolic doctrine, as we have demonstrated.[10]

2. In fact, all the apostles taught that there were two covenants in the two peoples, but one and the same God, who planned them both for the benefit of men who were to believe in God—for that the covenants were given.[11] This we demonstrated in the Third Book from the doctrine of the apostles.[12] Likewise, [we demonstrated] that the first Covenant was not given without purpose or meaning or by chance; no, it brought under the service of God those to whom it was given for their own benefit, for God did not need the service of men; but it [the covenant] manifested the type of the heavenly realities, since man could not yet look on the things of God by his own [power of] sight. It also outlined in advance the images of the things in the Church, that our faith might become firm. It contained, finally, a prophecy of future things, that man might learn that God has foreknowledge of all things.

Chapter 33
The True Disciple of the Apostles

1. Such a disciple, truly spiritual, who receives the Spirit of God—the Spirit who was with men in all God's economies from the beginning, and announced future things and pointed out present things and narrated past things—such a one *judges all men but is himself judged by no one.*[1] He judges the Gentiles, *who serve the creature rather than the Creator,*[2] and with *a base mind* consume all their energy without gain. He judges also the Jews, who do not receive the message of liberty,[3] and who refuse to go free, though they have the Liberator present; but who are out of date in pretending, [by practices even] beyond the Law, to serve God who is in need of nothing. They do not acknowledge Christ's coming, whom he made Man for the salvation of men; and they refuse to understand that all the Prophets proclaimed two comings of Christ. In the one, he became Man subject to stripes, knowing how to bear infirmity,[4] and sitting on the foal of an ass,[5] and rejected by the builders as a stone,[6] and led to slaughter like a sheep,[7] and who destroyed Amalech by stretching out his hands;[8] who gathered from the ends of the earth into the Father's sheepfold the children who had been scattered;[9] who remembered his dead who had fallen asleep before, and descended to them in order to free and save them.[10] In the second coming, however, he will come upon clouds,[11] and will bring on the Day which is like a burning furnace,[12] and will

strike the earth with the sword of his mouth, and will slay the wicked with the breath through his lips,[13]and will [14] *have a winnowing fork in his hands, and he will clear his threshing floor, and gather his wheat into the granary, but the chaff he will burn with unquenchable fire.*

2. The spiritual disciple will also judge the doctrine of Marcion. How does he hold that there are two gods, though they are separated from each other by an infinite distance?[15] Or how can he be good if he draws men who do not belong to him away from the one who made them and calls them to his kingdom? And why is his goodness deficient for not saving all? And why does he seem to be good toward men, but is most unjust toward him who made men, inasmuch as he deprives him of his possessions? Moreover, how could the Lord, if he is of another Father, rightly have professed that the bread from this creation of ours is his Body, and that the mixture of the chalice is his Blood?[16] And why did he acknowledge himself to be the Son of Man,[17] if he did not experience human birth? Again, how could he forgive us our sins,[18] for which we were responsible to our Maker and God? How, too, if he was not flesh, but appeared as man, was he crucified, and blood and water flowed from his side when it was pierced?[19] Since they buried his body, what was it that rose again from the dead?

3. The spiritual disciple will also judge all the followers of Valentinus,[20] who, though with the tongue they profess one God and Father and that all things are from him, assert that he who made all things is the fruit of degeneracy. Likewise, though with the tongue they profess one Lord Jesus Christ, God's Son, in their teaching they make a special emission of Only-begotten, and a special one of Word, and another of Christ, still another of Savior, with the result that according to them, though these are all spoken of as one, they are really all understood separately, and each has a special emission by his own conjugal couple.

And so only their tongues concede a unity; but their doctrine and thought, when examined thoroughly, fall short of unity; and they will fall into the multiform judgment of God, when they will be questioned about the things which they have thought up,—by the Christ, who, they assert, had a later birth than the Fullness of the thirty Aeons, and whose emission occurred after the degeneracy [of wisdom] and because of the passion that wisdom suffered, according to their assertion, at whose childbirth they themselves assisted.[21]

Now, Homer, their own prophet, will accuse them—by whom they have been instructed and in whom they have discovered such things. This is what he says, "In truth, a man who hides something in his heart, different from what he tells, is as much an enemy as the gates of Hades."[22] He [the spiritual disciple] will also judge the empty speeches of the depraved Gnostics,[23] showing them to be the disciples of Simon Magus.[24]

4. He [the spiritual disciple] will also judge the Ebionites:[25] How can they be saved unless God is the one *who worked their salvation upon the earth*?[26] How can man pass over to God if God has not passed over to man? How can men forsake the birth unto death if they are not regenerated by faith into the new birth, the one from the Virgin, that has been given in an unexpected manner by God, as a sign of salvation?[27] Or what sort of adoption can they receive if they remain in the human birth in this world? How did he possess more than Solomon and more than Jonah,[28] and how was he Lord of David,[29] who was of the same nature as they? How did he overcome him who was stronger than men, who had not only conquered man, but had held him subject under his power; and how did he conquer him who had conquered, but loosed man who had been conquered,[30] if he was not superior to man who had been conquered? Who else is superior to and more eminent than the man who was made after the likeness of God, if not God's Son, after whose likeness man was made? And for this reason he manifested the likeness in the last times, when God's Son was made man, assuming the ancient handiwork unto himself, as we have demonstrated in the preceding book.[31]

5. He will also judge those who hold that Christ is man only putatively.[32] For how do they think that they are truly debating if their Teacher was imaginary? Or how can they have anything secure from him if he was only putative and not the Truth? How can they truly partake of salvation, if he, in whom they claim to believe, showed himself as putative? So, if with them everything is putative, and not the Truth, then one might ask: Perhaps, since they themselves are not men but dumb animals, do they not parade before many as shades of men?[33]

6. He will also judge the false prophets, who have not received the grace of prophecy from God and do not fear God but, either because of vainglory, or because of some gain, or for some other reason according to the influence of the evil spirit, pretend to prophesy but are lying against God.

7. He will also judge those who bring about schisms and are devoid of God's love, who consider rather their own advantage than the unity of the Church, and for slight and chance reasons cut to pieces and divide the great and glorious Body of Christ and, as far as

is in their power, kill it.[34] They speak of peace, but wage war; they truly *strain out a gnat and swallow a camel.*[35] To be sure, they cannot bring about restoration that will be as great as the destruction of the schism.

He will also judge those that are outside the Truth, namely, who are outside the Church.[36] He, however, will be judged by no one. Really, all things are consistent for him. There is the faith intact in the one God Almighty, *from whom are all things.*[37] There is the secure persuasion in God's Son, Christ Jesus Our Lord, *through whom are all things,*[38] and in the economies relative to him, through which God's Son was made man. This [persuasion] is by God's Spirit, who furnishes us with *the knowledge of the Truth*[39] and has set forth the economies of the Father and the Son, by virtue of which he dwelt among men, for the benefit of men, in keeping with each generation,[40] just as the Father wills.

8. The true knowledge is the doctrine of the apostles, and the ancient constitution of the Church in the whole world,[41] and the distinctive character of the Body of Christ according to the succession of the bishops, to whom they [apostles] handed down the Church, which is in every place. This [knowledge] has come down even to us.[42] It is a safeguarding without fictional matter, the fullest account of the Scriptures, with neither addition nor subtraction; it is, likewise, a reading [of the Scriptures] without falsification; it is a correct and harmonious explanation according to the Scriptures, without danger and without blasphemy; it is, finally, the preeminent gift of love, which is more precious than knowledge, more glorious than prophecy, more excellent than all the rest of the charisms.[43]

9. On this account, the Church, because of her love for God, sends a multitude of martyrs ahead to the Father everywhere and always.[44] All these others not only have no such thing to show among themselves, but they claim that it is not even necessary to have such martyrdom (witness), because their doctrine is the true martyrdom (witness). Yet they might concede that during the entire time since Our Lord appeared on earth, one or two have at times borne the opprobrium of the Name together with our martyrs, as having obtained mercy and been led forth with them [to death], and as having been given to them as an adjunct. Really, only the Church upholds intact the opprobrium of those who suffer persecution for the sake of justice,[45] and who endure all the pains and are put to death on account of love for God and on account of the confession of his Son. She is always having members amputated, but soon increases her members and becomes whole again, just as her type, the salt statue of

Lot's wife.[46] They endure persecutions, just like the ancient Prophets, as the Lord said, *For so they persecuted the prophets before you,*[47] because, since the same Spirit rests upon her,[48] though in a new manner, she suffers persecution at the hands of those who do not accept the Word of God.

10. In fact, the Prophets also foretold, along with the rest of the things they prophesied, this: that those upon whomever God's Spirit would rest, and who would obey the Father's Word, and serve him according to [their] capacity, would suffer persecution and be stoned and killed.[49] Really, the Prophets prefigured all this in themselves, on account of the love for God and his Word. For, since they themselves were members of Christ, each one of them, according to his own membership, manifested a prophecy.[50] All of them, many as they were, prefigured the One [Christ], and announced the things that pertained to that One. For example, by our members the activity of the entire body is manifested; the shape, however, of the entire man is not manifested by one member, but by all. So all the Prophets prefigured the One, but each of them according to his membership fulfilled an economy and performed in advance that activity of Christ which was in keeping with his membership.[51]

11. Some of them saw him in glory and beheld his glorious mode of life *at the right of* the Father.[52] Others saw him *coming on the clouds like the Son of Man,*[53] and said of him,[54] *They will look on him whom they have pierced,* thus pointing out his coming. He himself said of his coming,[55] *When the Son of Man comes will he find faith on earth?* Paul, too, refers to this event when he says,[56] *God deems it just to repay with affliction those who afflict you, and to grant rest with us to you who are afflicted when the Lord Jesus is revealed from heaven with his mighty angels in flaming fire.* Others calling him[57] the Judge and the Day of the Lord a burning furnace, who[58] *gathers the wheat into the granaries but the chaff he will burn up with unquenchable fire, threatened the unbelievers.* Of these the Lord himself said,[59] *Depart from me, you cursed, into the eternal fire which my Father has prepared for the devil and his angels.* The Apostle speaks in the same strain,[60] *They shall suffer the punishment of eternal destruction from the presence of the Lord and from the glory of his might, when he comes on that day to be glorified in his saints, and to be marveled at in all who have believed in him.* There are those who said,[61] *You are the fairest of the sons of men; and, God, your God has anointed you with the oil of gladness about your fellows;* and, *Gird your sword upon your thigh, O mighty one. In your majesty and your beauty ride forth victoriously, and reign for the sake of truth and meekness*

and right. And whatever similar things were said of him pointed out the beauty in his kingdom, both the splendor and the majesty that are more radiant and more eminent than all who reign under him, in order that those who would hear this would long to be present there, doing what is pleasing to God.

Again, there were those who said,[62] *He is a man and who will know him?* and,[63] *I went to the prophetess, and she bore a son and his name will be called Wonderful, Counselor, God the Mighty*; as also those who preached that he would be *Emmanuel*,[64] born of *the Virgin.* These manifested the union of the Word of God with his handiwork; namely, that the Word would be flesh; and the Son of God, the Son of Man; that the pure One would open, in a pure manner, the pure womb that regenerated men unto God and that he himself had made pure.[65] So, though he was made what we are, still he is *God the Mighty* and has an *ineffable generation.*[66]

Then there were those who said,[67] *God roared in Sion, and uttered his voice from Jerusalem*; and,[68] *In Judah God is known.* These pointed out his coming in Judea. There were those who said[69] that *God will come from the South, and from the shady and dense mountain.* These spoke of his coming from Bethlehem, as we have shown in the preceding Book.[70] From there comes the one who is in charge of and shepherds his Father's people.[71] There were those, moreover, who said that at his coming[72] *the lame man shall leap like a hart, and the tongue of the dumb shall be free, and the eyes of the blind shall be opened, and the ears of the deaf unstopped, and the weak hands and the feeble knees shall be strengthened, and*[73] *that the dead who are in tombs shall rise; and,*[74] *he himself will bear our griefs, and will carry our sorrows.* These are the cures effected by him, which they announced.[75]

12. Some of them, moreover, prophesied his coming as Man, as he entered Jerusalem, where he suffered and was crucified and endured all things that were prophesied; namely, that he would be a man of griefs, and lacking in beauty, and one who would know how to bear griefs;[76] that he would enter Jerusalem riding on…the foal of an ass;[77] that he would bend his back to the scourge, and give his cheeks to the palms, and that he would be led like a sheep to slaughter,[78] and be given vinegar and gall to drink;[79] and would be forsaken by friends and relatives,[80] and extend his hands all the day long;[81] that he would be ridiculed and cursed by those who would look upon him, and his garments would be divided and lots cast for his tunic, and that he

would be brought down to the dust of death.[82] And all other similar things.

Others said,[83] "The Lord was mindful of his dead, who had fallen asleep in the dust of the earth, and he descended to them that he might raise them up for the sake of saving them"; by that they gave the reason for his suffering all those things. Some said,[84] *And it shall come to pass on that day, says the Lord, the sun will set at noon, and darkness will be over the earth in broad daylight; and will turn your feasts into mourning, and all your songs into lamentations.* They clearly announced the setting of the sun that took place when he was crucified from the sixth hour onward;[85] and that after this had happened the festivals that were according to the Law and the songs would be turned into grief and lamentation when they would be handed over to the Gentiles. Jeremiah pointed out the same thing still more clearly,[86] *She who bore has languished; she has swooned away; her sun went down while it was yet midday; she has been shamed and disgraced; and the rest of them I will give up to the sword before their enemies.*

13. Those, however, who said that he lay down and slept and rose again, for the Lord sustained him;[87] and those who commanded the rulers of the heavens to *open the eternal gates, that the King of glory may come in,*[88] heralded his resurrection from the dead through the Father and his reception into heaven. But when they said,[89] *Its rising is from the end of the heavens, and his circuit to the end of them; and there is nothing can hide from its heat,* they announced that he was taken up to the place from where he had come down, and that there is no one who will escape his judgment. Those who said,[90] *The Lord reigned, let the people be angry; he sits enthroned upon his cherubim; let the earth quake,*—they both prophesied the anger of all peoples against those who believed in him after his ascension, and the insurrection of the whole earth against the Church; and they prophesied that when he *will come from heaven with his mighty angels,*[91] the entire earth will quake; as he himself said,[92] *And there will be a great earthquake, such as has not been from the beginning.* Again when he says,[93] *Who is to be judged? Let him stand over against me. Who is to be vindicated? Let him come near the servant of the Lord*; and, *Woe to you, because you will wear out like a garment, and the moth will eat you up,* and[94] *the haughtiness of man will be humbled, and the Lord alone will be exalted in that day.* By this is pointed out that after his passion and ascension, God will subject under his feet all who were against him,[95] and he will be exalted above all, and there will be no one who can be vindicated or compared with him.

14. There were those, too, who would say that God would prepare *a new covenant* for men,[96] *not like* the one he *made with their fathers* on Mount Horeb, and that he would *give a new heart and a new spirit* to men;[97] and again,[98] *Consider not the things of old. Behold, I am doing new things; and now they spring forth, you shall know; and I will make a way in the wilderness, and rivers in the desert, to give drink to my chosen people, to the people whom I have formed, that they might declare my powers.* They clearly announced the liberty of the new covenant, and that[99] *the new wine, which is put into fresh wine skins* is the faith in Christ, the way of righteousness,[100] which has arisen in the wilderness and the rivers of the Holy Spirit in the waterless land, to water God's chosen race,[101] which he acquired, that his miracles might be declared, but not that they might blaspheme the God who made these things.

15. The man who is truly spiritual will explain that the Prophets spoke all the other things which we have demonstrated by such abundance [of Scripture texts].[102] He will point out regarding which feature of the Lord's economies each one of the things mentioned was spoken, and [he will manifest] the organic whole of the work of God's Son. He will always know the same God; he will always recognize the same Word of God, even though he has now appeared to us; and he will always recognize the same Spirit of God, even though in the last times he is poured out on us in a new manner, but [was poured out] on the entire human race from the creation until the end.[103] From him [the Spirit], those who believe in God and follow his Word, receive salvation that comes from him. Those, however, who separate from him, and hold his precepts in contempt, and by their deeds dishonor him who made them, and by their doctrines blaspheme him who nourished them, heap up against themselves a most just judgment.[104]

So, this [spiritual man] *judges all men; but is himself judged by no one.*[105] For he neither blasphemes his Father, nor sets aside as worthless his economies; nor makes accusations against the Patriarchs, nor dishonors the Prophets, nor says that the Prophets were from another god, or that the prophecies were from different substances.

Chapter 34
Against the Marcionites: The Prophets Speak of the One Christ.

1. Against all the heretics, and especially against the Marcionites and their ilk, who assert that the Prophets were from another god, we shall say: Read with greater care the Gospel that has been given us by the apostles, and read with greater care the Prophets, and you will find proclaimed in them all the deeds and all the doctrines and the entire passion of Our Lord.

If, however, a thought like this should come to mind and you should say: "What new thing, then, did the Lord bring by coming?" know that he who was heralded in advance brought something quite new by presenting himself. Really, this very thing had been heralded in advance that a newness would come to renew and give life to man. To illustrate, the coming of a king is heralded by servants who are sent ahead to prepare those who are to welcome their sovereign. But when the king comes, his subjects are filled with the joy that had been heralded; and when they have received his freedom, and have actually seen him, they have heard his discourses and have enjoyed his gifts, those who have any sense at all no longer ask, "What did the king bring that is newer than what the heralds of the coming announced?" To be sure, he brought himself and gave to men the blessings that had been predicted, *into which angels longed to look.*[1]

2. The servants would have been liars and not sent by the Lord if Christ had not fulfilled their words by coming just as he was heralded in advance. For that reason he said,[2] *Think not that I have come to abolish the law and the prophets. I have not come to abolish but to fulfill [them]. For truly, I say to you, till heaven and earth pass away, not an iota, not a dot will pass from the law until all is accomplished.* For by coming he fulfilled all things and still fulfills in the Church, until the consummation, the new covenant predicted by the Law. Paul, his Apostle, said the same thing in his Letter to the Romans:[3] *But now the righteousness of God has been manifested apart from law, although the law and the prophets bear witness to it; for he who is righteous lives by faith.* Now, the fact that *the righteous man lives by faith* was predicted by the Prophets.[4]

3. How could the Prophets predict the King's coming; how could they tell in advance about the good news of the liberty he would give; how could they announce beforehand all that was done by Christ,

both by words and by deeds, and his passion; how could they foretell the new covenant, if they had received prophetic inspiration from some other god, and had been ignorant, according to you, of the ineffable Father, of his kingdom, and of his dispensations, which God's Son fulfilled by coming on earth in the last days? You cannot, in truth, say that these things happened by some chance, as if the Prophets had said them of some other god, but they happened just like that to the Lord. For, all the Prophets foretold the same things, but they did not happen to any of the ancients. To be sure, if they had happened to any of the ancients, the later Prophets would not have foretold that they would take place in the last times.

More yet, there is no Patriarch or Prophet or ancient king who properly and specially experienced anything like these things. For, all of them prophesied Christ's sufferings; they themselves, however, were far from suffering things similar to what they prophesied. And the elements of the Lord's passion that were prophesied took place in no one else. For example, the sun did not set at the death of any of the ancients, nor was the veil rent in two, nor was there an earthquake, nor were the rocks split open, nor did the dead rise, nor did any of them rise, nor was any of them taken into heaven, nor on being taken up were the heavens opened, nor did the Gentiles believe in the name of any of them, nor did any of them die and rise again and then inaugurate a new covenant of liberty.[5] So the Prophets did not speak of anyone except the Lord in whom all the signs spoken of before converged.

4. Again, if anyone advocating the cause of the Jews should say that the new covenant is the building of the temple that took place under Zerubbabel, after the migration into Babylonia and the return of the people, after seventy-two years, let him know that at that time a stone temple was rebuilt—for the Law which had been given on stone tablets was still observed—but no new covenant was given. No, the Law which had been given by Moses was used until the Lord's coming. By the Lord's coming, however, the new covenant for the reconciliation of peace and the life-giving Law went out into the whole earth, as the Prophets had foretold:[6] *For out of Zion shall go forth the law, and the word of the Lord from Jerusalem. And he shall judge many peoples and they shall beat their swords into plowshares, and their spears into pruning hooks, neither shall they learn war any more.* Consequently, if another law and message went out from Jerusalem and brought so great peace to the nations that accepted it, and through them rebuked the imprudence of many

people, it seems to follow that the Prophets spoke of another god. On the contrary, if the Law of liberty, namely, the word of God [preached] by the apostles who went out from Jerusalem has been proclaimed to the whole earth, and has brought about such a change that they made *the swords and the war-lances into plowshares,* and that they changed them into pruning hooks for reaping grain, (that is), into peaceful tools, and no longer know how to wage war, but if *struck* would *offer the other cheek,*[7] then the Prophets did not say these things of some other god, but of him who made these things. But this is Our Lord, and *in that the word is true*;[8] for he it is who made the plow and brought the pruning hook, that is, the first planting of man which was the handiwork Adam, and the harvest gathered through the Word in the last times. And because he joined the beginning to the end, being Lord of both, he showed the plow in the end, the wood joined to iron, and thus he purged the earth, since the secure Word, having been united with the flesh, and with that form[9] was crucified and cleansed the savage earth. Now, in the beginning he prefigured the pruning hook by Abel, pointing out that there would be a gleaning of a righteous race of men. For he said,[10] *See, how the righteous man perishes, and no one understands; and the devout men are taken away, while no one lays it to heart.* These things were practiced in advance in Abel, but they were heralded by the Prophets and were fulfilled in the Lord. In us, too, it is the same, because the Body follows the Head.[11]

5. Such things are appropriate against those, too, who assert that the Prophets and Our Lord were from different gods, that they might in some manner finally desist from so great irrationality. Really, for that reason we exert ourselves to produce proofs from the Scriptures, that we may refute them by the very words, as far as we can, and restrain them from so great blasphemy, and from making such a foolish fabrication with a multitude of gods.

Chapter 35

The Confusion of the Heretics as to Which God Inspired the Prophets

1. So there are the Valentinians and the rest of the falsely so-called Gnostics, who assert that sometimes in the Scriptures things were spoken about by Supreme Power for the sake of the Offspring

that also comes from there but at other times about the middle regions, for the sake of the <audacious> Mother, Prunikos;[1] but at still other times many things were spoken about by the Maker of the world, from whom also the Prophets were sent. In opposition to these people we say that it is very irrational to reduce the Father of all things to so great need, as if he did not have his own means, by which the things that are in the Fullness might be announced intact. Really, whom did he fear that he would not of his own accord and independently make known his will, freely and without any association with the Spirit who was made in degeneracy and ignorance? Did he fear lest many should be saved when they would hear intact the things of the Truth? Or again, was he powerless to prepare for himself those who would announce the Savior's coming?

2. If the Savior, when he came to this earth, sent his apostles into the world to herald his coming intact and to teach his Father's will, [the apostles] would in no way have anything in common in doctrine with the Gentiles or the Jews. Then much more, while remaining in the Fullness, would he have appointed his own heralds who would announce his future coming to this world, without having anything in common with the prophecies that are from Demiurge? If, on the other hand, while he was in the Fullness, he had made use of the Prophets of the Law, and by means of them manifested his own things, much more would he have used these same teachers, when he came to this earth and would have announced the Gospel to us through them.

Therefore, let them no longer assert that Peter and Paul and the other apostles proclaimed the Truth, but that it was the scribes and the Pharisees and the rest, through whom the Law was preached. Now, if at his coming he sent his own apostles *in the spirit of truth, and not in the spirit of error*,[2] he did the very same with the Prophets, because the Word of God was always the self-same. Since, moreover, according to the rule of these men, the Spirit from the Supreme Power was the Spirit of light, the Spirit of truth, the Spirit of perfection, the Spirit of knowledge, while the Spirit of Demiurge was the Spirit of ignorance, degeneracy, error, and the offspring of a shadow, how could perfection and degeneracy, knowledge and ignorance, error and truth, light and darkness, be in one and the same Spirit? If, however, it was impossible for this to be so in the case of the Prophets—but that [as inspired] from the one God, they preached the Word of God, and proclaimed the coming of his Son—much more would the Lord himself never have held discourses, now about the Supreme Power, now about the Degeneracy rejected here below, thus acting as a teacher both of knowledge and of ignorance. Nor would he ever have glorified now the Creator of this world, now the Father who is above him, as Christ himself said,[3] *No one [takes] a piece from a new garment and puts it on an old garment; and no one puts new wine into old wine skins.* So, either let them lay off altogether from the Prophets, as from the ancients, and let them not assert that these were sent ahead by Demiurge and spoke some things about the message which is according to Supreme Power; or, on the contrary, they will be convicted by the Lord who says, *New wine is not put into old wine skins.*

3. From where could the Offspring of their mother get his knowledge about the mysteries within the Fullness and speak about them? To be sure, the mother was outside the Fullness when she gave birth to this Offspring. But what is outside the Fullness, they assert, is outside of knowledge, and that means it is ignorance. How, then, could the Offspring which was conceived as ignorance be able to announce knowledge? Or, how could the mother herself know the mysteries of the Fullness, formless and shapeless as she was, cast outside as an abortive child, and there fashioned and formed, and hindered by Limit from going within, and continuing till the consummation to be outside the Fullness, namely, outside of knowledge? Again, if they assert that the Lord's passion is a type of the straining forward of Christ from on high, who, when he strained forward, formed their mother by the aid of Limit, they are refuted in regard to other particulars, since they can no longer show a likeness of the type. For example, where was the Christ on high given vinegar and gall to drink? Or, where were his garments divided? Or, where was he pierced so that blood and water flowed? Or, where did he sweat drops of blood? And all the rest that happened to the Lord, and that the Prophets spoke of? From where, then, did either the mother or her Offspring divine the things that had not yet taken place but would take place?

4. Besides these things they assert that certain others were spoken by Supreme Power. But they are refuted by the things related in the Scriptures about Christ's coming. What these things were, they cannot agree on; they give different answers about them. In fact, if one would want to make an experiment with them and question their renowned men separately about some word, he would find him saying that the question is about Pre-father, namely, Profundity; another, about the Beginning of all things, namely, Only-begotten; another, about the Father of all things, namely, Word; again, another will say

that it is about one of the Aeons in the Fullness; another, that it is about Christ; and another, about Savior. But one who is more skilled than these, after having been silent for a long time, says it is said of Limit; another will say that Wisdom in the Fullness is manifested; another, that the mother outside the Fullness is announced; and still another will say it is God the Maker of the world. So great are the differences among them about the one [being], because they have various opinions about the same Scripture texts. And when a passage has been read, all wrinkle their eyebrows and shake their heads and say they are making a most profound discourse, but that not all are able to understand the greatness which is contained in it! And so, silence is of greatest importance among the wise. Really, the Silence that is above must have its pattern in the silence they are keeping. Thus all, many as they are, disperse, holding so many opinions about one being, and secretly carrying within themselves their clever excogitations.

So, when they agree among themselves on just what was predicted in the Scriptures, then we will refute them. In the meantime, by not thinking wisely, they convict themselves inasmuch as they do not agree on the same words. We, on the contrary, follow one and the same true Lord[4] as teacher, and possess his words as the Rule of the Truth,[5] and so we all speak the same things always about the same passages. We know that there is one God, the Creator of the universe; he sent the Prophets who led the people out of Egypt; he revealed his Son in the last times, that he might confound the unbelievers and search after the fruit of righteousness.

SECTION 3

HOW THE PARABLES OF CHRIST REFER TO THE GOD OF THE OLD COVENANT, WHO IS ALSO THE GOD OF THE NEW COVENANT

Chapter 36
The Patriarchs and the Prophets and Christ Are from One and the Same God the Father.

1. That God, the Lord did not reject.[1] He did not teach that the Prophets spoke on the authority of a god other than his Father, or that they are from different substances than from one and the same Father; or that someone other than his Father made the things that are in this world. He taught thus:[2] *There was a householder who planted a vineyard, and set a hedge around it, and dug a wine press in it, and built a tower, and let it out to tenants, and went into another country. When the season of fruit drew near, he sent his servants to the tenants to get his fruits; and the tenants took his servants and beat one, stoned another, and killed another. Again, he sent other servants, more than at first; and they did the same to them. Afterward he sent his son to them, saying, "They will respect my son." But when the tenants saw the son, they said to themselves, "This is the heir; come, let us kill him and have his inheritance." So they took him and killed him and cast him out of the vineyard. When therefore the owner of the vineyard comes, what will he do to those tenants? They said to him, "He will put those wretches to a miserable death, and will let out they vineyard to other tenants, who will give him the fruits in their seasons."* Again the Lord said, [3] *"Have you never read in the Scriptures, 'The very stone which the builders rejected has become the head of the corner; this was the Lord's doing, and it is marvelous in our eyes.' Therefore, I tell you, the kingdom of God will be taken away from you and given to a nation producing the fruits of it."*

By these things he evidently points out to his disciples that there is one and the same householder, namely, one God the Father, who made all things by himself; but that there are various farmers, some are *contumelious and proud*[4] and unprofitable and murderers of the Lord; others, in full obedience, return fruit in their seasons. He also [pointed out] that this householder is the same one who sometimes sends his servants, sometimes his Son. So the servants are sent by the same Father by whom the Son was sent to the tenants who killed him. Now, the Son, coming as he did from the Father, with supreme authority, used to say,[5] *But I say to you*; while the servants were sent by the Lord as servants, and so used to say,[6] *Thus says the Lord.*

2. The one, therefore, whom the former [Prophets] preached to the unbelievers as Lord, him Christ handed down as Father to those who obey him. And the God who had called the former, namely, in

the beginning through the Law of servitude, he received the latter by adoption later on. To explain, God planted the vineyard of the human race, first by the fashioning of Adam and the election of the Patriarchs. Then he handed it over to the tenants by the Law given by Moses and surrounded it with a hedge, that is, on all sides he determined what they were to produce; and he built a tower, chose Jerusalem, and dug a winepress, that is, he prepared a receptacle of the prophetic Spirit. And so he sent the Prophets before the exile in Babylon took place, and after the exile he sent others, even more than the first, who were looking for the fruit.

They said to them,[7] *Thus says the Lord, Amend your ways and your doings.*[8] *Render true judgment, show kindness and mercy each to his brother, do not oppress the widow, the fatherless, the sojourner, and the poor.* And,[9] *Do not recall your brother's evil in your hearts; and love no false oath.*[10] *Wash yourselves, make yourselves clean; remove the evil from your hearts; learn to do good, seek justice, defend the oppressed, defend the fatherless, plead for the widow. Come, now let us reason together, says the Lord.* And again,[11] *Keep your tongue from evil, and your lips from speaking deceit. Depart from evil, and do good; seek after peace, and pursue it.*

In preaching that, the Prophets sought the fruit of justice. And when the former did not believe, *he sent last of all his Son,*[12] Our Lord Jesus Christ, whom the evil tenants, when they had killed him, threw out of the vineyard. As a result, the Lord God delivered it, no longer hedged in, but scattered throughout the world, to other tenants who would return fruits in their seasons. The beautiful tower of election was raised everywhere, for everywhere there is the illustrious Church, and everywhere the wine press is dug round about, because everywhere are those who receive the Spirit.[13] For since they have rejected God's Son and cast him outside the vineyard, when they had killed him, God justly rejected them and gave the production of fruit to the Gentiles who were outside the vineyard. Just as the Prophet wrote,[14] *For the Lord has rejected and forsaken the people who did this, for the sons of Judah have done evil in my sight, says the Lord.* And again Jeremiah,[15] *I set watchmen over you, saying, "Give heed to the sound of the trumpet!" But they said, "We will not give heed!" Therefore the nations have given heed and those who herd the sheep among them.* So there is one and the same God the Father who planted the vineyard, who led the people forth, who sent the Prophets, who sent his Son, who gave the vineyard to other tenants, to those who return fruits in their seasons.

3. And on this account the Lord, preparing us as good laborers, said to his disciples:[16] *Take heed to yourselves, and always and at all times be watchful, lest your hearts be weighed down with dissipation and drunkenness and the cares of this life, and that day come upon you suddenly. For it will come as a snare upon all who dwell on the face of the earth.*[17] *Let your loins be girded and your lamps burning, and be like men who are waiting for their master to come home.* And[18] *as it was in the days of Noah, They ate and drank, bought and sold, married and were given in marriage, and they did not know until Noah entered the ark, and the flood came and destroyed them. Or as it was in the days of Lot. They ate and drank, they bought and sold, they planted and built, until the day that Lot went out from Sodom. It rained fire from heaven and destroyed them all. So will it be at the coming of the Son of Man.*[19] *Watch, therefore, for you do not know on what day your Lord is coming.*

He announced one and the same Lord, who in the days of Noah, on account of the disobedience of men, brought on the flood;[20] and who in the days of Lot, on account of the multitude of sins of the Sodomites, rained fire from heaven;[21] and who in the last days, on account of the same disobedience and similar sins, will bring on the day of Judgment, on which he said,[22] *it will be more tolerable for the Sodomites and Gomorrhites than for that town and house,* which did not accept the word of the apostles. He said:[23] *And you, Capernaum, will be exalted to heaven? You shall be brought down to Hades. For if the mighty works done in you had been done in Sodom, it would have remained to this day. But I tell you, it shall be more tolerable on the day of judgment for Sodom than for you.*

4. Because the Word of God is always one and the same, he gives to those who believe in him *a fountain of water unto eternal life,*[24] but suddenly dries up the unfruitful fig tree.[25] He justly brought on the flood in the days of Noah, in order to destroy the most wicked race of men who lived at that time, who no longer could bear fruit for God, because the angels who had transgressed had been united to them in marriage,[26] and to put a check on their sins; on the other hand, to preserve the archetype, the handiwork of Adam. In the days of Lot he rained fire and sulphur from heaven on Sodom and Gomorrah, an example of *the just judgment of God.*[27] He did these things that all might know that[28] *every tree that does not bear good fruit is cut down and thrown into the fire,* and that in the universal judgment he will deal with the Sodomites more tolerably than with those who saw the miracles that he performed and did not believe in him or accept his doctrine.[29] For, as by his coming he gave greater grace to those who have believed in him and are doing his will, so he also indicated that those who did not

believe in him would be given a greater punishment in the Judgment, since he is equally just to all. Of the ones to whom he gave more he will demand more[30]—"more" not in the sense that he will manifest the knowledge of another Father, as we have shown by so many and valid arguments, but because by his coming he poured out on the human race a more abundant gift of the Father's grace.

5. Now, if what we have already stated should not be sufficient proof for anyone to believe that the Prophets were sent by the One and same Father by whom also Our Lord was sent, let him open the ears of his heart and call upon the Lord Jesus Christ as Teacher, and listen to him saying:[31] *The kingdom of heaven may be compared to a king who gave a marriage feast for his son, and sent his servants to call those who were invited to the marriage feast. But when they refused to obey, Again he sent other servants, saying, "Tell those who are invited, Behold, I have made ready my dinner, my oxen and my fat calves are killed, and everything is ready; come to the marriage feast." But they made light of him and went off, one to his farm, another to his business, while the rest seized his servants, some they treated shamefully, and some they killed. But when the king heard of it, he was angry, and he sent his troops and destroyed those murderers, and burned their city. Then he said to the servants, "The wedding is ready, but those invited were not worthy. Go therefore to the thoroughfares and invite to the marriage feast as many as you find." And his servants went out and gathered all whom they found, bad and good, so the wedding was filled up. Now when the king went in to look at the guests, he saw there a man who had no wedding garment; and he said to him, "Friend, how did you get in here without a wedding garment?" And he was speechless. Then the king said to the attendants, "Take him by hands and feet, and cast him into the outer darkness; there men will weep and gnash their teeth." For many are called but few are chosen.*

Now, also by his words, the Lord points out clearly all things: both that there is one King and Lord, the Father of all, of whom he said before, *"Do not [swear] by Jerusalem, for it is the city of the great king"*;[32] and that from the beginning he made ready the nuptials for his Son, and that because of his immense goodness he invited the former people to the wedding banquet through his servants. When these refused to obey, he again sent other servants to invite them. Not even then did they obey him, but even stoned and killed those who brought the invitation. *He sent his troops and destroyed them and burned their city.* Then he invited people from all the roads, that is, from all the Gentiles, to the wedding banquet of his Son, as he said through Jeremiah:[33] *And I have sent to you all my servants the prophets, to say, "Turn now every one of you from his evil way, and amend your doings."* And again through the same [Jeremiah] he said:[34] *And I have sent all my servants the prophets to you, during the day and before the dawn, yet they have not listened to me, or inclined their ear. So you shall speak all these words to them, "This is the nation that did not obey the voice of the Lord," and did not accept discipline; faith has perished from their lips.*

The Lord,[35] therefore, who invited us from everywhere through the apostles, this same one invited the people of old through the Prophets, as is shown by the Lord's words. The Prophets were not from one god, while the apostles from another, even though they preached to various nations. But they were from one and the same God. Some announced the Lord, while others proclaimed the good news of the Father; some announced in advance the coming of God's Son, while others heralded him in advance as already present to those who were afar off.

6. Furthermore, he revealed that it was necessary for us to be adorned with the calling and the deeds of righteousness, in order that God's Spirit might rest upon us;[36] for that is the wedding present about which the Apostle wrote,[37] *not that we would be unclothed, but that we would be further clothed, so that what is mortal may be swallowed up by immortality.* But those who were invited to God's supper and did not share in the Holy Spirit, because of their evil mode of living, *will be cast into outer darkness,*[38] the Scripture says. He manifestly points out that the same King who invited the faithful from everywhere to the wedding of his Son and who gave to them the imperishable banquet likewise commands the one who has no wedding garment,[39] namely, a contemptuous person, to be cast into outer darkness. For just as in the first covenant, *with most of them [God] was not pleased;*[40] so now, too, *many are called, but few are chosen.*[41]

The God, then, who judges is not different from the Father who invites to salvation, nor is the God who gives eternal light different from the one who commands those who do not have on the wedding garment to be cast into outer darkness. No, it is one and the same God the Father of Our Lord, by whom also the Prophets were sent out. He invited those who were unworthy out of his immense kindness. But then he inspected those who had been invited to see whether they had on the proper garment, suitable for his Son's wedding, for nothing improper and evil pleases him. Just as the Lord said to the one who was healed,[42] *See, you are well. Sin no more, that nothing worse befall you.* For he who is good and righteous and pure and spotless will not tolerate anything evil or unrighteous or abominable in his bridal chamber.

That is the Father of Our Lord, through whose providence all things are in harmony, and by whose command all things are administered. He bestows gifts gratuitously on whom he ought. On the other hand, being a most just Rewarder, he repays according to deserts in a very exacting manner to those who are ungrateful and who do not acknowledge his kindness, and so he says,[43] *He sent his troops and destroyed those murderers, and burned their city.* He called them *his troops* because all men are God's.[44] *For the earth is the Lord's, and the fullness thereof; the world and all who dwell in therein.* With this in mind the Apostle Paul wrote in his Letter to the Romans:[45] *For there is no authority except from God, and those that exist have been instituted by God. Therefore he who resists the authority resists the ordinance of God; and those who resist will incur judgment. For rulers are not a terror to the good conduct but to the bad. Would you have no fear of him who is the authority? When you do what is good, you will receive his approval, for he is God's servant for your good. But if you do wrong be afraid, for he does not bear the sword in vain; he is the servant of God to execute his wrath on the wrongdoer. Therefore you must be subject, not only to avoid God's wrath but also for the sake of conscience. For the same reason you also pay taxes, for the authorities are the ministers of God, attending to this very thing.* So both the Lord and the Apostle announced one and the same God the Father; him who made the Law, who sent the Prophets, who made all things. And so he said, *he sent his troops,* since everyman, inasmuch as he is man, is his handiwork, even though he should be ignorant of God. In point of fact,[46] *he makes his sun rise on the evil and on the good,* and gives to all the gift of existence, *he also sends rain on the just and the unjust.*

7. He taught one and the same God not only by the passages mentioned but also by the parable of the two sons,[47] the younger of whom wasted his possessions by living luxuriously, living with harlots. For the Father allowed not even a goat for the older son, but for the sake of him who had been lost, the younger son, he ordered a fat calf to be killed and gave him the finest robe.[48] Likewise, by the parable of the laborers who were sent into the vineyard at different times,[49] He manifested one and the same Lord, who called some immediately from the beginning of the making of the world and others later; others at the middle of the times; others when the times had already progressed; similarly, others at the end. The purpose of this was that there might be many workers in their various epochs, but one householder

who calls them. For there is one vineyard, because there is also one righteousness; and there is one steward, namely, the one Spirit of God who disposes all things; likewise, there is one wage, for all received each a denarius with the king's image and inscription, namely, the knowledge about God's Son, which is imperishability.[50] For this reason he began giving the wage to the last ones, since the Lord was manifested in the last times and gave himself back again to all.[51]

8. The publican, too, who surpassed the Pharisee in prayer[52] received testimony from the Lord to the effect that he was justified more than the other, not because he worshipped another Father, but because he made his confession to that same God with great humility and without pride and boasting.

Likewise, the parable of the two sons who were sent into the vineyard manifests one and the same God.[53] The one refused his father and afterward repented when repentance did him no good. The other promised to go—he promised immediately—but he did not go (*Because every man is a liar.*)[54] *The will is ready, but one cannot bring himself to carry it out.*[55]

Also the parable of the fig tree. The Lord said of it:[56] *Lo, these three years I have come seeking fruit on this fig tree, and I find none.* Thus having pointed out his coming by means of the Prophets, through whom he came a number of times in search of the fruit of righteousness from them, but found none, he clearly manifested that the fig tree would be cut down on account of the reason stated. Again, without a parable, the Lord said to Jerusalem:[57] *O Jerusalem, Jerusalem, killing the prophets and stoning those who are sent to you! How often would I have gathered your children together as a hen gathers her brood under her wings, and you would not.* Now, what he had said by way of parable (*Lo, those three years I have come seeking fruit*) and what he said openly (*How often would I have gathered your children together*) would be a lie if we do not understand it of his coming through the Prophets, since he did come to them once, and that the first time. But that he who chose the Patriarchs is the same Word of God, both visiting them at all times through the prophetic Spirit and calling us from everywhere through his coming, besides what was said in truth, he expressed thus:[58] *Many will come from east and west, and sit at table with Abraham, Isaac, and Jacob in the kingdom of heaven, while the sons of the kingdom will be thrown out into the outer darkness; there men will weep and gnash their teeth.* So if those from the east and the west who, through the preaching of the apostles, believe in him will *sit at table with Abraham, Isaac, and Jacob in the kingdom of heaven,* partaking with them of the same banquet, one and the same God is manifested, who chose the Patriarchs, visited his people [the Jews], and called the Gentiles.

Chapter 37
Because of Free Will, Men Are Not by Nature Good or Bad.

1. That passage, *How often would I have gathered your children and you would not,*[1] makes the ancient law of human freedom manifest, namely, that God made man free from the beginning, possessing his own power as also his own soul for the purpose of voluntarily following God's teaching without being forced by him.[2] For God does not force anyone; but good counsel[3] is always at hand for him,[4] and so he gives good counsel to all. He placed in man the power of choice, as also in the angels—for the angels are intellectual[5]—in order that those who obey him would justly possess the good, which was given by God but preserved by them; those, however, who disobeyed will justly not possess the good and will receive a deserved punishment, since God in kindness bestowed a good on them, but they did not guard it with care or consider it precious, but despised his supereminent goodness. So, since they reject the good and, so to say, vomit it out, they all deservedly fall under God's just judgment. Paul the Apostle testified to this in his Letter to the Romans. He wrote thus:[6] *Or do you despise the riches of his kindness and forbearance and patience? Do you not know that God's kindness is meant to lead you to repentance? But by your hard and impenitent heart you are storing up wrath for yourself on the day of wrath when God's righteous judgment will be revealed. But,* he says, [7]*glory and honor to everyone who does good.*

So God gave the good, as also the Apostle testifies in the same letter, and those who do good receive glory and honor, for they did good when they had it in their power not to do so.[8] Those, however, who do not do good will receive God's just judgment, since they did not do good when they had it in their power to do so.

2. If some had by nature been made bad[9] and others good, the latter would not be praiseworthy for being good, because they were made such. Neither would the former be blameworthy, because they, too, were made such. But since all are of the same nature, both having

the power to retain and do the good, and both having the power to reject it and not do it, some are justly praised, even among men who are rightminded and how much more with God, and receive a worthy testimony for their choice of the good and perseverance.[10] Others, however, are blamed and receive the deserved punishment for rejecting what is just and good.[11]

For this reason the Prophets used to exhort men to observe righteousness and to do good, as we have shown by many passages. Since such [conduct] was in our power, and since we had fallen into forgetfulness because of great negligence and needed good advice, on that account the good God bestowed the good advice through the Prophets.

3. For this reason the Lord said,[12] *Let your light so shine before men that they may see your good works and give glory to your Father who is in heaven.* And,[13] *Take heed to yourselves lest your hearts be weighed down with dissipation and drunkenness and cares of this life.* And,[14] *Let your loins be girded about and your lamps burning, and be like men who are waiting for their master's return from the marriage feast, so that they may open to him at once, when he comes and knocks. Blessed are those servants whom the master on his return finds so doing.* And again,[15] *But that servant who knew his master's will, but did not act according to it shall receive a share beating.* And,[16] *Why do you call me, "Lord, Lord," and do not do what I tell you?* And again,[17] *But if that servant says to himself, "My master is delayed in coming," and begins to beat the menservants and to eat and drink, and get drunk, the master will come on a day when he does not expect, and will separate him and make him share the lot of the hypocrites.* And all such passages show that man has free will[18] and that God instructs him with advice, exhorting us to be submissive to him and deterring us from unbelief in him, but not forcing us by violence.

4. In fact, if anyone would refuse to follow the Gospel, he would be able to do so, but it would not be expedient. Certainly, disobedience to God and the rejection of good is in man's power, but that brings on no small injury and harm. On that account Paul says,[19] *All things are lawful, but not all are helpful.* By this he refers to man's freedom, by which all things are possible, since God does not force him. But this "it is not helpful" shows that we *should not misuse freedom as a cloak for evil*;[20] for that *is not helpful.* Again he says,[21] *Let everyone speak the truth with his neighbor.* And,[22] *Let no evil talk come out of your mouth, whether filthiness or silly talk or levity, which are not fitting; but instead let there be thanksgiving.* And,[23] *once you were darkness, but now you are light in*

the Lord. Walk as children of light becomingly, not in revelry and drunkenness, not in debauchery and licentiousness, not in quarreling and jealousy. And[24] *such were some of you. But you were washed, you were sanctified in the name of Our Lord.*

If, therefore, we did not have the power to do or not to do these things, what reason would the Apostle have and, long before him, the Lord himself, to give counsel to do some of them but to abstain from others? Since, however, man is endowed with free will from the beginning, and since God has free will—to whose likeness man was made—he is always advised to hold fast the good, which is perfected by obedience toward God.

5. And not only in works but also in faith did the Lord safeguard man's freedom and self-determining power, since he said,[25] *According to your faith be it done to you,* showing that it is man's faith because man has self-determining power. And again,[26] *All things are possible to one who believes,* and,[27] *Go, be it done for you as you have believed.* And all such passages show that man has self-determining power in regard to faith. For that reason,[28] *he who believes the Son has eternal life; he who does not believe him does not have eternal life, but the wrath of God rests upon him.* With that in mind, the Lord manifested his own good [free will] and pointed out that man is free and self-determining, when he addressed Jerusalem,[29] *How often would I have gathered your children together as a hen gathers her brood under her wings, but you would not. Behold your house is forsaken and desolate.*

6. Those, however, who hold opinions contrary to these introduce the Lord as powerless, namely, as if he could not carry out what he wills, or again, as ignorant, inasmuch as [men] are by nature clayish, as they say, and as such cannot receive his imperishability. But, it is said, it was necessary that he should not have made angels such that they could transgress, or men such that they immediately were ungrateful to him, since they were made rational with the power of examining and judging, and not as irrational and animal beings, which can do nothing by their will but are drawn to good by necessity and force. In them there is one "mind" and one mode of action. They are inflexible and without power of judgment who can do nothing else than what they have been made.

In that case, neither would the good be a pleasure to them, nor would the communion with God be precious.[30] Nor would the good be something greatly to be sought after, which would come to them without their own effort and care and striving, and would be implanted as spontaneous and effortless, with the result that their being good would be of no importance, because they would be such by nature rather than by volition, and their good would be spontaneous and not freely chosen. And so, they would not even understand that the good is beautiful, nor could they enjoy it, For what enjoyment of the good is there for those who are ignorant of it? And what glory is there for those who did not strive for the good? And what assurance is there for those who did not endure anything?[31] And what crown is there for those who did not acquire it as winners in a contest?

7. With this in mind the Lord spoke of the kingdom of heaven as of the violent *and those who do violence,* he said,[32] *take it,* that is, who are constantly vigilant take it by force and struggle. For this reason Paul too said to the Corinthians:[33] *Do you not know that in a race all the runners compete, but only one receives the prize? So run that you may obtain it. Every athlete exercises self-control in all things. They do it to receive a perishable wreath but we are imperishable. Well, I do not run aimlessly; I do not box as one beating the air; but I pummel my body and subdue it, lest after preaching to others I myself should be disqualified.* So, the good athlete [Paul] admonishes us in regard to the contest for imperishability, in order that we might receive the crown and might esteem the crown precious, namely, since it is won by us in a contest and is not spontaneously implanted in us. And the more precious it is, so much the more will we love it always.[34] On the contrary, the things that come to us spontaneously are not loved in the same manner as those that are discovered by much effort.

Since, then, it was in our power to love God more, both the Lord taught us and the Apostle handed down to us to discover this for ourselves by effort. Otherwise, we should not appreciate our good if we did not strive for it. Likewise, the power of seeing would not be so desirable if we had not realized what a great evil it is not to see; the experience of being sick makes good health more appreciated; the comparison with darkness [makes] light [more appreciated], and comparison with death makes life [more appreciated]. So the heavenly kingdom is esteemed more by those who realize what the earthly kingdom is. And the more it is appreciated, the more we love it; and if we have loved it more, we will be more glorious in God's presence.

The Lord, therefore, has permitted all these things for us, in order that we, having been instructed by all things, might preserve in all his love,[35] having been intelligently taught to love God. God shows himself magnanimous to man in his rebellion, and through it man has been taught, as also the Prophet said,[36] *Your apostasy will reprove you,* inasmuch as God determines all things beforehand for the perfection of man, and for the realization and revelation of [his] economies, in order that his goodness might be made manifest and his righteousness be accomplished, and the Church might be made *after the pattern of the image of his Son,*[37] and that, finally, man might reach maturity, growing to maturity by so great (economies) in order to see and comprehend God.[38]

Chapter 38
Why Man Was Not Made Perfect from the Beginning

1. If, at this point, someone says, "What then? Could not God have made man perfect from the beginning?," let him know that as far as God is concerned, since he is always the same and ingenerate,[1] all things are possible. But created things, by the very fact that they had a beginning or origin, must by virtue of this be inferior as creatures to him who created them, for things recently made could not have been ingenerate. For this very reason that they are not ingenerate, they are inferior to the Perfect Being, because inasmuch as they are of more recent origin, they are infantile; and as such they are unaccustomed to, and unexercised in, perfected discipline. For just as a mother can give solid food to her infant, but the infant is not yet able to take the more substantial food, so also God could have given man perfection from the beginning, but man was incapable of receiving it, since he was still an infant.[2] And for this reason Our Lord,[3] *recapitulating all things in himself,* came to us in these last times, not as he could have come, but as we were capable of beholding him. To be sure, he could have come to us in his ineffable glory, but we could by no means have endured the greatness of his glory. Therefore, he who was the perfect Bread of the Father[4] offered himself as milk to us who were like infants—that [milk] was his coming as Man—that we, having been fed from the breasts of his flesh, as it were, and having by such nourishment of milk become accustomed to eat and drink the Word of God, may be able to retain in ourselves the Bread of immortality, which is the Father's Spirit.[5]

2. And on this account Paul said to the Corinthians,[6] *I fed you with milk, not solid food, for you were not ready for it, that is, you learned the*

coming of the Lord in human nature, but God's Spirit had not yet rested on you, because of your weakness. For[7] *when there is jealousy and strife among you, are you not of the flesh, behaving like ordinary men?*, that is, because the Father's Spirit was not yet with them, because of their imperfection and weakness in their mode of living. So, just as the Apostle could have given them solid food—*for on whom the Apostles laid hands,*[8] these received the Holy Spirit, who is the solid food of life[9]—but they could not receive it because the faculty of perception of the mode of living that leads to God was still weak and unexercised.[10] And so, God was able in the beginning to grant perfection to man; but man, having been but recently made, could not receive it; nor, having received it, could he have comprehended it; nor having comprehended it, could he have retained it. And for this reason the Word of God, though he was perfect, became an infant together with and for man.[11] He made himself comprehensible in this wise, as far as man could comprehend him, not because of himself, but because of man's infancy. So, the impossibility and the need were not on God's part but on man's, who was but lately created and was not ingenerate.

3. In regard to God there are manifested at one and the same time power and wisdom and goodness: power and goodness, inasmuch as he created and made freely the things that did as yet not exist; wisdom, inasmuch as he gave order and harmony to the things that did exist. Some of these, through his immense kindness, receive an increase and continue for a long time, and then partake of the glory of the Ingenerate. God gives them what is good without being jealous. For, inasmuch as these things are created, they are not ingenerate; but inasmuch as they continue for long ages, they receive the power of the Ingenerate; God gratuitously bestows on them perpetual continuance.

In this way God will hold the primacy in all things, because he alone is ingenerate and prior to all and is the cause of existence for all things; whereas all things remain subjected to God. But subjection to God spells imperishability; and continuance of imperishability is the glory of the Ingenerate.[12] So by that order and by such harmony and such guidance, man, who has been created and fashioned, is made *according to the image and likeness*[13] of the Ingenerate God: The Father being well pleased and giving orders,[14] the Son administering and fashioning,[15] the Spirit nourishing and giving growth;[16] while man gradually makes progress and comes to the Perfect, that is, comes to the Ingenerate. For the Ingenerate is perfect, but that is God. Now, it was necessary for man to be first created and, having been created, to grow, and, having grown, to become mature, and having become mature to multiply, and having multiplied to grow strong, and having grown strong to be glorified, and having been glorified to see his Sovereign; for it is God who would be seen. The vision of God, however, effects imperishability, *but imperishability brings one near to God.*[17]

4. Those, then, who do not wait for the time of growth and ascribe to God the weakness of their own nature are altogether irrational. Certainly, they know neither God nor themselves; they are insatiable and ungrateful.[18] They refuse to be first that they were made, namely, men capable of suffering; they transgress the law of the human race, and before they are men, they already wish to be like God the Creator and believe that there should be no difference between the Ingenerate God and the recently created man. They are more irrational than the dumb animals. For these do not blame God for not having made them men; but each one of them, by the very fact that it was made, gives thanks to God for having made it. We, however, blame him because we were not made gods from the beginning, but first men and at length gods; although God acted thus out of his sheer goodness, lest anyone think him jealous or greedy. He declares,[19] *I have said, "You are gods, and all of you sons of the Most High."* Since we, however, could not sustain the power of the divinity, he adds,[20] *"Nevertheless, you shall die like men."* Thus he referred both to the kindness of his gift, and to our weakness, and that we have power of self-determination. For, in keeping with his great kindness, he endowed man well and made him like himself in giving him power of self-determination. Whereas, through his foreknowledge, he knew the weakness of men and its consequences, still, in keeping with his love and power, he will overcome the [weak] nature of creatures. It was necessary, however, that first nature should exist; then, what was mortal should be conquered and swallowed up by immortality and the imperishable by imperishability,[21] and that man, having received the knowledge of good and evil, should be made *according to the image and likeness* of God.[22]

Chapter 39

Man Is Endowed with Free Will to Observe God's Commandments and Prepare for His Own Reward.

1. It is good to obey God, to believe him, and to keep his commandment; and that is life for man; just as not to obey God is evil, and that is death for man. So, since God showed himself magnanimous, man knew both the good of obedience and the evil of disobedience in order that the eyes might experience[1] both, and might choose with discernment what is better, with the result that he might never become indolent and neglectful of God's command, and that he might learn by experience that to disobey God takes life away from him, and this is evil, and that he would never attempt this. On the contrary, that he might know that what preserves life, namely, to obey God, is good, and that he might guard it diligently with all care. For that reason he has a twofold perception and has knowledge of both, so that he might, with discernment, make choice of the better things. But how could he have the discernment of the good if he was ignorant of its contrary? For the understanding of things at hand is more secure and indubitable than conjecture that arises from guesswork. For example, as the tongue, through taste, experiences what sweet and bitter are; and the eye, through sight, discerns black from white; and the ear, through hearing, knows the difference in sounds; so too the mind, through experience of both kinds of knowledge, might receive discernment of the good and so be made more secure for its continuance, being obedient to God. By repentance,[2] it would first cast away disobedience as something bitter and evil, then it would learn by grasping what it really means to be contrary to good and sweet, so that it would never attempt to taste disobedience to God. Now, if anyone should try to escape from this knowledge of both kinds, and also from the twofold perception of the knowledge, he, unawares, kills himself as a man.

2. How, then, can he be a God who has not yet been made a man? How can he be perfect who has but recently been created? How can he be immortal who in his mortal nature did not obey his Maker? It is a fact that you must first preserve the order of man[3] and afterward partake of the glory of God.[4] For you do not make God, but God makes you. So if you are the work of God, wait for the hand [God's Word] of your Artificer, which will make all things in due time,[5] as far

as you are concerned who are created. Offer to him your heart pliable and docile, and guard the image according to which the Artificer patterned you since you have in yourself the Dew [the Spirit],[6] that you may not become hardened and lose the traces of his fingers [the Word and the Spirit].[7] By guarding what has been fashioned, you will ascend to the Perfect One; for by God's art the clay that is in you becomes hidden. His hand framed the substance in you. He will line you from within and from without with refined gold and silver[8] and will adorn you so much that the King himself will be enamored of your beauty.[9] If, on the contrary, you have become hardened immediately and reject his art and are ungrateful to him for having made you, since you have become ungrateful toward God, you have lost at the same time his art and his life. For it is proper to God's kindness to make; but it is proper to man's nature to be made.[10] So if you give to him what is your own, namely, faith in him and subjection, you will receive his art and will be God's perfect work.

3. If, on the contrary, you do not believe in him and flee from his hand, you will be the cause of imperfection in yourself—but not in him who called you—because you have not obeyed. For example, he sent those who should extend the invitation to the wedding; but those who did not obey him deprived themselves of the royal supper.[11] God's art, then, is not defective; for he has power to raise up children to Abraham from stones,[12] but he who does not accept that art is the cause of his own imperfection. For light does not cease because of those who have blinded themselves, but it continues such as it is by nature, while those who have blinded themselves are placed in darkness through their own fault. Light[13] will not subject anyone to itself necessarily; neither does God force anyone who does not wish to keep his art. So those who have apostatized from the Father's light and have transgressed the law of freedom have apostatized through their own fault, since they had been created with free will and power of self-determination.

4. God, who has foreknowledge of all things, prepared fit dwellings[14] for both classes. To those who search after the light of imperishability and return to it, he kindly grants the light they long for. But to the others who despised this light and turned themselves from it and flee from it and, so to say, blind themselves, he prepared darkness that is suitable to such as oppose the light; and those who flee from subjection to him he subjects to a suitable punishment. Now subjection to God is eternal rest so those who flee from the light will have

a place deserving of their flight, and those who flee from the eternal rest will have a dwelling suitable to their flight. Now, since all good things are with God, those who of their own free will flee from God deprive themselves of all good things. And if they have been deprived of all good things in respect to God, consequently, they will fall into God's just judgment. For these who flee from rest will justly spend their time in punishment; and those who flee from the light will justly dwell in darkness. Just as those who flee from material light enslave themselves in darkness, so that they themselves are the cause of their being deprived of light and of dwelling in darkness, and the light is not the cause of such a mode of living, as we have said, so those who flee from God's eternal light, which contains in itself all good things, are themselves the cause of their dwelling in darkness. Having been deprived of all good things, they have become their own cause of such a dwelling.[15]

Chapter 40
The One and Same God Rewards and Punishes.

1. There is, then, one and the same God the Father who prepares the good things that are with himself for those who desire communion with him and persevere in submission to him. But he prepares eternal fire for the author of the apostasy, the Devil, and for the angels who apostatized with him. *Into this fire,* the Lord said,[1] *those who are separated on his left will be cast.* The Prophet said the same thing,[2] *I am a jealous God. I make weal and create woe.* He makes peace and friendship with, and brings into unity, those who repent and turn back to him. For those, however, who do not repent and who flee from his light, he prepares eternal fire and outer darkness—which are indeed evils for those who fall into them.

2. Now, if the Father who grants rest were really different from the God who prepares the fire, their sons, too, would be different. The one would send people into his Father's kingdom; the other would send people into the eternal fire. But they are one and the same because the one and same Lord revealed that in the judgment the entire human race would be separated, as a shepherd separates the sheep from the goats,[3] and since he will say to some,[4] *Come, O blessed of my Father, inherit the kingdom prepared for you*; but he will say to the others, *Depart from me, you cursed, into the eternal fire, which my Father*

prepared for the devil and his angels.[5] Thus, one and the same Father is most clearly manifested who[6] *makes weal and creates woe,* preparing for both classes what is suitable, as one judge who sends both to their suitable places. This the Lord revealed in the parable of the cockle and the wheat, when he said:[7] *Therefore, just as the weeds are gathered and burned with fire, so will it be at the close of the age. The Son of Man will send his angels, and they will gather out of his kingdom all causes of sin and evildoers and throw them into the furnace of fire; there men will weep and gnash their teeth. Then the righteous will shine like the sun in the kingdom of their Father.* So the same Father who prepared the kingdom for the righteous into which his Son takes those who are worthy also prepared *the furnace of fire* into which the angels who were sent by the Son of Man at God's command will send those who deserve it.

3. The Lord, in fact,[8] *sowed good seed in his field—for the field, he said, is the world; but when the men were asleep, the enemy came and sowed weeds among the grain and went away.* Really, this angel and enemy has been a rebel since the day on which he envied God's handiwork and attempted to make him God's enemy.[9] Wherefore, God in turn separated from fellowship with himself him who of his own accord secretly sowed weeds, that is, who introduced the transgression. He had pity, however, on man who negligently and wickedly took upon himself disobedience and turned back upon the author of the enmity that enmity by which he wished to make man God's enemy. He did so by removing his own enmity against man and turning it back and putting it again against the Serpent. That is according to what the Scripture tells us God said to the Serpent:[10] *I will put enmity between you and the woman, between your seed and her seed. He shall observe your head and you shall observe his heel.* This enmity the Lord recapitulated in himself by being made man from woman,[11] and by *trampling on his [Serpent's] head,* as we have shown in the preceding Book.[12]

Chapter 41

Unbelieving and Disobedient People Are the Devil's Angels and Sons.

1. Since the Lord said that there are certain angels who belong to the Devil, for whom the eternal fire had been prepared;[1] and again, since he said in regard to the weeds that[2] *the weeds are the wicked sons,* it

is necessary to the author of this transgression. But it was not the Devil who made them by nature either angels or men. To be sure, we do not recognize that the Devil made anything at all, precisely because he is a creature himself, just like the rest of the angels; for God made all things. David, too, said the same of all these things:[3] *For he spoke and they were made; he commanded and they were created.*

2. Since, therefore, all things were created by God, and since the Devil is the cause of apostasy for himself and for the rest, rightly does Scripture always style such as continue in the apostasy the sons of the Devil and the angels of the wicked one. For, as someone before us remarked,[4] a son is understood in two ways. The one by nature, because he was born a son; the other is considered a son because he has been made; nevertheless, there is a difference between being born and having been made, inasmuch as the one is born from him, but the other has been made by him, either by virtue of creation or by virtue of teaching a doctrine. Really, one who is taught by someone by word is called the son of the teacher, and he his father. So by nature, that is, by virtue of creation, we are all, so to say, God's sons, because we have all been made by him.[5] By virtue of obedience and doctrine, we are not all God's sons, only those are who believe him[6] and do his will.[7] Those who do not believe and do not do his will are sons and angels of the Devil, inasmuch as they do the Devil's work.[8] That this is so he said in Isaiah,[9] *Sons have I reared and brought up; but they have rebelled against me.* Again, it says these children are foreigners:[10] *foreign children have lied to me*; namely, according to nature, inasmuch as they were made by him, they are his children; but according to their deeds they are not his children.

3. For example, among men children who are disobedient to their parents and are disinherited are still their children according to nature but are disinherited by law. They do not become heirs of the natural parents. The same is true with God. Those who do not obey him have been disinherited by him and cease to be his children. And so they cannot receive his inheritance, as David says,[11] *The wicked go astray from the womb. Their wrath is like that of the serpent.* On that account the Lord called those whom he knew to be the children of men *the brood of vipers*,[12] because of their likeness to these animals that walk about capriciously and injure others. For he said,[13] *Take heed of...the leaven of the Pharisees and the Sadducees.* And of Herod he said,[14] *Tell that fox,* thus pointing out his wicked cunningness and deceitfulness. For the same reason the Prophets David and Jeremiah said,[15] *Man when he*

is surrounded by pomp becomes like a senseless beast; and,[16] *They have become like lusty stallions toward women; each one neighing for his neighbor's wife.* And when Isaiah was preaching in Judea and disputing with Israel, he called them the rulers of Sodom and the people of Gomorrah,[17] pointing out a transgression that is like that of the Sodomites, and that their sins are the same as those of the Sodomites. He called them by the same name because of the similar action. But they were not made such by nature by God; rather, they had the power of acting righteously, Isaiah said when he gave the good advice to them:[18] *Wash yourselves, make yourselves clean; remove the evil from your lives before my eyes; cease to do evil*; namely, because these received the same reproof as the Sodomites when they transgressed and sinned; but when they had converted and repented and ceased from evil, they could be God's children, and could obtain the inheritance of imperishability which is bestowed by him.

And so according to this reasoning, he called those who believe the devil and do his works the Devil's angels and sons,[19] though they had in the beginning all been made by one and the same God. On the other hand, when they believe and are subject to God, persevere and keep his doctrine, they are sons of God. But when they have apostatized and have become transgressors, they are assigned to the Devil, the author [and] the one who became the cause of apostasy first for himself and then for the rest.

4. Now, since the Lord's words are many but all announce one and the same Father, the Creator of this world, it was necessary that we, too, for the sake of those who are held bound by many errors, refute them by many arguments, so that, having been refuted by many arguments, they could in some way be converted to the Truth and be saved.

It is necessary, after these words of the Lord, to add to this composition in the following Book the doctrine of Paul, and to examine his mind, and to explain the Apostle and to elucidate Paul's statements that have been given a different interpretation by the heretics who understand nothing at all of Paul; and to make known the insanity of their foolishness; and to show by means of the same Paul, from whom they make difficulties for us, that they are liars, but the Apostle is the preacher of the Truth; one God the Father who spoke to Abraham, who gave the Law, who sent the Prophets, who in the last times sent his Son and bestowed salvation on his creatures, namely, on the substance of the flesh.

In another book, then, we will dispose of the rest of the words of the Lord about the Father, which he taught not by parables but plainly, along with the explanation of the Letters of the Blessed Paul. Thus, God granting, we shall furnish you with the entire work of THE EXPOSÉ AND REFUTATION OF THE FALSELY SO-CALLED KNOWLEDGE. Then we have trained ourselves and you in five books in the refutation of all the heretics.

ST. IRENAEUS OF LYONS
AGAINST THE HERESIES

Book 5

PREFACE

Dear Friend, in the four preceding Books that we sent you,[1] we exposed all the heretics and brought to light their doctrines. Likewise, we refuted these men who thought up impious opinions. This we did, both by (exposing) the doctrine peculiar to each one of them, which has been left in their writings;[2] and by reasoning that proceeds from all kinds of illustrations.[3] Thus we have demonstrated the Truth and manifested the Church's teaching, which, as we have shown, the Prophets have heralded, which Christ brought to completion, which the apostles handed down to us, from whom the Church accepted it and alone safeguards it well throughout the whole world[4] and hands it down to her children.[5]

So, having solved all the difficulties that are proposed to us by the heretics, and having explained the doctrines of the apostles, and having manifested many things that the Lord said and did in parables,[6] we shall, in this Fifth Book of the entire work dealing with THE EXPOSÉ AND REFUTATION OF THE FALSELY SO-CALLED KNOWLEDGE, try to present proofs from the rest of the words of our Lord's teaching and from the letters of the apostles. We do this in keeping with your request and obedient to your command.[7] And we do it because we are appointed *to the ministry of the word.*[8] We shall make every effort in our power to offer you many arguments as an aid against the contradictions of the heretics;[9] moreover, we shall try to strengthen the minds of the neophytes, that they may guard secure the faith that they have received from the Church well guarded, and may by no means be turned away from those who teach them badly and try to mislead them from the Truth.

Now, it will be proper for you and all who read this writing to read more carefully what we have already said, that you may know the systems themselves against which we make the objections.[10] For by this you will both rightly refute them and, from what has been furnished, you will have counterproofs against them. By means of the heavenly faith, you will discard their doctrines as dung, and you will follow the only secure and true Teacher, the Word of God, Jesus Christ, Our Lord, who on account of his *immense love* was made what we are, in order that he might perfect us to be what he is.[11]

Section 1

PROOF OF THE RESURRECTION OF THE FLESH

Chapter 1
Christ Is Truly Our Savior.

1. Certainly, in no other way could we have learned the things of God unless our Teacher, who is the Word, had become man; for no one else but his own Word could have revealed to us the things of the Father.[1] *For who else has known the mind of the Lord, or who else has been his counsellor?*[2] Again, we could not have learned in any other way than by seeing our Teacher and hearing his voice with our own ears. Thus, having become imitators of his works and *doers of his words,*[3] we—we who were but recently created, we who have been made according to the likeness of himself, by himself who is the only good and excellent [God], and who has the gift of imperishability—might have communion with him,[4] and receive growth from him who is perfect and who is before all creation.[5] For we, we who as yet did not exist, had been predestined according to the Father's foreknowledge to have existence, but once we had been made we received a beginning as a creature,[6] in the times that were foreknown, according to the ministry of the Word, who is perfect in all respects, because he is the powerful Word and true Man.[7] He redeemed us rationally[8] through his blood.[9] *He gave himself as a ransom* for those who had been led into captivity.[10] And since the Apostasy ruled over us unjustly, since by nature we belonged to God who rules all things, and so alienated us against our nature and made us his disciples, the Word of God who is all-powerful[11] and not deficient in his justice, justly turned against the Rebellion itself and redeemed from it what is his very own. He did this not by force—as the Rebellion ruled over us in the beginning, by snatching away greedily what was not his own—but with persuasion, as becomes God who persuades to obtain what he wills. And he does not use force, so that what is just might not be crushed, or that God's ancient handiwork might not perish.[12]

Therefore, all the doctrines of the heretics crumble to ruins, since the Lord redeemed us by his blood, and gave his soul for our souls, and his flesh for our flesh,[13] and poured out the Father's Spirit to effect the union and communion of God with man, by bringing down God to men through the Spirit, and by bringing man up to God through the incarnation. By his coming, too, he gave us imperishability securely and truly through communion with himself.[14]

2. Really, those who assert that he appeared only putatively are senseless. These things, certainly, did not take place putatively, but in

true reality. If he, though not man, appeared as man, then neither did he remain what he truly was, Spirit-God,[15] because Spirit is invisible; nor was there any truth in him, for he was not what he appeared to be. We have already said that Abraham and the other Prophets were wont to see him in prophetic vision, prophesying by vision what he would be in the future. If, therefore, at present he appears such, but actually is not what he was seen to be, this, too, is a kind of prophetic vision[16] that has been made for men, and it is necessary that we await another coming of his, in which he will really be such as he is now seen in prophetic vision. We have shown, moreover, that it is the same to say that he appeared putatively and that he received nothing from Mary.[17] For he would not be man with true blood and flesh, by which he redeemed us, unless he had recapitulated in himself the ancient handiwork of Adam.[18] Senseless, therefore, are the Valentinians who give out this opinion, that they might exclude salvation of the flesh and reject God's handiwork.[19]

3. Senseless, too, are the Ebionites, who do not receive into their souls through faith the union of God and man, but continue in the ancient leaven of birth,[20] and refuse[21] to understand that[22] *the Holy Spirit came upon Mary and the power of the Most High overshadowed her, therefore the child born is holy, and the Son of God,* of the Father of all things, who wrought his incarnation and revealed a new birth.[23] The purpose of this was that, just as through the first birth we have inherited death, so through this birth we might inherit life. So these men reject the mixture of the heavenly wine, and they wish to be only worldly water.[24] By not taking God into their mixture, they remain in the Adam who had been conquered and cast out of paradise. They do not consider that, as in the beginning of our formation the breath of life, which was from God, was united with the handiwork and gave life to man, and showed him to be a rational animal;[25] so in the end the Father's Word and God's Spirit,[26] having been united to the ancient substance of the handiwork of Adam, made man living and perfect, capable of receiving the perfect Father.[27] The result was that, just as all had died in the natural man [Adam], so all are given life in the spiritual man [Christ].[28] For Adam will never escape God's hands, to whom the Father spoke when he said,[29] *Let us make man to our image and likeness.* And so in the end, his hands made man living and perfect, *not of the will of flesh, nor of the will of man, but of the will* of the Father,[30] that Adam might be to *the image and likeness* of God.[31]

CHAPTER 2
ON BECOMING MAN CHRIST CAME IN THE FLESH THAT BELONGED TO HIM. HE GAVE MAN SALVATION THROUGH REDEMPTION AND THROUGH THE EUCHARIST.

1. Senseless, too, are those who assert that the Lord came to what did not belong to him, as if he were greedy of others' possessions, in order to present the man who was made by another god to the God who neither made nor created anything, but who even from the beginning was deprived of a creation of men that was his own. Then, his coming, which according to them was into another's domain, was not just. Nor, if he was not truly made man, did he truly redeem us by his blood, restoring to his handiwork what was said of it in the beginning, namely, that *man was made to the image and likeness* of God, since he did not snatch away[1] deceitfully what belonged to another, but justly and kindly took back[2] what belonged to himself; as far as we who were redeemed are concerned, he did it kindly.[3] For we did not give to him anything beforehand, nor does he want anything from us as if he were indigent; but we need communion with him. For that reason he kindly poured himself out that he might gather us into the Father's bosom.

2. Altogether senseless are they who hold in contempt God's entire economy and deny salvation to the flesh and spurn its regeneration, asserting that it is not capable of imperishability. Now, if this flesh is not saved, neither did the Lord redeem us with his blood, nor is the cup of the Eucharist a communion in his blood, nor is the bread we break a communion in his body.[4] To be sure, blood is only from the veins and flesh and from the rest of the human nature, which, however, the Word of God truly became, and so he redeemed us by his blood. The Apostle, for example, says,[5] *In whom we have redemption through his blood, and the remission of sins.*

And since we are his members,[6] we are also nourished by the creation; he himself furnishes us with the creature by making the sun rise and making it rain as he wills.[7] He confessed[8] that the cup which is from the creation is his Blood, from which he gives growth to our blood; and he affirmed that the bread which is from the creation is his Body, from which he gives growth to our bodies.[9]

3. When, therefore, both the cup that has been mixed and the bread that has been made[10] receive the Word of God[11] and become the

Eucharist of the Blood and Body of Christ,[12] from which the substance of our flesh gets its growth and consistency,[13] how, then, can they deny that flesh is capable of receiving God's gift, which is eternal life—that flesh which is nourished by Christ's Body and Blood, and that is his member?[14] As the Blessed Paul said in his Letter to the Ephesians,[15] *Because we are members of his body, of his flesh and of his bones.* He did not say this of some spiritual and invisible man[16]—*for a spirit has not bones and flesh*—but of that composition which is a true man, which consists of flesh, nerves, and bones, and is nourished from the cup, which is his Blood, and gets its growth from the bread, which is his Body.

By way of illustration, a branch of the vine, when placed in the ground, will produce fruit in due time, *and the grain of wheat that falls into the ground* and decomposes rises multiplied, through God's Spirit, *who holds all things together.*[17] After that, all these things, through wisdom, serve the use of men.[18] Besides, when they receive the Word of God, they become the Eucharist, which is Christ's Body and Blood. Now, in like manner, our bodies, having been nourished by the Eucharist and buried in the earth, and decomposed into earth, will rise in due time, when the Word of God bestows resurrection on them *for the glory of God the Father,*[19] who truly surrounds this mortal body with immortality and gratuitously grants imperishability to the perishable.[20] [All this] is because God's *power is made perfect in weakness,*[21] so that we might not have life as if from ourselves, and become puffed up and extol ourselves against God, taking an ungrateful attitude; but that by experience we might learn that we possess perpetual continuance because of his greatness, but not because of our nature. Likewise, that we might neither be deprived at any time of the knowledge about God just as he is,[22] nor be ignorant of our nature, but that we might know both what God is capable of and what benefit man receives, and so might not stray at any time from the true understanding of the things that exist just as they are, that is, those of God and of man. And, perhaps, as we have already mentioned, God allowed our dissolution into earth that, having been disciplined in every respect, we might in the future be careful in all things and be ignorant neither of God nor of ourselves.

Chapter 3
God's Power Will Shine Forth in the Resurrection of Our Dust to Glory.

1. The Apostle has shown in the clearest way that man was handed over to his weakness, lest being puffed up at any time, he would stray from the Truth. In his Second Letter to the Corinthians he says:[1] *To keep me from becoming too elated by the abundance of revelations a thorn was given me in the flesh, a messenger of Satan, to harass me. Three times I besought the Lord about this, that it should leave me; but he said to me, "My grace is sufficient for you, for power is made perfect in weakness." I will all the more gladly boast of my weakness, that the power of Christ may rest upon me.* What then, someone will ask, "Did the Lord, therefore, wish his Apostle to be thus harassed and undergo such weakness?" "Yes," says the Word;[2] *for power is made perfect in weakness,* making him better who recognizes God's power through his own weakness. For how would man have learned that he was weak and mortal by nature, but that God is immortal and powerful, unless he had learned by experience what is in the one and the other? Surely, to learn of his own weakness by endurance is not evil; rather, it is something good not to go astray in one's nature. On the other hand, to have extolled himself against God and taken to himself a glory of his own in a presumptuous manner made man ungrateful and brought much evil on him, yet not so as to take away from him the Truth and the love, even the one toward his Maker.[3] Rather, the experience of both impressed on him the true knowledge about God and man and increased his love toward God. But where there is a growth in love, there greater glory will be made perfect by God's power for those who love him.

2. Those, therefore,[4] reject God's power and do not consider what the Word is, who look to the weakness of the flesh, but do not consider the power of him who raises the flesh from the dead. For if he does not give life to the mortal body and does not lead the perishable to imperishability, he is no longer the powerful God. But that he is powerful in all such things, we ought to understand from our own beginning, since God took the dust of the earth and made humans out of it. Indeed, it is much more difficult and incredible to give existence to nonexistent bones, nerves, veins, and the rest of the human composite, and to make man a sentient and rational animal, than to make whole again what had been made but was resolved into earth,

on account of the reasons already given, though it had passed into the elements from which in the beginning man, who had as yet not been made, was made. To be sure, he who in the beginning, when he willed, gave existence to him who as yet was not, much more, when he wills, will restore those who at one time existed, to the life that is given by him.

The flesh, which in the beginning accepted God's skill, will be found capable of receiving and accepting God's power.[5] The eye that sees, the ear that hears, the hand that touches and works, the sinews stretched tight and holding the limbs together, the arteries and veins, which are transits for blood and breath, the diverse entrails, and the blood that is the means of union between body and soul,—all these are different. What then? There is no end to enumerating the many members of man's composition[6] that was not made except by God's multiple wisdom.[7] But these members that partake of God's art and wisdom also partake of his power.[8]

3. The flesh, then, is not excluded from God's art and wisdom and power. For this *power*, which bestows life, *is made perfect in weakness*, that is, in the flesh.[9] Now those who assert that the flesh is not capable of the life given by God, let them tell us whether they say these things while they are at present living and partaking of life, or whether they will confess that they have absolutely nothing of life, but are dead even now. And if they are dead, how do they move and speak and do other things that are not the works of the dead but of the living? But if they are alive now, and if their entire body partakes of life, how do they dare say that flesh is not able to partake of life, since they profess to have life at present? That is just as if one would hold a sponge full of water, or a lamp full of light, and say that the sponge cannot partake of water; or the lamp of light.[10] In the same manner, these men, too, assert that they are alive and, boastingly,[11] are bearers of life in their members, but later contradict themselves and say that their members are not capable of receiving life. Now if the life that is temporary is so powerful to give life to our *mortal members*,[12] though it is much weaker than that eternal life, why does the life that is more efficient[13] and eternal not give life to the flesh that has already been exercised and accustomed to bear life?

Now, that flesh is capable of partaking of life is shown by the fact that it is living;[14] for it lives as much as God wills it to live. And that God has power to give life to it is evident; for, since he gives life to us who live, and since the Lord has power to give life to his handiwork, and since flesh is capable of being given life, what else is there that would prevent the flesh from receiving imperishability, which is a long[15] and unending life, given by God?

Chapter 4
There Is No Other God Besides the Creator Who Also Gives Salvation.

1. Those who imagine another Father, whom they call good, besides the Maker,[1] present the Maker (unawares to themselves) as weak and lazy and neglectful, not to say also envious,[2] inasmuch as they assert that the bodies are not given life by him. Certainly, when they say that things like the spirit and the soul continue immortal[3]—a point manifest to all—and that these are given life by the Father, but that the other (the body), which differs from those, but is not given life in any other way than that God bestows it, is devoid of life, it is clear that their Father is either powerless and lazy, or envious and neglectful.

In truth, since the Creator gives life to our mortal bodies here below and promises resurrection through the Prophets, as we will demonstrate,[4] which one is shown to be more concerned and stronger and truly good? Is it the Creator who gives life to the entire person, or is it their Father, falsely so-called, who imagines he gives life to the things that by nature are immortal, that, namely, are able to live by their nature; while to the things that need some aid from him in order to live, he is not kind enough to give life, but neglectfully leaves them dead? Is it, then, that their Father does not give life to them though he can give it, or because he cannot? Indeed, if he cannot, he is no longer powerful, nor more perfect than the Creator. For the Creator bestows what that one cannot bestow, as everyone can see. But if he does not bestow, though he can, he is manifested to be no longer good, but an envious and neglectful Father.

If, however, they assign some other cause why their Father does not give life to the bodies, that cause must necessarily appear greater than the Father since it prevails over the kindness, and his kindness will be powerless by reason of the cause which they assign. That the bodies, however, can receive life can be seen by all; for they live as long as God wills them to live. These men are, then, no longer able to say that the bodies can in no way receive life. So if on account of necessity or some other cause they who can partake of life are not given life, their Father will be a slave to necessity and to a cause, and he is no longer free, with self-determining power.[5]

Chapter 5

The Old Testament Offers Clear Examples That God Can Raise Up Our Bodies to Eternal Life.

1. Let these heretics read the Scriptures to learn that (our) bodies continued on for so long as it pleased God. They will find that some of our ancestors lived more than seven hundred, eight hundred, even nine hundred years. Their bodies attained length of days,[1] and they participated in life, so long as God willed that they live. And what do we say about the following? Enoch, for example, because he *was pleasing to God*, was transferred in the body in which he pleased him.[2] This revealed beforehand the transfer of the just. And Elijah, while he was in the substance of the created order, was assumed.[3] Thus he prophesied the assumption of the spiritual men.[4] Certainly, they received this assumption and transfer by the very hands by which they were fashioned in the beginning. For God's hands had become accustomed in Adam to order and govern and bear their own handiwork, and to transfer it and place it where it pleased them. Where, then, was the first man placed? In paradise, as the Scripture says,[5] *And God planted a garden in Eden, in the east; and there he put the man whom he had formed.* From there he was cast out into this world when he was disobedient. Wherefore the presbyters, who were the disciples of the apostles,[6] say that those who were transferred were transferred there. Really, paradise was prepared for the just and for those who possess the Spirit. The Apostle Paul was also carried to it, and he heard ineffable words,[7] ineffable as far as we are concerned. [The presbyters also say] that those who were transferred there remain there until the consummation, together awaiting the imperishability.

2. If anyone should think it impossible for men to live so long a time, and that Elijah was not assumed in the flesh[8] but that his flesh was consumed in the fiery chariot,[9] he should take note of the fact that Jonah was thrown out into the deep and swallowed into the whale's belly but was again vomited up safe on the earth by God's order.[10]

Likewise, Hananiah, Azariah, and Mishael, who were thrown into the fiery furnace that had been heated sevenfold, were not harmed in the least, nor was any smoke of fire on them.[11] God's hand was present with them, and it wrought in them things unexpected and impossible to men's nature. So what is strange if, serving the Father's will, it wrought something unexpected in those who were transferred? Now, this (hand) is God's Son. Scripture tells us Nebuchadnezzar said of him:[12] *Did we not cast three men into the fire? And I see four men walking in the midst of the fire and the appearance of the fourth is like the Son of Man.*

So, neither the nature of any created thing nor the weakness of the flesh will be stronger than God's will. For God is not subject to created things; no, they are subject to God, and all serve his will. For this reason the Lord said,[13] *What is impossible with men is possible with God.* Just as it seems incredible and impossible to men who are now living and who are ignorant of God's economy,[14] that a man could live so many years, and yet our ancestors did live and those who were transferred are living as a type of the future *length of days*;[15] and that some came out safe from the whale's belly and from the fiery furnace, and yet they did come out, being led out, so to say, by God's hand, in order to show his power. So at present, though some are ignorant of God's power and promise, and deny his salvation, because they think it impossible for God to raise up the bodies and bestow on them perpetual continuance, nevertheless, the incredulity of such does not make void the faithfulness of God.[16]

Chapter 6

God Will Glorify the Entire Man, Because the Word Assumed Our Entire Nature.

1. Now, God will be praised in his handiwork by fashioning it to conform and correspond to his Son.[1] For by the Father's hands, namely, the Son and the Holy Spirit, man, and not part of man, is made to the image and likeness of God. Now, the soul and the "Spirit" can be a part of man, but by no means the [whole] man; for the perfect man consists of the mingling and the union of the soul, which assumed the Father's "Spirit," and which has been united with the flesh, which was fashioned after the image of God.[2]

For this reason the Apostle declares: *We speak wisdom among the perfect.*[3] He calls those perfect who have received God's Spirit and who speak with all the tongues through the Spirit, as he himself spoke. We, too, hear many brothers in the Church who possess the prophetic charisms, and speak with all the tongues through the Spirit, and bring out into the open secrets of men for the benefit of others, and declare the mysteries of God. The Apostle calls them also spiritual,[4] since they are spiritual by virtue of the participation of the Spirit and not because they have been despoiled and deprived of their flesh. Really, if one would remove from someone the substance of the flesh, namely, of the handiwork, and would understand only the Spirit, such a one would no longer be a spiritual man, but man's spirit, or God's Spirit.[5] But since this spirit is mingled with the soul and both are united to the handiwork, man has become spiritual and perfect because of the outpouring of the Spirit.[6]

It is he who was *made after* God's *image and likeness.* But if the spirit is lacking to the soul, such a one is truly ensouled and, having been left carnal, he will be imperfect.[7] He has the image of the handiwork but has not assumed the likeness through the spirit. Just as such a one is imperfect, so, if anyone takes away the image and spurns the handiwork, this can no longer be considered man, but either a part of man, as we have said, or something other than man. For the handiwork of the flesh by itself is not the perfect man but the body of man and a part of man.[8] Neither is even the soul itself a man, but the soul of man and a part of man; nor is the Spirit man, for it is called spirit and not man. But the mingling and the union of all these makes the perfect man.

With that in view, the Apostle explained himself and made clear who is the perfect and spiritual man, who is saved. This he said in his First Letter to the Thessalonians,[9] *May the God of peace himself sanctify you to be perfect, and may your whole self, spirit and soul and body, be preserved blameless at the coming of our Lord Jesus Christ.* Really, what reason did he have to pray for these three—the soul, the body, and the spirit—that they be preserved as a whole[10] for the Lord's coming unless he knew that the restoration and the union of the three would be their one only and same salvation?[11] For this reason he called those *perfect* who present all three *blameless* to God. So those are *perfect* who continuously possess God's Spirit within themselves and *preserve* their souls and bodies *blameless,* that is, they keep the faith in God and practice justice toward their neighbor.[12]

2. Hence he also says that the handiwork is God's temple. *Do you not know,* he asks,[13] *that you are God's temple, and that God's Spirit dwells in you? If anyone destroys God's temple, God will destroy him; for God's temple is holy, and that temple you are.* He clearly calls the body the temple in which the Spirit dwells. The Lord said the same of himself:[14] *Destroy this temple, and in three days I will raise it up. But,* it says, *he spoke about his body.* Paul, too, knows that our bodies are not only a temple but the members of Christ, as he tells the Corinthians:[15] *Do you not know that your bodies are the members of Christ? Shall I therefore take the members of Christ and make them members of a prostitute?* He did not say that about some other kind of spiritual man, for such a one does not embrace a prostitute. But our body, namely, the flesh when it continues in holiness and purity, he called the members of Christ; but when it embraces a prostitute, it becomes the member of a prostitute. That is why he said,[16] *If anyone destroys God's temple, God will destroy him.*

So, how is it not the greatest blasphemy to say that God's temple, in which the Father's Spirit dwells, and the members of Christ do not partake of salvation but are to be reduced to ruins? That our bodies, however, are raised, not in virtue of their own substance, but by God's power, he tells the Corinthians:[17] *Now the body is not meant for immorality, but for the Lord, and the Lord for the body. And God raised the Lord and will also raise us up by his power.*

Chapter 7

Since Christ Rose in a Body Like Ours, We Too Shall Rise in Our Bodies.

1. Therefore, just as Christ rose in the substance of our flesh and showed the marks of the nails and the opening in his side to his disciples[1]—for these things are signs of his flesh, which rose from the dead,—so Paul said:[2] *He will raise us up by his power.*

To the Romans, too, he said:[3] *But if the Spirit of him who raised Jesus from the dead dwells in you, then he who raised Christ from the dead will give life to your mortal bodies.* Which then are the mortal bodies? Are they the souls? No, souls are incorporeal compared to the bodies. For,[4] *God breathed into man's nostrils the breath of life; and man became a living soul*; now, *the breath of life* is incorporeal. They cannot even call it [the soul] mortal, since it is *the breath of life*.[5] That is why David said,[6] *And my soul will live for him*, inasmuch as in him it [the soul] is the substance that is immortal.[7] Nor can they say that the mortal body is the Spirit. What, then, remains to be called the mortal body but the handiwork, namely the flesh, of which the Word said that God *will give life* to it? For this is the element that dies and dissolves, but not the soul. For to die is to lose the power of life and then to be breathless, soulless, devoid of motion, and to pass away into the things from which it got the beginning of its substance. But this does not happen to the soul, for it is *the breath of life*; nor to the spirit, for the spirit is not composed of parts, but simple, which cannot dissolve. It is, moreover, the life of those who receive it. So there is nothing left but to show that death is related to the flesh, which, after the soul has departed, becomes breathless and soulless and gradually dissolves into earth from which it was taken. The flesh, then, is what is mortal. It is that of which he also says,[8] *He will give life to your mortal bodies.* This, too, is why he says in the First Letter to the Corinthians,[9] *So is it with the resurrection of the dead. What is sown is perishable, what is raised is imperishable. What you sow,* he says, *does not come to life unless it first dies.*

2. But what is it that is sown as a grain of wheat and rots in the earth, except our bodies, which are placed in the earth into which also the seeds are cast? So he said, *It is sown* in dishonor, it is raised in glory. What is more dishonorable than dead flesh? Or, again, what is more honorable than the flesh that rises and receives imperishability?[10] *It is sown* in weakness, it *is raised in power.* "In weakness" that is its own; for, since it is earth, it returns to earth;[11] but "in power" that is God's who raises it from the dead.[12] *It is sown in a physical* body, it is raised a spiritual body. Without doubt he taught that he is not speaking of the soul or of the spirit, but of the dead bodies. For these are ensouled bodies, that is, they partake of the soul, which, once they have lost it, they are dead. Then when they rise through the Spirit, they become spiritual bodies, in order that continuing forever through the Spirit they may have life.

He says,[13] *Now our knowledge is imperfect, and our prophecy is imperfect, but then face-to-face.* Peter also said the same thing,[14] *Without seeing him you love him. Though you do not now see him, you believe him and exult with unutterable joy.* For our face will see the face of the Lord, and it will rejoice with an unutterable joy, namely, when it will see its joy.

Chapter 8
The Gifts of the Holy Spirit Make Us Spiritual and Prepare Us for Imperishability.

1. At present we receive a certain part of his Spirit[1] for the perfection and preparation of imperishability,[2] so we may gradually become accustomed to receiving and bearing God. The Apostle also called this a pledge, that is, a part of the honor that was promised us by God. In his Letter to the Ephesians he says:[3] *And in him you also who have heard the word of truth, the gospel of your salvation, and have believed in him, were sealed with the promised Holy Spirit, who is the pledge of our inheritance.* So that by thus dwelling in us, this pledge already makes us spiritual, and[4] *what is mortal may be swallowed up by the immortal.* He says,[5] *For you are not in the flesh, you are in the Spirit, if the Spirit of God dwells in you.* But this does not take place by the boasting of the flesh, but by communion with the Spirit. For those to whom he wrote were not without flesh; but they had assumed God's Spirit, through whom we cry,[6] *Abba, Father.* If, therefore, at present with the aid of the pledge[7] we cry *Abba, Father,* what will happen when on rising *we shall see him face-to-face,*[8] when all the members will overflow with a hymn of joy, glorifying him who raised them from the dead and gave them the gift of eternal life?[9] For if the pledge, by assuming man to itself,[10] already makes us say *Abba, Father,* what will the entire grace of the Spirit do, which will be given to man by God? It will make us like him and will perfect us by the Father's will; for it will make man *according to God's image and likeness.*[11]

2. The Apostle rightly calls those spiritual[12] who have the pledge of the Spirit, because God's Spirit dwells in them,[13] and they do not serve the lusts of the flesh but subject themselves to the Spirit and live according to reason in every respect. Now, incorporeal spirits cannot be spiritual men; our substance, however, that is, the union of soul and body, receiving God's Spirit, does constitute the spiritual man.[14] On the other hand, the Apostle rightly calls those carnal[15] who reject the counsel of the Spirit but serve the lusts of the flesh, and live senselessly and without restraint give themselves over to their own lusts,[16] since they have no inspiration from the divine Spirit, but live like pigs and dogs, because they think of nothing but carnal things.

The Prophets, too, for the same reason, likened them to irrational animals, because of their irrational mode of living. They said,[17] *They have become like lusty stallions toward women, each neighing for his neighbor's wife.* And again,[18] *When man was in honor he was like the beasts.* That is, because of his own fault, since he imitates their irrational life, he is likened to beasts. And even we customarily call such men beasts and irrational brutes.[19]

3. Now, the Law predicted all these things in types, describing man by means of animals.[20] It proclaims clean[21] whatever have a cloven hoof and chew the cud; but whatever lacks both or either of those, it sets aside as unclean. Who, then, are clean? Those who through faith securely journey toward the Father and the Son.[22] This is the security of those who have the cloven hoof, and[23] *meditate on the words of God day and night,* in order to be adorned with good works, because that is the power of those who *chew the cud.* Contrariwise, the unclean animals, which have neither *the cloven hoof* nor *chew the cud,* that is, who neither have faith in God nor meditate on his words—these are [a type] of the loathsomeness of the Gentiles. Those, however, who *chew the cud* but do not have *the cloven hoof,* are also unclean—these are a figurative description of the Jews, who certainly have the words of God in their mouth but do not have their root firmly fixed in the Father and the Son.[24] For that reason their race is liable to slip. Animals, namely, that have an uncloven hoof easily fall; those that have the cloven hoof are more secure, because their cloven hooves succeed each other as they step along, and so one hoof gives support to the other. Equally unclean are those who have the cloven hoof but do not chew the cud—this [type] manifests nearly[25] all heretics and those who do not *meditate on the words of God* and are not adorned with works of righteousness. Of them the Lord said,[26] *Why do you call me, "Lord, Lord," and do not do what I tell you?* Such people indeed say that they believe in the Father and the Son but never *meditate on the words of God* as is proper and are not adorned with the works of righteousness; but, as we have said, they have lived the life of pigs and dogs, giving themselves over to uncleanness and gluttony and the rest of the carefree life. Rightly, then, does the Apostle call carnal and animal[27] all such who on account of their unbelief and licentious living do not obtain the divine Spirit, and cast away, by their various traits, the Word that gives life, and live irrationally in their lusts. The Prophets, however, called them beasts and wild animals. Custom styled them brutes and irrational [animals], but the Law pronounces them unclean.

Chapter 9
"Flesh and Blood Cannot Inherit the Kingdom of God" (1 Cor 15:50).

1. The following, among others, is what was said by the Apostle,[1] *Flesh and blood cannot inherit the Kingdom of God.* This is adduced by all the heretics in their madness. From it they try to show that God's handiwork is not saved. They do not take note that there are three elements, as we have shown, of which the whole man consists—flesh, soul, and spirit.[2] The one saves and fashions, which is the spirit; the other is united and is fashioned, which is the flesh; but what is between these two, the soul, is at times raised up by him,[3] namely, when it follows the spirit; but at times it falls into earthly lusts, namely, when it consents to the flesh. Whoever, therefore, do not possess what saves and fashions unto life will rightly be *flesh and blood,* and will be called such, inasmuch as they do not have God's Spirit in themselves. For that reason such were also spoken of by the Lord as dead. He said,[4] *Let the dead bury their dead,* since they do not have the Spirit who gives life to man.

2. On the other hand, whoever fears God and believes in the coming of his Son, and who through faith establish God's Spirit in their hearts, such are rightly called men, *pure, spiritual,* and *living for God,*[5] because they have the Father's Spirit, who purifies man and elevates him unto God's life.[6]

For the *willing spirit* received testimony from the Lord just as the *weak flesh* did:[7] that is, whatever he is willing to do that he is powerful to accomplish.[8] So if anyone adds this willingness of the spirit to the weakness of the flesh as an impetus,[9] it is necessary, by all means, that the weak will be overcome by the powerful, so that the weakness of the flesh be absorbed by the strength of the spirit, and that such a one be no longer carnal but spiritual on account of communion in the Spirit.[10] In this way, therefore, the martyrs give their witness and despise death, not according to the weakness of the flesh but according to the willingness of the spirit.[11] For when the weakness of the flesh is [so] absorbed, it shows forth the spirit as powerful; moreover, when the spirit absorbs the weakness, he possesses the flesh in himself as an inheritance. Then out of both *a living man* has been formed—"living" on account of the communion in the Spirit, but "man" on account of the substance of the flesh.[12]

3. So the flesh without God's Spirit is dead, since it has no life; it has no power to *inherit the kingdom of God.* It is irrational blood; it is as water poured out on earth.[13] With that in mind, Paul said,[14] *As was the earthly man, such also are the earthly.* But where the Father's Spirit is, there is *a living man*: rational blood preserved by God to be avenged[15]; and flesh, which was inherited by the spirit and which, forgetful of itself, assumes the property of the Spirit and becomes conformed to the Word of God. And so he says,[16] *Just as we have borne the image of the earthly, we shall also bear the image of the heavenly.*

What, then, is "the earthly"? It is the handiwork. What is "the heavenly"? It is the Spirit. So he says,[17] just as at one time we lived in the flesh without the heavenly Spirit, inasmuch as we did not obey God, so now we have received the Spirit and *we walk in a new life,* inasmuch as we obey God. Since, therefore, we cannot be saved without God's Spirit, the Apostle admonished us to preserve God's Spirit through faith and a chaste manner of living, in order that we might not be without the communion of the Holy Spirit and lose the kingdom of heaven; and he cried out that *flesh and blood* by themselves cannot *inherit the kingdom of God.*

4. If we must speak the truth, flesh does not inherit but is inherited;[18] as the Lord said,[19] *Blessed are the meek for they shall inherit the earth,* as if the earth, whence also the substance of our flesh is taken, would be inherited in the kingdom. That is why he wills that the temple be clean, so that God's Spirit may delight in it, as the bridegroom delights in the bride. By way of illustration, the bride cannot take to herself the spouse, but she can be taken by the spouse when he comes to take her. In like manner, this *flesh* by itself, that is, all alone, *cannot inherit the kingdom of God*; but it can be inherited in the kingdom by the Spirit. For one who is alive can inherit the things of a dead person. And it is one thing to inherit, and another to be inherited. For the one has dominion and rules, and disposes the things he inherits just as it pleases him; but those things are subject to him who inherits, and obey him and are ruled by him, and are under his dominion.

What then is it that lives? It is God's Spirit. And what are the things of the dead person? They are a man's members, which will also perish in the earth. These are the things that will be inherited by the Spirit when they have been transferred to the kingdom of heaven. That is why Christ died, in order that, when the covenant of the Gospel had been opened and read to the entire world, he might first free his servants,[20] and then make them heirs of the things that belong to him, inasmuch as the Spirit possesses them as an inheritance, as we have shown. For one who is alive inherits, but the flesh is inherited. In order that we might not lose life by losing the Spirit who inherits us, the Apostle admonished us to communion in the Spirit. With reason he said, what has been quoted before, *Flesh and blood cannot inherit the kingdom of God.* That is the same as saying:[21] Do not err: for if the Word of God does not dwell in you, and the Spirit of God is not in you, and if you have lived without purpose or foresight, as if you were only *flesh and blood,* you *cannot inherit the kingdom of God.*

Chapter 10
The Wild and the Domestic Olive Tree

1. He made that statement so that we would not gratify the flesh and reject the graft on to the Spirit.[1] He said,[2] *You, a wild olive shoot, were grafted on a good olive and have become a sharer of the richness of the olive tree.* So, just as a wild olive, after being grafted, if it remains the wild olive it was before, it will be cut off and cast into the fire.[3] But if it holds fast to the graft and is changed into a good olive, it becomes a fruitful olive tree, as if planted in the king's garden. In the same way, if men have through faith made progress toward what is better and have received God's Spirit and produced his fruit,[4] they will be spiritual, as if planted in God's garden. But if they reject the Spirit and continue to be what they were before, wishing to belong to the flesh rather than to the Spirit, quite rightly is it said of such, *Flesh and blood cannot inherit the kingdom of God.* That is like saying that the wild olive is not received in God's garden. Wonderfully, therefore, did the Apostle manifest our nature and God's entire economy in the passage about flesh and blood, and the wild olive.[5]

By way of explanation, suppose that a good olive has been neglected and left for a time in a wilderness, it produces wild growth and of itself become a wild olive. On the other hand, suppose a wild olive is cared for and grafted, it returns to its pristine fruit-bearing. In the same way, if men have been neglected, as wild growth they produce carnal lusts and by their own fault become unfruitful in righteousness. For,[6] *while men are sleeping the enemy sows weeds.* That is why the Lord commanded his disciples to be vigilant.[7] Again, men who are unfruitful in righteousness and, so to say, covered with brambles, if they accept care and receive the Word of God as a graft, they return to man's pristine nature—that which had been made *according to the image and likeness of God.*[8]

2. Moreover, when the wild olive is grafted, it does not lose its nature of wood, but changes the quality of its fruit and gets another name, since it is no longer a wild olive but a fruitful olive, and it is called such too. In like manner, when man is grafted by faith and receives God's Spirit, he does not lose his nature of flesh but changes the quality of the fruit of his works and gets another name, which signifies the change into something better, since he is no longer flesh and blood, but a spiritual man, and he is called such too.

Another point, if the wild olive is not grafted, it remains useless for its master, because of its wild quality. It is *cut off* as an unfruitful tree *and is cast into the fire.* In like manner, man who by faith does not accept the graft of the Spirit remains what he was before, *flesh and blood,* and he *cannot inherit the kingdom of God.*[9]

So, the Apostle has expressed it well,[10] *Flesh and blood cannot inherit the kingdom of God,* and[11] those *who are in the flesh cannot please God.* Not that he rejects the substance of the flesh, but he adds the infusion of the Spirit. And for that reason he says,[12] *For this perishable nature must put on the imperishable;* and again,[13] *But you are not carnal but spiritual, if the Spirit of God dwells in you.* He makes that still clearer:[14] *The body it is true,* he says, *is dead because of sin, the spirit is life because of righteousness. If the Spirit of him who raised Jesus from the dead dwells in you, he who raised Christ from the dead will give life to your mortal bodies also through his Spirit which dwells in you.* Again, in the Letter to the Romans, he says,[15] *For if you live according to the flesh you will die.* By that he does not reject their living in the flesh, for he was in the flesh as he wrote to them; but he cuts off the lusts of the flesh that kill man. So he continues,[16] *But if by the Spirit you put to death the deeds of the flesh you will live. For all who are led by the Spirit of God are sons of God.*[17]

Chapter 11

Carnal and Spiritual People

1. The Apostle pointed out the deeds he considers carnal, and since he foresaw the calumny of the unbelievers, he also explained himself, lest any difficulty remain for those who in unbelief scrutinize him. In his Letter to the Galatians he says this:[1] *Now the works of the flesh are plain, adulteries, fornications, impurities, licentiousness, idolatry, sorcery,*

enmity, strife, jealousy, anger, quarreling, dissension, party spirit, envy, drunkenness, carousing, and the like. I warn you, as I have warned you before, that those who do things shall not inherit the kingdom of God. This way he preached more clearly to his hearers what is meant by this that *flesh and blood cannot inherit the kingdom of God.* Certainly, those who do these things really *walk according to the flesh* and cannot *live for God.*[2] He also added the spiritual deeds that give life to man, which is the grafting of the Spirit. He says,[3] *But the fruit of the Spirit is: love, joy, peace, patience, goodness, kindness, faithfulness, gentleness, continence, chastity: against such there is no law.*

Hence, just as one who has made progress toward what is better and has produced fruit of the Spirit is altogether saved because of communion of the Spirit, so one who continues in the aforementioned deeds of the flesh is considered truly carnal, because he does not accept God's Spirit and *cannot inherit the kingdom of God.* In the same strain the Apostle says to the Corinthians:[4] *Do you not know that the unrighteous will not inherit the kingdom of God? Do not be deceived; neither the immoral, nor idolaters, nor adulterers, nor male prostitutes, nor homosexuals, nor sodomites, nor thieves, nor the greedy, nor drunkards, nor revilers, nor robbers will inherit the kingdom of God. And such were some of you. But you were washed, you were sanctified, you were justified in the name of the Lord Jesus Christ, and in the Spirit of our God.* The Apostle most clearly shows by what man perishes if he continues to live according to the flesh,[5] and by what he is saved. The things that save, he said, are *the name of our Lord Jesus Christ* and *the Spirit of our God.*

2. Since, therefore, in this passage he enumerated the deeds of the flesh, which are without the Spirit and are deadly, in keeping with the things mentioned by him already, he exclaimed by way of summary at the end of the Letter [to the Corinthians]:[6] *Therefore, as we have borne the image of the earthly, we shall also bear the image of the heavenly. I tell you this, brethren, flesh and blood cannot inherit the kingdom of God.* Now, the statement, *Just as we have borne the image of the earthly* is like this one,[7] *But such were some of you. But you were washed, you were sanctified, you were justified in the name of the Lord Jesus Christ, and in the Spirit of our God.* When, then, did we bear *the image of the one who is earthly*? It was when the deeds of the flesh mentioned above were wrought in us. But when, on the other hand, *the image of the heavenly*? It was when, as he says, *you were washed,* and believed *in the name of the Lord* and received his *Spirit.* But we were *washed* by [washing away] not the substance of the body or the image of the handiwork,[8] but the former way of living

that resulted in emptiness. So in the very members in which we were perishing because we were doing the perishable deeds, in these we are given life because we do the deeds of the Spirit.

Chapter 12
On Giving Life to the Flesh Again

1. To explain, just as the flesh is capable of receiving perishability, so is it capable of imperishability; as it is capable of death, so of life. These things displace each other; and both cannot remain in one and the same being; the one is expelled by the other; when one is present the other ceases.[1] So if death, when it takes possession of a man, expels life from him and shows him to be dead, how much more does life, when it takes possession of man, expel death and restore him to God as a living being. For if death has killed, why, when life comes, should it not give life to man?[2] That is what the Prophet Isaiah says,[3] *Death swallowed up when it prevailed*; and again, *God wiped away every tear from all faces.* The pristine life was expelled because it was not given by the Spirit but by breath.

2. For *the breath of life* which makes man *a living soul* is one thing, while the Spirit who gives life and makes man spiritual is something else.[4] That is why Isaiah said:[5] *Thus says the Lord, who created the heavens and stretched them out, who established the earth and what comes from it, who gives breath to the people on it and spirit to those who walk on it.* He says that the breath was given in general to all people on earth, but the Spirit was given as something specific to those who walk in carnal lusts. Isaiah, therefore, distinguishes between the things mentioned when he says,[6] *For from me will proceed the Spirit, and I have made every breath.* He thus assigns the Spirit specifically to God, whom in these last times he poured out on the human race through adoption;[7] but the breath [he assigns] generally in creation, and showed it was something made. But what is made is different from the one who made it. So breath is temporal while the Spirit is eternal. And breath is vigorous for a while and continues on for some time, then it departs, leaving that [body], in which it was, breathless. The Spirit, however, envelops men from within and without. And of course, since he always continues, he will never forsake him. *But it is not the spiritual that is first,* says the Apostle[8] when speaking to us, but *the physical is first, and then the spiritual.* That is in keeping with reason. For it was necessary first that man

be fashioned; next, that what was fashioned receive the soul; then, that it receive communion of the Spirit. Wherefore, also[9] *the first Adam was made a living soul* by God, *the second Adam a life-giving Spirit.* Therefore, as he who was made a living soul lost his life when he turned to worse things, so this same one when he returned to better things by accepting the life-giving Spirit, will find life.

3. For it is not one thing that dies and one thing that lives, just as what is lost does not differ from what is found. The Lord came in search of the very sheep that had been lost.[10] What was it, then, that had died? It was, of course, the substance of the flesh, which had lost *the breath of life* and was breathless and dead. This is what the Lord came to give life to, in order that, as in Adam we all die, inasmuch as we are ensouled, so we may live in Christ, inasmuch as we are spiritual; by putting off, not God's handiwork, but the carnal lusts and by accepting the Holy Spirit.

Thus the Apostle says in his Letter to the Colossians:[11] *Put to death therefore what is earthly in you.* What these are he himself explains, *immorality, impurity, passion, evil desire, and covetousness, which is idolatry.* So, the Apostle preaches the laying aside of these things; and he says that those who do them are living as if they were only *flesh and blood* and *cannot inherit the kingdom of heaven.* For their soul inclines toward what is worse, and descends to earthly lusts, and so it shares the same name as they do. Again, he tells us in the same letter that we should lay aside such things:[12] *Put off the old man with his practices.* He said this not to get rid of the ancient handiwork; otherwise it would be necessary to kill ourselves and to cut ourselves off from the mode of life here below.

4. The Apostle himself, moreover, who was formed in a womb and came forth from the womb,[13] wrote to us, and by his Letter to the Philippians he acknowledged that[14] *to live in the flesh is the fruit of work.* But the Spirit's *fruit of work* is the salvation of the flesh. For what other visible fruit is there of the invisible Spirit than to make the flesh grow to maturity and to make it capable of imperishability? Therefore,[15] *if to live in the flesh is the fruit of work,* he did not despise the substance of the flesh when he said,[16] *Put off the old man with its deeds*: but he did point out we should put off our former way of life, the kind that grows old and perishes. For that reason he adds,[17] *and put on the new man, which is being renewed unto perfect knowledge after the image of his Creator.* Now, when he says, *who is better renewed,* he declares that the very man who was in ignorance before, namely, who was ignorant of God, is renewed by the knowledge that is about him. For the knowledge of God renews

man. And when he says, *after the image of his Creator*, he pointed out the recapitulation of the same man who was made in the beginning *after the image of God.*

5. That the Apostle himself is the one that was born from the womb, namely, from the ancient substance of the flesh, he himself tells us in his Letter to the Galatians:[18] *But when he who had set me apart from my mother's womb and called me through his grace, was pleased to reveal his Son to me, in order that I might preach him among the Gentiles.* The one who was born from the womb, as we have said, was not different from the one who proclaimed the good news of God's Son. No, it was the same who before was in ignorance and who persecuted the Church. But when he received a revelation from heaven, and the Lord spoke with him,[19] as we have shown in the Third Book,[20] he announced the good news of God's Son, Jesus Christ, who was crucified under Pontius Pilate. For then the past ignorance was destroyed by the subsequent knowledge.

By way of illustration, the blind people whom the Lord healed lost their blindness but received the substance of the eyes intact; and in the same eyes with which they could not see before they received sight, the blindness alone had been destroyed while the substance of the eyes was saved, with the result that they were again able to see with the eyes with which before they did not see, and that they might give thanks to him who had restored their sight to them. Likewise, the one whose withered hand was healed,[21] and absolutely all who were healed by him did not change the members which in the beginning were brought forth from the womb, but they received these very same members back sound.

6. For the Artisan of all things, the Word of God, who also in the beginning fashioned man, finding his handiwork infected by wickedness, healed it in every respect. At times he healed an individual member, just as it was fashioned in the beginning. At other times, he restored the entire man sound and whole all at once, thus preparing him, so made perfect, for himself, with a view to the resurrection. What reason did he have to heal members of the flesh and to restore them to their pristine state, if these members, which had been healed by him, were not to be saved? To be sure, if the benefit conferred by him was [only] temporal, he did not confer a very great benefit on those who were healed by him. Or, should flesh not be capable of receiving the life which flows from him, though it received healing from him? For life is brought about through healing, and imperishability through

life. He, therefore, who heals also [gives] life, and he who [gives] life also surrounds his own handiwork with imperishability.

Chapter 13
The Dead Whom Christ Raised Demonstrate the Possibility of the Resurrection.

1. Those who talk against us, rather who talk against their own salvation, should tell us in what bodies the following rose: the deceased daughter of the ruler of the synagogue,[1] the son of the widow who, when dead, was being carried near the gate,[2] and Lazarus, who had been in the tomb for four days?[3] Undoubtedly, they did so in the same bodies in which they had died. In fact, if it was not in the same bodies, then certainly the same ones who had died did not rise again. But Scripture says:[4] *The Lord took the hand of the dead one and said to him, young man, I say to you, arise; and he who was dead sat up and he directed them to give him something to eat, and he gave him to his mother.* Lazarus, too,[5] *He called with a loud voice, saying, "Lazarus, come out." And the dead man came out,* says the Scripture, *his feet and hands bound with bandages.* This is a symbol of man who had been bound by sins. That is why the Lord said,[6] *Unbind him, and let him go.*

Those, therefore, who were healed, were healed in the very members in which they had previously suffered, and the dead rose in the same bodies, because it was their members and bodies that were healed, and they received the life which is given by the Lord. Through the temporal things he prefigured the eternal and manifested that he is the one who can bestow healing and life on his handiwork, in order that also his word about the resurrection might be believed. In the same way, in the end, when the Lord will cry out with the last trumpet,[7] the dead will rise, as he says,[8] *The hour is coming when all who are in the tombs will hear the voice of the Son of God. And those who have done good will come forth to the resurrection of life, and those who have done evil, to the resurrection of judgment.*

2. Senseless, therefore, and truly wretched are they who refuse to see into things that are so manifest and clear; who, on the contrary, flee from the light of the Truth and, like the tragic Oedipus, blind themselves.[9] To illustrate, the untrained, when wrestling with others, grasp with their whole hands any part of the [other's] body but fall

down by the very part they hold on to, and though they fall, they think they are winning, simply because they are holding on, with a fighting spirit, to the part they first grasped—really, such are laughed to scorn for falling down.[10] In the same way, the heretics in regard to the famous passage,[11] *Flesh and blood cannot inherit the kingdom of God*, take two passages from Paul, but they neither understand the Apostle's mind, nor have they examined the meaning of the passages. Still they hold on to the bare statements, and so die because of them and, as far as in them lies, overthrow God's entire economy.

3. They assert that this passage is of flesh proper and not of carnal deeds, as we shall demonstrate. And so they show that the Apostle contradicts himself. For in this same Letter immediately afterward he says as follows, with clear reference to the flesh:[12] *This perishable body must put on imperishability, and this mortal body must put on immortality. But when this mortal body puts on immortality, then shall come to pass the saying that is written: "Death is swallowed up in victory. O death, where is they sting? O death, where is they victory?"* Now these things can rightly be said when this mortal and perishable flesh, about which [the talk of] death is, and which is oppressed by a certain dominion of death, ascends to life and puts on imperishability and immortality. For then death will truly have been overcome when flesh, which is held bound by death, has escaped from its dominion.

Again, he says to the Philippians:[13] *But our commonwealth is in heaven, and from it we eagerly await a Savior, the Lord Jesus Christ, who will change our lowly body, conforming it to his glorious body, as he is able*[14] *by the working of his power.* What, then, is the *lowly body* that the Lord *will change*, having made it *conformed to the glorious body*? It is obvious that it is the body that is flesh, which is made *lowly* when it falls into the earth. Its transformation is this, that though it is mortal and perishable, it becomes immortal and imperishable, not by virtue of its own substance, but by virtue of the Lord's working, by which he can clothe the mortal with immortality and the perishable with imperishability.[15] And for this reason he says in the Second Letter to the Corinthians,[16] *so that what is mortal may be swallowed up by life. He who made us perfect for this very thing is God, who has given us the Spirit as a pledge.* He most obviously refers to the flesh, for neither the soul nor the spirit is mortal. But what is mortal *will be swallowed up by life* when the flesh will no longer be dead but will continue to live and be imperishable, hymning God who has perfected us for this very purpose.[17] That, therefore, we are being perfected for this end, was well put by Paul to the Corinthians,[18] *Glorify God in your body.* But God is the author of imperishability.

4. That he is speaking of the body of the flesh, and not of some other body, he states clearly and indubitably and unambiguously to the Corinthians:[19] *Always carrying in our body the death of Jesus, so that the life of Jesus may also be manifest in our body. For if while we live we are being given up to death for Jesus's sake, it is so that the life of Jesus may be manifested in our mortal flesh.* That the Spirit embraces the flesh, he tells us in the same letter:[20] *You are a letter from Christ, delivered by us, written not with ink but with the Spirit of the living God, not on tablets of stone but on fleshly tablets of the heart.* So if at present the fleshly hearts become capable of receiving the Spirit, what is there surprising if in the resurrection they receive the life which is given by the Spirit? Of that resurrection the Apostle said this in the Letter to the Philippians:[21] [I have] *become likened to his death, that if possible I may attain the resurrection from the dead.* So, in what other mortal flesh can one understand life to be manifested except in this substance which is put to death because of confessing God? Of this the Apostle wrote as follows:[22] *What do I gain, if, humanly speaking, I fought with beasts at Ephesus? If the dead are not raised neither has Christ been raised; and if Christ has not been raised, then our preaching is in vain and your faith is in vain. We are even found to be misrepresenting God because we testified of God that he raised Christ, whom he did not raise. For if the dead are not raised, then Christ has not been raised; if Christ has not been raised, your faith is futile, and you are still in your sins. Then those also who have fallen asleep in Christ have perished. If in this life we who are in Christ have only hope, we are of all men most to be pitied. But in fact, Christ has been raised from the dead, the first fruits of those who have fallen asleep. For as by man came death, by man comes also the resurrection of the dead.*

5. In all these passages, therefore, as we said, either they assert that the Apostle holds a contrary opinion with regard to this,[23] *Flesh and blood cannot inherit the kingdom of God*; or, they will be forced to give a bad and distorted exposition of all the passages, in order to twist around and change the meaning of the passages. In fact, what sensible thing can they say, if they will try to interpret in a different way what Paul wrote,[24] *For this perishable body must put on imperishability, and this mortal body must put on immortality*: and,[25] *that the life of Jesus may be manifested in our mortal flesh*? And what of all the other passages in which the Apostle evidently and clearly preaches the resurrection and imperishability of the flesh? And so those who do not wish to understand one of these passages correctly will be forced to interpret all of them badly.

Chapter 14
If Flesh Were Not Capable of Salvation, the Word Would Never Have Assumed It.

1. The Apostle did not direct "*Flesh and blood cannot inherit the kingdom of God*"[1] against the very substance of *flesh and blood.* In fact, the same Apostle has everywhere used the words *flesh and blood* in reference to the Lord Jesus Christ. This he did both to prove his human nature[2] (for he called himself the Son of Man) and to confirm the salvation of the flesh. For if flesh could not be saved, the Word of God would by no means have become flesh.[3] And if the blood of the just could not be sought out, the Lord would by no means have had blood. But that blood cries out from the beginning, God said to Cain, when he had killed his brother,[4] *The voice of your brother's blood is crying to me.* And that their blood could be sought out, he said to the people around Noah,[5] *For I will require the blood of your lives at the hand of every beast.* And again,[6] *Whoever sheds the blood of man,* [his own] *shall be shed for that one's blood.* In like manner, the Lord said to those who would shed his blood:[7] *All the righteous blood shall be requited—[all] shed on the earth from the blood of innocent Abel to the blood of Zachariah, the son of Berechiah, whom you murdered between the sanctuary and the altar. Truly, I say to you, all this will come upon this generation.* Thus he pointed out the future recapitulation[8] in himself of shedding blood from the beginning, of all the righteous and the Prophets, and requiring their blood through himself. But this would not be required if it could not be saved. Nor would the Lord have recapitulated in himself these things unless he himself had been made flesh and blood after the original handiwork, thus saving in himself at the end what had perished in Adam in the beginning.

2. Now, if the Lord became incarnate for some other economy and brought his flesh from some other substance, he did not recapitulate man in himself, and what is more, he cannot even be called flesh. For flesh truly is that which is in the lineage of the first substance made out of clay.[9] Now if it had been necessary for him to have matter from another substance, the Father would in the beginning have worked to make man's formation from another substance. But as the case is, the saving Word has become the very thing which man who had perished was, thus through himself he wrought the communion [of man] with himself and the seeking out of man's salvation.[10] But

what perished did have flesh and blood; for God took clay from the earth and formed man; and the entire Economy of the Lord's coming is for the sake of man.[11] He himself, therefore, had flesh and blood, and he recapitulated in himself not some other kind, but the Father's original handiwork when he sought out what had perished. With this in mind the Apostle says in his Letter to the Colossians:[12] *You who once were estranged and hostile in mind, through your evil deeds, he has now reconciled in his body of flesh through his death, to present you holy and blameless and irreproachable before him. He says, You have been reconciled in the body of his flesh,* that is the holy flesh reconciled the flesh that was held captive by sin, and brought it into friendship with God.

3. If, according to that, anyone should say that the Lord's flesh differs from ours, since it neither sinned, nor was there *any deceit in his soul,*[13] but we are sinners, he says the truth. But if he imagines another substance of flesh for the Lord, then the word about reconciliation will no longer be consistent for him.[14] For that is reconciled which was at one time at enmity. Now, if the Lord brought flesh from some other substance, no longer is that reconciled which has been made his enemy through transgression. As the case is, the Lord reconciled man to the Father through communion with himself [Christ], by reconciling us to himself *through the body of his flesh,*[15] and redeeming us through his blood, as the Apostle tells the Ephesians:[16] *In him we have redemption through his blood, the forgiveness of sins*; and again he says to the same people:[17] *You who once were far off have been brought near in the blood of Christ*; and again:[18] *The hostility in the flesh, the law of the commandments in ordinances he abolished.* And so in every letter the Apostle testifies that we have been saved through Our Lord's flesh and through his blood.

4. So if it is flesh and blood that give us life, it was not said literally of flesh and blood that these *cannot inherit the kingdom of God,*[19] but of the aforementioned carnal acts, which turn man to sin and deprive him of life. This is why he says in the Letter to the Romans,[20] *Let not sin therefore reign in your mortal body, to make you obey its passions. Do not yield your members to sin as instruments of wickedness, but yield yourselves to God as men who have been brought from death to life, and your members to God as instruments of righteousness.* Hence, with the members with which we served sin and produced fruit unto death, with these same members he wishes us to serve righteousness that we might produce fruit unto life.[21] So, my dear friend,[22] recall that you have been redeemed by Our Lord's flesh and acquired by his blood. *Holding fast to the head,*[23] *from whom the whole body of the Church has been knit together and grows,* that is,

by confessing the coming of God's Son in the flesh, and God; and by firmly accepting his human nature,[24] also by using the proofs from Scripture, you will, as we have shown, easily overthrow all the tenets of the heretics, which have been concocted later on.

Chapter 15
Proofs from Isaiah and Ezekiel for the Resurrection

1. That he who created man in the beginning promised man a regeneration after he has been decomposed in the earth, Isaiah tells us as follows:[1] *The dead shall rise again, and those who are in the tombs shall rise, and those who are on the earth shall rejoice. For thy dew is health for them.* And again:[2] *I will comfort you, and you shall be comforted in Jerusalem. You shall see, and your heart shall rejoice; your bones shall flourish like the grass, and the hand of the Lord shall be known to those who worship him.*

Ezekiel puts it thus:[3] *The hand of the Lord was upon me, and he brought me out by the Spirit of the Lord and set me down in the midst of a valley; it was full of bones. And he led me round among them on every side; and behold there were very many upon the valley, and lo, they were very dry. And he said to me, "Son of man, do you think these bones can live?" And I answered: "O Lord God, thou knowest, thou who made them."*[4] Again he said to me: Prophesy to *these bones, and say to them: "O dry bones, hear the word of the Lord. Thus says the Lord God to these bones: Behold I will cause breath [Spirit] to enter. And I will lay sinews upon you, and will cause flesh to come upon you, and cover you with skin, and put breath [Spirit] in you, and you shall live; and you shall know that I am the Lord." So I prophesied as he had commanded me; and as I prophesied there was an earthquake. And the bones came together, each one to its joint. And as I looked, there were sinews on them, and the flesh had come upon them, and skin had covered them; but there was no breath [Spirit] in them. And he said to me: "Prophesy to the breath, O Son of man, and say to the breath: 'Thus says the Lord God: Come from the four winds, O breath, breathe upon these slain, that they may live.'" So I prophesied as he commanded me, and the breath came into them and they lived, and they stood up upon their feet, an exceedingly great host.*

And again he said:[5] *Thus says the Lord God: "Behold, I will open your graves, and raise you from your graves. And I will bring you home into the land of Israel. And you shall know that I am the Lord, when I open your graves, to bring my people back from the graves, and I will put my Spirit with you, and you shall know that I, the Lord, have spoken and I will do it, says the Lord."* In this passage, therefore, the Creator gives life to our dead bodies, as can be seen, and promises them resurrection, and raises them from the graves and the tombs, and gives them imperishability. *For their days will be as the tree of life,* he says.[6] The one God who made those things is manifested in this passage, and he is the good Father himself, who kindly grants life to those who do not have life of themselves.

2. That is why the Lord most clearly revealed to his disciples himself and the Father who each is,[7] that they might not look for another God besides the one who formed man and gave him the breath of life, and that they might not reach such a height of insanity as to concoct another Father above the Creator. As a fact, he healed by word all the rest who happened to have an ailment due to their transgression; <and so> to these he said,[8] *See you are well. Sin no more, that nothing worse befall you.* By that he reveals that ailments came upon men because of the sin of disobedience. But to him who was blind from birth he restored sight, not by word, but by action. He did this, not without aim or plan, but that he might manifest God's hand (the Word) who fashioned man in the beginning. And so, when the disciples asked him the reason why the man was born blind, whether because of his own or his parents' sin, he said,[9] *It was not that this man sinned, or his parents, but that the works of God might be made manifest in him.* Now, God's work is the handiwork, that is, man. For he made this by an action, as Scripture says,[10] *And God took clay from the earth, and formed man.* Wherefore, the Lord *spat on the ground, made clay and smeared* it on the eyes,[11] showing how the ancient handiwork had been made and manifesting God's hand to them, that they could understand by what hand man was formed from clay. For what the Artificer, the Word,[12] had omitted to form in the womb, this he completed in the open. He did this in order that God's works might be made manifest in himself, and that we might no longer look for another hand by whom man was formed, or another Father. Instead we would know that the hand that had formed us in the beginning, and forms [us] in the womb, also in the last times sought us out who had been lost. He won back his own sheep that had been lost, and took it on his shoulders, and with joy restored it to the fold of life.[13]

3. That the Word of God forms us in the womb he told Jeremiah:[14] *Before I formed you in the womb I knew you, and before you were born I consecrated you; I appointed you a prophet unto the nations.* Paul, in like manner,

said:[15] *But when he who had set me apart from my mother's womb was pleased [to reveal his love to me]*[16] *in order that I might preach him among the Gentiles.* Since, therefore, we are formed in the womb by the Word, it is this very same Word who re-formed[17] the sight for the man who had been blind from birth. Thus he made manifest our hidden Fashioner, that the Word himself was made manifest to men. He also made known the ancient handiwork for Adam, both how he was made and by what hand he was fashioned, thus manifesting the whole by the part. For the Lord who formed the sight is one who formed the whole man, ministering to the Father's will. Then, because man had transgressed in the handiwork that is Adam and needed *the bath of regeneration*,[18] the Lord, after having smeared clay on his eyes, said to him,[19] *Go to the pool of Siloam, and wash*; thus he restored both the handiwork and the regeneration through the bath at one and the same time. On this account, when he had washed, he came seeing, that he might recognize the Fashioner, and that man might learn of the Lord who gave him life.[20]

4. And so all the Valentinians err when they say that man was not formed from this earth, but from a fluid and diffused matter.[21] For it is manifest that the Lord fashioned man in the beginning from the same earth from which he formed his eyes. Really, it is not logical that the body and the eyes should have been formed from different substances; just as it is not logical for one [God] to have formed the body and another the eyes. No, the same one [the Word] who in the beginning fashioned Adam and to whom the Father said,[22] *Let us make man after our image and likeness*, refashioned the sight for the blind man, who <descended> from Adam,[23] when in the last times he manifested himself to men. For this reason Scripture points out what would happen in the future, when Adam had hidden himself because of the disobedience. It says that the Lord came, toward evening, and called out to him, and said,[24] *Where are you?* This means that in the last times the same Word came to call man, thereby he reminded him of his deeds, in which he was living when he hid himself from God. For just as at that time God sought out Adam and spoke to him in the evening, so in the last times he sought out his offspring and visited him through the same voice.[25]

Section 2

UNITY OF GOD SHOWN THROUGH LIFE OF CHRIST

Chapter 16
The Word Incarnate Is the Pattern for the First Man.

1. It was because the handiwork, Adam, was from our earth that Scripture says God spoke to him:[1] *In the sweat of your face you shall eat bread, till you return to the earth, from which you were taken.* If, then, after death our bodies return to some other earth, it would follow that they also had their substance from there. But if they return to this same earth, it is evident that they were fashioned from this earth. The Lord made this manifest when he re-formed his eyes from this [earth]. And so the hand by which Adam was fashioned, and by which we, too, were fashioned, has been very clearly[2] revealed as God's. Further, since there is one and the same Father whose voice was present with his handiwork from the beginning, and since the substance of our handiwork has been clearly manifested by the Gospel, we ought no longer to go in search of another Father besides this one, or another substance of our handiwork besides the one mentioned and manifested by the Lord, or another hand of God besides the one which forms us from the beginning to the end, and prepares us for the life, and is present to his handiwork, and perfects it *after the image and likeness of God.*[3]

2. This, however, was manifested to be thus when the Word of God became man, making himself like man and man like himself, so that by his likeness to the Son man might become precious to the Father. For in former times it was said that man was created *after the image of God,* but the image was not shown; for the Word, after whose image man had been created, was as yet invisible. For this reason man easily lost also the likeness. When, however, *the Word of God became flesh,*[4] he made both [image and likeness] secure: for he truly showed forth the image, since he himself became what his image was; and he securely restored the likeness by making man like the invisible Father by means of the visible Word.[5]

3. The Lord manifested himself and the Father, not merely by the things already mentioned, but also by his passion. For he undid the disobedience of man, which happened in the beginning by means of the tree, by becoming *obedient to death, even to the death on a cross.*[6] Thus he healed the disobedience that happened on a tree by the obedience on a tree. But he would not have come in the same image to undo the disobedience against our Fashioner if he had announced

another Father. Since, however, he brought obedience and consent to his word by means of the very things by which we did not obey God and did not believe his word, he clearly manifested him to be God whom we offended in the first Adam by not keeping his commandment, but to whom we were reconciled in the Second Adam, *who became obedient unto death.* In fact, we were not debtors to anyone else, but to him whose commandment we had transgressed from the beginning.

Chapter 17

By Forgiving Sins Committed against God, Christ Proved Himself to Be God's Son.

1. The Creator is the one who in respect to love is the Father, in respect to power the Lord, and in respect to wisdom our Maker and Fashioner.[1] It was his commandment that we transgressed and became his enemies. For this reason, in the last times the Lord restored us to friendship through his incarnation, having been made *Mediator between God and man.*[2] On our behalf he appeased the Father against whom we had sinned; and he came to the aid of disobedience by his obedience,[3] granting us the gift of living with our Maker and of being subject to him. That is why he taught us to say in prayer,[4] *and forgive us our transgressions*; certainly, because this is our Father, whose debtors we were because we had transgressed his commandment. But who is this? Is it some unknowable[5] Father who never gives a commandment to anyone? Or is it the God who is preached by the Prophets[6] and whose debtors we were because we transgressed his commandment? The commandment was given to man by the Word. *For Adam,*[7] Scripture says, *heard the Voice of the Lord God.* Correctly, then, does his Word say to man,[8] *Your sins are forgiven.* It is the same one against whom we had sinned in the beginning who grants us remission of sins in the end. Now, if we transgressed the commandment of someone else than the one who said, *Your sins are forgiven,* such a one is not good or truthful or just. Really, how is he good if he does not give of his own things? Or how is he just if he steals what does not belong to him? And how are the sins truly forgiven unless the very one against whom we have sinned grants *remission through the heart of our God's mercy,* by which he *visited us* through his Son?[9]

2. In keeping with this, when the paralytic had been cured, it [Scripture] says,[10] *When they saw it they glorified God, who had given such authority to men.* Now which God did the people who were standing around glorify? Was it the unknown Father who was thought up by the heretics? Then, how did they glorify him who was totally unknown by them? So it is manifest that the Israelites glorified him who was preached as God by the Law and the Prophets, who is also the Father of Our Lord. That is why he taught men by their senses through the signs he worked, to give glory to God. But if he had come from one Father, and the men who saw his power glorified another Father, he would have made them ungrateful toward that Father who had sent the cure. But since it is from the Father who is God that the Only-begotten Son came for the salvation of men, he invited unbelievers, by the signs he worked, to give glory to God. On the other hand, he said to the Pharisees who did receive the coming of his Son, and so did not believe in the remission of sins through him,[11] *That you may know that the Son of Man has authority to forgive sins.* And when he had said this, he ordered the paralytic to take up his bed on which he had been lying and go to his house. By this action he confounded the unbelievers and pointed out that he is the voice of God, through which man on earth[12] received the commandments that he transgressed and by which he became a sinner; for paralysis was a consequence of sin.

3. By remitting sins, then, he cured the man and clearly manifested who he himself is. In fact, no one can forgive sins except God alone. And if the Lord used to forgive them and heal men,[13] it is evident that he was the Word of God who became the Son of Man and had received authority from the Father to forgive sins,[14] since he was both man and God. Thus as Man he suffered with us, and as God he had mercy on us and forgave us our debts, which we owed God our Creator.[15] That is why David foretold,[16] *Blessed are they whose transgressions are forgiven, and whose sins are covered. Blessed is the man to whom the Lord imputes no iniquity.* Thus he manifested in advance the forgiveness [that would be given] through his coming,[17] by which *he cancelled the bond* of our debt *and nailed it to the cross,* so that, just as through a tree we had become debtors to God, so through a tree we might receive forgiveness of our debt.

4. This fact has been strikingly manifested by many other examples, especially by the Prophet Elisha. When his companion Prophets were cutting down trees for making a tent, the iron shook off the axe and fell into the Jordan and could not be retrieved by them. When

Elisha learned about the accident, he came to the place and threw a piece of wood into the water. When he had done this, the iron of the axe floated to the top, and they who had lost it picked it up from the surface of the water. By this action the Prophet showed that God's firm Word, which we had lost through the tree[18] because of neglect, and which we could not find, we would receive again through the economy of the tree. Now, since God's Word is like an axe, John the Baptist says of it,[19] *The axe is already laid to the root of the trees.* Jeremiah expressed himself in the same manner,[20] *The word of the Lord cleaves the rock like a two-edged sword.* So, as we have said, the tree of the economy manifested this word which was hidden from us. Since we lost it through a tree, it was again made manifest to all by a tree, which shows in itself the height, the length, the breadth,[21] and—as one of the presbyters said—by stretching out the arms it gathered the two peoples to the one God.[22] There were two arms, because the two peoples had been scattered to the ends of the earth; but one head in the center, because there is *one God who is above all, and through all, and in us all.*[23]

Chapter 18

Through His Own Power, Namely, through His Son and Spirit, God Created All Things.

1. He did not make this great and excellent economy by means of someone else's creatures, but by his own; nor by those who were made from ignorance and degeneracy, but by those that had their substance from the Wisdom and the Power of his Father. To be sure, he is not wicked so that he covets what does not belong to him. Nor is he in need so that he would not give life to his own creatures by means of his own creatures, using his own creation for man's salvation. For the creature [the cross] could not have borne him if he had been a product of ignorance and degeneracy. For we have shown by many texts that the Word of God himself, having become incarnate, was suspended on a tree. The heretics themselves acknowledge that he was crucified.

How, then, could the emission of ignorance and degeneracy bear him who possesses knowledge of all things and is true and perfect?[1] Or how did the creation which was hidden from the Father and quite separated have borne his Word?[2] But suppose these things were made by the angels, who either did not know of the God who is above all things or who did know, how could this creation of the angels have endured to bear the Father and the Son at the same time, since the Lord said,[3] *For I am in the Father and the Father is in me*? And how did the creation which is outside the Fullness receive him who contains the entire Fullness? Since all these things are impossible and cannot be proven, that preaching of the Church alone is true that says that his own creation, which exists through the power and art and wisdom of God, bore him. This creation is borne by the Father in an invisible manner; but his Word bears it in a visible manner. And that is true.

2. By way of explanation, the Father bears the creation and his Word at the same time; and the Word, who is borne by the Father, bestows the Spirit on all, just as the Father wills;[4] to some, in keeping with creation, he gives that [spirit] which pertains to creation, which is made; to some, in keeping with adoption, [he gives] that [Spirit] who is from the Father, who is generated.[5] And so one God the Father is manifested who *is above all, and throughout all, and in all*.[6] The Father is *above all*, and he is the Head of Christ;[7] the Word is *throughout all*, and he is the Head of the Church;[8] the Spirit is *in all of us*, and he is *the living water* that the Lord bestows on those who rightly believe in him[9] and love him and know that there is *one God the Father who is above all and throughout all and in all of us*.[10]

John, the Lord's disciple, on his part, bears witness to these things in the Gospel when he writes as follows:[11] *In the beginning was the Word, and the Word was with God, and the Word was God. He was in the beginning with God. All things were made through him, and without him was not made anything*. Then, of the Word itself he said,[12] *he was in the world, and the world was made through him, yet the world knew him not. He came to his own, and his own received him not. But to all who received him, who believed in his name, he gave power to become children of God*. Next, pointing out his economy in human nature, he said:[13] *And the Word became flesh and dwelt among us*; to which he added, *And we have beheld his glory, glory as of the Only-begotten of the Father, full of grace and truth*. He clearly pointed out to those who are willing to hear, that is, to those who have ears, that there is one God the Father *above all*, and one Word of God, who is *throughout all, through whom all things were made*; and that this world is his own, and was made by him according to the Father's will, and not by angels, or by the rebellion, degeneracy, or ignorance; or by some power, Prunikos, whom some also call Mother;[14] or by any other maker of the world who was ignorant of the Father.

3. For the Maker of the world is truly the Word of God. He is also our Lord, who in the last times became man, who is in this world and in an invisible manner contains all things created and is inscribed in the form of a cross on the entire creation,[15] inasmuch as he is the Word of God who governs and disposes all things. Therefore, *He came to his own* in a visible manner[16] and *became flesh* and hung on a tree,[17] that he might *recapitulate in himself all things.*[18] *And his own people received him not.*[19] Moses made this very thing clear to the people:[20] *And your life shall hang in doubt before your eyes, and you shall have assurance of your life.* Those, therefore, who did not accept him did not receive life:[21] *To all who received him he gave power to become children of God.* For it is he who has power from the Father over all things,[22] since he is the Word of God and true Man, ruling over invisible things in a rational manner,[23] and in an intelligent manner making a law that all things should continue in their own order; over visible and human beings, however, he rules in a visible manner, and passes deserving and just judgment on all. David pointed out his visible coming in these words:[24] *God comes manifestly and does not keep silence.* Then he pointed out the judgment that is passed by him. He said,[25] *Before him is a devouring fire; round about him a mighty tempest. He calls to the heavens above, and to the earth, that he may judge his people.*

Chapter 19

Eve's Disobedience Is Remedied by Mary's Obedience.

1. The Lord, therefore, came manifestly into his own possessions. Thus his own creation, which was borne by him, bears him; and he recapitulated the disobedience that was by means of a tree, through the obedience that was by means of a tree. Thus the deception by which the virgin Eve, who was already wedded to a man, was wickedly deceived, was destroyed through the truth, by which the Virgin Mary, who was already wedded to a man, was brought the good news by the angel.[1] For just as the former was deceived by an angel's word, so that she fled from God upon having transgressed his word, so the latter, too, was brought the good news by an angel's word, that she might bear God upon being obedient to his word. And as the former was deceived to disobey God, so the latter, too, was persuaded to obey God,

in order that the Virgin Mary might become the advocate of the virgin Eve. And just as the human race was put in bonds to death through a virgin, it was loosed through a virgin. Thus the virginal disobedience was balanced by the virginal obedience.[2] Moreover, the sin of the First-fashioned man was rectified by the correction of the First-born. Thus the Serpent's cunning was overcome by the dove's simplicity;[3] and the bonds by which we were bound to death were loosed.

2. All the heretics are uninstructed and ignorant of God's arrangements and unaware of his economy in human nature. Of course, since they are blind in regard to the Truth, they speak against their own salvation. Some introduce another Father besides the Creator. Some assert that the world and its matter was made by certain angels. Some say that the matter was far distant from him who, according to them, is Father and blossomed of itself and was born spontaneously. Some claim that the world had its matter from among the things contained by Father, because of degeneracy and ignorance. Some hold the Lord's visible coming in contempt by not accepting his incarnation. Some, again, are ignorant of the economy about the Virgin, and assert that Christ was begotten of Joseph. And some certain ones assert that neither man's soul nor his body can receive eternal life, but only the inner man can. This, they claim, is the mind that is in themselves, which alone, they decree, ascends to the Perfect. Some assert that, though the soul has been saved, yet their body will not partake of the salvation which is from God, as we have explained in the First Book.[4] In that book we have also exposed the tenets of all of them, while in the Second Book we showed their weakness.[5]

Chapter 20

Only the Shepherds to Whom the Apostles Committed the Church Have the True Doctrine.

1. In point of fact, all these [heretics] are of later date than the bishops to whom the apostles have handed on the Churches. This we have shown with all care in the Third Book.[1] So these [heretics], since they are blind to the Truth, are constrained to go astray by different roads; and for this reason the traces of their doctrines are scattered about without harmony or order.[2] But the path of those who belong

to the Church encircles the whole world, since it possesses the secure tradition from the apostles, and grants us the privilege of seeing that the faith of all is one and the same, since all receive one and the same God the Father and believe in the same economy of the incarnation of God's Son, and all acknowledge the same gift of the Spirit[3] and practice the same commandments. All safeguard the same structure resulting from order in the Church.[4] All await the same coming of the Lord, and all hold the same salvation of the entire man, namely, of soul and body.[5] The preaching of the Church is therefore true and secure. Within her, one and the same way of salvation is manifested in the whole world. For to her was committed God's Light; and so also God's Wisdom, by which he saves all men,[6] *cries aloud in the streets; in the market places she raises her voice; on top of the walls she cries out; at the entrance of the city gates she speaks firmly.* Really, the Church preaches the Truth everywhere, and she is the seven-branched lamp, bearing the light of Christ.[7]

2. Now, those who forsake the preaching of the Church accuse the holy presbyters with lack of intelligence. But they do not consider how much more valuable an unlettered pious person is than a blasphemous and bold sophist.[8] Such are all the heretics and those who think they discover something more than the Truth when they follow the things we have already mentioned. They travel the path in varied and different and foolish manners. They do not always hold the same doctrines about the same things, and so they are like blind men who are led about by the blind; deservedly they fall into the ditch of ignorance that lies open before them.[9] They are always in search of truth but never find it.[10]

It is, therefore, necessary to avoid their doctrines and be on guard more intently, lest we be injured by them anywhere. With all diligence we must take refuge in the Church[11] and be reared in her bosom and nourished by the Lord's Scriptures. Really, the Church, as a garden, is planted in this world. So says God's Spirit,[12] *from every tree of the garden you shall eat the food*; that is, you shall eat of every Scripture of the Lord. But you shall not eat with a haughty mind,[13] and you shall not touch any faction of the heretics. These men profess that they themselves possess the knowledge of good and evil,[14] and they boastfully raise their impious thoughts above the God who made them. So, their thoughts are not kept within the bounds of reason.[15] To this the Apostle says,[16] *Let no one think of himself more highly than he ought, but let him think with sober judgment,* so that we may not eat their knowledge and be wiser than it behooves and be thrown out of the garden of life. The Lord leads those who obey his preaching into this garden, *recapitulating in himself all things, both those in the heavens and those on the earth.*[17] Now, the things *in the heavens* are the spiritual; those, however, *on the earth* are the human economy. These things, therefore, he recapitulated in himself; by uniting man to the Spirit and placing the Spirit in man, he himself was made the Head of the Spirit, and makes the Spirit the head of man; for through the Spirit we see and hear and speak.

Chapter 21

Christ Is the Head of All Things: It Was Fitting That He Should Assume Human Nature and Be Tempted by Satan, and Carry Off a Glorious Victory.[1]

1. Therefore, in recapitulating all things, he has also recapitulated the battle against our enemy. He both challenged and dashed to pieces[2] him who in the beginning led us captive in Adam; and he tramples on his head. This you have given in Genesis where God said to the serpent:[3] *I will put enmity between you and the woman, and between your seed and her seed; he shall observe your head, and you shall observe his heel.* To explain, ever since then he who was to be born of the Woman, the Virgin, according to the likeness of Adam, was heralded as observing the head of the serpent. This is the Offspring of whom the Apostle wrote in his Letter to the Galatians:[4] *The law of works was enacted until the offspring should come to whom the promise had been made.* He makes this still clearer in the same letter when he says,[5] *But when the fullness of time had come, God sent his Son made of a woman.* Certainly, the enemy would not have been justly conquered,[6] unless a man born of a woman had conquered him. For it was through a woman that he got dominion over man in the beginning, setting himself up as man's Adversary. For that reason, too, the Lord confessed himself to be the "Son of Man," inasmuch as he recapitulated in himself the original man, out of whom was made the Handiwork [Christ] that is according to a woman. This he did in order that, just as our race descended to death through the man who was conquered, so we might again ascend to life through the man who was victorious. And just as death received the

palm over us through the man, so we in turn might receive the palm over death through man.[7]

2. The Lord would not have recapitulated in himself that ancient and original enmity against the serpent, thus fulfilling the Creator's promise and carrying out his commandment, if he had come from some other Father. But since he who in the beginning fashioned us and who in the end sent his Son is one and the same, the Lord carried out his commandment when he was *made of a woman* and destroyed our Adversary and perfected man *after the image* and likeness *of God.*[8] On this account he did not destroy him by any other means than by the words of the Law, having used the Father's commandment as an aid for destroying and exposing the Rebel Angel.

First,[9] *He fasted forty days,* as also Moses and Elijah had done, then he was hungry, that we might understand that his human nature is true and unshakable;—for it is a characteristic of a man who fasts to be hungry[10]—and that the Adversary might have an occasion for attacking him. For just as in the beginning by means of food he deceived man, who was not hungry, to transgress God's commandment, so in the end he was not able to dissuade Man, who was hungry, to take food that was from God. For when he tempted him and said,[11] *If you are the Son of God, command these stones to become loaves of bread,* the Lord repelled him by the commandment of the Law, saying,[12] *It is written, "Man shall not live by bread alone."* To his statement, *If you are the Son of God,* he did not answer; but he blinded him by acknowledging himself to be a man, and he nullified the first attack by the Father's word. So the satiety of man in the garden by the twofold tasting of the food was undone by the indigence in this world.[13]

When he had been vanquished by the Law, he too, by lying attempted to make an attack by using the Law. He led him up to the highest point of the temple and said:[14] *If you are the Son of God, throw yourself down; for it is written, "God has given his angels charge of you, and on their hands they will bear you up, lest you strike your foot against a stone."* He concealed a lie under a Scripture text, as all heretics do.[15] For this that *He had given his angels charge of him* was indeed written; but this, *throw yourself down,* no Scripture text says of him. No, the Devil got this advice from himself. And so the Lord confounded him by the Law by quoting,[16] *Again, it is written, "You shall not tempt the Lord Your God."* By this statement from the Law he showed first, with reference to man, that man ought not to tempt God; then, with reference to that one [the Devil], that he should not tempt the Lord his God in the man whom he was seeing.[17] And so the pride of the mind that was in the serpent was undone by the humility that was in the man. Already twice was the Devil overcome by Scripture, when he was exposed as advising things contrary to God's commandment and was shown to be God's Adversary by his opinion. Then, having been signally confounded, he, so to say, gathered himself together and threw all his strength into a lie, and third, *showed him all the kingdoms of the world and the glory of them,*[18] adding, as Luke reminds us,[19] *All these I will give to you if falling down you will worship me.* At that the Lord exposed him for what he is. *Begone, Satan,* he said,[20] *for it is written, "You shall worship the Lord your God, and him only shall you serve."* He exposed him by his name and also showed who he himself is; for the Hebrew word *Satan* means a rebel.[21] So, having conquered him for the third time, he drove him away from himself for good as one who had been vanquished by the Law; and the transgression of God's commandment that occurred in Adam was undone by the command of the Law, which the Son of Man kept by not transgressing God's commandment.

3. Who, then, is the Lord God to whom Christ gives testimony, whom no one may tempt, and whom all must adore, and alone serve? It is, by all means and without any doubt, the God who also gave the Law. For these things were foretold in the Law, and by means of the word of the Law the Lord showed that the Law announces the true Lord who is from the Father. On the other hand, the Rebel Angel is destroyed by his voice, when his identity was exposed and he was vanquished by the Son of Man who kept God's commandment. For since in the beginning he persuaded man to transgress the Creator's commandment, he had him in his power. But this power is transgression and rebellion, and by these he put man in chains. So contrariwise, it was necessary that by man himself he should be conquered and be put in the same chains by which he had bound man, in order that man, having been loosed, might return to his Lord, by leaving to that one the chains by which he had been bound, that is, by the transgression. For, putting Satan in chains means loosing man, since[22] *no one can enter the strong man's house, and plunder his goods, unless he first binds the strong man.* Therefore the Lord exposed him in matters contrary to the word of God who made all things, and subdued him by means of a commandment—God's Law is a commandment.[23] Now, in his human nature[24] he showed him to be a fugitive from, and transgressor of, the Law and an apostate from God.[25] Thereafter[26] the Word kept him securely bound as a fugitive from himself and took as spoils

his tools, that is, those men who were held captive by him, whom he exploited unjustly. Justly is he led captive who before had led man captive unjustly; but man who had before been led captive has been withdrawn from the power of the possessor by the mercy of God the Father, who had pity on his handiwork and gave him salvation, restoring it through the Word, namely, through Christ, in order that man might learn through actual experience that he receives imperishability not of himself but as a gift from God.

Chapter 22

The Law Reveals the True Lord and God. The Gospel, Too, Manifests Him.

1. Our Lord clearly showed that the Lord is the true and only God, who was revealed by the Law. For the one whom the Law preached as God, him Christ revealed to be the Father, whom alone the disciples of Christ must serve. The Lord also defeated our Adversary by the words that are in the Law. But the Law commands us to praise the Creator as God and to serve him alone.[1] So it is no longer necessary to look for another Father besides this one, or above this one,[2] *For there is but one God who will justify the uncircumcised on the ground of their faith, and the circumcised because of the faith.* For if there were some other perfect Father above this one, he [Christ] would not have defeated Satan by the words and commandments of this one. For one ignorance cannot be cancelled by another ignorance; just as one degeneracy cannot make void another degeneracy. If, then, the Law comes from ignorance and degeneracy,[3] how can the words that are in it be made void by the Devil's ignorance, and how can the strong man be overcome? For the strong man cannot be overcome by one less strong or equally strong, but by one who has a greater power. Now the Word of God has greater power than all other things. He is proclaimed loudly in the Law:[4] *Hear, O Israel, "The Lord your God, is one Lord; and you shall love the Lord your God with all your soul; and him shall you adore, and him only shall you serve."* Now in the Gospel the Lord by means of these same statements destroyed the rebellion, and by the Father's word he overcame the strong one. By his words, too, he acknowledged the commandment of the Law, saying,[5] *You shall not tempt the Lord your God.* Really, he did

not destroy his Adversary[6] and overcome the strong one by another's word, but by his Father's word.

2. By his commandment, he taught us who have been set free that when we are hungry we should take the food that is given by God; and that, if we are placed at the heights of every charism, or if we are confident in the works of justice, or if we have been decorated with the highest administrative office, we should never be elated or tempt God. No, we should think humbly in all things and have ready at hand this, *You shall not tempt the Lord your God.* The Apostle taught the same,[7] *Do not be haughty,* he said, *but associate with the lowly.* He meant that we should not be taken in by riches, worldly splendor, and temporary fancy; but we should know that it is necessary *to adore the Lord your God, and to serve only him*; and not to believe him who falsely promises things that are not his, saying,[8] *To you I will give all these things, if you will fall down and worship me.* Why, he himself confesses that to worship him [the Devil] and to do his will is to fall away from the glory of God. And in what pleasant or good thing can one who has fallen share? Or what else can such a one hope for and await except death? For one who has fallen, death is near. Then, as a matter of course, he will not give what he promised. For how can he who fell give anything? God has dominion over man, and over him [Devil] too, since not even a sparrow falls to the ground unless our Father in heaven wills it.[9] Thus the [Devil's] statement,[10] *All these things have been delivered to me, and I give them to whom I will,* he said as one who is puffed up with pride. For the creation is not under his power, since he himself is one of the creatures. Nor can he give the kingdom of men to men; no, all other things and all things pertaining to men are disposed according to the order of God the Father. Now, the Lord says,[11] *The devil is a liar from the beginning, and has nothing to do with the truth.* So if he *is a liar, and has nothing to do with the truth,* he certainly did not say truthfully, *All these things have been delivered to me, and I give them to whom I will.* No, he told a lie.

Chapter 23

The Devil Is a Liar. God Is the Truth.

1. The Devil was already accustomed to lie against God for deceiving men. For in the beginning God had given man much food but had commanded him not to eat of one tree only. As Scripture tells

us:[1] *God said to Adam, "You may freely eat of every tree of the garden; but of the tree of knowledge of good and evil you shall not eat, for in the day that you eat of it, you shall die the death."* But the Devil lied against the Lord and tempted man. As Scripture tells us, the serpent said to the woman,[2] *Why has God commanded you that you should not eat of any tree of the garden?* But she exposed the lie and restated the command simply by saying,[3] *We may eat of the fruit of the trees of the garden; but of the fruit of the tree which is in the midst of the garden God has commanded us that we should not eat; and that we should not touch it, lest we die.* When he had learned God's commandment from the woman, he used his cunning and told another lie:[4] *No you shall not die the death; for God knows that in the day that you eat of it, your eyes will be opened, and you will be like God, knowing good and evil.* First he disputed in God's garden about God, as if he were absent; for he was ignorant of the immensity of God. Then when he had learned from her that the Lord had said they would die if they ate of the tree mentioned, he uttered the third lie, *"No, you will not die the death."* But the effect, namely, that death came upon those who ate, made it clear that God is truthful and that the serpent is a liar. For together with the food, they also took death into themselves, because they were disobedient and ate; but disobedience to God brings death. For that reason, from that time on, having become debtors to death, they were handed over to it.

2. And so they died on the same day that they ate, and were made debtors of death, since a day of creation is one. Scripture says,[5] *For there was evening and there was morning, one day.* Now on this very day they ate, and on it they died too. In the cycle and course of the days one is called a first day, another a second day, and another a third day. If anyone wishes to ascertain carefully on which of these seven days Adam died, he will find out from the Lord's economy. For by recapitulating in himself the entire human race from the beginning to the end, he recapitulated also his [Adam's] death. And so it is clear that the Lord suffered death in obedience to his Father on that day on which Adam died because of his disobedience to God. But he ate on the same day that he died. For God said,[6] *For on the day that you eat of it, you shall die the death.* So the Lord recapitulated the death in himself and came to the passion the day before the Sabbath—which is the sixth day of creation, the day on which man was fashioned—in order to give him a second creation through his passion, which freed him from death.[7]

Certain ones place the death of Adam in the thousandth year; for,[8] *since a day of the Lord is as a thousand years,* he did not overstep the thousand years, but died within them, fulfilling the sentence of the transgression. So, whether [we consider the transgression] according to the disobedience, which is death; or, the fact that they were then handed over and made debtors of death; or, according to the one and same day on which they ate and died, since a day of creation is one; or, according to the cycle of days, because they died on the day on which they ate, that is, on the day of preparation, which is called the clean supper,[9] namely, the sixth day, which the Lord manifested by dying on it; or, according to the fact that he did not overstep the thousand years—according to all these things that are pointed out, God is truthful; for they who tasted of the tree died. But the serpent was shown to be a liar and a homicide. This the Lord said of him:[10] *He was a murderer from the beginning and has nothing to do with the truth.*

Chapter 24
The Devil Is a Perpetual Liar; He Apostatized from God.

1. Just as the devil lied in the beginning, so he lied at the end too, saying,[1] *All these things have been delivered to me, and I give them to whom I will.* To tell the truth, not he but the Lord institutes the kingdoms of this world:[2] *For the king's heart is in the hand of God.* And through Solomon he says,[3] *By me kings reign and the rulers decree what is just; by me princes are exalted, and by me the nobles govern the earth.* To this end the Apostle Paul said,[4] *Let every person be subject to the governing authorities; for there is no authority except from God, and those that exist have been instituted by God.* And again he says of them,[5] *For he does not bear the sword in vain; for it is the servant of God, an avenger to execute his wrath on the wrongdoer.* But that he did not say this of the angelic powers or of invisible rulers, as certain ones dare to explain, but of human authorities, he says,[6] *For the same reason you also pay taxes, for they are the ministers of God, attending to this very thing.* The Lord confirmed this by not doing what the devil advised but ordered the tax collectors to pay the taxes for himself and for Peter,[7] since *they are ministers of God, attending to this very thing.*

2. Since man, having become apostatized from God, became so much like a wild beast that he considered even his kin as an enemy and engaged in every kind of restlessness, homicide, and avarice without fear, God imposed the fear of men on him—for they did not

acknowledge the fear of God—that having been subjected to human authority and educated by their law,[8] they might attain some justice and show moderation toward one another, because they would fear the sword dangling before their eyes, as the Apostle says,[9] *He does not bear the sword in vain, for it is the servant of God, an avenger to execute his wrath on the wrongdoer.* And for this reason the magistrates, too, have the laws as a mantle of justice and will not be questioned in regard to matters they have done justly and lawfully, nor will they be punished. On the contrary, whatever they have wickedly and impiously and unlawfully and tyrannically done for the overthrow of the just, in these things they will also perish; for the just judgment of God comes equally on all and is not wanting in anything. So the earthly kingdom has been established by God for the usefulness of the Gentiles—not by the Devil who is never altogether quiet. Why, he does not want even the Gentiles to live tranquilly—in order that they might fear the kingdom of men, and not devour one another like fish,[10] but might by the passing of laws beat back the multiple wickedness of the Gentiles. And according to this they *are ministers of God.*

3. Now, <if they are ministers of God>, who exact taxes of us, *attending to this very thing*; <and if> *the authorities that exist have been instituted by God,*[11] it is manifest that the devil lies in saying,[12] *They have been delivered to me, and I give them to whom I will.*[13] Really, kings are established by order of the same One by whose order men are born; and they are suited to the ones who are ruled by them at that time.[14] For some of them [rulers] are given for the correction and usefulness of the subjects and for the preservation of justice; but some are given for fear and punishment and reproof; and some for deception, dishonor, pride, which they also deserve; whereas God's just judgment, as we have remarked, comes equally upon all. The Devil, however, Angel that he is, can only accomplish this—what he did also in the beginning—to deceive and draw the mind of man to transgress God's commandments, and gradually to blind the hearts of those who begin to serve him, that they might forget the true God but adore him *as if he were God.*[15]

4. That is like a rebel who would seize a region in a hostile manner and would stir up trouble among these who are in it and usurp the king's glory among those who are ignorant that he is rebel and a thief. That is how the Devil acts, since he is one of the angels who has been put over the spirit of the air, as the Apostle Paul revealed in his Letter to the Ephesians.[16] He became envious of man, and so he

became a rebel from the divine law; for envy is foreign to God. And since his rebellion was exposed by man, and since man became the test of his sentiments, he set himself more and more in opposition to man, envying his life,[17] and he wished to include him in his own rebel power. But the Word of God, the Artificer of all things, vanquished him by man and showed him to be a rebel and, contrariwise, subjected him to man. He says,[18] *Behold, I give you authority to tread upon serpents and scorpions, and over all the power of the enemy,* so that, just as he had dominion over man by rebellion, so his rebellion would be made void by man's returning to God.

SECTION 3

UNITY OF GOD SHOWN THROUGH EXEGESIS OF SCRIPTURES ABOUT THE END TIMES

CHAPTER 25

PAUL AND DANIEL DESCRIBE THE FRAUD, THE PRIDE, THE TYRANNICAL KINGDOM OF THE ANTICHRIST.

1. Not only by the things already mentioned but also by the things that will exist under the Antichrist is it manifest that, though he is a rebel and a thief, he wants to be adored as God, and though he is a servant, he wants to be heralded as a king. For this one [the Antichrist] will take on the Devil's power and will come not as a just king, nor as a law-abiding subject of God, but as wicked and lawless,[1] as a rebel, and unjust and murderous, as a thief, recapitulating in himself the diabolical rebellion. He will depose idols to persuade men that he himself is God; but thus he will exalt himself as the only idol, having in himself the multiple error of all the rest of the idols, in order that those who worship the Devil by means of many idols may serve him by means of this one idol. In regard to this the Apostle says in the Second Letter to the Thessalonians as follows:[2] ...*unless the rebellion comes first, and the man of lawlessness is revealed, the son of perdition, who opposes and exalts himself against every so-called god, or object of worship, so that he takes his seat in the temple of God <as God>, showing himself to be God.* Clearly, therefore, does the Apostle show up his *rebellion* and that *he extols himself against every so-called god or object of worship,* namely, against every idol—for these are indeed called gods by men, but in reality are not—and that he will try in tyrannical fashion to *show himself to be God.*[3]

2. Besides that, he revealed also this—a thing we have demonstrated by many arguments—that the temple in Jerusalem was made by an order of the true God.[4] For the Apostle himself on his own name called it absolutely God's temple. Now, also in the Third Book we showed that the apostles in their own name call no one God except him who is truly God, the Father of Our Lord, by whose order the temple of Jerusalem was made for the purpose mentioned by us.[5] In this temple the Adversary will sit and attempt to show that he is the Christ. That is what the Lord said:[6] *So when you see the desolating sacrilege spoken of by the Prophet Daniel, standing in the holy place (let the reader understand), then let those who are in Judea flee to the mountains; let him who is on the housetop not go down to take what is in his house. For then there will be great tribulation, such as has not been from the beginning of the world until now, and never will be.*

3. Daniel, too, seeing the end of the last kingdom, namely, the last ten kings, among whom is divided the kingdom of those upon whom the son of perdition will come, says that ten horns will issue from the beast, and that another small horn will issue in the center, and three of the former horns will have their roots in his forehead. He says:[7] *And behold, in his horn were eyes like the eyes of a man, and mouth speaking great things. And his face was greater than the rest. As I looked this horn made war against the saints, and prevailed over them, until the Ancient of Days came and judgment was given for the saints of the Most High, and the time came when the saints received the kingdom.*

Then, for the interpretation of the visions he was told:[8] *As for the fourth beast, there shall be a fourth kingdom on the earth, which shall be greater than all the kingdoms, and it shall devour the whole earth, and trample it down, and break it to pieces. As for the ten horns, out of this kingdom ten kings shall arise, and another shall arise up after them; he shall be mightier than the former ones and shall put down three kings. He shall speak words against the Most High and shall oppress the saints of the Most High; and shall think to change the times and the laws; and they shall be given into his hand for a time, and two times, and half a time.* That means for three years and six months, during which time he will come and reign on the earth.

The Apostle Paul also spoke of this in the Second Letter to the Thessalonians and announced at the same time the reason of his coming. This is what he said:[9] *And then the lawless one will be revealed, and the Lord Jesus will slay him with the breath of his mouth and destroy him by the manifestation of his coming. And his coming by the activity of Satan will be with all power and with pretended signs and wonders, and with all wicked deception for those who are to perish, because they refused to love the truth and so be saved. Therefore God sends upon them a strong delusion, to make them believe what is false, so that all may be condemned who did not believe the truth, but had pleasure in unrighteousness.*

4. The Lord, too, spoke the same things to those who did not believe him:[10] *I came in my Father's name, and you did not receive me; if another comes in his own name, him you will receive.* By *another* he meant the Antichrist, because he is estranged from God, and he is the lawless judge of whom the Lord said that he *neither feared God, nor regarded man,* to whom the widow, namely, the earthly Jerusalem, who had forgotten God, will flee, for avenging the enemy.[11] This he will also do in the time of his reign. He will transfer his kingdom to her [Jerusalem] and will sit in the temple, deceiving those who worship him, as if he himself were the Christ.

Wherefore, Daniel says again:[12] *And he shall make desolate the sanctuary; and sin was offered as sacrifice; and justice was cast down on the earth, and he has acted and prospered.* And the Angel Gabriel, when explaining this vision, said about this very one:[13] *And in the latter end of their rule, a king of bold countenance, one who understands riddles shall arise; his power shall be great and admirable. He shall cause fearful destruction and shall succeed in what he does, and destroy mighty men and the people of the saints; and the yoke shall be prosperous as a necklace; deceit in his hand and in his heart shall be exalted; and by deception he shall kill many; and he shall rise up for the ruin of many, and as an egg he shall crush them with the hand.* Then he points out the time of his tyranny, at which time the holy people will be put to flight who offer a clean sacrifice to God:[14] *And in half the week my sacrifice and my libation shall fail, and there shall be in the temple the desolating sacrilege; and the desolation shall continue until, and end with, the consummation of time.*

5. By all this, not only the things pertaining to the rebellion are revealed, and what belongs to him who recapitulates in himself every diabolical error, but also that there is one and the same God the Father, who was heralded by the Prophets and made known by Christ. For if the things about the end that were prophesied by Daniel were confirmed by the Lord—he did say:[15] *When you see the desolating sacrilege spoken of by the Prophet Daniel*—then one and the same God is most clearly shown. (The Angel Gabriel gave Daniel the interpretation of the visions, but he is the Archangel of the Creator and the same one who brought the good news to Mary about the visible coming and the incarnation of the Christ.)[16] It is he who sent the Prophets and sent the Son[17] and called us to his knowledge.

Chapter 26

John and Daniel Predicted the Fall of the Roman Empire.

1. Still more clearly in the Apocalypse has John, the Lord's disciple, pointed out the things about the last times, and the empire which now reigns will be divided among the ten kings. He explained what the ten horns seen by Daniel were. He affirmed that this is what was said to him:[1] *And the ten horns that you saw are ten kings who have not yet received royal power, but they are to receive authority as kings for one hour*

together with the beast. These are of one mind and give over their power and authority to the beast; they will make war on the Lamb, and the Lamb will conquer them, for he is Lord of lords and King of kings, and those with him are called and chosen and faithful. Hence, it is evident that he who is to come will kill three of these, and the rest will be made subject to him; he himself will be the eighth among them. They will lay Babylon waste, and will burn her with fire, and will give her kingdom to the beast, and will put the Church to flight. After that they will be destroyed by the Lord's coming. In fact, the Lord said that the kingdom must be divided and thus perish:[2] *Every kingdom divided against itself is laid waste, and no city or house divided against itself will stand.* So it is necessary that the kingdom and city and house be divided into ten parts. For this reason he already prefigured the partition and division.

Daniel, too, said carefully that the end of the fourth kingdom is the toes of the statue that was seen by Nebuchadnezzar, against which the stone cut off without hands fell. He says:[3] *And its feet were partly iron and partly clay, till the stone that was cut off without hands smote the statue on its feet of iron and clay, and broke them in pieces completely.* Then for the interpretation he said:[4] *And as you saw the feet and the toes partly of potter's clay and partly of iron, it shall be a divided kingdom; but some of the firmness of iron shall be in it, just as you saw the iron mixed with miry clay. And the toes of the feet were indeed partly iron and partly clay.* So the ten toes are the ten kings among whom the kingdom will be divided, of which some are strong and energetic, while others will be weak and idle,[5] and they will not agree among themselves. Of this Daniel said:[6] *The Kingdom shall be partly strong and partly brittle. And as you saw the iron mixed with miry clay, so will they mix with one another in marriage, but they will not hold together, just as iron does not mix with clay.* And that the end will come he tells us:[7] *And in the days of those kings the God of heaven will set up a kingdom which shall never be destroyed, nor shall his sovereignty be left to another people. It shall break in pieces all these kingdoms and bring them to an end, and it shall stand for ever, just as you saw that a stone was cut from a mountain by no hands, and that it broke in pieces the clay and the iron and the bronze and the silver and the gold. The great God has made known to the king what shall be hereafter. The dream is true and its interpretation sure.*

2. If, therefore, the great God pointed out future things through Daniel, and confirmed them by his Son; and if Christ is the stone which was cut off without hands who will destroy the temporal kingdoms and bring on the eternal kingdom, that is, the resurrection of the just—Scripture says:[8] *In those days God will set up a kingdom of heaven,*

which shall never be destroyed—then let those who reject the Creator and do not agree that the Prophets have been sent in advance by the Father (from whom also the Lord came), but affirm that the prophecies came from various powers, let them come to their senses, since they have been put to shame.

Certainly, the things that were in like manner predicted by the Creator through all the Prophets, these Christ brought to completion in the end, ministering to the Father's will and fulfilling the economies regarding the human race.[9] Therefore, those who blaspheme the Creator either in so many words and openly, as the Marcionites do, or by twisting the thought,[10] as do the Valentinians and all falsely so-called Gnostics, should be recognized by all God-fearing people as tools of Satan, through whom Satan at present, and not before, is seen to blaspheme God who has prepared the eternal fire for every rebellion.[11] For he does not dare by himself to blaspheme his Lord openly, just as in the beginning he deceived man by means of the serpent, as if being hidden from God.[12]

3. Justin has said correctly[13] that before the Lord's coming into the world, Satan never dared blaspheme God, since he did not yet know about his own condemnation, because the Prophets spoke of him in parables and allegories. However, after the Lord's coming he ascertained clearly from the words of Christ and of the apostles that eternal fire had been prepared for him who of his own will departed from God and for all who unrepentant continue in rebellion.[14] By means of such men he blasphemes God who sets the sentence, as if he were already condemned, and he imputes the sin of rebellion to his Creator and not to his own free choice.[15] That is how those act, too, who transgress laws and then when they suffer punishment they blame the lawgivers but not themselves. In the same manner these men, who are full of the diabolical spirit, make innumerable accusations against their Creator—who gave us also the Spirit of life, and made a suitable law for all—and who deny that God's judgment is just. Wherefore, they concoct some other Father, who does not care for or provide the things that concern us, or who even approves all sin.

Chapter 27

In the Future Judgment by Christ, Some People Will Be Separated from God, Others Will Be United with Him.

1. If, then, the Father does not judge, either judgment is not his right or he approves all things that happen. Now, if he does not judge, all persons will be equal and will be classed in the same state. In that case, Christ's coming will be useless, even contradictory, since he does not judge. For he[1] *has come to set a man against his father, and a daughter against her mother, and a daughter-in-law against her mother-in-law*; and,[2] *when there will be two men in one bed, to take one and to leave the other; and, where there will be two women grinding at the mill, to take one and to leave the other*; and,[3] at the end to give orders to the harvesters to gather up the weeds first, bind them in bundles and burn them with unquenchable fire, but to gather the wheat into the barn; and,[4] to call the lambs into the kingdom that has been made ready, but to throw the goats *into the eternal fire prepared* by his Father *for the devil and his angels.*

And why that? The Word came for *the fall and the rising of many.*[5] Yes, *for the fall* of those who do not believe him, whom he has threatened with even greater punishment in the judgment than the Sodomites and Gomorrhites,[6] but *for the rising* of those who believe and *do the will of his Father who is in heaven.*[7] If, then, the Son's coming is to all in the same manner, but if he judges and separates the believers and the unbelievers—since the ones believe by free choice and do the Father's will, while the others are disobedient by free choice and do not accept his teaching—it is evident that his Father, too, made all of them alike, each one having self-determination and free choice. For he has regard for all things and provides for all:[8] *He makes his sun rise on the evil and on the good, and sends rain on the just and on the unjust.*

2. Therefore, he bestows communion with himself on all who preserve their love for him. But communion with God means life and light and enjoyment of the good things that are with him.[9] On the contrary, he will establish the separation which they have chosen of themselves, having of their own choice rebelled against him. But separation from God is death, and separation from light is darkness; and the separation from God is loss of all good things that are from him. Hence, those who by rebellion have lost the things mentioned, since they are deprived of all good things, experience every punishment.

God himself did not originally punish them, but punishment followed them because they deprived themselves of all good things. On the other hand, the good things that are from God are eternal and endless; and for that reason also their loss is eternal and endless.[10] To illustrate, those who were in the endless light but have blinded themselves or have been blinded by others are always deprived of the joy of light, not because the light brought them the punishment of blindness, but because blindness itself brings the calamity on them. For this reason the Lord said,[11] *he who believes in me, is not condemned*; that is, is not separated from God, for he is united with God by faith. *He who does not believe,* he adds,[12] *is condemned already, because he has not believed in the name of the Only-begotten Son of God*; that is, he separated himself from God by his own free choice. And[13] *this is the judgment that the light has come into the world, and men have loved darkness rather than light, because their deeds were evil. For everyone who does evil hates the light, and does not come to the light, lest his deeds should be exposed. But he who does what is true comes to the light that it may be clearly seen that his deeds have been wrought in God.*

Chapter 28

Separation of the Good and the Evil; the Rebellion of the Antichrist at the End of the World

1. Since, then, in this world some people come running to the light and unite themselves to God through faith, whereas others stay away from the light and separate themselves from God, the Word of God came to supply a suitable dwelling for all: for the ones in the light, that they might enjoy it and the good things that are in it; for the others in darkness, that they might partake of the calamities that are in it. That is why he said that those who are on his right will be called into his Father's kingdom, while those who are on his left will be thrown into eternal fire;[1] for they had deprived themselves of all good things.

2. For this reason the Apostle said:[2] *Because they refused to love the truth and so be saved. Therefore God sends upon them a strong delusion, to make them believe what is false, so that all may be condemned who did not believe the truth, but had pleasure in unrighteousness.* For he will come

and of his own choice he will recapitulate the apostasy. He will work whatever he does work by his own free will and choice, and sit in the temple of God, so that those who are led astray by him would adore him as Christ, for which he will be justly thrown into the pool of fire.[3] But God knows all things by his foresight, and at the proper time he would send him who was to be such *to make them believe what is false, so that all may be condemned who did not believe the truth but had pleasure in unrighteousness.*[4]

John, in the Apocalypse, pointed out his coming in this manner:[5] *And the beast that I saw was like a leopard, its feet were like a bear's feet, and its mouth was like a lion's mouth. And to it the dragon gave his power and his throne and great authority. One of its heads seemed to have a mortal wound, but its mortal wound was healed, and the whole earth followed the beast with wonder. Men worshipped the beast, saying, "Who is like the beast, and who can fight against it?" And the beast was given a mouth uttering haughty and blasphemous words, and it was allowed to exercise authority for forty-two months; it opened its mouth to utter blasphemies against God, blaspheming his name and his dwelling, that is those who dwell in heaven. And authority was given it over every tribe and people and tongue and nation, and all who dwell in the earth will worship it, everyone whose name has not been written before the foundation of the world in the book of life of the Lamb that was slain. If any man has an ear, let him hear. If anyone is to be taken captive, to captivity he goes; if anyone slays with the sword, with the sword must he be slain. Here is a call for the endurance and faith of the saints.*

After that he said about the armor bearer, whom they call the false prophet:[6] *It spoke like a dragon. It exercises all the authority of the first beast in its presence, and makes the earth and its inhabitants worship the first beast, whose mortal wound was healed. It works great signs, even making fire come down from heaven to earth in the sight of men. And it deceives those who dwell on earth.*

Let no one think that he works those signs by divine power; no, he does so by magical power. And it is not surprising that he works signs through the demons and rebel spirits, since they serve him. By these signs he deceives the inhabitants of earth. He said,[7] *And it ordered an image to be made for the beast. And it was allowed to give breath to the image of the beast, so that the image of the beast should even speak, and to cause those who will not worship the image of the beast to be slain. Also it causes to be marked on the right hand or on the forehead, so that no one can buy or sell, unless he has the mark, that is, the name of the beast or the number of its name and its number is six hundred and sixty-six,* that is, six times one hundred and six times ten, and six times one. That is in view of the recapitulation of his entire rebellion which happened in six thousand years.

3. For as many days it took to make this world, so many thousands of years will it be in coming to an end. With this in mind the Scripture of Genesis says:[8] *The heavens and the earth were finished, and all the host of them. And on the sixth day God finished his work which he had done, and he rested on the seventh day from all his work which he had done.* This is both an account of things made previously, just as they had been made, and a prophecy about future things. *For with the Lord a day is as a thousand years.*[9] But the things that were created were finished in six days. So it is evident that the year of their completion is the six thousandth.

4. For this reason, in every age, man, who in the beginning had been formed by God's hands, namely, by the Son and the Spirit, is *made after the image and likeness of God,*[10] when he has discarded the straw, which is apostasy, but *has gathered the grain into the barn,*[11] which is those who make faith bear fruit for God. Hence, tribulation is necessary for those who are saved, that having been, in a sense, ground fine,[12] and kneaded together with patience by the Word of God, and baked, they may be fit for the King's banquet. As one of our own who was condemned to the beasts because of his testimony to God, said,[13] "Christ's wheat I am, and by the teeth of wild beasts I am to be ground that I may prove God's pure bread."

Chapter 29

All Things Are for the Just, but All Evil Is Summed Up in the Antichrist.

1. In the preceding books we have given the reasons on account of which God permitted these things to happen thus. We showed that all such things were made for man who is saved. Those things would make his free will and self-determining power grow to the mature state of immortality and would prepare it for a more suitable eternal submissiveness to God. For this reason creation is at the service of man. Man, indeed, was not made for the sake of creation, but creation was made for the sake of man. For, Scripture rightly accounted *the nations like a drop of water from a bucket, and as the dust on the scales, and as nothing,*[1] because they, too, did not lift their eyes to heaven, or give thanks to their Creator, or wish to see the light of the Truth, but were

as blind mice hidden in the depths of stupidity. They were, however, of use and service to the just, to the extent that the stem is of use to the growth of the wheat, and as its straw is of use for fire in making gold. For this reason, when in the end the Church will of a sudden be taken hence, [Scripture] says,[2] *There will be tribulation such as has not been from the beginning no, and never will be.* For this is the last contest of the just. If they are victorious in it, they will be crowned with imperishability.

2. When, then, the beast comes, there will be in it a recapitulation[3] of all evil and of all deceit, so that all rebel power might flow into it, and be shut up in it, and be cast into the fiery furnace.[4] Fittingly, too, its name will consist of a number, six hundred and sixty-six, recapitulating in itself all the mess of evil which existed before the flood, which resulted from the rebellion of the angels.[5] For Noah was six hundred years old and the flood came upon the earth and "destroyed the living being of the earth" on account of the most wicked generation that lived in Noah's time.[6] He also recapitulated all the lying error of the idols that existed after the flood, and the killing of the Prophets and the burning of the just. For the statue set up by Nebuchadnezzar had a height of sixty cubits and a width of sixty cubits.[7] Because Hananiah and Azariah and Mishael did not worship it, they were thrown into the fiery furnace,[8] and by the event they prophesied the burning of the just that would take place at the end. Really, the entire statue was a prefiguring of the coming of this One, who decreed that he alone should be worshipped by absolutely all people. So the six hundred years of Noah, under whom the flood occurred because of the rebellion, and the number of the cubits of the statue, on account of which the just were thrown into the fiery furnace, signify the number of the One in whom are recapitulated every rebellion of the six thousand years, and injustice and wickedness and false prophecy and deception; on account of which will come also the deluge of fire.

Chapter 30

The Antichrist's Number Is Certain, Though Its Meaning Is Uncertain.

1. That is the state of the case. This number is found in all the trustworthy and ancient writings.[1] Those who saw John face-to-face testify to it.[2] Reason[3] teaches us that the number of the beast according

to a calculation of the Greeks, by means of the letters that are in it, will amount to six hundred and sixty-six. That means that the decade is the same as the hundred, and the hundred is the same as the unit; for the number that is called six is kept the same throughout. So this [number] shows the recapitulation of the entire rebellion, which was in the beginning, and in the intermediate periods, and which will be at the end. I do not know how some have erred by following the common mode of speech and have set aside the middle number of the name, subtracting fifty, and wish it to be one decade instead of six decades. This I think was the mistake of a scribe, as is wont to happen, and since numbers are expressed by letters, the Greek letter that expresses the number sixty was easily expanded into the letter iota of the Greeks. After that, some without any examination accepted this reading. Some in their simplicity and lack of education used the number ten; while others through ignorance dared to look for names that would have the false number of the erroneous reading. Now we think that God will grant pardon to those who have done this in their simplicity and without malice. But whoever through vainglory establishes names that contain the false number, and who decree that the name invented by them is the name of him who will come, will not depart without harm since they have deceived both themselves and those who believed them. First, it is harmful to fall away from the truth, and to believe that a thing which does not exist, does exist. Then, whoever adds or subtracts from Scripture will endure not a light punishment; such a person must necessarily fall into such [a punishment]. Moreover, another danger, and not a small one, will follow those who falsely presume to know his name. For if these men think up a name, but if when the Antichrist comes, he will have another name, they will easily be deceived by him, as if he were not yet present, against whom they ought to be on guard.

2. These men, then, ought to learn the true number of the name and return to it, so they will not be classed with the false prophets. But knowing the secure number that is announced in the Scripture, that is, 666, they ought first to hold fast the division of the kingdom into ten. Then, when they [the kings] are ruling and beginning[4] to straighten out their affairs and to strengthen their kingdom, they ought to know that he who will come unexpectedly to vindicate for himself the kingdom and will terrify the kings mentioned, since he has the name contained in the number mentioned, is *the desolating sacrilege.*[5] This too is what the Apostle says,[6] *When people say, "There is*

peace and security," then sudden destruction will come upon them. Jeremiah revealed not only that his coming will be sudden but also the tribe from which he will come. He says,[7] *The snorting of his horses is heard from Dan; at the sound of the neighing of his stallions the whole land quakes. He shall come and devour the land and all that fills it, the city and those who dwell in it.* And for this reason this tribe is not enumerated in the Apocalypse with those who are saved.[8]

3. It is, therefore, safer and without danger to await the outcome of the prophecy than to guess and divine any names when many names can be found to express the number mentioned and when the difficulty would remain the same. For if many names can be found which express this number, which name, may we ask, will he have who will come?

It is not for want of names expressing this number that we say this, but on account of reverence for God and zeal for the truth. For example, *Evanthus*[9] has the number in question, but we do not affirm anything in regard to it. Also Latins express the number 666; and it is very probable that the last kingdom has this name, for the Latins are the ones who hold sway at present. But we will not boast of this. And *Teitan*[10] is of all the numbers found among us the most worthy of credence. For it contains the number mentioned, and consists of six letters, with three letters to each syllable. The word itself is ancient and unusual. In fact, we called none of our kings Titan. Neither does any of the idols that are worshipped publicly among the Greeks or barbarians have this number. Likewise many consider this name divine, so that those who now hold sway call even the sun Titan.[11] Again, it manifests, in a sense, the revenge, and the one who will carry out the vengeance, since he [the Antichrist] pretends to vindicate those who had been mistreated. Besides, this name is ancient, worthy of credence, kingly, and above all a tyrant's name. Since, therefore, this name Titan has so much to recommend it, it has so much probability, that, of the many names, we can gather that the one who will come will be called Titan. Nevertheless, we will not take any risk with it, neither will we give out as certain that he will have this name, since we know that if his name ought to be preached clearly at the present time, it would have been proclaimed by the one [John] who saw [its] revelation. For it is not such a long time ago since it was seen, but almost in our own age, namely, at the end of the reign of Domitian.[12]

4. But as the case is, he gives the number of the name, so that when he comes, if we know who he is, we might be on guard against

him. In regard to his name, however, he was silent, because it was not deserving to be announced by the Holy Spirit. For if it had been announced by him, he [Antichrist] would perhaps have remained a long time. As the case is, however, since he *was, and is not, and is to ascend from the bottomless pit, and go to perdition,*[13] just as if one does not exist, his name is not announced; for the name is not announced of one who has no name.

But when the Antichrist will have laid waste everything in this world, he will reign for three years and six months, and *will sit in the temple at Jerusalem.*[14] Then the Lord *will come from the heavens upon clouds,* in the glory of the Father, to throw him and those who obey him into the pool of fire.[15] On the other hand, he will inaugurate the times of the kingdom for the just, that is, the period of rest, the seventh day that was sanctified; and he will restore the promise of the inheritance to Abraham. In this kingdom, according to the Lord,[16] *many will come from east and west, and will sit at table with Abraham, Isaac, and Jacob.*

Chapter 31

The Imperishability of the Body Is Confirmed by Christ. There Will Be an Intermediate Kingdom.

1. Certain people who are thought of as orthodox believers go beyond the plain order for the promotion of the just. They are also ignorant of the methods of disciplining themselves for imperishability.[1] They harbor within themselves heretical thoughts. For heretics hold God's handiwork in contempt and do not admit salvation for their flesh; and they despise God's promise and pass over and beyond God altogether in their thinking. They assert that as soon as they die, they pass over and beyond the heavens and the Creator and go to Mother [Wisdom] or to their imagined Father. Now they reject total resurrection and, as far as they are able, put it out of existence. It is strange they do not know the order of resurrection, since they refuse to understand that if things were as they say, the Lord, in whom they profess to believe, would certainly not have risen on the third day. Instead, when he expired on the cross, he would directly have departed on high, leaving the body on earth. But as it is he stayed three days in the place where the dead were,[2] just as the Prophet says of him:[3] "The

Lord remembered his holy dead, who had previously fallen asleep in the earth, and he went down to them to liberate them and save them."

And the Lord himself said:[4] *For as Jonah was three days and three nights in the belly of the whale, so will the Son of man be in the heart of the earth.* And the Apostle says,[5] *But in saying "He ascended" what does it mean but that he had also descended into the lower parts of the earth?* David, too, prophesied of Christ,[6] *Thou hast delivered my soul from the depths of Sheol.* Moreover, when he rose on the third day, he appeared first to Mary and said to her:[7] *Do not hold me, for I have not yet ascended my Father; but go to the disciples and say to them: "I am ascending to my Father and to your Father."*

2. Consequently, if the Lord observed the law for the dead, so that he might be *the Firstborn of the dead*[8] and sojourned until the third day in the lower parts of the earth, and then rose in the flesh that he might show the prints of the nails to the disciples,[9] and in that manner ascended to the Father, how are they not confounded who assert that the lower parts are this world of ours, and that their inner man leaves the body here below, while it ascends to the supercelestial place? For since the Lord departed to *the midst of the shadow of death,*[10] where the souls of the dead were, and then rose bodily, and after the resurrection was taken up, it is evident that also the souls of his disciples, on account of whom the Lord wrought these things, will go to the invisible place determined for them by God and will sojourn there until the resurrection, awaiting the resurrection. Then they will receive their bodies and rise integrally, that is, bodily, so that just as the Lord rose, they also will come to the vision of God.[11] *For*[12] *a disciple is not above his teacher, but every one when he is fully taught will be like his teacher.* Consequently, as our Teacher did not directly fly away but awaited the time of his resurrection as appointed by the Father, which was also disclosed by Jonah, and then rose after three days and was taken up, so we too ought to await the time of our resurrection appointed by God, which was foretold by the Prophets, and on rising thus be taken up, [that is] all whom the Lord will deem worthy of this.

Chapter 32

The Saints Will Be Rewarded in the Very Bodies in Which They Suffered. All Creation Is Awaiting This, Which Was Promised to Abraham and His Posterity.

1. Since, therefore, the opinions of certain people are derived from heretical discourses, and since they are ignorant of God's economies and of the mystery of the resurrection and of the kingdom of the just, which is the beginning of imperishability,[1] and by means of which [kingdom] those who are worthy gradually become accustomed to receiving God, it is necessary to talk about these things.

It is necessary that the just, when they rise at the Lord's appearance, first receive the inheritance, promised by God to the forefathers, in this creation which is being renewed, and to reign in it. After that will be the judgment of all men.[2] For it is proper that they receive the fruits of their suffering in the creation in which they labored, having been tested by every mode of suffering; and to be brought to life in the creation in which they were killed for the sake of God; and to reign in the creation in which they endured the servitude. For God is rich in all things, and all things belong to him. Therefore, it is proper that the creation itself, after being restored to its pristine state, be of unhindered service to the just. The Apostle revealed this in his Letter to the Romans:[3] *For the creation waits with eager longing the revealing of the sons of God; for the creation was subjected to futility not of its own will but by the will of him who subjected it in hope; because the creation itself will be set free from its bondage to decay and obtain the glorious liberty of the children of God.*

2. And so also the promise that God made to Abraham remains assured. This is what he said:[4] *Lift up your eyes, and look from the place where you are, northward and southward and eastward and westward. For all the land which you see I will give to you and to your descendants forever.* And he added:[5] *Arise, walk through the length and the breadth of the land, for I will give it to you.* Yet he did not receive the inheritance in it, not even one footstep, but he was always *a pilgrim and a stranger* in it.[6] And when his wife Sarah died, and the Hittites wished to give him a place of burial gratis, he refused to take it; instead he bought a monument from Ephron the son of Zohar the Hittite. He gave four hundred didrachmas for it.[7] [He showed that] he waited for the promise of God, not wishing to appear to take from men what God had promised

to give to him, when he also said to him:[8] *To your descendants I give this land, from the river of Egypt to the Euphrates River.* And he counted up ten nations that dwelled in all that country.[9]

Consequently, if God promised him the inheritance of the land, and he did not receive it during his entire sojourn, it is necessary that he receive it in the resurrection together with his offspring, that is, those who fear God and believe in him. But the offspring is the Church which through the Lord receives the adoption relative to him [Abraham].[10] That is what John the Baptist said,[11] *For God is able from these stones to raise up children to Abraham.* The Apostle, too, says in the Letter to the Galatians,[12] *But you, brethren, like Isaac, are children of the promise.* Again, in the same letter he clearly states that those who believe in Christ will receive through Christ the promise to Abraham. He says:[13] *The promises were made to Abraham and to his offspring. It does not say, "And to offsprings," referring to many; but, referring to one, "And to your offspring," which is Christ.* To confirm what he said, he remarked:[14] *Thus Abraham "believed God, and it was reckoned to him as righteousness." So you see that it is men of faith who are the sons of Abraham. And the Scripture, foreseeing that God would justify the Gentiles by faith, preached the gospel beforehand to Abraham saying, "In you shall all the nations be blessed." So then, those who are men of faith are blessed with Abraham who had faith.* As a consequence, men of faith will be blessed with Abraham who had faith, and it is they who are the children of Abraham. But God promised the inheritance of the land to Abraham and his offspring. Now neither Abraham nor his offspring, that is, those who are justified through faith, do at present receive the inheritance in this land; but they will receive it in the resurrection of the just. For God is true and reliable in all things;[15] and so he called *the meek blessed, for they shall inherit the earth.*[16]

Chapter 33

The Promises to the Patriarchs Will Be Fulfilled in the New Earth.

1. In keeping with this, when he came to his passion, in order to announce the good news of the inauguration of the inheritance to Abraham and to those with him, he gave thanks over the cup, drank from it and gave it to his disciples, the while saying to them:[1] *Drink of it, all of you; for this is my blood of the new covenant, which is being poured*

out for many for the forgiveness of sins. I tell you, I shall not drink again of the fruit of this vine, until that day when I drink it new with you in my Father's kingdom. He himself will renew the inheritance of the earth and restore the mystery of the glory of the sons of God, as David says,[2] *Who will renew the face of the earth.* In that [inheritance] he promised to drink of the fruit of the vine with his disciples. Thus he manifested two things: the inheritance of the earth in which the new fruit of the vine is drunk, and the bodily resurrection of his disciples. For the flesh that rises new is the one that receives the new cup. Nor can we understand that he would drink the fruit of the vine in the supercelestial place on high; nor, on the other hand, that those who would drink it would be without flesh, for it is characteristic of the flesh, not of the spirit, to receive the drink of the wine.[3]

2. With this in mind the Lord said:[4] *When you give a dinner or a banquet, do not invite your friends, or your brethren or your kinsmen or your rich neighbors, lest they also invite you in return, and you be repaid. But when you give a feast, invite the poor, the maimed, the lame, the blind; and you will be blessed, because they cannot repay you. For you will be repaid at the resurrection of the just.* This, too, he said:[5] *Everyone who has left lands or houses or parents or brothers or children for my sake, will receive a hundredfold in this world, and inherit eternal life in the next.* Now, what are the hundredfold of this world and the dinners given to the poor and the banquets offered? These things will take place in the times of the kingdom, that is, on the seventh day which was sanctified, on which God rested from all the works he had made.[6] This is the true Sabbath of the just, on which they will not do any wearisome work but will have at hand a table prepared by God, who will feed them with every kind of food.[7]

3. Isaac's blessing, with which he blessed Jacob, the younger son, has the same meaning. *See,* he said,[8] *the smell of my son is as the smell of a plentiful field, which the Lord has blessed. But the field is the world;*[9] and so he added:[10] *May God give to you of the dew of heaven, and of the fatness of the earth, and plenty of grain and wine. Let peoples serve you, and nations bow down to you. Be lord over your brothers, and may your mother's sons bow down to you. Cursed be everyone who curses you, and blessed be every one who blesses you.* Now if anyone does not refer these things to the times of the "kingdom" mentioned before, he will fall into a great contradiction and opposition, just as the Jews fell and are involved in every perplexity. For not only in this life do the Gentiles not serve this Jacob, but after the blessing he himself went forth and served Laban his Syrian uncle for twenty years.[11] And he was not only not made the lord of his

brother, but even reverenced Esau his brother when he returned to his father from Mesopotamia and offered Esau many gifts.[12]

And how did he who, on account of the famine in the land in which he dwelt, emigrate to Egypt and become subject to Pharaoh who then reigned in Egypt?[13]How did he inherit here below the abundance of wheat and wine? The aforementioned blessing, then, belongs indubitably to the times of the "kingdom" when the just will rise from the dead and will reign, and will have been honored by God through the very resurrection,[14] when the creation, after it has been renewed and liberated, will produce an abundance of every kind of food because of the dew of heaven and the fertility of the land, as the Presbyter, who had seen John, the Lord's disciple, recalled that they had heard from him that the Lord taught these things about the times, and said:[15] "Days will come when the vine will sprout, each one having ten thousand branches and every branch ten thousand twigs, and on each branch ten thousand shoots, and on each shoot ten thousand clusters, and on each cluster ten thousand grapes, and in each grape when pressed twenty-five measures of wine. And when any of the saints will take hold of a cluster, another cluster will cry out, 'I am a better cluster, take me, and bless the Lord through me.' In like manner, a grain of wheat will sprout ten thousand ears of wheat, and each ear will have ten thousand grains, and each grain will furnish ten pounds of clean white flour. Likewise, the rest of the fruits and the seeds and the herbs will produce in proportion to these; and all the animals who use these foods which are gotten from the earth will live in peace and harmony among themselves, completely subject to men."

4. Papias, who was an old man, John's auditor, and Polycarp's companion, testifies in writing to the same things in the fourth of his books. (He wrote five books.)[16] This is what he added: "These things are credible to believers," he said, "Judas, the traitor, who did not believe, and who asked, 'How, then, can things that will produce so plentifully be made by the Lord?' got this answer from the Lord: 'Those who come to them, will see.'"

Prophesying of these times, Isaiah said:[17] *The wolf shall pasture with the lamb, and the leopard shall lie down with the kid, and the calf and the bull and the lion shall pasture together, and a little child shall lead them. The cow and the bear shall pasture together, and their young shall be together, and the lion shall eat straw like an ox. The suckling child shall be over the hole of the asp; and shall thrust his hand into the den of the young asps; and they shall not hurt, nor shall they be able to destroy anyone in my holy mountain.*

He summed it up again this way:[18] *The wolves and the lambs shall pasture together; and the lion shall eat straw like the ox; and ground shall be food for the serpent. They shall not hurt or destroy in my holy mountain, says the Lord.*

I am not unaware that certain people try to transfer these things to wild men, who, coming from various nations and diverse occupations, became believers and once they believed they lived in concord with the just. But even though at present this happens among certain people, who from various nations unite in the one doctrine of faith; nevertheless, in the resurrection of the dead it will happen to those animals, exactly as it was said. For *God is rich in all things.*[19] And it is proper that, once creation has been renewed, all the animals obey and be subject to man, and return to the first food that was given by God, just as before the disobedience they were subject to Adam, eating the fruit of the earth. For the rest, it is not possible at present to point to any lion who feeds on straw. But by this he pointed out the size and richness of the fruits. For if that animal, the lion, feeds on straw, what will the wheat itself be like, if its straw will be suitable food for lions?

Chapter 34
The Millennium Is Proved from the Prophets and the Parables.

1. Isaiah himself announced such future joy in the resurrection of the just. He spoke as follows:[1] *The dead shall rise, and those who are in the tombs shall rise, and they shall rejoice who are on the earth. For your dew is health to them.* Ezekiel said the same:[2] *Behold, I will open your graves, and raise you from your graves, and I will bring you home into the land of Israel. And you shall know that I am the Lord, when I open your graves. I will raise my people from the graves, and I will put my spirit within you, and you shall live, and I will place you upon your own land; then you shall know that I am the Lord.* And again, the same one said: *Thus says the Lord God, "When I gather the house of Israel from the peoples among whom they are scattered, and manifest my holiness in the midst of the Gentile peoples, then they shall dwell in their own land, which I gave to my servant Jacob. And they shall dwell securely in it, and they shall build houses, and plant vineyards. They shall dwell securely when I execute judgments upon all their neighbors who have treated them with contempt. Then they will know that I am the Lord their God, and the God of their fathers."*

Shortly before, we showed that the Church is the offspring of Abraham, for this reason,[3] too, that we may know that <there is one God> in the new covenant and the old who will assemble from all the Gentiles those who will be saved—*raising up children from stones.* Jeremiah said:[4] *Behold, the days are coming, says the Lord, when it shall no longer be said, "As the Lord lives, who brought up the people of Israel <out of the land of Egypt"; but, "As the Lord lives who brought up the children> out of the north country, and out of all the countries where he had driven them, and he shall restore them to their land which he gave to their Fathers."*[5]

2. Isaiah declares that the whole creation, according to God's will, will tend toward growth and development, so that it can produce and ripen such fruits:[6] *And upon every lofty mountain and every high hill there will be brooks of running water, in the day of the slaughter of many, when the towers fall. Moreover, the light of the moon will be as the light of the sun, and the light of the sun will be sevenfold, in the day when the Lord binds up the hurt of his people, and heals the wound inflicted by his blow.* Now, the pain comes from the wound by which man was struck in the beginning in Adam when he was disobedient; that is, death, which God healed by raising us from the dead and restoring us to the inheritance of the Fathers, as is contained in the blessing of Japheth[7] *"God enlarged Japheth, and let him dwell in the tents of Shem."* Isaiah also spoke of that:[8] *Then you shall delight in the Lord, and he will make you ride upon the whole earth; and he will feed you with the heritage of Jacob.*

That is what the Lord also said:[9] *Blessed are those servants whom the master finds awake when he comes; truly, he will gird himself, and have them recline at table, and he will come and serve them. If he comes in the second watch, or in the third, and finds them so, blessed are those servants!*

John too, spoke of the same thing in the Apocalypse:[10] *Blessed and holy is he who shares in the first resurrection.* Isaiah announced even the time when these things would happen:[11] *Then I said, "How long, O Lord?" Until cities lie waste without inhabitants, and houses without men, and the land is utterly desolate. And the Lord removes men far away, and they are multiplied that were left on the earth.*

Daniel, likewise, said the same thing:[12] *And the kingdom and the dominion and the greatness of the kings under the heavens shall be given to the saints of the Most High, and his kingdom shall be everlasting, and all dominions shall serve him and obey him.* And lest the promise be thought to have been given for the present time, the Prophet was told:[13] *But you go your way, and you shall stand in your allotted place at the end of the days.*

3. Now the promises were announced not only to the Prophets and the Patriarchs but also to the churches gathered together from the nations, which the Spirit calls also islands, because they are placed in the midst of a turbulence and endure the tempests of blasphemies, and are safe ports for those in dangers and a refuge for those who love the height [of Truth] and who try to shun the profundity of error.[14]

Jeremiah puts it thus:[15] *Hear the word of the Lord, O nations, and declare it on the islands afar off; say, "He who scattered Israel will gather him, and will keep him as a shepherd keeps his flock. For the Lord has ransomed Jacob, and has redeemed him from the hands too strong for him. They shall come and sing aloud on the height of Zion, and they shall come to the good things of the Lord, to the land of grain and wine and fruits and herds and flocks; their life shall be like a fruitful tree, and they shall be hungry no more. Then shall the maidens rejoice in the company of the young men, and the old men shall be merry; and I will turn their mourning into joy, and I will make them rejoice; and I will magnify and feast the soul of the priests of the sons of Levi; and my people shall be satisfied with good things."*

In the preceding Book we have shown that the Levites and the priests are all disciples of the Lord, who also profane the Sabbath in the temple, and that, without fault.[16] So, such promises most clearly signify a feast with this creation in the kingdom of the just—a feast God promises to serve them.

4. Likewise, Isaiah said of Jerusalem and its king:[17] *Thus says the Lord: Blessed is he who has children in Zion, and servants in Jerusalem. Behold a king will reign in righteousness, and princes will rule in justice.* And of the preparation by which it will be renewed he said:[18] *Behold I will prepare for you a precious stone, and [lay] your foundations with sapphires, and I will make your pinnacles of agate, and your gates of carbuncles, and your well of precious stones. All your sons shall be taught by the Lord, and great shall be the prosperity of your sons. In righteousness you shall be established.*

Again, the same one said:[19] *Behold I will rejoice in Jerusalem, and [be glad] in my people; no more shall be heard in it the sound of weeping, and the cry of distress. No more shall there be in it an infant or an old man who does not fill out his time, for the young man shall be a hundred years old, and a sinner a hundred years old on dying shall be accursed. They shall build houses and inhabit them; they shall plant vineyards and eat their fruits. <They shall drink wine>. They shall not build and another inhabit; they shall not prepare the ground and another eat; for like the days of the tree of life shall the days of my people be; and they shall <make use of> the works of their hands.*

Chapter 35
The Testimonies Are Not to Be Understood Spiritually of the Heavenly Blessings, but of the Kingdom of the Millennium.

1. Now, if certain ones would attempt to understand these things in an allegorical sense, they could not be found consistent in all things. They would be refuted by the statements that say,[1] *Until cities lie waste without inhabitants, and houses without men, and the land be utterly desolate.* Isaiah says,[2] *Behold, the day of the Lord comes, cruel, and full of wrath and fierce anger to make the earth a desolation; and to destroy its sinners from it.* And again he says,[3] *Let him be taken that he may not see the glory of the Lord.* And when these things will have happened, he says,[4] God *shall remove men far away, and they who were left on the earth shall be multiplied.* And[5] *they shall build houses and inhabit them, they shall plant vineyards and eat their fruit.*

Surely, such things are without doubt said of the resurrection of the just, which will take place after the coming of the Antichrist, and after the destruction of all the nations who will be under his dominion. At that [resurrection] the just will reign on the earth, they will gain growth because of the appearance of the Lord, and through him they will become accustomed to receiving the glory of God the Father; and in the "kingdom" they will have companionship with the holy angels and will have communion and union with the spiritual beings. Those, too, whom the Lord will find on the earth in the flesh awaiting him from heaven, and who have suffered affliction and have escaped the hands of the evil One, are the ones of whom the Prophet says, *They who were left on the earth shall be multiplied.* And all from among the Gentiles whom God prepared for this: to multiply those who were left on the earth, for belonging to the reign of the saints, and for serving in Jerusalem.

The Prophet Jeremiah pointed out still more clearly about Jerusalem and the "kingdom" in it. He said:[6] *Look about you, O Jerusalem, to the east: and behold the joy that comes to you from God himself. Behold your children whom you had sent away are coming, they come gathered together from east to west, rejoicing in the glory of God at the word of the Holy One. Take off, O Jerusalem, the garment of your mourning and affliction; and put on the beauty of the glory of your God for ever. Wrap yourself in the double mantle of justice; and put on your head the crown of everlasting glory. For God will show your glory to every [creature] under heaven. For your name, given by God himself for ever, shall be "Peace of justice" and "Glory of divine worship." Arise, O Jerusalem, and stand on the heights, and look about to the east, and behold your children gathered together from the rising of the sun to its setting, by the Word of the Holy One, rejoicing that God remembers them. For they left you on foot, led by the enemies, but the Lord will bring them to you borne aloft in glory as (on) the throne of the kingdom. For God has decreed to level every high mountain and the everlasting hills, and to fill up the valleys to make the earth a plain, so that Israel may walk safe in the glory of God. The woods, moreover, and every fragrant tree have by an order of God cast a shadow over Israel. For God will joyfully go before Israel by the light of his glory, with mercy and justice that come from him.*

2. All these things cannot be understood as supercelestial matters. He says:[7] *For God will show your glory to every creature under heaven.* These things must be understood of the times of the kingdom, when the earth has been renewed by Christ and Jerusalem has been rebuilt according to the pattern of the Jerusalem on high, of which the Prophet Isaiah says,[8] *Behold, I have graven your walls upon my hands, and you are always in my sight.* The Apostle writing to the Galatians spoke in a similar strain.[9] *But the Jerusalem above is free, and she is the mother of us all.* He did not say this of an imagined Aeon that had strayed, nor of any power that rebelled against the Fullness and Prunikos, but of the Jerusalem that was organized in God's hands.

John, in the Apocalypse, saw it coming down upon the new earth. For, after the times of the "kingdom," he says:[10] *I saw a great white throne, and him who sat upon it; from his presence earth and sky fled away and no place was found for them.* And he explains the details of the general resurrection and judgment; he said he saw[11] *the dead, great and small. And the sea gave up the dead in it, and Death and Hades gave up the dead in them; and the scrolls were opened. And the book of life, too, was opened; and the dead were judged by what was written on the scrolls, by what they had done. Hades and Death were thrown into the lake of fire.* This is known as Gehenna, which Christ called eternal fire.[12] *If anyone,* he says,[13] *was not found written in the book of life, he was thrown into the lake of fire.*

After that he continued:[14] *Then I saw a new heaven and a new earth; for the first heaven and the first earth had passed away, and the sea was no more. And I saw the holy City, New Jerusalem, coming down out of heaven from God, prepared as a bride adorned for her husband; and I heard, he said, a great voice from the throne saying: "Behold, the dwelling of God with men. He will dwell with them, and they will be his people, and God will be with them as their God; and he will wipe away every tear from their eyes, and death shall be no more, neither shall there be mourning nor crying nor pain any more, for the former things have passed away."* But Isaiah said the same thing:[15] *For behold, there will be a new heaven and a new earth, and the former things shall not be remembered, or come to mind. But they shall find gladness and rejoicing in her.* And that is precisely what the Apostle said:[16] *For the form of this world is passing away.* The Lord said something similar,[17] *Heaven and earth will pass away.*

When, therefore, these things have passed away, John, the Lord's disciple, said that *the Jerusalem from on high will come down on the new earth, as a bride adorned for her spouse,* and that this is God's dwelling, in which God dwells together with men. The image of this Jerusalem is that Jerusalem on the former earth, in which the righteous are disciplined beforehand for imperishability, and are made ready for salvation. Moses received the pattern of this tabernacle on the mountain.[18]

Nothing of these things can be taken in an allegorical sense, but all are reliable and true, and represent reality, and were made by God for the enjoyment of the righteous people. For, just as he is truly God who raises men up, so man rises from the dead, really and not allegorically, as we have shown by so many arguments. And as he really rises, so also is he really disciplined beforehand for imperishability and will grow and flourish in the times of the "kingdom," that he might become capable of receiving the Father's glory. Then, when all things have been renewed, he will in all reality dwell in the city of God. For he said:[19] *And he who sat upon the throne said, "Behold, I make all things new."* And the Lord said, *"Write <all>, because these words are trustworthy and true, and he said to me, 'It is done.'"*

Chapter 36
The Earth Will Be the Dwelling of the Righteous.

1. That is according to reason, too. To explain, since they are truly men, it is necessary that their transfer be also true,[1] and that they do not pass away into nonexistence but make progress in existence. For neither the substance nor the matter of creation is to be brought to nought—for the one who established it (creation) is true and trustworthy—but *the form of this world is passing away;*[2] that is, the

things in which the transgression was committed, since man grew old in them. For that reason this *form* was made temporary, since God foreknew all things, as we have shown in the preceding Book. We have shown, too, as far as possible, what the reason for the temporary things in the creation of the world was. But when *the form passes away,* and man has been renewed and matures for imperishability, so as not to grow old, there will be *a new heaven and new earth,* in which man will continue on, always conversing in a new way with God. That these things will always continue without end, Isaiah put in these words:[3] *For as the new heaven and the new earth, which I am making, shall remain before me, says the Lord; so shall your descendants and your name remain.*

And as the presbyters said: Then those who are worthy of the life in heaven will be transferred there, that is, to heaven; others however will share the delights of paradise; others still will enjoy the beauty of the city. God, however, will be seen everywhere to the degree to which those who see him are worthy.

2. They say that there is this distinction between the dwelling of those who produced a hundredfold and of those with sixty, and of those with thirty:[4] certain ones of them will be taken into heaven; others will live in paradise, others will dwell in the city. For this reason the Lord said,[5] *there are many mansions with my Father.* For all things belong to God who gives to all a suitable dwelling. As his Word says, The Father has distributed to all to the extent that each one is worthy or will be.[6] And that is the couch on which those who were invited to the wedding[7] will recline and feast.

The presbyters, the disciples of the apostles, assert that this is the order and the method for those who are saved, and that by means of these steps they make progress, and through the Spirit they ascend to the Son and through the Son to the Father.[8] Finally, the Son hands over his work to the Father, as was said by the Apostle:[9] *For he must reign until he has put all his enemies under his feet. The last enemy to be destroyed is death.* For in the times of the "kingdom" the righteous man on the earth will forget to die. He said,[10] *But when it says, "All things are put in subjection under him," it is plain that he is excepted who put all things under him. When all things are subjected to him, then the Son himself will also be subjected to him who put all things under him, that God may be everything to everyone.*

3. With precision, therefore, John saw in advance the first resurrection of the righteous, and the inheritance of the land in the kingdom. But this agrees with what the Prophets had foretold about it. For

these things the Lord taught, when he promised that he would drink a new mixture of the cup in the kingdom with the disciples.[11] And[12] he also said that the days would come *when the dead*[13] *in the tombs will hear the voice of the Son of man* and come forth. *Those who have done good [will come] to the resurrection of life, and those who have done evil, to the resurrection of judgment.* He said, those who have done good would rise first and will go to their rest; then those would rise who are to be judged. Thus the Scripture of Genesis has it:[14] The end of this world is the sixth day, that is, the six-thousandth year; and then the seventh day will be the one of rest.[15] David says of it,[16] *This is my resting place, the righteous shall enter it.* That is the thousandth year of the kingdom of the righteous, in which they shall be disciplined for imperishability, once creation has been renewed, for those for whom this has been reserved.

The Apostle, too, acknowledged that the creation would be freed from the servitude of perishability for the liberty of the glory of the sons of God.[17]

In all these things and by means of all of them, the same God the Father is manifested who formed man and promised the inheritance of the land to the Patriarchs, who will give it in the resurrection of the righteous, and who will fulfill the promises in the kingdom of his Son, who later in a fatherly way will bestow those things which *no eye has seen, nor ear heard, nor the heart of man conceived.*[18]

Certainly, there is one Son who carried out his Father's will; and one human race in which God's mysteries are accomplished, *into which angels long to look.*[19] But they cannot probe the Wisdom of God by which his handiwork, conformed to and incorporated into his Son, is brought to perfection; namely, that his Firstborn Son, the Word, should descend to his creature, that is, to his handiwork, and that it should be embraced by him; and that the creature should embrace the Word and, passing beyond the angels, should ascend to him and be made after the image and likeness of God.[20]

NOTES

Introduction

1. Address of His Holiness Pope Francis to the Saint Irenaeus Joint Orthodox–Catholic Working Group, October 7, 2021, https://www.vatican.va/content/francesco/en/speeches/2021/october/documents/20211007-gruppo-ortodossocattolico-santireneo.html.

2. Pope Benedict XVI, General Audience: Saint Irenaeus of Lyons, March 28, 2007; https://www.vatican.va/content/benedict-xvi/en/audiences/2007/documents/hf_ben-xvi_aud_20070328.html.

3. Benedict XVI, St. Irenaeus of Lyons.

4. I refer you to Steenberg's superb introduction for the history of the work on these volumes. I would like to note that, like Steenberg and Dillon, I have left Unger's voice to speak throughout Books 4 and 5. I have added some updated bibliographic material in the notes and smoothed out some translations.

5. See Robert M. Grant, *Irenaeus of Lyons* (New York: Routledge, 1997). Eric Francis Osborn, *Irenaeus of Lyons* (Cambridge: Cambridge University Press, 2001). Scott D. Moringiello, *The Rhetoric of Faith: Irenaeus and the Structure of the Adversus Haereses* (Washington, DC: Catholic University of America Press, 2019).

6. As you would expect, Irenaeus's discussion of the "rule of faith" has garnered much scholarly discussion. Albert Ebneter, "Die 'Glaubensregel' des Irenaeus als oekumenisches Regulativ," in *Unterwegs zur Einheit*, ed. Johannes Branchtschen, Heinrich Stirnimann, and Pietro Selvatico, 588–608 (Freiburg: Universitätsverlag, 1980); William Reuben Farmer, "Galatians and the 2d Century Development of the Regula Fidei," *Second Century: A Journal of Early Christian Studies* 4, no. 3 (1985): 143–70; Philip J. Hefner, "Saint Irenaeus and the Hypothesis of Faith," *Dialog* 2, no. 4 (1963): 300–306; Norbert Brox, "Irenaeus and the Bible," in *Handbook of Patristic Exegesis: The Bible in Ancient Christianity*, ed. Charles Kannengiesser, 483–506 (Boston: Brill, 2004).

7. Irenaeus also discusses this in A.H. 4.35 and *Proof* 3.

8. Irenaeus did not seem to know the third epistle of John, Paul's letter to Philemon, and the Epistle of Jude. André Benoît, *Saint Irénée; Introduction à l'étude de sa Théologie* (Paris: Presses universitaires de France, 1960), 105.

9. The fact that Christians do not all agree on whether certain books are inspired does not negate Irenaeus's point.

10. For a particularly helpful discussion of this, see John Behr, *Irenaeus of Lyons: Identifying Christianity* (Oxford: Oxford University Press, 2013), 112–13.

11. See Jacques Fantino, *La théologie d'Irénée: lecture des Ecritures en réponse à l'exégèse gnostique : une approche trinitaire* (Paris: Editions du Cerf, 1994), 117–18.

12. On this point, see Moringiello, *The Rhetoric of Faith*, generally and especially 21.

13. See A.H. 4.20.7. Barbara Aland, "Fides und Subiectio: zur Anthropologie des Irenäus," in *Kerygma und Logos* (Göttingen: Vandenhoeck & Ruprecht, 1979); Mary Ann Donovan, "Irenaeus: At the Heart of Life, Glory," in *Spiritualities of the Heart* (Mahwah, NJ: Paulist Press, 1990); Antonio Orbe, "Gloria Dei Vivens Homo (Analisis de Ireneo, Adv Haer IV, 20, 1–7)," *Gregorianum* 73 (1992) 205–268; Thierry Scherrer, *La Glorie de Dieu dans l'Oeuvre de Saint Irénée* (Rome: Editrice Pontifica Universita Gregoriana, 1997).

14. This schematic comes from Mary Ann Donovan's discussion of Phillipe Bacq's magisterial study of Book 4. See Mary Ann Donovan, *One Right Reading? A Guide to Irenaeus* (Collegeville, MN: Liturgical Press, 1997), 285–86. Donovan notes her indebtedness to Bacq. For Behr's division of the book, which mirrors this one, see Behr, *Irenaeus*, 98.

15. Here I follow the editors of the *Sources Chrétiennes* edition. I should note, though, that in his analysis of the book, Overbeck divides Book 5 this way: (a) 1–14, (b) 15–20, (c) 21–30, and (d) 31–35. Winfried Overbeck, *Menschwerdung : eine Untersuchung zur literarischen und theologischen Einheit des fünften Buches "Adversus Haereses" des Irenäus von Lyon* (New York: P. Lang, 1995). Behr divides Book 5 this way: (a) 1–14, (b) 15–24 (c) 25–36. See Behr, *Irenaeus*, 103. Antonio Orbe, *Teología de San Ireneo, Comentario al libro 5 del Adversus Haereses*, 3 vols., Biblioteca de Autores Cristianos (Madrid: Editorial Católica, 1985).

16. See A.H. 1.11.1. On this point, see Lance Jenott, "The Gnostics: Myth, Ritual, and Diversity in Early Christianity," *The Catholic Biblical Quarterly* 74, no. 3 (2012): 589–91.

17. Michael A. Williams, *Rethinking "Gnosticism": An Argument for Dismantling a Dubious Category* (Princeton: Princeton University Press, 1996); Karen L. King, *What Is Gnosticism?* (Cambridge, MA: Belknap Press of Harvard University Press, 2003); David Brakke, *The Gnostics: Myth, Ritual, and Diversity in Early Christianity* (Cambridge, MA: Harvard University Press, 2010).

Book Four

Preface

1. *Sources chrétiennes*, vol. 100 (Paris 1965), published its scholarly edition of Book 4 of *Adv. Haereses*, done by the team A. Rousseau, B. Hemmerdinger, L. Doutreleau, and C. Mercier. (The *Sources chrétiennes* volumes will be abbreviated SC.) There scholars can find a complete discussion of the text, especially of the Armenian version. There seems no need for me to go into the matter here, beyond the treatment found in my Book 1. I am in close contact with their text and notes throughout my translation and Notes. Where I decide against the Armenian version will be noted in the Notes. See also follow-up study on textual problems that was done by B. Hemmerdinger, (*Observations critiques sur Irénée, IV: (Sources chrétiennes 100), ou les Mésaventures d'un philologue* [Oxford: Oxford University Press, 1966]) to which I refer a number

of times in my Notes. L. Doutreleau also published some observations on the text in "A propos d' Irénée, Adv. haer., livre IV," *RSR* 53 (1965) 589–99.

2. For the title to the whole work, as given here, see the discussion in Book 1, Introd., pp. 2–3.

3. The aim of Book 4 is to prove by the Lord's words, as promised in A.H. 3.25.7, that there is only one God the Father.

4. The Latin here reads *profundum*, which is a translation of the Greek Βυθός, which is one of the Aeons in the Valentinian system Irenaeus describes in Book 1. See A.H. 1.1–8.

5. Lat. Iren. has the second person singular (*facias*), as if the addressee (a preacher) would try to convert the heretics. That fits the idea that the addressee is to accept (*accipias*) Irenaeus's writings, and then (as in #2 also) be said to attempt converting the heretics. But Arm. Iren. has the third person plural, referring to the heretics, who can then avoid falling into the Deep and avoid being swallowed up by the sea of ignorance; rather, they will, turning back to the harbor of the Truth, obtain salvation. SC preferred that against the Latin. But I still think the Latin fits better in the context, and the Armenian translator changed the approach. SC also introduced "in" with *pelago*, as in Arm. Iren. Lat. Iren. does not need "in." It is not a question of being drowned *in* the sea, but of being swallowed up *by* the sea.

6. Once for all, note that when the Latin has a doublet joined by *sive* and the Armenian has only one term, only the first has been translated, while the second is considered the translator's clarification.

7. Arm. Iren., as SC points out, has here a confused translation. The Latin is clear and standard in Irenaeus; cf. 1.P.2; 13.3; 3.17.4. Too bad we do not have an indication as to who Irenaeus's predecessors were. Possibly Justin is one.

8. See A.H. 2.31.1

9. Cf. A.H. 1.1–4; 2.19.9.

10. Cf. A.H. 1.2.6. SC, following Arm. Iren., would read *in labe*, in place of Lat. Iren. *a labe*, citing other cases where *in labe* occurs; e.g., 2.14.9; 19.9; 16.8. But in those cases the verb is *facti sunt*, with which *in* is correct, whereas here the verb is *emissi sunt*, with which *ab* is correct. Besides, just before our passage we read both *a labe* and *ex labe*. I stay with the Latin as quite correct.

11. Cf. Luke 1:5.

12. For Irenaeus's use of this term, see also A.H. 1.P.1; 3.15.2; 3.17.4; 5.P.

13. "Foresaw" is according to Lat. Iren. (supposing *προιδόντες*). Arm. Iren. supposes *προειδόντες* (foreknew). Either could be correct. Someone misread the Greek. "Announced beforehand" is according to Lat. Iren. (*praedicaverunt*). Arm. Iren. has "commanded beforehand." Both suppose the same προειδὸτες but give it a different translation. SC opts for Arm. Iren. as better. Possibly. But again the Latin is quite good in context.

14. 2 Cor 11:3; Gen 3:5. There might be an allusion to the Ophites. Bacq notes the eschatological context this allusion sets up. Bacq 37n.2 See A.H. 3.4.4. On the Dragon see A.H. 2.31.3; 3.23.7; 5.25–36.

15. Cf. Rev 12:9; 20:2; Gen 3:15.

16. Arm. Iren. has "flesh" made to God's likeness, whereas Lat. Iren. has "man." SC thinks Arm. Iren. is better, because that is the more difficult

reading and fits the immediate context better; and in A.H. 5.6.1, "flesh" is said to be modeled on the *image* of God. Yet here it is not image but likeness, and in Irenaeus likeness is referred to the spirit, that is, to man made spiritual through the Spirit's grace. For the composition of man see Orbe, *Antrop.* 34–74; Joppich 27–37, who has a detailed analysis of the terms. For man made after God's likeness see Orbe, *Antrop.* 75–77; Joppich 86–98; and chap. 20, note 6 below.

17. Cf. Gen 1:26. The first-person plural of Gen 1:26 is not a proof for the Trinity of Persons. The plural is one of perfection of being and power which God has. Yet, given the revelation of the Trinity in the New Testament, it is just this Trinity of Persons that best explains the perfection of being in God. The early churchmen quite generally referred this plural to the Trinity. Irenaeus often speaks of the consultation of the Father with the Word and the Spirit implied in this plural. Cf. *Proof* 11.

18. Cf. Wis 2:24.

19. Cf. A.H. 3.16.6, for instance. The Son of God made the entire economy of salvation for the sake of humanity, who is God's handiwork. See A.H. 4.5.1; 7.4; 5.29.1; 8.1; also Joppich 43, 80ff. One must, however, not interpret this as if God became man primarily for man's sake, excluding Christ's human nature, which was the very first recipient of salvation.

20. For more on Irenaeus on adoption, see A.H. 3.51.; 3.6.1; 3.9.1; 3.15.3. Bacq 38n1.

Chapter 1

1. Cf. A.H. 3.6.1. "In his own name" was added from Arm. Iren., as noted by SC.

2. Justin has a close parallel to this sentence in *Dialogus* 56.15 (MG 6.597).

3. Cf. Matt 23:9; also John 10:35. Irenaeus is developing a theme he began in A.H. 3.6–8.

4. "In reality...by name" is *naturaliter...verbotenus* in Lat. Iren. Arm. Iren. is more literal, supposing θέσει, that is, "by nature...by convention." This pair is found already in A.H. 1.23.3. See SC (201).

5. "Mythologists" is *grammatici* in Lat. Iren. Above, these were branded as *perversissimi sophistae,* and in #2 as *Pandora perversissimi sophistae.*

6. Cf. A.H. 1.5.3.

7. Cf. John 10:35

Chapter 2

1. Deut 32:1.
2. Pss 120 (121):2; 123 (124):8, from which "our help" comes.
3. Isa 1:2.
4. Isa 42:5.
5. Matt 11:25; Luke 10:21.
6. Deut 6:4.

7. John 5:46–47.
8. Luke 16:31.
9. Luke 16:19.
10. Cf. Isa 5:11,12, where the subject is not "they" but "you."
11. Cf. 1 Cor 15:24. Lat. Iren. has *Dominum*, but Arm. Iren. has *Christ*, which seems correct, because of the contrast in the context between Christ and Jesus against Irenaeus's opponents.
12. Col 1:18.
13. As Bacq notes, Irenaeus constantly argues against his opponents' belief that one can separate Christ from Jesus. See Bacq 53n1.
14. Cf. Matt 11:27; Luke 10:22.
15. Matt 5:34–35.
16. Isa 66:1.
17. For the "great King" see Matt 5:34–35. See also A.H. 3.5.1; 4.2.5.
18. Mark 11:19; Matt 21:13; Mark has "have made" according to Lat. Iren. and Arm. Iren., but Matt has "made."
19. Cf. Matt 5:17. Of course, this is central to Irenaeus's argument.
20. Isa 1:23. "Rebels" is *indicto audientes* in Lat. Iren., which occurs also in A.H. 4.16.3; 5.27.1; and in 4.27.4, *indicto audientia* for disobedience; and in 4.41.2, *dicto audientia* for obedience. That, of course, comes from a very literal translation of the Greek.
21. Jer 4:22.
22. Matt 10:6.
23. John 4:41. As Bacq notes (55n2), this might also be an allusion to Matt 10:5–6.
24. Rom 11:26.
25. Gal 3:24.
26. St. Augustine quotes this to the end of the paragraph, in *Contra Iulianum* 1.35 (ML 44.644).
27. Cf. Num 21:8; John 3:14–15.
28. Cf. Rom 8:3.
29. John 12:32 and 3:14–15.
30. Cf. John 5:21.

Chapter 3

1. Cf. Isa 66:1 and Luke 21:33.
2. Bacq notes that Irenaeus makes this type of philosophical argument in A.H. 2.1.1–4. Bacq 56n1.
3. 1 Cor 7:31.
4. Arm. Iren. has only "this form," not "the form of this world," which seems to have slipped into Lat. Iren. from the preceding quote of 1 Cor 7:31. In A.H. 5.36.1, we read the same Greek, with which both the Lat. Iren. and Arm. Iren. agree, as noted by SC.
5. Ps 101 (102):26–29.
6. Irenaeus extends this argument in A.H. 5.36.1. See Bacq 56n2.
7. Isa 51:6.

CHAPTER 4

1. Matt 5:35; Ps 47 (48):3.
2. Cf. Isa 1:8.
3. Cf. A.H. 2.28.1.
4. Cf. Gal 4:24–31.
5. Rom 5:14.
6. Irenaeus will discuss this at much greater length at A.H. 4.9.1 and 4.12–16.
7. This statement implies the catholicity of the Church. See also 1.10.1 and 4.34.4.
8. Isa 27:6, but not as in the Vulgate.
9. Rom 9:5.
10. Lat. Iren. MSS have *ad impletionem eius advenerat Christus.* That makes sense, as has been translated here, and nothing is then missing. "Since" is implied. SC 100.420 corrected the Latin to *idimpletio enim eius,* according to Arm. Iren. and the one MS *Ottoboniensis,* second hand at that. Such a scribal mistake could have been possible; yet the change is probably not necessary. Other attempts at correcting the text through a supposed Greek (cf. Harvey) are not necessary either.
11. Cf. Luke 16:16. The historical reference in the following sentence is to 2 Kgs 5:7.
12. Cf. Wis 11:20: "But you have arranged all things by measure and number and weight." In his allusion to this, Irenaeus has "order" in place of "number." "unplanned" is *incompositum ametron.* In A.H. 3.16.7, Lat. Iren. has *incomptum* (no Greek extant). So, literally, "unnumbered." Ἀναρίθμητον does not mean reconsider, as if compounded with the prefix 'ανα. The first alpha is a negative prefix. Nu was inserted to avoid running two alphas together.
13. "Comprehend" is *capit.* So Lat. Iren. contrasts a noun and a verb. Arm. Iren. has "since he is his comprehension," contrasting two nouns (*mensura...comprehensio*), and is possibly original. See also Bacq 58n2.
14. Isa 1:8. In place of the Vulgate *umbraculum* Lat. Iren. has *casa*; and in place of *custodiarium, tugurium.*
15. Cf. 1 Cor 7:31.
16. Mal 4:1. The Vulgate and Aquila have "all the proud and all that do wickedly. LXX has "strangers," which is a misreading of the Hebrew *zarim* for *zedim* (sinners).
17. Matt 3:11–12.; Luke 2:16–17.
18. Rationality makes man like God. That is really the explanation of the image of Gen 1:26, though here Irenaeus does not refer explicitly to that passage. Of course, the body belongs to that whole man who has reason. Cf. Tertullian, *Adv. Marcionem* 2.5–6 (CCL 1.479–82). We should note in the next clause the clear expression on freedom of the will.
19. Ps 48 (49):21. Arm. Iren. quotes only part of the psalm verse, as in my translation. Lat. Iren. has the full verse, but that must have been an adaptation of the translator, because in A.H. 4.41.3 and 5.8.2 the verse is quoted only partially also by Lat. Iren. SC (425n1) thinks "prophet" was Jeremiah, not David. True, Irenaeus never calls David a prophet, but he does present him as

prophesying; cf. 3.10.4; 3.22.2; 5.17.3; and in 4.5.2 the author of Ps 44 (David) was given as a prophet.

Chapter 5

1. Isa 34:4.
2. Ps 103 (104):30.
3. Man, therefore, can cooperate with God in achieving heavenly immortality, which is the result of a good life, as ripe fruit is of a good tree. This immortality is obviously supernatural imperishability, because it is due to a good life. There is no question here of natural immortality of the soul, implying that it could be not immortal. On this whole problem see Orbe, *Antrop.* 395–480, for an ample treatment.
4. Cf. Eph 2:7. "Unsearchable" is from Arm. Iren. The Bishop could have gotten that adjective from Eph 3:8, where the Vulgate has *investigabiles.* Lat. Iren. has *inenarrabiles.* In this chapter, Irenaeus summarizes the errors of his opponents. Bacq 61n1.
5. Isa 43:10–12 LXX.
6. Isa 41:4.
7. "It was impossible to learn of God without God" is a kind of theme song in Book 4. Irenaeus means, as he brings out later in 6.4.–5, that the incarnation was needed, not absolutely, but because God willed it for the facility of man. And all this speaks forcefully for the incarnation in God's original plan, prior to the foreknowledge of sin. See Unger, FS 14–18. For the soteriological value of revelation through the Word as the beginning of salvation that leads eventually to imperishability, see Jossua 58–62, and Houssiau 80–82.
8. Matt 22:29.
9. Matt 22:29, 31–32. Irenaeus rightly ascribes the last words to Christ.
10. Exod 3:3–6.
11. Dan 14:5.
12. Dan 14:25.
13. Luke 20:36.
14. John 11:25.
15. Ps 44 (45):17. Cf. chap. 4, note 19 on "prophet." In A.H. 3.22.4, Lat. Iren. quotes the same phrase thus: *Pro patribus nati sunt tibi filii* (without *tui*). In the present passage it is: *Pro patribus tuis facti sunt tibi filii tui,* as if Irenaeus were saying that in place of the forefathers, who were also Christ's (*tuis*), sons were born to him and were his sons. Arm. Iren. has: In place of the fathers that were there were born sons of yours. SC claims the context demands the idea that they who were Christ's fathers in the flesh became his sons in the spirit; that context does not demand this idea: Your sons were born in place of (in the place left vacant by) the fathers. That is true, but there is no reason why the Lat. Iren. cannot carry that same meaning in the sense that in place of the forefathers according to the flesh, sons of Christ's were born according to the spirit, and among these sons were also the forefathers.
16. Christ is certainly divine, clearly identified with God, just as the Father is. See Dominic J. Unger, "The Divine and Eternal Sonship of the Word According to St Irenaeus of Lyon." *Laurentianum* 14 (1973): 357–408.

17. John 8:56.

18. Rom 4:3; Gal 3:6; Gen 15:6. Hemmerdinger (311) would restore here *Quid enim dicit Scriptura* from Rom 4:3. That would fit, but there is no warrant in the MSS for it, and it is not needed at all. Irenaeus asks for the reason for the Gospel statement of John 8:56 and gives the answer from Rom 4:3.

19. Cf. Gen 14:22; 2 Ezra 9:6.

20. Cf. Gen 15.5; Heb 11:12.

21. Phil 2:15. Cf. *Proof* 35, where Irenaeus quotes Gen 15:5 and then adds "and setting up lights in the world those who believe in him."

22. "Traveled as pilgrims" and "dwell as citizens" are each given in Greek by one verb. Irenaeus presents Abraham on pilgrimage in this world in search of the Word to live with him and follow him freely through faith (see also note 97). This contains the essential elements of Christian living as developed later in monasticism. Cf. E. Lanne, "La *Xeniteia* d'Abraham dans l'oeuvre d'Irénée: Aux origins des themes monastiques de la *peregrinitio*," *Irenikon* 47 (1974): 163–87. Irenaeus seems to have a link here with Philo, but he Christianizes the matter.

23. Luke 5:11.

24. Gen 22:6; Luke 9:23.

25. Cf. Gen 22:1–18. This is a clear statement of redemption through the cross, which some scholars, wrongly, think Irenaeus slighted too much. Cf. also 4.8.2; 14.2; 33.12; 20.2. Jossa (101–8, 122, 167–69) speaks somewhat disparagingly of Irenaeus's grasp of Pauline soteriology. González (215–19) and Joppich (108 f) defend Paul. That Abraham was our forerunner in faith is also expressed in A.H. 4.21.1; 25.1.

26. Lat. Iren. has *per quem.* The antecedent must be *Dominus,* because in the following sentence it is stated that the Lord was not unknown to Abraham. So it is the Lord, through faith in him, who saves. But SC, supposing the Greek to have been κύριον, took "passion" πάθους as the antecedent. κύριον is neuter; the relative could have been read as neuter. But in the context that is not correct. Irenaeus ascribes salvation directly to Christ, not to his passion.

27. Gen 14:22. The last phrase is according to LXX, which here, as in Prov 8:22, translates the Hebrew *qanah* with "created" instead of "possessed." That Abraham was a prophet is noted also in *Proof* 44.

28. Matt 11:27 is the text referred to; he will speak of it at length in chap. 6.

Chapter 6

1. Matt 11:27; Luke 10:22. The mutual knowledge of Father and Son is noted also in *Proof* 7. There is no object for the last Greek verb in Christ's statement. So the question is asked, Whom does the Son reveal? It would seem that he reveals both the Son (himself) and the Father. Irenaeus consistently holds that the Son reveals the Father only by revealing himself, and when he does reveal himself he reveals the Father too. So directly the object is the Son, but indirectly it is also the Father. Cf. also A.H. 6.3 5.7; 5.15.2; 16.3. See Unger "The Divine and Eternal Sonship of the Word According to St Irenaeus of Lyon." *Laurentianum* 14 (1973): 357–408 (1973), 376–380.

2. Mark's present Gospel does not have this passage. Perhaps Irenaeus's copy did, or maybe he took it from a book of Testimonies, where it was interpolated from Matthew or Luke.

3. Cf. A.H. 1.20.3 for Irenaeus's discussion of Ptolemy, who, Irenaeus argues, says this. For further bibliography see Bacq 68n4.

4. The main point of difference between his opponents' version of Christ's statement and Irenaeus's is this: Christ used the present "knows," his opponents read it in the aorist, "knew." The entire context is about Irenaeus's opponents claiming that no one *knew* the Father before Christ's coming, and they bolster that view by their version of this text. For a longer discussion of this text see R. Luckhardt, "Matthew 11:27 in the *Contra Haereses* of St. Irenaeus," *Revue d'Université d'Ottawa* 23 (1953): 65–79.

5. Justin's work *Syntagmata against Marcion* quoted is not extant. See Eusebius, *Hist. Eccl.* 4.18.9 (GCS 9.366). Scholars are not agreed on how much of this paragraph comes from Justin. Some hold that only the first sentence does, namely, what is given by Eusebius. The rest is Irenaeus's own explanation. Thus Wilhelm Bousset, *Kyrios Christos; a History of the Belief in Christ from the Beginnings of Christianity to Irenaeus* (Nashville: Abingdon Press, 1970), n51; J. A. Robinson, "On a Quotation of Justin Martyr in Irenaeus," JTS 21 (1930): 374–78. Others hold that the rest of the paragraph is a quotation from Justin. Thus Friedrich Loofs, *Theophilus von Antiochen Adversus Marcionem und die Anderen Theologischen Quellen bei Irenaeus* (Leipzig: J. C. Hinrichs, 1930), 225–27, 359; E. Scharl, "Der Rekapitulations-begriff des hl. Irenäus und seine Anwendung an díe Körperwelt," *Orientalia Christiana Periodica* 6 (1940): 400–401. This view was presented already by Adolf von Harnack, *History of Dogma* (New York: Russell & Russell, 1958), 2.220, n1; and it is considered possible by Wingren 81. This is of some importance. In the second opinion Irenaeus would have gotten the kernel of his teaching on recapitulation from Justin but developed it extensively. In the first opinion Justin is not a source of Irenaeus for the doctrine on recapitulation.

6. Irenaeus uses the phrase "good pleasure of the Father" many times in the A.H. See, e.g., 4.6.3; 4.6.4; 4.7.3; 4.20.4; 4.20.5; 4.20.6.

7. Lat. Iren. has *et indeterminabilem* after *invisibile,* which is missing in Arm. Iren. The Armenian seems to be the original, as more balanced: "knows...invisible...ineffable...declares."

8. Matt 11:27; Luke 10:22. Bacq connects Matt 11:27 with John 1:18. The plural *quibuscumque* of Lat. Iren. is matched by the simpler *quibus* in Arm. Iren.

9. "What he is" is according to Arm. Iren., for which Lat. Iren. has *sicut est.* In A.H. 5.15.2 there is a parallel case, in which Arm. Iren. again has *quid sit,* while Lat. Iren. has *quidem,* which seems a corruption. See SC, note to p. 445.1.

10. On "Gnostics" see the introduction to this volume.

11. See A.H. 1.2.5.

12. Cf. chap. 6, note 16 below on revelation of God through the Incarnate Word as part of God's original plan.

13. The idea that a sinner makes his own punishment is prominent in Irenaeus: see A.H. 2.34.3; 4.39.4; 5.27.2.

14. Irenaeus speaks of having a natural knowledge about God through the Word, because he and other churchmen considered creation itself as an image of the Word; the Word left his traces on creation. So all knowledge about God, natural as well as supernatural, is ascribed to the Word.

15. Cf. John 11:9.

16. The Greek is not extant. Lat. Iren. is very cryptic: *invisibile etenim Filii Pater, visibile autem Patris Filius.* Literally: whatever of the Son is invisible is the Father; whatever of the Father is visible is the Son. Arm. Iren. seems to have struggled with the construction and placed the second clause first. It seems to have caught the correct meaning but expressed it rather clumsily. According to SC's Latin version: *videri enim filium patris est, non-videri autem patrem filii. Etenim* indicates that this double, contrasted phrase is an explanation of what preceded, where we read: "all saw the Father in the Son." Hence, I think it better, as in my translation, to take *Pater* and *Filius* as subjects, and *invisibile* and *visibile* as predicates, not the other way round. As a key we must remember that the Father is in himself invisible, but he can be revealed, made visible, in and by the Son, and so the Son contains in himself what is invisible of the Father. As such the Son Incarnate is visible, and as such he can reveal the Father. Hence the Son is the visible element of the Father. This is the passage that gave the title to Ochagavia's study on revelation according to Irenaeus. For revelation of the Father by the Word see also Houssiau 63–128; González 43–59; 141–160; and the dissertation (of which only one chapter was published) by J. T. Ford, "St. Irenaeus and Revelation. A Theological Perspective" (Notre Dame, IN, 1962). This dissertation was done at the Gregorian University in Rome. One would wish the whole dissertation could have been published. The author treats the subject from a theological, not an apologetic point of view. "Chooses to reveal" has, according to A.H. 4.6.7, the Father as subject; but according to Matthew it is the Son, as Irenaeus has elsewhere. Actually both are true. See SC 100, 451n1. See also Bacq 71n1 for further bibliography.

17. Mark 1:24; Luke 4:34.

18. Mark 4:3; Luke 4:3.

19. My translation follows the extant Greek, with which Arm. Iren. agrees. Latin Iren. has *comprobatur.* This too can be brought in line with the Greek if one takes that as a variant translation, as it may be taken, of *testimonium accipere.*

20. Even non-Christians have testified to Christ, as for instance, Josephus, though the extent of his testimony is disputed. See Raymond E. Brown, Joseph A. Fitzmyer, and Roland Edmund Murphy. *The New Jerome Bible Handbook* (Collegeville, MN: Liturgical Press, 1992), 68, 116; and G. Ricciotti, *The Life of Christ,* trans. Al Zizzamia (Milwaukee: Bruce, 1944), 81–82.

21. Lat. Iren. MSS have *singulaca testificationis,* which has always created a problem and given rise to many guesses; e.g., Massuet chose *singularia,* which was used by BVK and ANF. Grape already took *sigilla* and it makes good sense; but *signacula* is a better guess, which, according to SC, is found in Ottobonensis MS. Arm. Iren. reads: "according to your testimony," which makes no sense. Harvey wrongly suggested "single witnesses."

22. Cf. 1 Cor 15:27.

23. Cf. 1 Cor 15:25–26. "The enemy" is the Devil; cf. Matt 13:39. Note also the expression of man's union with God in Christ.

24. "The Son's administration for the Father may not be twisted to imply a subordination to the Father, because Irenaeus clearly teaches the eternity and strict equality of the Son with the Father." Cf. Unger, 1973.

25. Lat. Iren. has: *Agnitio enim Patris Filius, agnitio autem Filii in Patre et per Filium revelata.* The *in Patre* creates a problem. One would expect a perfect parallel in construction, and so it should be *Pater.* But Irenaeus did not want such a perfect parallel, because he could indicate better that our knowledge about the Son comes from the Father. Arm. Iren. has "by the Father," which SC accepted. Ochagavia changed to *Patris.* I think that even *in Patre* can have the same meaning, namely, that the Father sends the Son and so gives us knowledge of him. Cf. A.H. 3.11.6: *et iterum Pater per Filium, Filii sui dat agnitionem his qui diligent eum.*

26. Matt 11:27; Luke 10:22. Irenaeus had quoted it exactly before; why he now says it was written this way is not clear.

27. Cf. Eph 4:6.

Chapter 7

1. Cf. Gen 14:22. But "as the stars" is from Gen 22:17; 15:5.

2. "Apparition" is *repraesentatio* in Lat. Iren., which I think genuine, referring to the apparition of the three messengers who appeared to Abraham, one of whom Abraham worshipped (cf. Gen 18:2–3). *Repraesentatio* is used in A.H. 1.29.2 in the sense of image or likeness, that is, of a great light. According to SC, Arm. Iren. does not have a word equivalent to *repraesentatio.* It rendered the passage so: "having learned of the coming of God's Son among men." That missed "a man." SC thinks Arm. Iren. correct, and that Lat. Iren. used two words (*repraesentatio* and *adventus*) for the one Greek word, παρουσία, to avoid an ambiguous reference of *per quem* to *Filius* or *adventus.* No, I think Arm. Iren. did not grasp the reference to the apparition of messengers to Abraham, by which he learned of the Son's coming. *Repraesentatio* is scarcely a synonym for *adventus. Praesentia* would be; cf. 2.18.8. Harvey thought that because of the preceding scriptural allusion, this refers to the interview with Melchizedek.

3. Gen 17:17; John 8:56. See A.H. 4.5.5; 4.20.8.

4. Luke 2:32–33, where Lat. Iren. has *oculorum* for the Vulgate *gentium,* which is certainly erroneous for *populorum,* as Grabe already suggested. Arm. Iren. has "people." Cf. 3.16.4, which confirms the view that Irenaeus considered Christ himself the Light and the Glory.

5. Luke 2:10.

6. Luke 1:46ff. Lat. Iren. ascribes the *Magnificat* to Elizabeth in the Clermont and Voss MSS, as does Arm. Iren. Since two important MSS of the Latin agree with the Arm. Iren., the evidence is strong that this was already in the Greek copy. So the question arises: Did Irenaeus himself write it, deliberately or inadvertently, or did a later scribe write it? Since this reading is not in the Greek or the Armenian Bible, the scribes could not have taken this from their Bibles. Maybe the Lat. Iren. was influenced by his Old Latin Bible in

which three MSS have Elizabeth. But how did it get into the Arm. Iren.? Inadvertently? That would be an odd coincidence, but not impossible. Certainly, Irenaeus has Mary in all the MSS of 3.10.2., see A.H. 3, chap. 10, n10. So his Bible had the correct reading. SC sides with Elizabeth here.

7. Luke 2:8, 17.

8. John 8:56.

9. Cf. 1 John 1:1. "Touchable" is from Arm. Iren. Lat. Iren. has *passibilis*, which seems an evident scribal error. The pair *visibilis et palpabilis* is found also for the Ptolemaic Savior's body in A.H. 1.6.1; 9.3; of the Word in 4.6.6; 24.2. Interestingly, in 1.6.1 *passibile* is a third term.

10. Cf. Gen 22:17; 15.5.

11. Matt 3:9; Luke 3:8.

12. He drew us away from idolatry, from worshipping stone statues. Cf. *Proof* 92; and Book 3, chapter 6, note 22.

13. "Ideas" follows *cogitationibus* of Lat. Iren., which fits the context quite well, about false ideas in idolatrous religions over against true knowledge of Christ. Because of the idea of kinship to Abraham in the previous context the Arm. Iren. got "relationship" in here. If that was original, it is hard to see how Lat. Iren. could have got *ideas* from it. As far as sense is concerned, faith would scarcely transfer us from unfruitful kinship; but faith could draw us away from unfruitful ideas.

14. Rom 4:12, 16; 9:8; Gal 4:28.

15. Cf. A.H. 3.3.4; 3.4.3; 3.11.2.7.9; 3.12.5.12; 3.14.4; 4.6.4; 4.33.2–3; 4.34–5; 5.26.2.

16. Phil 2:15.

17. Matt 5:14; cf. Dan 12:3.

18. John 14:6–7. Irenaeus uses this passage in a similar context at A.H. 3.13.2.

19. Gen 18:1.

20. Exod 3:7, 8. Irenaeus also speaks about Moses's encounter with the Word at 4.5.2. For another use of the expression *descendi liberare*, see 3.6.2. Bacq 76n3.

21. "For giving form…for disposing." Lat. Iren. has *ad fabricationem et dispositionem. Et* was inserted from Arm. Iren. Cf. A.H. 4.20.1: "the angels neither created nor formed us." *Dispositio* does not mean "economy" here, as SC takes it, but "dispositing," shaping up and arranging.

22. SC in the French translation and the restored Greek put "His hands"/in place of *figuratio.* Hemmerdinger (315) supports that again. However, Daniélou in *RSR* 57 (1969): 87, with support from Orbe, insists on retaining *figuratio.* And rightly so, the plural "His hands" would not fit the pair: "His Offspring (obviously the Word) and His hands." This pair is explained immediately with another pair "the Son and the Holy Spirit." *Figuratio* is a name for the Spirit, just as *figura* in 4.20.1. Other second-century writers, as Daniélou notes, used *figuratio* for the Spirit. SC's idea that "Offspring" is a collective noun and so matches the plural *hands* is chimerical. The Fathers thought of the Spirit as the likeness of the Son just as the Son is of the Father.

23. See Bacq 76n4 on the difficulty of this passage.

24. Heb 1:13; 2:5ff. Thus is indicated the equality of the Son and Spirit as God, whom the angels serve. Angels were not only not needed by God in creating; they must even serve God's Word and Spirit. See also *Proof* 10.

CHAPTER 8

1. Cf A.H. 1.27.3.
2. Rom 4:3; Gal 3:6; Gen 15:6.
3. Matt 3:9; Gen 15:6.
4. Luke 13:29, but "of heaven" is from Matthew's account (8:11).
5. Luke 13:28. As Bacq notes, in arguing against Marcion, Irenaeus draws on Luke's Gospel, which Marcion did not accept. See also A.H. 1.27.2; 3.11.7.9; 3.12.12. Cf. Tertullian *Adv. Marc.* 4.1.1 CCL p. 544; Epiphanius *Panarion,* 42, 9; *GCS,* 104–5. Irenaeus then joins this to a passage from Paul, which Marcion does accept. Bacq 77n3.
6. Irenaeus clearly holds that the people of the Old Law belonged to the Church of Christ. Lat. Iren. reads: *semen eius quod est Ecclesia, per Christum Iesum cui et adoption redditur.* The antecedent of *cui* is not *Christus Iesus,* but *Ecclesia.* It is not unusual for Lat. Iren. to have the antecedent of a relative some distance away. Arm. Iren. agrees with that in general, but it has "which receives adoption." SC points out a close parallel in 5.32.2 and remarks that the adoption here is not the divine adoption but one relative to Abraham. That idea needs being completed. A pagan becomes an adopted son of Abraham through Christ. But such an adoption *through Christ* must be one of faith and grace. There is no other adoption through Christ.
7. Luke 13:13–15.
8. For Irenaeus on circumcision see also A.H. 4.12.1 and 4.16.2.
9. John 7:22–23.
10. Irenaeus gives three notes of this miracle: it took place at Siloam; cures were effected there often on the Sabbath; many people sat around waiting for a cure. But what is the exact translation? Harvey and ANF would change *etiam* to *et iam,* because they think Siloam is definitely an ablative of place. However, in John 5 the waters of the pool did the curing in the unusual miracle, while Christ cured the lame man with a mere command. So Siloam, the pool, can be the subject of "cured," even though a few sentences earlier Christ is subject of *curans.* Really, Irenaeus is proving that the Law did not forbid all work on the Sabbath, and he gives instances of works done by the Jews prior to Christ. Among these were the frequent and customary cures at the pool of Siloam. If Irenaeus had said that Christ worked many miracles there on the Sabbath, he would have been begging the question. It is the Law which is represented as not forbidding those works. The Law, here as in the preceding and the following, is the subject of *curavit.* And then reference is definitely to John 5, and Irenaeus merely confused the name of the Probatic pool with that of Siloam. Siloam was involved in the miracle of John 9. But the circumstances of John 9 do not fit those given by Irenaeus here. In John 9 only one cure is recorded, and Christ did not find the man at the pool waiting for a cure; but he sent him to the pool from elsewhere; further, there were no crowds at the pool waiting. So of this cure in John 9 nothing fits the

case of Irenaeus except the name Siloam. In John 5, however, Christ cured a man lame for many years, at the pool of Bethsaida, on a Sabbath. There were crowds waiting for a cure. So John 5 fits the case described by Irenaeus, except for the name of the pool, which is Probatic, not Siloam. It seems certain then that Irenaeus had in mind John 5, and that he got the wrong name of the pool (as Massuet held), or some transcriber exchanged the names. Grabe's suggestion that Irenaeus had knowledge of a tradition about many cures at Siloam is useless guesswork.

11. Lat. Iren. has *reliquo terreno actu* (deed); Arm. Iren. reads *reliqua terrena arte* (skill). SC, without any explanation, accepts Arm. Iren. I am not so sure that is correct. Irenaeus has often spoken of deeds, actions, or practices, but not of skills. Here, as a complement to "business," it would seem quite correct. These are deeds of the body, paralleled below by deeds (*opera*) of the soul. *Actu* and *opera* could stand for the same Greek πράξις.

12. Cf. Matt 5:17.

13. Here Unger follows the Armenian, which is an explicit allusion to the old covenant. See Bacq 81n3.

14. "Exiled." Arm. Iren. has the same idea, but a slavish analysis of the Greek ἐξαφορισθεὶς, a word that is unusual, found only in Irenaeus, to my knowledge. It is supposed, according to SC, also in 4.4.3; and 4.27.4. It is attested for 4.20.12 by a fragment.

15. Num 35:25; Josh 20:6. This is a clear expression of redemption by appeasement, by a propitiatory death.

16. Luke 6:1:3–4 [*sic.* Probably Luke 6:1–4 intended]; from 1 Kgs 21:4ff.

17. "Recognized" is *scitus* in Lat. Iren., which in itself could come from *scio* (I know) or *scisso* (I decree or appoint). Harvey claims it comes from *scisso* and means that God appointed David as priest. But the Bible has no record of such appointment. Nor does BVK's "kundiger Priester" give the precise meaning either. It seems Irenaeus wished to say that David was recognized before God as a priest because he was a just man, even though Saul persecuted him, since Irenaeus adds as reason (*enim*) that every just man is of priestly rank. So there is no question of an appointment, but of a recognition.

18. Matt 12:3–4; Luke 6:3–4; cf. 1 Sam 21:4–7.

19. Deut 33:9. *Novi* agrees with the Vulgate *nescio*; LXX and Arm. Iren. have *non vidi.* Because of scribal adaptations or mistakes it is impossible to know what Irenaeus had originally. Cf. A.H. 4.16.1.

20. Num 18:20; Deut 10:9, but not verbatim.

21. Deut 18:1.

22. Phil 4:17.

23. Cf. Matt 10:10.

24. Matt 12:5, which has the present tense (*violant...sunt*). Arm. Iren. also has the present. SC (477n1) has a long explanation in favor of the Arm. present. I still believe Irenaeus was quoting directly and verbatim, but he changed the tense because he was taking it as a historical witness.

25. Num 15:32, 36.

26. Matt 3:10; 7:19; Luke 3:9.

27. 1 Cor 3:17.

Chapter 9

1. For a brief commentary on A.H. 4.9.1–3 see M. F. Berrouard, "Servitude de la Loi et liberté d'´Evangile selon S. Irénée," *Lumiére et Vie* 61 (1963): 41–45.

2. Matt 13:52.

3. Lat. Iren reads: *servis quidem et adhuc indisciplinatis.* The *et* was dropped by SC because it is not in the Voss MS and seemingly not in Arm. Iren. Yet it is sufficiently attested in Latin, better, in fact, than in the next line, where SC retains it. In both places there seem to be two groups, with two modifiers: *Servi...indisciplinati: liberi...justificati.* In Paul (cf. Gal 4:1–2) servants and children under a tutor are the same in relation to justification, so here too. "undisciplined" could represent *ἀπαιδεύτους*, as 2 Tim 2:23. Slaves, even when instructed, would not be free.

4. As Bacq notes, for Irenaeus the servitude of the law is replaced by freedom thanks to the coming of Christ. See 4.13.2; 416.5; 4.28.2; *Proof* 96.

5. Matt 23:24.

6. Pss 95 (96):1; 97(98):1.

7. Isa 42:10,12, as in LXX, and not a quotation from memory as Harvey notes.

8. Jer 31:31–32, as in LXX, but the words in brackets were skipped, and the phrase "on mount Horeb" is a shortened form of what is in LXX about leading the Israelites by the hand out of Egypt. See also A.H. 5.34.3.

9. Cf. Rom 6:4; 5:15; 17,20; Gal 4:31.

10. Matt 12:6.

11. According to SC, Arm. Iren. has "the grace of liberty is therefore superior to the law of servitude," with reference to John 1:17, where the law is said to have come from Moses, but grace from Christ. In A.H. 3.12.11 the Law is of Moses; but grace, of the N.T. I am not sure that Arm. Iren. is correct. It could have been adjusted to the N.T. idea. Irenaeus actually could have spoken of the law for slaves (namely, of the O.T.) and of the "precepts" for the N.T. The illustrations *aqua ab aqua, lumen a lumine* suppose the same noun in both parts of the comparison, that is, the law in the O.T. and the law in the N.T.

12. Cf. Matt 12:6, 42, 41. See also A.H. 3.20.1 where Irenaeus talks about the sign of Jonah.

13. John 1:50. The promise Christ made to Nathaniel alone is given by Irenaeus as made to all the disciples.

14. Phil 3:12.

15. 1 Cor 13:9–10.

16. Matt 5:8.

17. Isa 25:9 LXX.

18. 1 Pet 1:8. Lat. Iren. has: *Quem non videntes diligitis, inquit, in quem nunc non videntes credidistis.* Arm. Iren, according to SC, amounts to: *videntes inquit in quem non videntes creditis.* SC prefers this and translates: "Lorsque vous verrez celui en qui, sans le voir encore, vous croyes." Cf. A.H. 5.7.2: *Quem cum non videritis diligitis, in quem nunc quoque non videntes creditis.* The Greek of Peter has a present participle for *creditis* (of Vulgate) as well as for *videntes,* and both modify a present tense verb. So it seems *creditis* is correct.

19. Rom 8:15. See also A.H. 5.8.1.

20. Cf. 1 Cor 13:12. Paul has "face to face," as does Lat. Iren., but Arm. Iren. has the equivalent of the supposed Greek αὐτοψίᾳ, which SC accepts. The context is different in 1 Cor and in Iren. In 1 Cor it is about "seeing"; in Irenaeus it is about enjoying. So it would have been natural for Irenaeus, though alluding to 1 Cor 13, to change to αὐτοψία. Lat. Iren. would have harmonized Irenaeus with Paul because of the allusion. So argues SC. To me that is not convincing. Arm. Iren. could just as easily have done the adjusting. Lat. Iren. has *muneribus*, while Arm. Iren. has *bonis*, which SC prefers. Yet *donat* and *donans* in the context here, and *muneribus* in #3 make this word just as probable at this point. One should take note of the equality here of the Spirit with the Father and the Son.

21. See also, A.H. 4.6.3.

22. That God gradually led man to perfection through various steps is an idea dear to Irenaeus in this Book 4 particularly; see chap. 38.

23. As Bacq notes, this is a sort of preview of A.H. 4.12–16

24. Cf. 2 Tim 3:7.

25. There is subtle irony in this allusion to the Profundity who is incomprehensible.

26. Matt 15:3–4. As Bacq notes, this is, in effect, Irenaeus's argument against the Jews. See also A.H. 4.2.6; 4.11.4; 4.12.4; 4.33.1. Bacq 92n1.

27. Matt 15:6.

Chapter 10

1. John 5:39–40.

2. For the Greek here, see Bacq 93n1. Irenaeus uses the same word at A.H. 3.12.7; 4.23.1. See also SC (291n1).

3. John 5:46.

4. Irenaeus agrees with the many ancient writers that Christ was spoken of in the entire O.T., and that very often.

5. Gen 18:5. See Bacq 93n2–6 for the many references Irenaeus makes here.

6. Gen 6:15.

7. Gen 3:9.

8. Gen 18:13ff.

9. Gen 31:11ff.

10. Exod 3:3ff.

11. *Ipsa quae* has no expressed antecedent, which must be feminine. SC rightly took *dies*, which occurs both before and after this sentence. It is taken as a masculine before in Latin, but *ipsa quae*, feminine, follows the Greek syntax where it was feminine. Irenaeus, as many other ancient church writers, seems to have included the idea of suffering in the term *Pasch.* See Tertullian, *Adv. Iudaeos* 10.18 (CCL 2.1380); Gregorius Nazianz., *Oratio* 45, *de Paschate* (MG 36.636C). Harvey denies this for Irenaeus, claiming that he knew Hebrew, about which he is certainly wrong; and he overlooks the fact that the reference need not be seen in a relation between

pascha and *paschein.* It is rather in the circumstances of the Pasch, and not in the accidental play on words, much less in the real etymology.

12. Deut 16:5–6.

13. Gen 49:10–12, according to LXX; but the *cui repositum* is in the singular, whereas the regular LXX text has the plural. *Laetifici oculi eius a vino* is according to the Alexandrian recension of the LXX. The Vatican MS has the comparative with "above" as in the Hebrew. See also *Proof* 57. Justin *Ap* 32.1–3. Bacq 92n1.

14. Deut 32:6.

15. Deut 28:66.

16. Deut 32:6.

Chapter 11

1. Matt 13:17.

2. Cf. 1 Pet 1:4.

3. Gen 1:28.

4. "Growing and maturing" is *adiectionem et augmentum.* SC omits *adiectionem,* according to Arm. Iren. But the pair occurred at the end of #1, *augmentum et incrementum;* and a little lower in #2 we read: *homo vero profectum percipiens et augmentum.* Without the Greek original, it is difficult to say whether the same Greek pair were involved always. SC supposed *akme* for *augmentum.* Daniélou (RSR 57 [1969]: 87) says that does not fit the idea of a constant growth. See also Bacq 96n2.

5. Cf. A.H. 1.12.2; 2.13.3; 2.28.4. Clement *Strom.* 8.1.5.5.

6. Cf 3.19.3. Bacq argues this may be an allusion to Phil 3:9–10; Bacq 97n1.

7. Matt 25:21, 23.

8. God offers more grace but not more knowledge. That is, Christ does not offer secret knowledge that was previously unavailable.

9. Cf. A.H. 4.9.2; 4.11.4; 4.34.1 Bacq 98n2.

10. Ps 34 (35): 9. Irenaeus views this as prophetic of the sufferings of Christ.

11. Lat. Iren. reads: *Omnes qui errant in via David in dolore animae,* as if it should mean: "All who were in the David Street with sorrowful soul." The cryptic *in via David* makes little sense, and *in dolore animae* does not fit the context of rejoicing. Arm. Iren., according to SC, reads: *Omnes in via qui a David ardentes desiderantes anima* (*erant*). The two participles are a couplet that seem to emphasize the desire. That would mean: All people who followed David in a strong desire. With that clue I believe the Latin can support the same idea: all who were on the way of David, that is, who followed David, without any reference to a street. The idea of desiring is in keeping with the remote context of chap. 11 and the proximate of #3 about seeing Christ, as SC observes. "Desiring in soul" is found in Ps 41:2 and in Ps 83:3: ἐπιποθεῖ ἡ ψυχή μου and in Ps 119:20 as ἐπεπόθησεν ἡ ψυχή μου. As SC has it, Irenaeus's Greek must have been the same as this last. If that was misread as ἐπιποθοῦωτες τῆς ψυχῆς, it is easy to see how *in dolore animae* got into the Latin.

12. Matt 21:8–9; Cf. Ps 117:25–26.

13. Cf. Matt 18:29–30; Luke 16:1ff.

14. Matt 21:16; Ps 8:3; Luke 19:38.

15. Here Irenaeus stresses that Christ is part of the economy of salvation. Of course, this is a central part of his argument in Book 4. If Christ is part of the economy of salvation, if Christ's Father is the creator of the universe, then those who would say Christ does not belong to the created order are wrong.

16. Ps 8:2.

17. Cf. Col 2:17; Heb 10:1.

18. "More diligent." Lat. Iren. has: *tanquam diligentiam suam etiam ipsi Deo praeferentibus*: that, they place their own diligence above God's, Arm. Iren. gives that clearer by a comparative: *diligentiores ipsis de Deo*: "as if they were more diligent than God." It is not clear to me whether Lat. Iren. does not represent the original Greek, which Arm. Iren. tried to clarify.

19. Cf. Matt 23:25, 28.

Chapter 12

1. Isa 1:22 LXX.

2. Arm. Iren. has nothing corresponding to: *id est aggredientes legem adulteram et contrariam legi*.

3. Matt 15:3.

4. This is an important passage for Irenaeus to raise. Obviously, he is in favor of the tradition of the Church. But, like Jesus, he wants to discern what the proper tradition is.

5. Lat. Iren. does not have a noun with "Pharisaical" but it seems evident that this should be *lex*, which is found at the end of the paragraph. "Transgression" stands for *praevaricationem*. One might have expected Irenaeus to say that they set at nought God's law by their tradition, instead of by their transgression. But it amounts to the same thing, as is indicated at the end of the paragraph, "for transgressing God's precept by the tradition." By following their tradition they transgressed God's law.

6. "Especially" is *singulariter* in Lat. Iren. Coming between *utunțur* and *magistri*, its reference is doubtful. I read it with *magistri*, as did SC. But BKV has "besonders dienen."

7. Cf. Gal 3:24. Bacq points out how these two Pauline passages go together. A.H. 4.2.7; 4.12.5; 4.13.2; 4.13.3–4.16.5. Bacq 107n1.

8. Cf. John 7:22–23.

9. "Precept" is in Lat. Iren. *praeceptum*, which in Greek had the definite article. In #2 it is explained as "the first and greatest precept." The presence of "precept" in #2 almost demands its presence in #1, otherwise something of the sense would be missing. SC inserted *praecipium* in place of *praeceptum* from Arm. Iren. in the sense of "the essential of the Law." Again, I believe Arm. Iren. did not understand the Greek. Either the Latin *praeceptum* by itself, according to all MSS, is correct, or *praecipium* as an adjective implies its noun *praeceptum*. I opt for the first: They transgressed the precept of God and did not have *the* precept of the Law.

10. Arguably, Irenaeus's most important point is that the identity of God in the old and new covenants rests on love.

11. Matt 22:37–40.

12. Arm. Iren. does not speak of the precept as being God's, but simply as being the Legislator's. Lat. Iren. has: *non eo (praecepto) uti quod a Deo Legis fuisset datum.* SC finds this surprising, since Irenaeus has a stereotyped expression "the Law by Moses." Yet, in #1 Irenaeus constantly stresses this as God's Law, against the man-made traditions. So it is not surprising to speak of this precept as being given by the God who gave the Law. Again, Arm. Iren. did not grasp the construction or the thought, nor did SC.

13. Rom 13:10.

14. 1 Cor 13:13.

15. 1 Cor 13:2ff.

16. Cf. A.H. 4.9.2; 4.11.2.

17. Matt 23:2–4.

18. Arm. Iren. has "devoid of love," supposing a longer expression than Lat. Iren. has *sine dilectione.* In 4.33.7 even Lat. Iren. has this longer form: *qui sunt inanes, non habentes Dei dilectione.* So, maybe here too the Greek was longer, and Lat. Iren. had difficulty expressing it.

19. Isa 29:13 LXX.

20. Rom 10:3–4.

21. Exod 3:7–8. Cf. A.H. 4.7.4.

22. Matt 19:17.

23. Matt 19:18–19.

24. Matt 19:20.

25. Matt 19:21.

26. Irenaeus has discussed all of this in Book 1. See AH 1.1–8.

27. Luke 19:8.

Chapter 13

1. The place of the Law in Irenaeus's thought is important. His opponents want to argue that the Law has no place in Christian life or in Christian history. In contrast, Irenaeus argues that the Law is part of Christian life and history and that Christ has fulfilled the Law. Cf. Tertullian, *Adv. Iudaeos* 2. 6–7 (CCL 2, 1342) for a similar idea.

2. Matt 5:21, 27–28.

3. Matt 5:21–22.

4. Matt 5:33, 34, 37. Lat. Iren. has: *Sit autem vobis sermo, etiam etiam, et non non,* which is close to our Greek Bible. But Arm. Iren. has "Let your yes be yes, and your no be no." SC claims that could not have come from the Arm. Bible, and since Lat. Iren. tends to harmonize Irenaeus with the Bible, Arm. Iren. could have attempted to clarify the matter without regard to the exact wording of the Greek, as it did in other cases.

5. Matt 5:20.

6. Cf. Matt 23:3.

7. "Corporal means" is simply *corporalia,* namely, the external ceremonies that affected the body more directly than the soul.

8. "Serve" is according to Lat. Iren. *servire Deo.* Arm. Iren. has *assentire Deo.* That would mean to obey God, and there would be a tautological

duplication: obey God...obey the commands. Yet, just below we have *sequi Deum,* and in 4.13.4 *assentire et assequi.* So Arm. Iren. could be correct.

9. Cf. A.H. 4.14.2–3; 4.15.1.

10. Matt 5:21–22.

11. Matt 19:21.

12. Matt 5:43–44.

13. Luke 6:29, 30, 31.

14. Matt 5:41.

15. Matt 5:45. Cf A.H. 4.36.6; 5.2.1; 5.2.2; 3.25.3.

16. See a parallel in Justin, *Dialogus* 93.3 (MG 6.697). B. Alfonsi, "Su un passo di Ireneo (Adv. haer. 4.13.4)," *VC* 12 (1958): 225–26, thinks Irenaeus borrowed and adapted this from Caecilius, who wrote: *homo homini deus est, si suum officium sciat,* or, since Irenaeus knew Greek, possibly from Menander, Caecilius's predecessor.

17. John 15:15.

18. Cf. Jas 2:23. Cf. A.H. 4.5.4.

19. Irenaeus addresses this theme in other contexts. See A.H. 14.1.2.3; 4.16.4; 4.17.1; 4.18.1.3.6. See also Philo of Alexandria *Spec Leg* 1.271; Clement of Rome *Cor* 52.1; Barnabas. *Ep* 2.; Athenagoras, *Supplique pro Christianis* 13; *Ep to Diogenes* 3.4; Justin, *1 Apol* 13; *Dial.* 22.1; Clement *Strom.* 7.3.14.6–15.1.

20. "Imperishability." The noun is correct. Arm. Iren. has *incorruptibiles fiunt.* This adjective suggests the correct noun *incorruptibilitas* not *immortalitas.* Iren. did at times misread *athanasia* for *aphtharsia.* In A.H. 1.4.1 the Greek is "imperishable" but Lat. Iren. has *immortalitas.*

Chapter 14

1. This paragraph contains some beautiful Irenaean theology; for instance, that God's salvific will began with the creation of humanity. See for this A. Bengsch, *Heilsgeschichte und Heilswissen: Eine Untersuchung zur Struktur und Entfaltung des theologischen Denkens im Werke Adversus haereses des hl. Irenäus von Lyon,* Erfurter Theologische Studien 3 (Leipzig: St Benno-Verlag, 1957), 91–108; González 152–55; 160–61; Berrouard, "Servitude de la Loi et liberté de l'évangile," 41–60. This is an old idea in Christian theology that is gaining favor again today. See *General Catechetical Directory,* 51. That God's goodness is the reason for man's creation is taught also in # 2, and in A.H. 2.25.3; *Proof* 4, 5, 6. See François Vernet, "Irénée (saint)," *Dictionnaire de Theologie catholique,* 7.2 (Paris: Letouzey, 1927), 2476–78.

2. John 17:5.

3. Arm. Iren has a pair of active verbs (*illuminant et illustrant*) that match the other pair, *illuminantur et illustrantur,* and so are probably authentic. See Hemmerdinger 315.

4. "Demands" as in Lat. Iren. *exquirit.* This idea occurs also in 5.2.1, 4 (3 times). It is certainly correct against Arm. Iren., which has the idea that God needs service from man. SC explains that the Greek most likely was χρήζει, which bears both meanings. This is another case where the Arm. Iren. did not understand the clear teaching of Irenaeus.

5. John 15:16.

6. John 17:24.

7. Isa 43:5, 6, 7 LXX.

8. Matt 24:28.

9. The idea of man's bearing God's Spirit is also in A.H. 4.20.6, and *Proof* 7.

10. Cf. Luke 15:22–23.

11. "Symphony" is for *consonantia,* which quite probably stands for συμφωνία. Since immediately before this there is an allusion to the story of the prodigal son, SC rightly suggests that this term comes from that story (cf. Luke 15:25), where it has a musical meaning. Irenaeus seems to have had a musical meaning here too, since he speaks immediately after of the voices of the many waters of Christ, which he adds as an explanation of the preceding. The idea is truly beautiful: the entire plan of salvation is a harmonious whole, a symphony, literally and musically, giving glory to God.

12. Rev 1:15.

13. In Scripture the Spirit's gifts and graces are referred to several times as water or an effusion of water; cf. John 4:14; 7:37–9. See Unger, *Laur.* (1972): 313–14.

14. "Rich and abundant" is according to Lat. Iren., but for "abundant" the Latin is *magnus.* Arm. Iren. has "multiple." That seems correct since the pair "rich and abundant" occurs elsewhere: 3.10.6; 16.7. In A.H. 4.20.11, "abundant" is used alone with the Word. A.J. de Aldama, "Polypousios dans le Protoévangile de Jacques et l'A.H. de s. Irénée," *RSR* 50 (1962): 86–89, thinks this is a hendiadys, meaning "very rich."

15. "Purifications" is from Arm. Iren. Most of the Lat. MSS read *monitiones*; Voss has *munitiones.* But these are scribal errors out of context.

16. Exod 25:40; Heb 8:5.

17. 1 Cor 10:4.

18. 1 Cor 10:11.

19. Irenaeus's discussion of types—and the difference between types and allegories—is important. See Scott D. Moringiello, "Allegory and Typology in Irenaeus of Lyon," in *SP* 93(Leuven: Peeters, 2017), 255–64.

Chapter 15

1. In Lat. Iren. "training" is before "prophecy," but in Arm. Iren. the order is inverted. SC follows the order of the Arm. Iren., on the score that that is the order announced just before and the order followed thereafter in cc. 15ff. On the contrary, just before this sentence, Irenaeus stated *per typos, ergo discebant timere Deum.* That refers to the learning-training process. Then all of chap. 15 is about the precepts given for their training. Only in chap. 16 does Irenaeus begin discussing the signs, which were, typically, also prophecies. So Lat. Iren. does have the correct order. On Irenaeus's use of 1 Cor 10, see Bacq 120n2. Cf A.H. 4.14.3; 4.11.4; 4.19.1; 4.32.2.

2. Deut 5:22.

3. Ezek 20:24. "The desire of their heart" of Irenaeus is neither altogether according to LXX or the Hebrew. The Hebrew Bible has: "after the idols of their fathers." The LXX, by reading the consonants for "idols"

differently, got: "after the desires of their fathers." Irenaeus made *desire* singular, and, by a different reading of the consonants for "fathers," got "of their heart." But how Irenaeus, who knew very little Hebrew, got to that reading is a mystery. There is no MSS evidence for it in the Hebrew Bible or LXX. Maybe the book of *Testimonies* is responsible for this too.

4. Stephen is a key figure for Irenaeus. Stephen's speech in Acts before his martyrdom recounts the entire economy of salvation. Bacq connects 14:4–15:1, p. 119–21.

5. Acts 7:38–43. Lat. Iren. retained the transcribed *martyrium*, which seems to indicate that already at so early a date this common word for witness had acquired the specific usage of witness by shedding of blood. The earliest references to this meaning given by A. Blaise, *Dictionnaire Latin-Françaís des auteurs chrétiens* (Turnhout: Brepols, 1954), s.v., are Tertullian and Cyprian.

6. Exod 33:2–3.

7. Matt 19:7–8.

8. Cf. Heb 3:5.

9. 1 Cor 7:12.

10. 1 Cor 7:6.

11. 1 Cor 7:25.

12. 1 Cor 7:5.

13. I followed Arm. Iren., which in the Latin of SC reads: *salutarem Decalogi absorbentes hamum et detenti ab eo.* That differs considerably from Lat. Iren.: *salutem Decalogi observantes, munera dent ei, et detenti ab eo.* These changes were possibly made at different times. *Observantes* is a misreading for *absorbentes.* I can offer no explanation of how *hamum* became *munera dent ei.*

14. Matt 20:16.

15. Matt 7:15.

16. "Would be crowned" is from Arm. Iren. Lat. Iren. has *honorentur.* Here too Irenaeus stresses human free choice and its bearing on eternal punishment and reward.

Chapter 16

1. Gen 17:9, 10, 11.

2. Ezek 20:12. See also, A.H. 3.12.11; 4.15.1; 4.16.3.

3. Exod 31:13.

4. Col 2:11.

5. Deut 10:16 (LXX).

6. Cf. A.H. 2.22.2; *Proof* 96.

7. Rom 8:36, from Ps 43 (44):22.

8. A.H. 4.8.2; 4.8.3; 4.30.3; 4.18.2 *Proof* 96.

9. Cf. Matt 6:19.

10. A.H. 4.33.2; 5.34.3; 4.20.10.

11. Jas. 2:23; Rom 4:3; Gen 15:6.

12. Gen 19:17.

13. Gen 9:27, and chap. 10. Even Scripture gives the impression that the human race had a second beginning with Noah at the head. Hemmerdinger (311) thinks *mundi secundae generationis* is an interpolation. The sense would

be complete without them, and the Arm. Iren. does not have them. Arm. omitted the conjunction *sed et* and took *secundum* (for *secundae*) as an adverbial conjunction. But Daniélou (*RSR* 57 [1969]: 87) insists on retaining them and thinks this was inspired by Clement, *Epistola* 9.4. (ACW 1.14).

14. Cf. Gen 5:22, 24; Heb 11:5. "a legation to the angels" is from the apocryphal Book of Enoch, sect. 2., c. 71. 5–17 (R. H. Charles, *The Book of Enoch* [Oxford: Clarendon Press,1893], 184–85.) Hemmerdinger 308 thinks this reference to Enoch indisputable. That the angels who sinned fell to the earth seems a certain reference to Rev 12:9: "he was thrown down to the earth, and his angels were thrown down with him."

15. Deut 5:2–3.

16. 1 Tim 1:9.

17. Cf A.H. 4.12.2–3.

18. Exod 3ff.

19. Deut 8:3. Cf. 1 Cor 10:3–4

20. Deut 5:22.

21. Deut 10:12.

22. Cf. Rom 3:23. Irenaeus will speak of God's glory at much greater length below at A.H. 4.20.7.

23. Deut 30:19–20.

24. Cf. A.H. 4.16.3; 4.12.5.

25. Cf. A.H. 4.13.1; 4.13.3.

26. Deut 4:14. "disciplining" is from Lat. Iren., *eruditioni sive castigationi*, where the second noun is the translator's explanation, as Arm. Iren. confirms.

27. Cf. *Proof* 26.

28. Cf. 4.36.2, 4.26.5, *Proof* 96.

29. Matt 12:36.

30. Matt 5:28.

31. Matt 5:22.

32. Cf. A.H. 3.25.2.

33. 1 Pet 2:16.

34. Cf. A.H. 1.6.1–2; 3.15.2; 3.25.4; 4.37–39.

Chapter 17

1. 1 Sam 15:22.
2. Ps 39 (40):6.
3. For a chart showing prophetic antitheses, see Bacq 132n2.
4. Bacq connects A.H. 4.17.1 with 4.17.4 132n1.
5. Ps 50 (51):18–19.
6. Ps 49 (50): 9–13.
7. Ps 49 (50):14–15.
8. Isa 1:11.
9. Isa 1:16–18 LXX.
10. This is a partial quotation from Ps 50 (51):19, but the rest is in no canonical Scripture. It is not from Eccl 39:14 LXX as Massuet suggested, because the only thing in common is "odor of sanctity." It is quoted also by Clement of Alexandria in *Pedagogus* 3.12.90 (GCS 1.286). But it is found

already in Ps–Barnabas 2.10 (ACW 6.39). H. Windisch, *Der Barnabas Brief* (Tübingen, 1920), 313, thought Irenaeus took it from Ps–Barnabas. That was accepted as certain by L. Froidevaux, "Les trois textes cités par saint Irénée," *RSR* 44 (1956) 418. SC (581n1) observes that some wish to attribute this to the *Apocalypse of Adam* (cf. James, *The Apocrypha* [1893] 145), but that attribution is unfounded. Now it was Hemmerdinger (309) himself who put that into his MS for SC 100. Yet both Irenaeus and Ps–Barnabas could have gotten it from the book of *Testimonies.* This is confirmed by the fact that here Irenaeus, whose authority is normally the LXX, follows the order of the OT Books according to the Hebrew canon. Thus A. Benoit, "Irénée *Adv. haereses* IV, 1–5 et les Testimonia," *Studia patristica* 4 (TU 79, 1961.2): 20–27.

11. Jer 6:20 LXX.

12. Jer 7:2–4 LXX.

13. Jer 7:21–25.

14. Jer 9:24.

15. Isa 43:23–24 LXX.

16. Isa 66:2 LXX.

17. Jer 11:15 LXX.

18. Isa 58:6–9 LXX.

19. Zach 7:9–10 LXX. The Twelve Minor Prophets were treated as a special group and quoted as such by Irenaeus. See also paragraph 5 below.

20. Zach 8:16–17 LXX.

21. Ps 33 (34):12–14.

22. Hos 6:6.

23. Matt 12:7.

24. "First-fruits" is evidently used here of the Eucharist. But how is the Eucharist called so? Harvey thinks it is because it is the Easter offering, just as the "first-fruits" of the Old Law were the Paschal offerings. But that was really the offering for the Pentecost; cf. Exod 23:14, 16, 19; 34:22; Num 28:26. It seems that the eucharistic offering is called the first-fruits because it is an offering of wheat, the first-fruits of which were offered to God in the Old Law, and which were most pleasing to God and, in a sense, the best offering. Yet, Christ himself is called the first-fruits offering because of his offering on the cross. It seems quite probable that Irenaeus calls the Eucharist the first-fruits offering because it does contain Christ and reproduces the offering on the Cross.

25. Cf A.H. 4.17.5; 4.18.1; 4.18.3; 4.18.6.

26. Matt 26:26; Luke 22:19–20; 1 Cor 11:23ff. Irenaeus remarks for both the bread and the wine that these are from our creation. In other words, against his opponents, he is saying that the earth and its products are good, coming from the good God. They are worthy of becoming the very Body and Blood of the Lord and then serve as food of our souls as well as the finest sacrifice to God. That is the theme of A. W. Ziegler, "Das Brot von unseren Feldern: Ein Beitrag zur Eucharistielehre des hl. Irenäus," in *Pro Mundi Vita,* Festschrift zum Eucharistischen Weltkongress (Munich, 1960), 21–43.

27. In this passage Irenaeus teaches several points about the Eucharist. a) The elements are bread and wine. b) The offering of these by Christ at the Last Supper was a true sacrifice because it was in place of the sacrifices of the Old Law, and he calls it a first-fruits sacrifice and speaks of the offering of wine

as "a new oblation of the new covenant," and because he quotes Mal 1:10–11, where there is certainly question of a true sacrifice, and because he says as a comment on Malachi that the Old Law sacrifices have ceased, but that there is an offering of a clean sacrifice in every place. c) Moreover, this sacrifice of Christ is continued in the Church; in other words, the eucharistic sacrifice of the Church is a true sacrifice: it is the same sacrifice that Christ offered, and it "is offered in the whole world." In #6 the Bishop states that the Church offers an oblation in the whole world according to the instruction of the Lord, which is a certain allusion to "Do this in memory of me." In 4.18.2, he contrasts the Old Law sacrifices with that of the New, making it plain that this is as real as those. d) This sacrifice is also received in communion because he says it is given to us by God "as nourishment." He does not speak *ex industria* at this point about communion, concerned as he is with the idea of sacrifice. e) The bread and wine are Christ's flesh and blood in the sacrifice. For the bread Irenaeus simply quotes the words of Christ, "This is my Body." But the identity of Christ with what appears as bread is thereby asserted most evidently. In regard to the wine he makes the identification explicitly: "Christ acknowledged (the chalice) to be his blood." It is a clean sacrifice not because it remains bread and wine, but because it becomes the Body and the Blood of Christ. See also A.H. 4.18.4,5; 5.2.2,3. These studies may be consulted: A. Scheiwiler, "Die Elemente der Eucharistie in der ersten drei Jahrhunderten," *Forschungen zur christlichen Literatur- und Dogmengeschichte* (1903): 17–26, 43–56. P. Radopoulos, "Irenaeus on the Consecration of the Eucharistic Gifts," *Kyriakon, Festschrift Johannes Quasten* (Munster: Aschendorff, 1970), vol. 2:844–46, who stresses the realism of Irenaean eucharistic teachings. F. R. M. Hitchcock, "The Doctrine of the Holy Communion in Irenaeus," *Church Quarterly Review* 129 (1939.40): 206–25, who, in keeping with the tenets of his church about the Eucharist, denies that Irenaeus taught the real presence of Christ by a change of the elements and that it was a sacrifice.

28. *Didache* 14.1–3; Justin *Dialogue* 12.8.41 & 117. Mal 1:10–11 (LXX). Irenaeus considers this prophecy fulfilled in the Eucharist of the Church.

29. John 17.

30. Lat. Iren. reads: *Et quoniam proprii Filii eius est et ab eo factus est homo, suum illum vocat.* At first sight *homo* seems justified, for *homo* is in the context immediately before it occurs in *et homo glorificatur*. But that makes the sense of the whole clause obscure and complicated. Most of all, Irenaeus gives an illustration of this, as a policy, below and in it "the image" illustrates "name," but "image" both belongs to the son and was made by the king. And so in our clause "name," which belongs to the Son, was also made by the Father. *Nomen* is subject of *factum est*. SC, 595n1, gives an explanation of how *homo* entered the text; but I think it simpler to hold that because *homo* is in the preceding clause, seemingly calling for entrance into the explanation, *homo* was introduced as the subject.

31. God "made" the name of his Son "Jesus" by having it written into Scripture. There is here an evident allusion to Matt 1:21, where God, through Matthew, wrote the name and gave as an explanation of the name that he was to be Savior of humankind. See also Luke 1:31; and Acts 4:12.

32. Lat. Iren. has: *et in deo omnipotente per Iesum Christum offert Ecclesia.* Arm. Iren. agrees with that. Scholars, however, have found the construction

odd. It would mean that the Church offers by (in) the power of God. So changes have been suggested. SC inserts, from the context of Mal 1:11, quoted as an explanation, *omni loco.* Thus: *in <omni loco> Deo omnipotenti per Iesum Christum offert Ecclesia.* I accepted that in my translation. In the context the offering is made *to* God, not *by* the power of God. See #6: *nomini meo*; and 18.1.

33. Mal 1:11.

34. Rev 5:8.

Chapter 18

1. Matt 5:24–25.

2. Deut 16:16.

3. This is a puzzling sentence. Lat. Iren. reads: *ut in quibus gratus exstitit homo, in his gratus ei deputatus, eum qui est ab eo percipiat honorem.* One senses something is wrong. What? Arm. Iren. has, in place of *gratus exstitit, ingratus factus est.* SC rejects that as unacceptable, because it expresses an idea that is completely foreign to the context: in no part of this chapter is there even an allusion to human ingratitude. Yet, I think a more careful reading of chaps. 17 and 18 shows that Irenaeus is proving that God did not need man, and he uses as proof that God rejected the sacrifices of the Old Covenant. The rejection of these sacrifices is stated at least sixteen times in chap. 17. They were not acceptable to God because of the sins of the people; and so the people ("man") was not acceptable to God either. God demanded sinless conduct. See especially chap. 17.3–4, and chap. 18.2. Now, in order that man might not remain fruitless spiritually and be unaccepted, God has him offer the Sacrifice of the New Covenant (17.5); but not because God is now in need.

So there is more than enough reference to the fact that man was unacceptable, and even the idea of being displeasing can be seen in the term *ingratus.* In classical and ecclesiastical Latin *gratus* has as first meaning "pleasing," not "grateful": and *ingratitude* is displeasure; *ingratus,* displeasing. So in the context about people who were displeasing to God, this meaning is quite correct. Arm. Iren. is, then, quite accurate, and Lat. Iren. should read: *in quibus ingratus exstitit.*

4. This is a certain statement that the Church has a true sacrifice. See chap. 17, n27.

5. Lat. Iren. has: *nihil enim otiosum neque sine signo sive argumento. Argumento* is the translator's explanatory addition. Cf. 4.21.3: *nihil enim vacuum neque sine signo.* Also 4.16.1: *non autem sine symbolo erant signa, id est, sine argumento, neque otiosa.* Here too *sine argumento* seems to be the translator's note. A *signum* is a *symbolum* inasmuch as it has significance and can be used as a proof. In 4.21.2, *non sine significatione non inanes, significatione* must represent the same Greek as σύμβολον.

6. Cf. *Proof* 96; A.H. 4.13.2–3.

7. Luke 21:4; also Acts 2:44–45. In my preceding sentence, Lat. Iren. has *non* in the phrase *dantes ea non quae sunt minora,* as if the lesser things were not to be offered. But Irenaeus is actually stressing the giving of lesser goods, as the widow's mite. So Arm. Iren. is correct in omitting that *non.*

8. Gen 4:4–5.

9. Gen 4:7 LXX.

10. See Bacq's remarks on love and the Eucharist. Bacq 140n1.

11. Lat. Iren. reads: Sec *cessatio mali, quod est intus conceptum, ne per assimilatam operationem, magis autem peccatum, ipsum sibi homicidam faciat hominem.* What is the subject of *faciat*? Certainly not *hominem*, though BKV translated that way. Nor can *cessatio mali* be subject, since that is something good, whereas the subject of *faciat* is bad, a murderer. The more remote subject is *quod est intus conceptum*, sc. *malum*; not its simulated, that is, external, operation, but the inner sin; so the proximate subject is *peccatum*. This inner sin is what makes a man a real homicide, a murderer of a brother man. Thus Harvey and ANF. There is no question here of suicide, as ANF implies. The whole context is about killing another. And Irenaeus's explanation below makes it clear it is the inner sin that makes a man a killer. Mere external offerings make a man a hypocrite who hides jealousies that will cause someone's death. SC, following Arm. Iren., omits *magis autem*: but it is needed for the full understanding of the sentence. H. Elfers, *Die Kirchenordnung Hippolyts von Rom* (Paderborn 1938) 262–78, explains how Irenaeus's spiritual living ties in with his teaching on the Eucharist. God does not need us at all, but we need God and are obliged to even heroic obedience in offering ourselves in service for others.

12. Matt 23:27–28.

13. Cf. Jas. 5:6. Grant, in a review of SC 100, *VC* 22 (1968): 143, claims the reference is rather to Acts 7:52. I do not think so. In Acts Stephen is speaking directly about their killing the Prophets. In James the direct object of the killing is the Just One.

14. Cf. A.H. 4.11.3.

15. Matt 23:26.

16. Jer 22:17 LXX.

17. Isa 30:1 LXX.

18. Gen 4:7.

19. John 19:11.

20. Cf. A.H. 4.18.5.

21. Isa 66:3 LXX.

22. Phil 4:18.

23. Irenaeus insists that the Church's eucharistic offering is a true sacrifice, and that the Church alone has such a sacrifice. See chap. 17, n27: "Of his creation," that is, the bread and the wine. "with thanksgiving" is an allusion to the prayer of consecration. But it also refers to the offering as one of thanksgiving. Cf. below where, in contrast, the heretics are said to offer God an insult.

24. Cf. Isa 1:15.

25. Because C and V omit *per* before *quod*, Massuet and BKV dropped it, with the result that the Word is offered. But it is in the other MSS, and Harvey retained it. It is also confirmed by Arm. Iren.

26. Cf. Mark 4:27–28, though with some transposition of words. Irenaeus informs us that the heretics attempted to offer a eucharistic sacrifice with bread and wine, and that they believed this to be the body and the blood of Christ. See also 4.18.5. But they were inconsistent in holding that it was not

the body and blood of the Son of God, or of the Word, but of the Demiurge. Indirectly, Irenaeus states his faith, and that of the Church, in the real presence of Christ in the Eucharist. "The chalice is his blood" is according to Arm. Iren., which has *sanguinem*, making this construction parallel to that of the bread. Lat. Iren. has *sanguinis*, namely, the chalice is of his Blood, which also gives good sense.

27. The Eucharist as Communion is contained in the words: "the flesh is nourished by the Lord's Body and Blood," not by the bread. And so those words also imply the real presence of Christ. Irenaeus is arguing *ad hominem* against the heretics: if Christ is really present in communion, as the heretics admit, how is it possible that the body of the communicant will not share in the everlasting resurrection of Christ himself?

28. My translation follows the Latin, with *doctrina* as subject and *Eucharistiae* as indirect object. The Greek excerpt has Eucharist as subject and doctrine as indirect object. That misses the contrast intended. The Bishop wishes to say that our doctrine that the Word-Christ is the Creator of the elements of the Eucharist harmonizes with the idea that the Eucharist is the Body and Blood of the Word-Christ. And the fact that the Eucharist is the Body and Blood of the Word-Christ confirms the doctrine that he created the elements. That is splendid recapitulation. Irenaeus uses the word "Eucharist" for the Sacrifice and the Sacrament of the Body and Blood of the Lord. Cf. Th. Schermann, "*Eucharistia* und *eucharistein* in ihrem Bedeutungswandel bis 200 nach Christus," *Philologus* 69 (1910): 375–410.

29. "Harmoniously" is *congruenter*, and ἐμμελῶς in the Greek excerpt. The idea Irenaeus wishes to convey is that there is harmony here as he had just stated. What does he mean by the union of the flesh and the spirit? The *enim* in the following gives the clue. There he says our bodies, mortal in themselves, become imperishable through the Eucharist. If that is to be a parallel case to what he had just said, then flesh is our natural selves, mortal in themselves; spirit is our supernatural selves. This is a regular Irenaean idea. It fits in with Pauline theology as expressed in 1 Cor 15. Spirit is the whole person endowed with the grace of the Spirit. In the rest of the paragraph Irenaeus applies his point to the body and does not mention the spirit. Instead he speaks of the Eucharist, supposing that either the Eucharist in us is the "spirit" or that it gives the Spirit, who will entitle us to imperishable bodies. Cf. A.H. 4.20.4: *ut complexus homo Spiritum Dei in gloriam cedat Patris.*

30. "Invocation" follows the Latin *invocationem*, which supposes the Greek ἐπίκλησις, used elsewhere by Irenaeus (cf. A.H. 1, chap. 13, n6). But the Greek fragment has εκκλήσις, which editors generally take as a scribal error. Yet M. Jugie, "La forme du sacrament de l'Eucharistie d'aprés saint Irénée," *Mémoriale Chaine* (Bibliothéque de la Faculté catholique de théologie de Lyon 5 [Lyon 1950]), 223–33, claims that this is the original reading and that it refers to the formula of consecration, which is simply Christ's words identifying the Eucharist as his Body and Blood. That these words are the eucharistic formula according to Irenaeus I agree. See also A.H. 4.33.2. But that is true even if one does not accept ἐκκλήσις as the original reading, because ἐπίκλησις would at that early date not refer to a specific prayer of invocation to the Word or the Spirit, nor even to the whole *anaphora*. On the epiclesis see also A.H.

1, n311, and the study of J. P. de Jong, "Der Ursprüngliche Sinn von Epiklese und Mischungsritus nach der Eucharistielehre des hl. Irenäus," *Archiv für Liturgiewissenschaft* 9 (1965): 28–47; de Jong, "Epiklese," LTK 3 (1959): 935–37.

31. This sentence has been a *crux interpretum*, chiefly because of the difficulty of identifying what the earthly and what the heavenly is in the Eucharist. Irenaeus offers this parallel as an illustration (*enim*) of what preceded, and that was this: Flesh and spirit are happily united through the Eucharist, namely, in the resurrection. Just as the Eucharist which is Christ's Body (glorious, of course) is made up of a double element, bread and God's word that it receives, so the imperishable body is made up of the mortal body made imperishable in hope by the Eucharist it received. The parallel cannot be expressed perfectly because the imperishable body is not effected immediately by the reception of the Eucharist; that will come only at the final resurrection. Now it exists in hope. Nor could Irenaeus say that the imperishable body consists of an earthly and a heavenly element, because the glorious body is not the earthly element, nor does the mortal body exist any more as the earthly part. The mortal body is only the subject matter from which the imperishable was made; and in that sense it could be the earthly element, namely, in the state of becoming. In the accomplished state of the imperishable body the Eucharist is not a component part; only its effect continues in the imperishable body. And so, if Irenaeus meant the contrast of earthly and heavenly to be applied to the imperishable body in the accomplished state, this can be true only in the sense that something of what was the mortal body remains, but it was changed.

At this point we need say no more about the change of the bread into the Body of Christ, and not merely a coexistence of Christ with the bread, an impanation. Such a theory does not do justice to the wording of Irenaeus, here and in A.H. 5.2.2–3. Irenaeus's emphatic identifying of Christ's Body with the bread before him, and his saying explicitly that it is no longer common bread, demand a change of the bread into the "no longer common bread," but Christ's Body. See also A.H. 4.33.2 on the explicit identification of the bread and wine of the Eucharist as Christ's Body and Blood. See Bacq 143–46.

32. "Give thanks for the gift." Authors claim there is here an allusion to the introductory prayers to the Preface of the Mass, a hymn of thanksgiving. We are certain that at St. Cyprian's time such introductory prayers existed: cf *De dominica oratione* 31 (CSEL 3, part 1. 289). Maybe Irenaeus is alluding to such prayers. But maybe he is alluding in general to the Canon of the Mass, which was known as *actio gratiarum* in Tertullian's day; cf. *Adv. Marcionem* 4.9.9 (CCL 1.560).

33. "Gift" is according to the A and S MSS, which have *donationi* as a dative of means. Arm. Iren. has *de donatione*, which might have the same sense. SC accepts that. The C and V MSS have *dominationi*, which could give a correct meaning, namely, that we give thanks for God's lordship over us. That would be expressive of a very profound note about adoration. I took the dative as one of advantage, *donationi*.

34. Prov 19:17.

35. Matt 25:34–6.

36. As is clear from the next sentence, introduced by *ergo*, the altar here is a symbolic altar in heaven. The *oblationes* that are to be offered up frequently

are prayers and other things mentioned. But since Irenaeus has been speaking at length about the eucharistic sacrifice, this may also be included in this admonition about offering frequent sacrifices.

37. Cf. Rev 11:9. In the Roman Canon in the prayer that begins *supplices* after the consecration there is mention of carrying the gifts to the heavenly altar. Could it be possible that St. Irenaeus is here alluding to such an idea? But he may be alluding merely to Rev 11:9. See Ignatius Martyr, *Ad Philadelphenses* 4 (ACW 1.86); Gregory Nazianz., *Oratio 42, in Pascha* 23 (MG 36.656B).

38. Rev 11:19.

39. Rev 21:3.

Chapter 19

1. For "Moses on the Mount" see Exod 25:40. For "glorified among the nations" see Mal 1:10–11, of which there is an evident allusion here, and so the glorification of God in the Church is through the Eucharist, because Irenaeus is speaking of the sacrifices of the Old Covenant as mere types of that of the New. This was, of course, stated more clearly before, with an explicit quotation from Mal 1:11.

2. Lat. Iren. has *sermo,* which stands for *Logos.* Arm. Iren. skipped the whole phrase. SC (619n1) thinks this *sermo* refers to the Scriptures, which are in fact being quoted. Yet Irenaeus also knows that the Word spoke in the Scriptures, as did the Spirit. And so this Sermo-Logos could very well be the Word.

3. Isa 40:12. In the next sentence the underlined words could be alluding to Eph 3.18. "circumference" is for *circummensurationis,* which is well authenticated in the Latin MSS. It supposes the Greek περιμέτρου, which is found in A.H. 1.17.1. Arm. Iren. has *de mensura,* and so Hemmerdinger 311 thinks this could be a marginal title, in Greek περί μέτρου, which slipped into the text.

4. Of whose heart and mind is Irenaeus speaking: God's, or man's? ANF thought it is man's, here and in #3; namely, God cannot be measured by the heart of man or comprehended by his mind. BKV refers these words to God, and rightly so, because there is a contrast here: God's hand cannot be comprehended, much more so cannot he himself be comprehended in his heart or mind. It would be a strange contrast if he had said: "God's mind cannot be comprehended, much more so can he not be comprehended by man's heart and mind."

5. A rather graphic picture of God's immensity.

6. Eph 1:21.

7. Cf. Jer 23:24.

8. Cf. Dan 3:55.

9. Cf. Dan 3:55.

10. Jer 2:23–24, also Acts 17:27.

11. Cf. Rev 2:23. From this it is clear that the personified Hand of God is the Word. Cf. chap. 7, n22.

Chapter 20

1. God is in his nature so immense that man cannot know him as such even naturally; but when God in his love permits, man can know him through his creatures. So Irenaeus is here not denying to man a natural knowledge of God. Naturally, man can have only an indirect knowledge of God through creatures. Cf. A.H. 4.20.4.

2. Hemmerdinger 308 says he had suggested that this sentence from "and it is He who..." is from Hermas, but SC did not accept that.

3. Gen 2:7.

4. For "Word of God" Clermont MS has *Verbum Domini* while the Salamanca has *Verbum Dei* Arm. Iren. with its *verum Deum* suggests *Dei* as correct; but *Verbum* of Latin is quite likely correct. Irenaeus is pairing the Word and the Spirit with various figurative titles.

5. Gen 1:26.

6. Since the Hands are the Word and the Spirit, it seems, in context, that the Exemplar is the Word, and the Shape is the Spirit, because elsewhere the shaping of things is ascribed to the Spirit. See #2: He "made all things by his Word, and adorned them by his Wisdom" (the Spirit). Cf. also A.H. 4.20.4; 3.24.2; *Proof* 5. For the Incarnate Word as the ideal Man, the image after which man was made, see A. Orbe, "El hombre ideal en la teología de s. Ireneo," *Greg.* 43 (1962): 449–91; and Orbe, *Antrop.* 89–148. On God's creating through his hands see Orbe, *Antrop.* 34–47; Laurence Regnault, "St. Irénée de Lyon," *Dictionnaire de La Spiritualité* 7, no. 2 (Paris: Beauchesne, 1971), 1938–69.1944. Irenaeus does not teach pantheism when he says that God took from himself the substance of the creatures, because in the next paragraph he says explicitly that God created out of nothing. What he means is that the substance of creatures comes simply from the omnipotent will of God who creates out of nothing. In scholastic terms, he is the efficient cause, not the material cause. Through his Word he is also the exemplary cause.

7. For a full discussion see Bacq 166n2 This quotation is found in *The Shepherd of Hermas* Book 2, *Similitudo* 1. Irenaeus introduces it as Scripture. Authors have long concluded that Irenaeus considered it part of the Bible. That is a false inference. In *Proof* 4, Irenaeus also quotes Hermes, *Mandatum* 1, verbatim, but he adds "the Father" to "God," which he does not have here or in 4.20.2. Smith (ACW 6, n28) claims it is a question in *Proof* 4 of God's immensity, not of his incomprehensibility. True, but spatial incomprehensibility is also Irenaean. As the parallel in 4.20.2 shows, it is not a question of sustaining all things, as Barthoulot has in *Proof* 4. See Smith, 138n28. In Lat. Iren. the three verbs connected by "and" (*constituit et consummavit et fecit*) would seem to give a false sequence of actions, putting creation out of nothing after "establishing and adorning or arranging." The Greek excerpt preserved by Eusebius stops after the first two verbs, which are aorist participles. If the third is also an aorist participle, it could indicate time prior to the other two verbs, as I have translated it, and then the sequence would be good: creation out of nothing, then establishing things (through the Word) and arranging or adorning them (through the Spirit). For *consummavit* the Arm. Iren. Has *adaptavit,* which is more exact. Cf. A.H. 1.15.5; 1.22.1; 2.10.2; 2.30.9; 4.20.1; 4.20.2, 3, 4, and 6. *Proof* 4.

8. Mal 2:10. The two clauses are inverted in RSV and in Irenaeus.

9. Eph 4:6.

10. Matt 11:27.

11. Clearly, since God created through the Word, the created things belong to the Word and not to someone else, as Irenaeus's opponents held. See also A.H. 5.2.1; *Proof* 3.

12. Cf. Heb 2:8.

13. Acts 10:42.

14. Rev 3:7.

15. Rev 5:3, 6, 9, 12.

16. John 1:14. "By the God" is according to the reading suggested by Hemmerdinger (316) in keeping with the Arm. Iren. *ab eo Deo,* which Lat. Iren. wrote incorrectly as *ab odem.*

17. Cf. Col 1:18, where the Vulgate has *primatum,* but Lat. Iren. *principatum.*

18. 1 Pet 2:22.

19. Col 1:18. The idea of triple dominion agrees with the threefold realm expressed in Phil 2:10.

20. See also A.H. 3.9.1.

21. Bacq argues that the "Father's light" is given as the incarnation of the Son. Bacq 167n2.

22. This is a beautiful idea about Christ as the mediator of our glory. Note that it was first given to Christ, namely, for his own glory. Then from Christ it passes on to us. From this we can rightly conclude to the Absolute Primacy of Christ in God's plan of creation and salvation. Moreover, Irenaeus tells us that the incarnation took place that men might "see their King"; that is, Christ was intended as the mediator of man's knowledge of God on earth and in glory. See Unger, FS 14–18. On the incarnation as a new mode for being led gradually to the vision of God, see E. Lanne, "La vision de Dieu dans l'oeuvre de saint Irénée," *Irenikon* 33 (1960): 314–20.

23. On the preexistence of the Son see also 2.25.3; 2.30.9; 3.11.1–6.

24. The eternal existence of the Holy Spirit is given here in unmistakable terms; so he must have been divine in the strict sense.

25. Prov 3:19–20.

26. Prov 8:22–25, as in LXX for its punctuation of vs. 23 and the beginning of vs. 24. "Lord" is according to Lat. Iren.; Arm. Iren. has "God."

27. Prov 8:27–31 LXX, with some phrases omitted.

28. This is an important theme in Irenaeus. Ultimately, creatures know God through his love.

29. Cf. Bar 3:27.

30. *Proof* 12: "And so fair and goodly was the Garden, the Word of God was constantly walking in it; he would walk round and talk with the man, prefiguring what was to come to pass in the future, how he would become man's fellow, and talk with him, and come among mankind, teaching them justice" (ACW 16.55). Irenaeus stresses the truth that the incarnation took place so that man could be united with God on earth and in heaven and actually see him. He stresses this in such a manner that he must have considered it part of the original plan of God. See Unger; ES 13–14, 17.

31. Luke 1:71.

32. Luke 1:75.

33. Irenaeus did not define a prophecy by its most basic function, namely, speaking in God's name (as the Hebrew *nabi'* and the Greek προ-φήμι *pro-phemi* indicate etymologically), but by a frequent function of speaking for God about the future happenings. See also A.H. 4.20.12; *Proof* 34.

34. Matt 5:8.

35. Exod 33:20. "Ineffable" (supposing *inenarrabilem*) is according to Arm. Iren., against Lat. Iren. with *mirabilem.*

36. Vision is an important, if understudied, theme in Irenaeus's writings. See Scott D. Moringiello, *The Rhetoric of Faith: Irenaeus and the Structure of the Adversus Haereses* (Washington, DC: Catholic University of America Press, 2019) for connections between Irenaeus's discussion of vision and the Greco-Roman rhetorical context in which Irenaeus wrote. See also Bacq 169–72.

37. Luke 18:27.

38. The steps to perfection are found again in A.H. 5.36.2, and *Proof* 7. Human life develops only in communion with the triune God. The triple adverbial construction (*prophetice...adoptive...paternaliter*) had to be changed in order to get a readable translation.

39. See Bacq 328.

40. "By men" is according to Arm. Iren. and Lat. Iren. The Greek excerpt has ζωοποιήσῃ. There is a textual difficulty in the number of terms and their order. Arm. Iren. is the most complete and has the three positive terms in the same order as the matching negative terms. Someone might suspect that Arm. Iren. adjusted the text to be so consistent. But the number of the terms in Arm. Iren. is correct. Lat. Iren. omits *invisibile,* which is quite certainly authentic since it is in the Greek and Arm. Iren. The Greek excerpt omits *visibile,* which is carried by Lat. Iren. and Arm. Iren. As for the order, if we suppose the order of the negative terms in the Greek to be original, with which the Latin agrees, once we have restored *invisibilis* in third place, *incomprehensibilis* would be the middle term, just as in the positive side *comprehensibilis* is the middle term. If on the positive side we restore *visibilem* to the Greek in first place as it is in Arm. Iren. and Lat. Iren., then we could have the end terms inverted on the positive side, with the whole forming a kind of chiasmus, as in my translation. This was the suggestion already of G. M. Lee, "Notes on Irenaeus (*Adv. haereses* 4, 34.6)," VC 25 (1971): 29–30, and is followed by SC 100, in the French translation. All this is beautiful and harmonious doctrine. That the true life of a creature consists in partaking of the Creator's life is a masterful thought.

41. "Who bear the Spirit," see chap. 14, n9.

42. Deut 5:24 LXX; but Lat. Iren. and Arm. Iren. both have "we see," in place of the Bible's "we know."

43. Matt 6:10.

44. Hos 12:11. See also A.H. 3.2.13.

45. 1 Cor 12:4–7.

46. John 1:18. Lat. Iren. has *unigenitus Filius,* which seems an adaptation of the Latin translator, because Arm. Iren. has "only-begotten God," which Lat. Iren. also has two times in A.H. 4.20.11. Introducing this quotation, Lat.

Iren. has *in evangelio scriptum est,* while Arm. Iren. has "the Lord says." SC defends this Arm. reading as "incontestably original," noting that in A.H. 4.20.11 both Lat. and Arm. Iren. have this two times. SC thinks if the Greek had had "in the Gospel" it would be difficult to see how Arm. Iren. got "the Lord says"; but it can equally be retorted: if the Latin translator had in his Greek copy "the Lord says," it is difficult to explain how he got *in evangelio scriptum est.* SC's suggestion that Lat. Iren. did not understand how this quotation, actually a statement by the evangelist John, could be ascribed to the Lord, so he changed it. That is not convincing at all. He would have had to make the same change twice in A.H. 4.20.11. So either reading could have been original here.

47. For more on "only Begotten" see Bacq 324.

48. Cf. 1 Cor 12:4–7. A.H. 3.16.7.

49. Cf. A.H. 2.6.1.

50. See Bacq 174n1 and 320. See also A.H. 3.6.1; 4.5.1.

51. "Disciplined" renders *praemeditaretur.*

52. Tertullian, *De carnis resurrectio,* 28.1 (CCL 2.957); *Sicut vocibus, ita et rebus prophetatum est.* Augustine, *Contra Faustum,* lib. 4, c.2 (ML 42.219): *Ita illorum hominum non tantum lingua, sed et vita prophetica ait.*

53. Isa 6:5.

54. Ps 21 (22):15.

55. Exod 4:6–7 LXX.

56. Num 12:8; Exod 33:11.

57. Exod 33:21, 22, 20 (LXX, with some omissions, but with the addition of "high places"!).

58. Matt 17:3.

59. 1 Kgs 19:11–12 (LXX, with the omission of "on the mountains.")

60. Isa 42:3.

61. See also A.H. 5.35.1; 5.35.2; 5.36.2. And compare these texts with A.H. 4.9.2; 4.20.10; 4.26.1.

62. "Perfectly" is according to Arm. Iren., which seems certain, since Irenaeus here alludes to 1 Cor 12:9–12, about partial knowledge. Lat. Iren. has *proprie.* See 1 Cor 13:12 and A.H. 4.9.2.

63. Ezek 1:1, 5–25.

64. Ezek 2:1.

65. John 1:18. Cf. A.H. 4.20.6.

66. *Loc. cit.*

67. Cf. AH. 1.10.3.

68. Cf. A.H. 3.21.7.

69. Dan 3:92.

70. Dan 2:34.

71. Dan 7:13–14.

72. Cf. A.H. 4.33.1; 4.33.11.

73. Rev 1:12–17 "in the revelation" is not the title of the book, as SC notes, but the revelation that was accorded to John and recounted in Rev. He did not *see* in his book, but in the visions.

74. Exod 28:4; Lev 8:7. For more on types see chap. 19, n1 above.

75. 2 Pet 3:7.

76. Rev 1:17.

77. Exod 33:20.

78. John 13:25. Irenaeus identifies the disciple who reclined on Christ's bosom with John the apostle as the author of the Fourth Gospel and of Revelation.

79. Rev 1:17–18.

80. Rev 5:6.

81. Rev 19:11–17.

82. Lat. Iren. has *visus*. SC's critical apparatus is not complete here. It printed *usus* in the text, seemingly on the authority of Arm. Iren. But God did not *use* the Prophets through visions and speeches and in actions. He was, however, *seen* by the Prophets (dative of agent in Greek) through visions and speeches and *in* actions. Hence the change to the preposition *in*. The burden of the entire section before this is that the Son was *seen by* the Prophets in those visions and words.

83. Hos 1:2–3.

84. 1 Cor 7:14.

85. Bacq wonders whether Christ is the faithful husband and the Church the unfaithful spouse. See Bacq 180n1.

86. Hos 1:6, 9.

87. Rom 9:25–26; Hosea 1:10; 2:23. "It was said." *Eliberata* of Lat. Iren. (*liberata* in Clermont MS) must be wrong. Arm. Iren. (and SC followed that) omits it. Grabe already recommended omitting it as a marginal explanation to "might obtain mercy." Massuet and Harvey claim it supposes ἐρρύθη ("was freed"), which was a false reading for ἐρρέθη ("it was said"), in that case a doublet.

88. Cf. A.H. 1.10.3.

89. Exod 2:21.

90. Rom 11:17.

91. Irenaeus teaches the ancient doctrine that the Word entered into nuptials with the Church. Hence, the Church is the mother of the Gentiles. I translated "the Church which is from among the nations." That is what Lat. Iren. and the Greek have, and the context speaks of the Church and not of a calling. But Arm. Iren. has "the calling of the Gentiles." That supposes ἡ ἐξ ἐθνῶν καλλέω in place of ἡ ἐξ ἐθνῶν ἐκκλεσία. In *Proof* 21 the same idea and words occur. Smith (ACW 16. Note 114) thinks this was correct also in our place. Hardly; in our place there is no mention of a call in the context, and that would scarcely fit into the construction. In *Proof* the call had been mentioned in the previous context, and so it could be correct there. But it could also have slipped into the second place by a mistaken reading of the Greek.

92. Num 12:10–14.

93. Jos. 2.

94. Matt 21:31. Likewise an odd accommodation. Irenaeus, just like Clement and Justin, makes *Rahab* the Church; but Origen and Cyprian took her *house* for the Church. Cf. J. Danielou, "Rahab, figure de l'Eglise," *Irenikon* 22 (1940): 26–45. See also A.H. 4.20.12; 4.30.4.

Chapter 21

1. Gal 3:5–9.
2. See also A.H. 4.5.3–5; 4.7.2; 5.32.2.
3. Rom 9:10–13.
4. Gen 25:23. Other Fathers give the same explanation. See Tertullian, *Adv. Iudaeos* 1.4 (CCL 2.1340); Origen, *Hom. in Gen* 12.1 (GCS 6.107 Bährens).
5. Dan 13:42.
6. Rom 9:13, from Mal 1:2.
7. Gen 25:26.
8. Rev 6:2. Cf. A.H. 3.23.7.
9. Gen 25:32.
10. Cf. Col 1:15. On the "first born" see Bacq 331.
11. John 19:15.
12. Gen 35:16ff., only eleven sons were born to him outside of Palestine; Benjamin was born near Ephrata.
13. The earth is the foreign land of Christ. The twelve-pillared foundation is the apostles, since they are people, the verb *generate* is quite correct.
14. Gen 30:32ff.
15. Ps 2:8.
16. Lat. Iren reads: *Et quoniam multitudinis filiorum Domini prophetae fiebant Iacob, necesse fuit ex duabus sororibus eum filios facere. Multitudinis* is according to the Clermont and Voss MSS; the other Latin MSS have *multitudines.* Neither can be correct. Arm. Iren. has *multitudine,* which makes sense; and *fiebant* should be singular, with Jacob as subject. Thus also SC.
17. Cf. Gen 30:3, 9 and Gal 4:31.
18. Cf. John 6:64; 1 Cor 15.45; 2 Pet 3:18; Justin, *Dialogus* 134 (MG 6.785, 788).
19. Gen 29:17; Cf. Song 1:15.
20. Cf. Eph 5:32.

Chapter 22

1. Gal 4:4, 7. Cf. A.H. 3.22.4.
2. Isa 4:4.
3. John 13.5.
4. On the phrase "heir to God" see also A.H. 4.21.3.
5. In this sentence the phrases have been variously separated and joined, with a variation of meaning. Lat. Iren. and Arm. Iren. agree on: *Hic est enim finis humani generis heredificantis Deum, uti quemadmodum sic in vitam veniant Dei.* SC (685n1) gives a conjectural Greek original and then interprets it as meaning: "the end" is "to inherit God," and the *uti* clauses are result clauses. That would mean that *heredificantis* would be a genitive absolute with *humani generis* as the noun. But that is impossible because *humani generis* is a subjective genitive controlled by *finis.* Nor can the present participle (also in Greek) be a purpose clause, meaning "which would inherit God." Arm. Iren. is of little help here. So the simple solution seems to be:

"the end of the human race" is not "to inherit God," but "to come to the life of God." "First men" are certainly Adam and Eve, because they are said to be the ones through whom we inherited "the debt of death." "The last men" are rightly judged by SC to be the apostles, the foundation of the "last times." (SC, 687n1). Yet, in #2, there is a contrast between "the first" and "we." So maybe the "last men" include not merely the apostles but all people in the apostolic era, that is, till the end of time.

6. This is a spurious passage, not contained in any canonical book. For a full note on this, see Bacq 186n2. Irenaeus refers to Pseudo-Jeremiah six times (A.H. 3.20.4; 4.22.1; 4.33.12; 5.31.1; *Proof* 78). There is also an attribution in Justin, *Dial.* 72.4.

7. Matt 26:40ff.; Mark 14:37ff.; Luke 22:45ff.

8. Eph 4:9.

9. Matt 13:17; Luke 10:24.

10. Cf. Titus 2:12.

11. I followed Lat. Iren., taking *primo...quam reliquos* as a comparative expression. The Arm. Iren. *ex aliis* seems to be the same. SC (689) suspects that there is here a hint of millenarianism. I doubt that very much.

12. Rom 3:30.

13. Lat. Iren. has *deformari.* That has no pejorative sense here. See A.H. 4.25.3, in a similar context: *secundum formationem Christi.*

CHAPTER 23

1. John 4:35–36.

2. "Instructed by the prophets" (Lat. Iren.) and "confused by the Scriptures" (Arm. Iren.) are both partly wrong. "Confused" should be corrected to "instructed" as SC does. "Scriptures" is correct, because the examples given come not merely from the Prophets but also from the Gospels and the Acts. Besides, at the end of chap. 24 we read: *sine instructione Scripturarum.* And at the end of c.23.1, it is the Scriptures of which they are said to be ignorant.

3. Matt 1:20–21.

4. Matt 1:22–23.

5. Isa 7:12. A very clear statement that shows Irenaeus considered Isa 7:14 a literal and exclusive prophecy about Mary the Virgin.

6. Matt 2:14, 21–23.

7. On this phrase, see also A.H. 3.16.2.

8. Luke 3:23.

9. Luke 4:18. That was obviously at Nazareth. Yet both Lat. and Arm. Iren. have Capernaum; so that must have been in the Greek copy from which they translated, and even in Irenaeus's original. His memory could have failed him. See also, A.H. 3.9.3; 3.17.1; 3.18.3.

10. Luke 4:21.

11. Acts 8:26–39. Arm. Iren. adds "apostle" to Philip's name. SC (695n2) thinks that was an error of Irenaeus. But why then was it not also in Lat. Iren.?

12. Cf. A.H. 3.12.8.

13. Here and in A.H. 4.24.1 Irenaeus clearly indicates that catechizing before baptism was a practice of the Church at that time.

14. Matt 10:6.
15. Matt 16:17.
16. Acts 2:41; 4:4; he is really using the entire section of Acts 2–4.

Chapter 24

1. 1 Cor 15:10.
2. Cf. Luke 16:31.
3. Col 1:18; Rev 1:5. On catechizing before baptism see chap. 23, n13.
4. Acts 3:15; 5:31. SC (701n1, pp. 258–61) has a long and interesting note about Irenaeus's combining the texts from Col 1.18 and Acts 3.15, to stress the primacy of the risen Christ, the conqueror of death, the source of divine life for humankind. Having compared the four places where Irenaeus uses this combination (sc. AH. 2.22.4; 3.22.4; 4.24.1 [present passage]; *Proof* 39) he concludes that there is continuity of thought but also progress in insight. In 3.22.4, he does not have "the Author of life" but he does have "unto life of God" and "the beginning of the living." "Beginning" here comes from Col 1:18, the very text that has "Firstborn of the dead." And so "the Beginning of the living" is actually a profound insight into "Firstborn of the dead." Combining these texts is not chance, but the result of a personal reflection on them by the Bishop of Lyons. SC shrewdly observed that the Letter of the Churches of Vienne and Lyons also used this combination, and almost verbatim as in 4.24.1 and *Proof* 39. For the author of the Note in SC this is a good indication that Irenaeus wrote that Letter.
5. Exod 17:10.
6. Cf. Num 21:9 and John 3:14–15.
7. See A.H. 3.13.
8. Lat. Iren. has: *reformasse quidem humanum genus, destruxisse autem et vicisse*, as I translated. Arm. Iren. has: *pugnavisse pro humanitate, vicisse autem,* which SC adopted, but which does not seem correct.
9. Cf. Mark 10:19..
10. Eph 1:21.
11. Phil 2:8.

Chapter 25

1. Cf. Matt 3:9.
2. Lat. Iren. has: *Sic enim oportuerat filios Abrahae, quos illi...excitavit Deus, et fecit assistere ei.* Arm. Iren. omitted *oportuerat* and *quos illi.* SC adopted that. But I believe Arm. Iren. did not grasp the Greek underlying *oportuerat,* and so simplified what was a more complicated construction. The Latin, as I translated, makes good sense. One need merely supply *esse* with *oportuerat.* The parentheses as introduced by Harvey are not correct.
3. Rom 4:11, 12, 16.
4. Cf. A.H. 4.5.3–4; 4.7.2; 4.25.1.
5. Eph 2:20.
6. Heb 1:3.

7. Cf. A.H. 3.25.5.

8. Gen 38:28ff.

9. Hemmendinger (312) had suggested that some words fell out here to complete the triple phrase: *paternaliter et legaliter <a iudicibus, et prophetice> a prophetis.* In A.H. 4.20.5 we have the idea: *haec prophetice significabant prophetae,* where it is a question of gathering witnesses from the Prophets and not from the Law section of the Old Testament. The division of the Old Testament into Patriarchs, Law, and Prophets was current for Irenaeus. In A.H. 4.20.4, we have a trinitarian process of salvation expressed by three adverbs: *prophetice, adoptive, paternaliter.* That is not the same as in our passage, where the triple adverb would refer to chronological stages. However, I might add that in A.H. 5.21.2 *legaliter* refers to Christ's refuting Satan by quoting from the Law (Deut 8:3). Now since Moses was considered a prophet by Irenaeus, maybe *legaliter a Prophetis* does make sense, and the Latin would be good as it is in the MSS.

10. John 4:37.

11. Cf. Isa 55:10; 2 Cor 9:10.

12. 1 Cor 3:7.

13. Jer 9:2.

14. John 4:36.

Chapter 26

1. Of course, this is a central theme in A.H., which we have discussed at length. For Irenaeus, all the Scriptures—from the Old Covenant and the New—refer to Christ.

2. Matt 1:44, 38.

3. I followed the Greek fragment, which differs from Lat. Iren. It is in keeping with the following where Irenaeus clearly states that the prophecy before its fulfillment is an enigma. Hence the negative is needed. Yet the Latin could be a rhetorical question, demanding a negative answer; it would then have the same meaning as the Greek.

4. Dan 12:4, 7 (Theodotion).

5. Cf. Jer 23:20.

6. Matt 13:44.

7. Dan 12:3 (Theodotion). *A multis iustis* is a slavish rendering of the Greek partitive phrase, used as subject.

8. Cf. Luke 24:26, 46.

9. Matt 13:52. Irenaeus also quotes this passage at A.H. 4.9.1.

10. Cf. A.H. 3.3.2.

11. See Bacq 202n2 on the phrase "certain charism of the Truth" and the scholarly debate on whether this applies just to the bishops or to the Church as a whole.

12. This passage, which speaks of the entire episcopate, is very similar to that in A.H. 3.3.2, which speaks of the Roman episcopate. For a full discussion of this see A.H. 3, 126n3. *Loco* (supposing *topoi* of the Lat. MSS) is surely a faulty reading for *modo tropoi,* as is clear from Arm. Iren. and from the parallel in A.H. 3.3.2.

13. Lev 10:1–2.

14. Num 16:33.

15. 1 Kgs 14:10ff. An emphatic statement on the unity of the true Church.

16. "Pride of principal succession" would be the Lat. Iren. with *successionis.* It would be the apostolic succession of the bishops; but that would make no sense here, because the heretics did not pride themselves in that at all. So Arm. Iren. comes to our aid with "the pride of priority seating" (*consessionis*).

17. Dan 13:20.

18. Isa 11:3.

19. Dan 13:56, 52–53; Exod 23:7.

20. Matt 24:48–51; Luke 12:45–46. Irenaeus's variants from the accepted text of the Bible are found in some minor MSS of the Bible.

21. *Doctrina* of Lat. Iren. supposes διδαχὴν; but Arm. Iren. has "succession," supposing διαδοχὴν. SC adopts Arm. Iren., as a remarkable parallel to 4.26.5. But that parallelism is not so remarkable, except in favor of *doctrina.* Irenaeus does not speak of guarding succession, but he does speak of guarding doctrine and faith, and he has both of these concepts in this paragraph.

22. Num 16:15.

23. 1 Sam. 12:2–5.

24. 2 Cor 2:17; 7:2.

25. Isa 60:17 LXX.

26. Matt 24:45–46.

27. 1 Cor 12:28.

28. Cf. Titus 2:8. Irenaeus wishes to say that the authentic bishops are found in the Church only; cf. 4.26.2; 3.3.2.

Chapter 27

1. The scholarly literature on Irenaeus has spent a great deal of time discussing the Presbyter in the A.H. See Charles E. Hill, *From the Lost Teaching of Polycarp: Identifying Irenaeus' Apostolic Presbyter and the Author of Ad Diognetum,* Wissenschaftliche Untersuchungen zum Neuen Testament (Tübingen: Mohr Siebeck, 2006). Followed by John Behr, *Irenaeus of Lyons: Identifying Christianity* (Oxford: Oxford University Press, 2013). See also Bacq 205–7. Lat. Iren. has: *Presbyter cui audierat ab his qui apostolos viderant, et ab his qui didicerant.* He himself did not hear the apostles, but he learned from those who had seen them and who had learned from them. Now, are these one group of disciples who both saw and learned from the apostles; or were there two groups, one who saw the apostles, the other who learned from those who saw the apostles? Irenaeus actually knew of two kinds of disciples: those, like Mark and Luke, who saw the apostles (cf. A.H. 3.10.1; 3.1.1; 1.101; 3.12.3; 15.3); and those who lived in the postapostolic age, the presbyters to a great extent, who also had special authority to teach (cf. A.H. 5.5.1; 36.1). Arm. Iren. has the Presbyter seeing the apostles, as I translated; but he also learned from the later disciples. Polycarp was such a disciple. Adolf von Harnack, *Der Presbyter-Prediger des Irenäus : IV, 27,1–32,1 ; Bruchstücke und Nachklänge der ältesten exegetisch-polemischen Homilieen* (Berlin: Trowitzsch, 1907), 138, claims that this section of chaps. 27—32 was the Presbyter's discourse. W. Bousset, *Judisch-christlicher*

Schulbetrieb in Alexandria und Rom: Literarische Untersuchungen Neuen Testaments, N.F. 6 (Göttingen: Vandenhoeck & Ruprecht, 1915), 273, thinks Irenaeus indicates (e.g., 4.32 at the end: *si scripturas diligenter legerit*) that he had not merely a discourse of the Presbyter but a treatise on messianic prophecies.

2. Cf. Acts 10:34.
3. 1 Sam 18ff.
4. 2 Sam 11:27.
5. 2 Sam 12:1–7.
6. 2 Sam 2:13; Ps 50.
7. Cf. 1 Kgs 3:5, 28; 4:29–34. Lat. Iren. has *enarraret sapientiam,* which should have been *peteret,* as in Arm. Iren.
8. 1 Kgs 5–6, and 8.
9. Cf. 1 Kgs 8:15–53, 55–61.
10. Ps 71 (72):7–8.
11. 1 Kgs 4:32.
12. 1 Kgs 4:33.
13. 1 Kgs 8:27.
14. 1 Kgs 4:34.
15. 1 Kgs 10:1–10.
16. Matt 12:42.
17. 1 Kgs 11:1, 4, 6, 9.
18. 1 Cor 1:29. The words are Paul's not the Presbyter's.
19. 1 Peter 3:19–20.
20. Rom 3:23.
21. 1 Cor 10:11; 1 Pet 4.7.
22. Rom 6:9.
23. Matt 24:30; 25:31.
24. Matt 25:14–30; Luke 19:12–27; 12:48.
25. Cf. Heb 6:4–6.
26. Rom 11:21, 17.
27. 1 Cor 10:1–12. The quotations are from Exod 13:21; 14:19–22; Num 14:16; 25:1–9; 21:5; 14:2, 36.
28. 1 Cor 10:5; cf. Ps 94 (95):7b–11, and Heb 3:7–18.
29. Matt 22:14. Cf. A.H. 4.15.2.
30. 1 Cor 10:8–10.
31. Matt 25:41.
32. 1 Cor 6:9–10. Cf. A.H. 4.22.1; 4.27.1; 4.37.4.
33. 1 Cor 6:11.
34. Cf. Matt 18:8–9.
35. 1 Cor 5:11.
36. Eph 5:6–7.
37. 1 Cor 5:6.
38. Rom 1:18.
39. Exod 14:28.
40. Luke 18:7–8.
41. 2 Thess. 1:6–10. Cf. A.H. 4.33.11.
42. 2 Thess. 1:9 *a facie Domini* has usually been interpreted as if the punishment would consist in being *separated from* the face of the Lord. As SC points out (755n1), Irenaeus interprets Paul by Ps 33:17 (A.H. 4.28.1), in the

sense that the source of this punishment, God's anger, will be the face of the Lord. Irenaeus must have taken *a facie* in that sense also here. I indicated that by inserting "coming" into the text of RSV.

Chapter 28

1. Rom 1:18; 2 Thess. 1:9.
2. Ps 33 (34):17.
3. Cf. Mark 5:19.
4. Luke 6:49.
5. Matt 26:24.
6. Matt 10:15; Luke 10:12. Cf. A.H. 4.33.11
7. Cf. Matt 15:19; 12:36; Eph 5:4.
8. Not as if it was not eternal under the Old Covenant, but that in the New Covenant, after rejecting Christ, there is no new era of repentance. Cf. Heb 10:26–31. SC changed *solum* to *iam* according to Arm. Iren., which I followed. But Hemmerdinger (318) claims *solum* is correct.
9. Matt 25:41.
10. Matt 25:34.
11. Lat. Iren. reads: *exciderunt sibi*, while Arm. Iren. has *nec sciverunt se praedictos*. The Armenian translator did not understand the Greek, which is correct in Latin, that they "went out of their minds." It does not mean that they were unawares, as SC (761n1) thinks.
12. "Forgive," etc. is *demittentem eos quos demittit* in Lat. Iren., for which Arm. Iren. has, erroneously, *perdentem eos quos perdit*. The freeing of the Israelites from Egypt as a figure of the freeing of the Gentiles is also in *Proof* 46.
13. Matt 26:50, 55; John 19:34.
14. Cf. John 15:22; Matt 23:34–35; Rom 11:3.
15. Cf. Acts 12, and passim.
16. Cf. 1 Cor 1:18, 23–35.
17. 2 Cor 2:15–16.
18. Num 14:30.
19. Matt 2. Arm. Iren. has the bracket addition, which SC accepted with the remark that there is something missing in Latin. Rather, the Latin does read well without the addition, but it would be difficult to explain how this was added in Arm. if it was not in the Greek already.
20. 1 Cor 14:20. Bacq notes a parallel passage at *Proof* 96. Bacq 211n1.

Chapter 29

1. Exod 9:35.
2. Matt 13:10–16; Luke 8:10; 10.23; from Isa 6:10. This mixture is also in Arm. Iren. Against his usual practice, Irenaeus here does not quote LXX but the Heb. text, through the use of *Testimonies*, it would seem.
3. Cf. A.H. 2.27.2; 4.6.5; 4.39.3; 5.13.2; 5.27.2.
4. In A.H. 3.7.1, we have the same interpretation.
5. 2 Cor 4:4.

6. Rom 1:28.
7. 2 Thess 2:11–12.
8. Exod 3:19.
9. The Finger of God is the Word.

Chapter 30

1. The theme of the "spoils of the Egyptians" is common in early Christian writings. It becomes a metaphor for early Christian authors to borrow the learning of the Greek and Romans—philosophy, rhetoric, and so forth.—for the proclamation of Christian truth.

2. Luke 16:9.

3. Even some of the royal family were Christians at this time. That has been the usual interpretation of this clause by scholars of all persuasions. But G. Clarke, "Notes and Observations: Iren. A.H. 4.30.1," *HTR* 59 (1966): 95–97, thinks the reasoning is not convincing. *In regali aula* need not mean the Roman court. In his letter to Florinus, who need not have been more than a local functionary, Irenaeus speaks of Florinus's having been in the imperial court, which was simply the governor's court in Asia Minor. True, but Irenaeus is writing Book 4 in Lyons and would more likely have in mind the Roman Court, from which also the persecutions of the Lyonese people had issued. See A.H. 1, Introd., p. 4, on the date of Book 4.

4. Exod 1:13–14.

5. Exod 1:11.

6. The long protasis in Lat. Iren. was taken as an independent question by Harvey. But ANF and BKV read it as I did in the translation. In the Latin, the Jewish people are the *populo*, who are accused of taking a few things, while the Egyptians do not blame themselves for ungratefulness to the ancient Jews. Arm. Iren. has the Jews accuse the Egyptians, as the *populus*, for getting so little, but do not blame themselves for ingratitude toward the pagan nations to whom they owe so much. SC follows that and appeals to 4.30.1 for the same idea, with the remark that the Latin does not fit the context.

7. There seems to have been a period of peace in the Roman Empire when this was written. See A.H.1, Introd., p. 4.

8. Matt 7:5.

9. The Israelites are a type of the Christians.

10. Matt 7:1–2.

11. Luke 3:11.

12. Matt 25:35–36.

13. Matt 6:3. Cf. A.H. 4.13.3.

14. Luke 16:9. Cf. A.H. 4.18.6; 5.35.2.

15. Cf. Rev 15–16. Cf. A.H. 5.35.2.

Chapter 31

1. Cf. Gen 9:25.
2. Matt 10:24.

3. The advice of the Presbyter is very edifying.
4. Gen 19:26.
5. Gen 10:33, 35.
6. Gen 19:31–32.
7. Other churchmen are on record for having excused the daughters.
8. Deut 32:6.
9. Matt 11:19.
10. Ps 3:6.
11. Jer 21:26, LXX 38.
12. Matt 5:13. A. Orbe, "Ecclesia, sal terrae, según san Ireneo," *RSR* 60 (1972): 219–40, discusses the source of this symbolic application as possibly having been a Jewish Haggadic interpretation made after the Barkocheba War, which the Jewish Christians later adapted, as did also some of the so-called Gnostics. See also A.H. 4.10.2
13. Cf. 1 Tim 3:15; Eph 4:29.

Chapter 32

1. "By someone else" is *ab* as an independent agent; e.g., Demiurge; "through someone else" is *per*, as an instrument of God, e.g., the angels. That is a demonstration of Irenaean precision.
2. Lat. Iren. has: *ne victi salvari periclitentur.* I accept SC's observation that in Greek κινδυνεύσωσιν takes the object σωθῆναι. The reason for the danger to their salvation is rather simple. Their salvation comes through *gnosis*; so if their theory is refuted, their whole system falls, and they cannot talk about salvation.
3. "Believes," according to Lat. Iren. (*credat*). Arm. Iren. has *teneat,* which SC adopts. This stresses the contrast better to *transmoveatur a factore*; and *tenens caput* is in the Pauline quote. But *credat* fits too, and I see no need to depart from it.
4. Gen 1:3. God's *saying* was the means of creating through the Word.
5. John 1:3.
6. Eph 4:5–6.
7. Col 2:19.
8. Eph 4:16.
9. Lat. Iren. has *ei,* namely, it is consistent for him. Arm. Iren., which SC (799n3), again accepts has "every word *of his* will be consistent." But see a parallel to the dative again in A.H. 4.33.7: *omnia enim ei constant.*
10. Cf. A.H. 3.3.2; 4.26.1, 4, 5. Here there is question of episcopal teaching.
11. This sentence is poorly phrased in Lat. Iren. and in Arm. If in Latin the *qui* clause is read with *hominum,* that is, before the parenthetical clause *secundum quod Testamenta dabantur,* all reads well.
12. Cf. Book 3, especially cc. 9–15.

Chapter 33

1. 1 Cor 2:15. See Scott D. Moringiello, "The Pneumatikos as Scriptural Interpreter: Irenaeus on 1 Cor 2:15," *Studia Patristica* 65 (2013): 105–18. Bacq 218–26.

2. Rom 1:25, 28. Cf. A.H. 2.9.1; 2.27.2; 4.6.6.

3. Cf. A.H. 4.2.6; 4.7.4; 4.12.4; 4.18.4.

4. Isa 53:3; 1 Pet 3:23–24.

5. Zach 9:9.

6. Ps 117 (118):22; 1 Pet 3:7.

7. Isa 53:7; cf. 1 Pet 2:19.

8. Exod 17:11.

9. Isa 11:12.

10. 1 Pet 4:19. Cf. A.H. 3.20.4, for the noncanonical writing; also A.H. 1 Introd., pp. 8–10.

11. Dan 7:13; Matt 27:64.

12. Mal 4:1.

13. Isa 11:4; cf. 2 Thess 2:8.

14. Matt 3:12; Luke 3:17. Bacq 219n1 notes the echoes to this type of argument in Justin *Dial.* 1.8; 32.1–2; 49.2; 53.1–3; 86.1; 110.2; 120.4 and Tertullian *Adv Iud.* 14.1–19.

15. Cf. A.H. 1.27.2–4.

16. Matt 26:27; Mark 14.22; Luke 22:19; 1 Cor 11:23–24. Irenaeus certainly holds the real presence of Jesus in the Eucharist. Even his opponents admitted that, but quite inconsistently, since they denied the reality of Christ's body.

17. Matt 26:24, 64, and parallels.

18. Cf. John 20:23; Matt 9:6.

19. Matt 28; Mark 16; Luke 24; John 20–21. Cf. Tertullian, *De Carne Christi* 5 (CCL 2.880–83); and passim in *Adv. Marcionem* (CCL 1.441ff.).

20. Cf. A.H. 1.1–8.

21. Cf. A.H. 1.12.3, where the Greek is extant for *obstetricasse*, and it means first to deliver a child as by a midwife, and second, of a mother herself delivering her child. The first meaning applies here. SC (811n1) thinks it is wrong to take this in the sense that Irenaeus's opponents claimed the profession for themselves. Yet, Irenaeus ironically attributes that to them because they seem to know so much about the emissions from the conjugal couples. They never claimed to have been mothers in confinement either.

22. *Iliad* 9.312–313 (Loeb 1.404).

23. Here Irenaeus seems to be referring to a specific school, not to his opponents generally.

24. For the other places in which Irenaeus discusses Simon, see A.H. 1.23.1–2; 1.27.4; 2.P.1.; 2.9.2.

25. Cf. A.H. 1.26.2. Irenaeus is the first to use the word *Ebionites.* See Bacq 220n1.

26. Ps 73 (74):12.

27. Lat. Iren. would make good sense if one were to suppose a verb like *transeat* (from the preceding phrase) before *in novam generationem*, as older

authors tried to correct the text. However, Arm. Iren. has *regeneratur* in place of *regenerationem*; as also *relinquent* for *relinquet*. That makes very good sense. A detailed treatment of this passage can be found in Unger, *ME* 3–108. I shall give a summary of that. The context is this: The Ebionites will be judged because they deny the virginal conception of Jesus, and so deny the reality of his human nature, and so deny the possibility of salvation. To escape from death, incurred by the first generation from Adam, one must believe in the new generation, that is, the virginal generation of Jesus. The Virgin in question is certainly Mary the Mother of Emmanuel. It is not the Church alone, as some have held, nor even the Church together with Mary. Since the incarnation of God's Son from the Virgin was necessary for salvation, according to Irenaeus, Mary's faith-filled consent to be the Mother of Jesus indirectly makes her the mother also of all who would be saved by faith in Jesus. The older opinions, based on the Lat. Iren., which held that Mary is *directly* involved here as spiritual mother of all believers, is not tenable. This is, of course, not the only passage of Irenaeus for Mary's spiritual motherhood. On the soteriological value of the incarnation by uniting humanity to God, but not being fully achieved except through the Pasch, especially the resurrection, see Jossua 122–40; 271–72. Union with God through the incarnation is a rebirth that makes humanity like to God. That is Irenaeus's way of saying that humanity is divinized, a term he does not use although it is frequent among the Greek writers. See Lawson, 154–63. For the relationship between the divine and the human natures in Christ, indicated in our present passage, see Wingren, especially 110–12.

28. Matt 12:41–42.

29. Matt 22:43; Ps 109 (110):1.

30. Matt 22:24; Luke 11:21–22.

31. Cf. A.H. 3.16.6, 7; 18.1–2; 5.1.3, where the bishop speaks still more clearly: humanity was created to the image of Christ, who would become incarnate. Definitely Christ was in God's plan before Adam was. See Unger, FS 6–9.

32. Here Irenaeus refers to the so-called Docetists, who believed that Jesus Christ was not truly a human being. See A.H. 1, 164n6, 185n9, and 252n6.

33. "Parade" is according to *perferant*, the reading preferred by Massuet, according to the C and V and Q MSS. Earlier editions had *proferant*, which agrees with Arm. Iren. and was accepted by SC. Grabe, guided by the abbreviation in the A MS, thought it should be *praeferant*. Already Ignatius of Antioch said of the Docetists: "Surely if those things were done by our Lord as a mere make-believe, then I in my chains, too, am a make-believe" (ACW 1.917).

34. This is a grand expression of the Mystical Body, especially of its unity. The phrase "the great and glorious Body of Christ" was used by Pius XII in his encyclical letter on the Mystical Body (n.100). For more on the Body of Christ in Irenaeus see Wingren 159–70, but also 147–59 as a preliminary.

35. Matt 23:24.

36. This equation between Truth and the Church is excellent. It is true because only the Church has the whole Truth. Cf. A.H. 3.24.1.

37. 1 Cor 8:6.

38. 1 Cor 8:6.

39. 1 Tim. 2:4.

40. Cf. John 1:14. I followed the Greek. Lat. Iren. has: "He was present with the human race."

41. Irenaeus stresses the antiquity of the Church along with the apostolicity and the catholicity. He contrasts the consistent doctrine of the apostles with the inconsistent doctrine of his opponents. See A.H. 2.19.8; 3.22.1; 4.12.5; 5.19.2.

42. This important passage on the Church and its doctrinal authority is difficult to translate accurately, though substantially the meaning is certain. To follow the discussion more easily it will be good to see the Latin text before us:

> Agnitio vera est apostolorum doctrina, et antiquus Ecclesiae status in universo mundo, et character corporis Christi secundum successiones episcoporum, quibus illi eam quae in unoquoque loco est Ecclesiam tradiderunt, quae pervenit usque ad nos.
>
> Custoditio [or, custodita] sine fictione, Scripturarum, plenissima tractatio, neque additamentum neque ablationem recipiens, et lectio sine falsatione, et secundum Scripturas expositio legitima et diligens et sine periculo et sine blasphemia; et praecipuum dilectionis munus, quod est....

Now, as must be apparent, this sentence is rather oddly structured; but because of scribal errors in handing down the text some points are doubtful.

Tractatio should be nominative. Only one MS (Arundel) has the ablative; obviously the scribe tried to make sense out of the whole clause since he read *custodita.* The really troublesome reading is *custoditio* or *custodita. Custodita* is presented by Arundel, Salamanca MSS, and Erasmus, which Harvey adopted. Vatican MS alone has *custoditio,* which could be a corruption of either the noun or the feminine participle. The Clermont and Voss MSS and Feuardent (accepted by Massuet) have *custoditione,* which is the closest to *custoditio,* witnessed to by the Lone Mercier II MS, but the Arm. Iren. agrees with it, and SC accepted it. So from the MSS evidence alone the matter remains doubtful. Grammatically a variety of constructions are possible. If *custoditio* is correct, it is the first of four nouns explaining *agnitio*; *tractatio,* since it is not joined by a conjunction, must be in apposition to it. *Sine fictione* is an adjective in Arm. Iren, and quite certainly was also in Greek. To catch the effect of the adjective I shall use *non-ficta* here. Since it is an adjective, the genitive *Scripturarum* cannot be immediately dependent on it, as if the Scriptures were somehow made fictional. In Irenaeus's explanations the fictitious element always exists separately from the Scriptures, and these are joined to it by Irenaeus's opponents. So we cannot read *sine fictione* directly with Scripture. Hence, Irenaeus could have meant it to read: *custoditio* [*nempe*] *plenissima Scripturarum tractatio non-ficta.* But I doubt that he would call the *tractatio* (account or course) nonfictional. One could read also: *custoditio non-ficta,* [*nempe*] *plenissima Scripturarum tractatio. Scripturarum* would, of course, be implied with *custoditio.* I followed that arrangement. One could also read: *custoditio Scripturarum non-ficta,* [*nempe*] *plenissima tractatio.* It seems SC followed this way. Hemmerdinger (319) objects to SC's comma after *Scripturarum* and so seems to agree with my reading.

If *custodita* is the correct reading, it could follow *quae-agnitio* and end the sentence after *usque ad nos.* But that is not so likely, because when Irenaeus uses that phrase it is not modified by a participle: *pervenit usque ad nos* (3.3.3); *permanente apud nos* (3.5.1). And so, if *custodita* is correct, it most likely began a new clause and modified *tractatio.* In that case *non-ficta* could modify only *tractatio.*

As far as the word usage is concerned, Irenaeus does not use *custoditio,* but he has *conservatio* in 4.31.2, where Arm. Iren. has the same word as it does in our passage. So both Latin words must stand for the same Greek word, and it is quite possible that he used a noun here. Most frequently he uses a verbal construction for this safeguarding, either in the active or passive voice. Since in our passage it would be passive, I note that the present *custoditur* is used in A.H. 3.2.1 for the guarding of tradition; the past participle *conservata* in A.H. 3.3.2 also for guarding tradition; *custodita* itself is used in A.H. 5 Prf. for the guarding of faith. So, whether the noun or the participle was original, both have substantially the same meaning here. For the rest, this passage puts into relief again the apostolicity of the Church and its doctrine, as well as the catholicity.

43. Cf. 2 Cor 8:1; 1 Cor 13.

44. Irenaeus here develops the need of martyrs in the Church to testify to her holiness. Then, as now, only the true Church boasts of many, many martyrs. See also A.H. 3.18.5; 4.31.3.

45. Matt 5:10. The Arm. Iren. *amputata* perhaps expresses more exactly than the Lat. Iren. *debilitata,* the idea of the Church diminishing by people martyred but increased by new members.

46. Gen 19:26; cf. above 4.31.1, 2. Other church Fathers, too, have this idea; cf. Justin, *Dialogus* 110, 4 (MG 6.729); Tertullian, *Adv. Scapulam* 5.4 (CCL 2.1132).

47. Matt 5:12.

48. Cf. 1 Pet 4:14. The reading is not clear, but the sense remains practically the same. Lat. Iren. has *idem Spiritus requiescens,* with which Arm. Iren. agrees. Hemmerdinger 319 explains it as a nounal phrase that is normal in Greek. Doutreleau, "*A propos d' Irénée, Adv. haer., livre IV,*" 592 considers it corrupt and changed it in SC to *eodem spiritu requiescente,* getting a hint for this from the Salamanca MS: *eo idem spiritu requiescente.*

49. Cf. Matt 23:34, 35, 39.

50. So the "body of Christ" existed somehow already in the Old Testament times, just as the Church did.

51. "Performed in advance" is for *praeformabant* of the Clermont MS, which is backed partially by *reformabant* of the Voss MS. SC chose *prophetabant,* seemingly according to Arm. Iren. But in the context, Prophets fulfilled the economies by their actions, which favors *praeformabant.*

52. Isa 6:1–4; Ps 109:1; Cf. John 12:41. Irenaeus cites this psalm numerous times. See A.H. 2.28.7; 3.6.1; 3.10.6; 3.12.2; 3.16.3; *Proof* 49 and 85.

53. Dan 7:13; Matt 24:30; 26:64.

54. Zach 12:10; John 10:37.

55. Luke 18:8.

56. 2 Thess 1:6–8.

57. Cf. Ps 49 (50):6; Mal 4:1.

58. Matt 3:12; Luke 3:17.

59. Matt 25:41.

60. 2 Thess 1:9–10.

61. Ps 44 (45):2, 7, 3, 4. Irenaeus cites this psalm at A.H. 3.6.1 and *Proof* 47.

62. Jer 17:9 (LXX).

63. Isa 8:3; 9:6.

64. Isa 7:14.

65. This text was studied in great detail in Unger, *ME* 108–20. See also the work of A. J. de Aldama, *Maria en la patrística de los siglos I y II* (Madrid: La Editorial Católica, 1970), 218–22. To give the highlights, since the word *purus,* is used as an adjective three times and as an adverb once, we should note that it means something is intact and/or unblemished. That is the consistent meaning throughout the works of Irenaeus. Three things are said here: The Son of God, become Son of Man, who was himself pure, opened the pure womb in a pure manner; second, that womb regenerates men unto God; third, God's Son had made that womb pure. Now, who is this woman? It can be no other than the Virgin Mother of the Emmanuel spoken of in the immediate context. A. Müller, *Ecclesia-Maria. Die Einheit Marias und der Kirche,* 2nd rev. ed., *Paradosis* 5 (Freiburg: Universitätsverlag, 1955), 63–75, made a special effort to show that this woman is Mary and the Church, but unconvincingly. God's Son is pure, namely, intact and unblemished in his eternal generation. Mary's womb is pure, too, namely, it is intact and unblemished. Her Son opened that womb. This is a scriptural term that simply expresses the birth of the firstborn of a woman. In its original use it meant, of course, that the mother was no longer a virgin; but in its later usage it could be said of even Mary as ever Virgin (see Luke 2:23). Irenaeus adds that Christ opened that womb in a pure manner (*pure*), namely, Mary remained intact. This is then an explicit reference to Mary's giving birth in a virginal manner. Aldama holds that *pure* does not modify *eperiens,* but *puram.* I am not convinced of the sense of that here. Yet, Aldama holds that Irenaeus teaches the virginal birth of Jesus.

The third point the Bishop makes is that God's Son made Mary's womb pure, that is, intact and unblemished. One can be said to make something intact even though it was never impure. Besides, there is nothing here that would prevent one from referring this to Mary's own conception as innocent and pure. And now the second point: that pure woman regenerates men unto God. Since Mary is the woman, she is thus our spiritual mother. She regenerates us in a virginal manner at the same time that she generates God's Son. This is clear and certain. One cannot reject this on the score that the spiritual motherhood of Mary was not known then. The answer is simple: Irenaeus does know of it, here and in other passages, and he teaches it. See other passages in Book 3 and in Book 5.

66. Isa 53:8.

67. Joel 3:16; Amos 1:2.

68. Ps 75 (76):2.

69. Hab 3:3.

70. Cf. A.H. 3.20.4.

71. Also Matt 2:6; Mic 5:2.

72. Isa 35:5, 6, 3.
73. Isa 26:19.
74. Isa 53:4.
75. As we have seen many times, Irenaeus believes that the Prophets of the old covenant speak with the voice of Christ.
76. Isa 53:2–4.
77. Zach 9:9.
78. Cf. Isa 53:6–7.
79. Ps 68 (69):22.
80. Isa 37:12.
81. Isa 65:2.
82. Cf. Ps 21:8, 16, 19.
83. See SC (829n1).
84. Amos 8:9–10.
85. Cf. Matt 27:45.
86. Jer 15:9.
87. Cf. Ps 3:6.
88. Cf. Ps 23:7.
89. Ps 18:7.
90. Ps 98:1.
91. Cf. 2 Thess 1:7.
92. Matt 24:21.
93. Isa 50:9.
94. Isa 2:7.
95. Cf. Ps 8:7; Heb 2:8.
96. Jer 31:31–32.
97. Ezek 36:26.
98. Isa 43:19–21.
99. Matt 9:17.
100. Cf. Rom 3:22.
101. Cf. John 7:37–39.
102. Lat. Iren. has *per tantem serie Scripturae,* and Arm. Iren. does not. The Latin makes good sense here.
103. Lat. Iren. has *a conditione* while Arm. Iren has *a genesi.*
104. Rom 2:5.
105. 1 Cor 2:15.

Chapter 34

1. 1 Pet 1:12. Cf. A.H. 4.11.3.
2. Matt 5:17–18. Cf. A.H. 4.2.6; 4.8.2; 4.13.1; 34.13.3.
3. Rom 1:17.
4. Hab 2:4.
5. See also A.H. 3.10.5; 3.12.14; 4.16.5; 4.33.14 on Irenaeus's discussion of the new covenant of liberty.
6. Isa 2:3–4; Mic 4:2–3.
7. Matt 5:39.
8. John 4:37.

9. "Form" here translates *habitu.* Perhaps Irenaeus is making a reference to Phil 2:7.

10. Isa 57.1.

11. Here Irenaeus is likely drawing on themes in Paul's letters (cf. 1 Cor, Col). Of course, in doing this he directly takes on Marcion, who argues that Paul obviated the need for the old covenant.

Chapter 35

1. For Irenaeus's discussion of the Valentinians see A.H. 1.1–8.
2. 1 John 4:6.
3. Luke 5:36–37.
4. Of course, Irenaeus here distinguishes between the false god his opponents proclaim and the true Lord that he, following Jesus and the apostles, teaches.
5. Bacq notes that this is the first time in the text that Irenaeus uses the term "rule of truth." It also appears at A.H. 4.26.5; 4.33.7–9; 4.33.13. Bacq 231n1.

Chapter 36

1. For the organization of the text, see the Introduction.
2. Matt 21:33–41. For another place where Irenaeus connects a discussion of the vine with the Spirit, see A.H. 4.33.14 and 5.1.3. And for other places where Irenaeus connects the Holy Spirit with the end times, see A.H. 3.17.2–3; 4.33.15; *Proof* 89.
3. Matt 21:42–44; Ps 117:22–23.
4. Rom 1:30.
5. Matt 5:22.
6. Of course, there are numerous passages where this is written.
7. Jer 7:3.
8. Zech 7:9–10.
9. Zech 8:17.
10. Isa 1:16–18.
11. Ps 33:14–15.
12. Matt 21:37.
13. Arm. Iren has "Spirit of God."
14. Jer 7:29–30.
15. Jer 6:17–18.
16. Luke 21:34–35.
17. Luke 12:35–36.
18. Luke 17:26; Matt 24:37–39.
19. Matt 24:42.
20. Cf. Gen 11.
21. Cf. Gen 19.
22. Matt 10:15; Luke 10:12.
23. Matt 11:23–24.

24. John 4:14.
25. Cf. Matt 21:19.
26. Cf. Gen 6:2–4.
27. 2 Thess 1:5.
28. Matt 3:10; 7:19; Luke 3:9.
29. The variant Latin reading here has "believed" (*credebant*) his doctrine.
30. Cf. Luke 12:48.
31. Matt 22:1–14.
32. Matt 5:35. Cf. A.H. 3.5.1; 4.2.5.
33. Jer 35:15.
34. Jer 7:25.
35. Reading *Dominus* rather than *Deus.*
36. Cf. Isa 11:2.
37. 2 Cor 5:4.
38. Matt 22:13.
39. Bacq notes Irenaeus's connection of the wedding garment with the works of justice. Cf. 4.36.6. Bacq 248n2.
40. 1 Cor 10:5.
41. Matt 22:14.
42. John 5:14.
43. Matt 22:7.
44. Ps 23:1.
45. Rom 13:1–7. Cf. A.H. 5.24.1.
46. Matt 5:45. Cf. A.H. 2.22.2; 3.25.4; 4.13.3; 4.36.6; 5.2.2; 5.27.1.
47. Cf. A.H. 3.11.8; 4.14.2.
48. Luke 15:11.
49. Matt 20:10.
50. Cf. A.H. 3.17.3.
51. This is likely a reference to the parable of the Workers in the Vineyard. See Matt 20:1–16. The translation here prefers the original Greek ἀποκατέστησεν to the Latin *repraesentavit.* In the later patristic tradition, ἀποκατέστησεν has salvific connotations.
52. Luke 18:10–14.
53. Cf. Matt 21:28–32.
54. Ps 115:2.
55. Rom 7:18.
56. Luke 13:6.
57. Luke 13:34–35; Matt 23:37–38.
58. Matt 8:11–12. Cf. A.H. 4.8.1; 5.30.4.

Chapter 37

1. Matt 23:37.
2. Lat. Iren. has by God (*a deo*). Arm. Iren has by him (*ab eo*).
3. Bacq argues that the "good counsel" of God is equivalent to the teaching of the Prophets. See Bacq 255n1 and 255n2.
4. We have the original Greek of this sentence from John of Damascus's

Sacra Parallela. There the sentence reads Βία θεῳ οὐ πρόεστιν ἀγαθη δὲ γνώμη πάντοτε συνπαρεστιν αὐτῶι.

5. Reading Arm. Iren here *rationabiles sunt* for Lat. Iren. *etenim angeli rationalibes.*

6. Rom 2:4–5.

7. Rom 2:10. Irenaeus makes a similar argument at *Proof* 8.

8. There is a slight difference here between Lat. Iren. and Arm. Iren. The main point, however, is that Irenaeus stresses that human begins have free will. His opponents, Irenaeus believes, deny that. All goodness, however, comes from God. Irenaeus does not get caught up in debates that would occupy later authors.

9. Irenaeus has discussed this possibility at A.H. 1.6.1–4 and 1.7.5.

10. The Greek here is ἐκλογῆς καὶ ἐπιμονῆς.

11. The Greek here is τοῦ καλοῦ καὶ αγαθοῦ.

12. Matt 5:6.

13. Luke 21:34.

14. Luke 12:35–36.

15. Luke 12:47.

16. Luke 6:46.

17. Luke 12:45–46; Matt 24:48–51.

18. Variant Latin reading has *talia et suae potestates quae liberum hominem ostendunt.* Greek reading is τάυτα τὸ αὐτεξούσιν ἐπιδείκνυσι τοῦ ανθρωποῦ.

19. 1 Cor 6:12.

20. 1 Pet 2:16.

21. Eph 4:25.

22. Eph 4:29.

23. Eph 5:8; Rom 13:13.

24. 1 Cor 6:11.

25. Matt 9:29.

26. Mark 9:23.

27. Matt 8:13.

28. John 3:36.

29. Matt 23:37–38.

30. Here Irenaeus is making an anti-Valentinian argument. See A.H. 1.6.3–4; 1.13.6.

31. See SC (937n1).

32. Matt 11:22.

33. 1 Cor 9:24–27. Irenaeus also discusses this passage at A.H. 4.15.2 and 5.29.1.

34. Cf. A.H. 4.9.2–3; 4.12.2; 4.13.3.

35. Cf. John 15: 9.

36. Jer 2:19.

37. Rom 8:29. Arm. Iren. reads *ad conformis* rather than *ad figuram.* See also A.H. 5.6.1.

38. Irenaeus's point here is that through the economy of salvation, human beings mature into the image of God. The economy of salvation is one long pedagogy to enable human beings to see (that word again) and comprehend God. Cf. A.H. 3.20.1–2; 4.39.1; 5.2.3; 5.3.1; 5.29.1.

Chapter 38

1. The Latin here reads *cum semper sit idem et innatus*. The Greek reads ἀεὶ κατὰ τὰ αὐτὰ ὄντι καὶ αγενητῳ ὑπαάρχοντι. Cf. 4.11.2; 3.8.3.

2. Here Irenaeus echoes a theme found in Paul about human maturity for receiving the Word of God. Cf. 1 Cor 3:2. Cf. A.H. 4.37.6; 4.37.7; 4.38.1; 4.38.2.

3. Eph 1:10.

4. Irenaeus continues the theme from 1 Cor 3:2 here, and now he links Paul's words there to the Eucharist. Irenaeus will quote Paul's passage below.

5. Although it is anachronistic to talk about Irenaeus's trinitarian theology, he certainly sees the work of the Son and the Spirit in human immortality. Cf. A.H. 5.1.1; 3.10.2; 3.16.3; 3.19.1; 3.20.2; 5.36.3.

6. 1 Cor 3:2.

7. 1 Cor 3:3.

8. Acts 8:17–19.

9. Cf. Heb 5:14.

10. SC (951n1) ἀγύμναστα…τὰ αἰσθητήρια. This is an allusion to Heb 5:11–14. Of course, this theme obviously chimes with the theme from 1 Cor 3:2.

11. Here Irenaeus links Christ's work in saving human beings with Christ's humanity. In doing so, he brings together the passages from 1 Cor 3:2 and Heb 5:11–14.

12. Latin has *perseverantia [est] incorruptelae [autem] gloria infecti*. Greek has ὑποταγὴ δὲ θεοῦ ἀφθαρσία καὶ παραμονὴ αφθαρσίας δόξα ἀγενήτον.

13. Gen 1:28.

14. Cf. Gen 1:26.

15. Cf. Gen 2:7.

16. Cf. Gen 1:28.

17. Wis 6:19.

18. Such people are "insatiable and ungrateful" because ultimately they are irrational. See Bacq 264n4.

19. Ps 81:6.

20. Ps 81:7.

21. Cf 2 Cor 5:4; 1 Cor 15:53.

22. Gen 1:26–28.

Chapter 39

1. Bacq notes the importance of the word *experience* (*experimentum/πεῖρα*) in this paragraph and in A.H. 3.20.2; 5.2.3; 5.21.3.

2. As Bacq notes, when Irenaeus discusses repentance, he has the biblical idea that it is a change of one's life. See also 3.5.2; 3.9.1. This is in contrast to his opponents' views, see A.H. 1.31.3; 3.14.4.

3. Irenaeus discusses this theme at *Proof* 14.

4. This is an important theme in Irenaeus. See also A.H. 4.16.4; 4.20.4; 4.20.8; 5.2.3; 5.35.1.

5. See also A.H. 3.16.7; 4.20.7.
6. See also A.H. 2.17.2–3.
7. See also A.H. 5.1.3; 5.16.1–2; 5.36.3.
8. Cf. Exod 25:11. C.f. A.H. 5.12.2.
9. Ps 44:12.
10. Irenaeus continues a theme that we have seen throughout the text, namely, the distinction between God the Creator and created human beings. Cf. A.H. 3.8.3; 4.11.2.
11. Matt 22:3.
12. Matt 3:9.
13. See also A.H. 4.20.5; 4.29.1; 5.27.2.
14. Cf. John 14:2.
15. Irenaeus is keen to stress here that punishment is a result of the choices human beings make. Human beings are free to reject God's light and dwell in darkness if they so choose. Cf. A.H. 5.27.2–28.1.

Chapter 40

1. Matt 25:41.
2. Isa 45:7.
3. Matt 25:32. Cf. A.H. 4.28.2; 5.27.1; 5.28.1.
4. Matt 25:34.
5. For other places where Irenaeus discusses Satan, see A.H. 5.21.1–3; 3.23.7, as well as 3.18.1,2,7; 3.23.1; 5.24.4.
6. Matt 25:41.
7. Matt 13:40–43. Orbe *Parabolas* I. 354–386.
8. Matt 13:28.
9. Lat. Iren. reads *et inimicum illum Deo facere aggressus est.* Greek reads καὶ εχθροποιῆσαι αὑτον πρὸς τὸν θεὸν ἐπεχείρησε.
10. Gen 3:15.
11. Gal 4:4 Cf. A.H. 3.23.7.
12. In Book 3, chaps. 21–22, Irenaeus discusses Jesus's birth from Mary and how it fits into the economy of salvation.

Chapter 41

1. Matt 25:41.
2. Matt 13:38. Cf. A.H. 3.23.3.
3. Ps 33:9. Cf. A.H. 2.2.5; 3.8.3.
4. See SC (985n1).
5. Arm. Iren. has *a deo*, "by God." Lat. Iren. has *ab eo*, "by him."
6. Cf. John 1:12.
7. Cf. Matt 12:50.
8. John 8:41.
9. Isa 1:2.
10. Ps 17:46.
11. Ps 58:3.

12. Matt 23:33.
13. Matt 16:6.
14. Luke 13:32.
15. Ps 49:21. Cf. A.H. 4.4.3; 5.8.2.
16. Jer 5:8.
17. Isa 1:10.
18. Isa 1:16.
19. Matt 25:41; Matt 13:38.

Book Five

Preface

1. "Sent" as in Arm. Iren. This agrees better with *tibi*, and with the parallel cases in 3 Prf. (*misimus tibi*), and 4.P.4 (*transmittens tibi*). There is no need of asking why Lat. Iren. has *editi*. It is most likely just one of his variations. "Exposed" and "refuted" indicate the twofold aim of the entire work, expressed in the longer title with *exposé* and *refutation*. See A.H. 1, Introd., pp. 2–3.

2. About the writings of Irenaeus's opponents, see A.H.1, Introd., pp. 5.

3. "By reasoning that all kinds." Lat. Iren. has *ratio*, that is, reasoning or method of argumentation, which fits very well. Arm. Iren. has *logos*. SC has a long note defending this as better. But if *logos* was the Greek original, then *ratio* is not only a possible but in this context a very good translation. "All kinds" refers to the type of argumentation in Book 2 (from reason) and in Book 3 (from the apostles), and in Book 4 (from the Lord's parables chiefly).

4. "Safeguard it," that is, the doctrine handed down to the Church, an idea that is prominent here. It implies the unerring character of the Church as described in A.H. 3.3.2; 4.26.4, 5. See A.H. 3, Introd., pp. 9–11. That the Church hands down the teaching is a commonplace in Irenaeus: see, e.g., 1.10.2; 3.3.4. "Throughout the whole world" comes close to the term *catholic* since in Greek this was probably καθ'τὸν κοσμόν. See A.H. 1, chap. 10, n2.

5. "Her children"—so the Church is our mother. See A.H.3, Introd., pp. 11–12, and Jossa 202–18.

6. Those three steps represent the three books already sent: Book 2: "having solved all the difficulties"; Book 3: "having explained the doctrines of the Apostles"; Book 4: "having manifested many things which the Lord said and did in parables."

7. In A.H. 1, Introd., pp. 4–6, I indicated from this passage that the reader for whom Irenaeus wrote this work must have been someone in authority, a bishop. And these books were *sent* to him, so he seems not to have been in the immediate vicinity.

8. See Acts 6:4; 20:24.

9. "Make every effort." See A.H. 1.P.3 (*elaboravimus*). Arm. Iren. has *efferentibus*, which is certainly not correct.

10. It is clear here that Irenaeus intends for his readers to know what he has already written in the previous books. As we will see, he will refer to previous books throughout his argument (as he has done before).

11. "Immense love"; cf. Eph. 3:19. The idea of God's becoming man that man might become like God is capital in Irenaeus. It is the summary of his doctrine on recapitulation. It is stressed so much as the purpose of the incarnation that one cannot help but hold that it was in God's original plan to deify man through the Incarnate Son of God. See Unger, FS 9–14, 18–20.

Chapter 1

1. Cf. John 1:14, 18.
2. Rom 11:34.
3. Cf. James 1:22.
4. Cf. 1 John 1:6 and A.H. 5.27.2.
5. Cf. Col 1:16.
6. "A beginning as a creature" as in Lat. Iren., *initium facturae*, a genitive of apposition. This is not an allusion to James 1:18, where the Vulgate has *initium creaturae*, but the Greek is *first-fruits of creatures*. Irenaeus is alluding to what he said in A.H. 4.37–38, namely, that all creatures have a beginning, and are not "un-made," like the Creator. This whole sentence differs in Lat. Iren. and Arm. Iren. For a bird's eye view we print it here, with the omissions of the Arm. Iren. in angular brackets:

Praedestinuti quidem	facturi [autem
ut essemus,	initium facturae accepimus]
qui nondum eramus,	in praecognitis temporibus,
secundum praescientiam Patris	secundum ministrationem Verbi
	[qui est perfectus in omnibus].

From this it should be clear that by omitting the *autem*, Arm. Iren. lost the balance in the acts (verbs), and most likely omitted the rest because the translator did not understand the construction or content. Contrary to SC, the Latin is not at all incomprehensible and is in fact quite balanced, while Arm. Iren. is not. We were predestined *ut essemus*; that was *de facto* realized when we got the *initium facturae*. We who *nondum eramus* got existence "in the times that were foreknown." Just as the predestination was according to God's foreknowledge, so the beginning as creatures was according to the ministration of the Word. All these ideas are thoroughly Irenaean. Arm. Iren. also omitted *qui est perfectus*, but incorrectly, because the *quoniam* phrase needs this phrase, which explains that the Word "is perfect in every respect," because (*quoniam*) he is both "powerful Word and true Man." See A.H. 4.38.3 for a parallel.

7. Cf. Eph 1:5, 11–12; 1 Pet 1:2. In Irenaeus's theology the incarnation was needed for bringing the knowledge of God to man because God had planned it so. See A.H. 4, chap. 5, n7.

8. "Rationally" is in Lat. Iren. *rationabiliter*, which must have been *logikos* in Greek, with a nice play on *Logos*. SC (19n2) argues strongly for this play on words and contends that, besides meaning "rationally," it also means "in a way befitting the Word." Yet the deliberate play on words does not necessarily mean

that *logikos* here alludes directly to *Logos*. That meaning must be got from the context, in which Irenaeus shows that the Word redeemed.

9. Cf. Col 1:14.

10. 1 Tim 2:6; Matt 20:28. We call attention to Irenaeus's expression here of Pauline redemption; see A.H. 4 chap. 5, n25.

11. Lat. Iren. has *Dei omnipotentis*. That adjective is not superfluous, as SC thinks. *Potens* with *Verbum* shortly later is there for a different reason: the Word, because it was *potens*, was able to redeem us from the devil justly, while God is designated as "all-powerful" because of his creating us.

12. On man's not being coerced by God see A.H. 4.37.

13. Cf. Matt 20:28; Clement, *Epistola* 1.49.6 (ACW 1.39–40), has the same words.

14. Lat. Iren. has *per*, which is certainly correct against the *propter* of Arm. Iren. *Per* is contained by the parallel idea in A.H. 5.14.3. The Bishop has a fine combination of incarnational and redemptive salvation. Jossua (especially 63–72) correctly holds that for Irenaeus the incarnation is soteriological and that the salvation is incarnational. Salvation is begun by the incarnation but it reaches its climax only in the Pasch and in our sharing in the Pasch through the resurrection. Likewise he insists that the Savior's actions were theandric (89–92; 95–97), in other words, the Savior had to be God and man. As Wingren asserts (89), to discard the humanity of Christ would mean a simultaneous loss of the divinity. For salvation as communion with God see González (25–42).

15. "Spirit-God": This is not the third Person, but God who is spirit. Cf. *Proof* 71: "Christ being the spirit of God." In A.H. 2.13.3; 28.4, Irenaeus argues that God is "total spirit." Orbe 1:83–84.

16. Orbe 1:84–85.

17. Cf. A.H. 1.25.1; 26.1.

18. Throughout this section Irenaeus is proving the reality of Christ's human nature, taken from the Virgin Mary on the supposition that the redemption was real, because otherwise we were not really redeemed. See also *Proof* 32.

19. "Salvation" as in Lat. Iren. The Greek excerpt and Arm. Iren. has "life." SC (25n1) thinks this fits better with "exclude," which in Greek takes the genitive: "exclude life from the flesh." True, in A.H. 5.12.1 Lat. Iren. also has *expulit ab eo vitam*; but Arm. Iren. translated that inexactly by "expelled his life." But in our passage there is a parallel construction between *excludant salutem carnis* and *reprobant plasmationem Dei*. *Carnis* could have been a genitive of separation in Greek, which Lat. Iren. translated literally. Besides, the whole context is about the possibility of salvation for the flesh, which Irenaeus's opponents deny. If the Greek actually had ζωή, it is difficult to see how Lat. Iren. got σωτερία. Greek excerpts are often inaccurate.

20. Cf. 1 Cor. 5:7. For this old birth see a different expression in A.H. 4.33.4.

21. "Refuse" in Lat. Iren. *non volentes*. Though MS has *valentes*, which agrees with Arm. Iren., SC (25n3) rightly notes that Arm. Iren could as easily have misread the original as V misread *valentes* for *volentes*. *Non volentes* gets support also from A.H. 5:13:2; 4:33:1; 5:1:3.

22. Luke 1:35.

23. "A new birth," not "the new birth." This new birth is not only the incarnation; it includes also baptism, through which, together with the incarnation, we receive new life.

24. Lat. Iren. reads: *Reprobant itaque hi commixtionem vini coelestis et solam aquam saecularem volunt esse.* The MSS vary considerably here. C has *sola aqua saecularem,* which is certainly faulty, the accusative at the end would seem to indicate that the other two words should be accusative, as they are in V, which Massuet and Stieren accepted. But since Erasmus has all in the nominative (C had the first two words nominative), and A and Q have *sola aqua qua saeculares* (sic), Harvey and Joppich (67n61) and SC have the nominative, which agrees with Arm. Iren. In this second reading (nominative) Irenaeus would be saying that the heretics reject the mixture of wine (implicitly holding that they do not wish to be such) and hold that *they* are only worldly water. In the first reading they would reject the mixture of wine and admit only worldly water; implicitly they could be applying both parts to themselves. I like to think Irenaeus either made the application in both parts or in none explicitly. So I chose the first reading of Lat. Iren. Arm. Iren. could have misread the Greek here as so often. The mixture of the heavenly wine is a symbol of God united with man, which brings salvation; the worldly water is man unredeemed, because he is not united with God. This mixture, of course, took place already in the incarnation itself. The Ebionites and Tatianites used only water for consecration. See Epiphanius, *Panarion* 30.16 (GCS 1.353). By mentioning the mixture Irenaeus alludes to the offering ceremony in the Church of his day.

25. Cf. Gen 2:7. Irenaeus's is a classical definition of man in the early Church. See A.H. 5 chap. 6, n2 below.

26. The pair of phrases "Father's Word" and "God's Spirit" have in Lat. Iren. the verb in the singular (*adunituseffecit*), which is regular for Greek syntax, namely, that the verb may follow the number of the nearest subject. Hence, as SC (27n5) observes, that is no argument in favor of holding that the Word and Spirit are identical. Immediately after, there is mention of the "hands of God" in a construction that is parallel to the present; but those hands are certainly the Word and the Spirit. So here too they are distinct persons.

27. Orbe argues that Irenaeus is here making a distinction between the apostolic and Valentinian understanding of the Father. See A.H. 1.2.2 and 2.18.6–7. Irenaeus also discusses this theme at A.H. 4.12.2 and 5.22.1. Orbe 1:109.

28. Cf. 1 Cor 15:22. Also compare the parallel in A.H. 5.12.3.

29. Gen 1:26.

30. Cf. John 1:13.

31. The "living and perfect Man" is Christ. In God's plan the incarnation was needed to make man according to the image and likeness of God. See Unger, FS 6–9.

Chapter 2

1. "Snatch away" is *diripiens.* Since he snatches it for himself, this is a usurpation, which Arm. Iren. expressed literally. See SC (31n1).

2. "Took back," *assumens.* The idea of taking *back again* might have been contained in the Greek preposition *ana* if the verb was *analaben.* Arm. Iren. is *suos fructos recondens,* which misses the thought totally.

3. The reason behind Irenaeus's statement is that all things belong to God through creation. See A.H. 4, chap. 19, n1. On the devil's rights theory see A.H. 3, chap. 18, n42.

4. Cf. 1 Cor. 10:16, "cup of blessing," which is another indication that "blessing" and "thanksgiving" were taken synonymously in the early Church. Here again Irenaeus shows that in his day already the sacrament of the Body and Blood of Jesus was known as the Eucharist. Cf. A.H. 4.18.4, 5; 5.2.3. This paragraph is a clear proof that Irenaeus identified the bread and wine with the Body and Blood of Jesus. The wording itself is unmistakable: Christ "confessed" that "the cup, which is from the creation (the wine) is his blood"; and he "affirmed that the bread, which is from the creation, is his body." Likewise, that real identity and presence emerges from his Pauline statement that we really communicate in the Body and the Blood of Christ. Moreover, his entire argumentation demands that identity and presence, because from it he proves the reality of Christ's body and blood while he was on earth. See A.H. 4, chap. 17, n24. The Eucharist is also a sacrament that is food for the soul. We are nourished by Christ's Body and Blood; the Blood of Christ dews our blood, and his Body gives growth to our bodies, not, as is self-evident, in a material sense, but by preparing them for the glorious resurrection.

5. Col 1:14. This paragraph initiates the theme of this Book: the flesh can be saved. See the full study of this by Joppich and Gonzáles.

6. Cf. 1 Cor 6:15; Eph 5:30. I followed the Greek construction where the parallels are clearer.

7. Matt 5:45; cf. Luke 22:28, 19.

8. 1 Cor 11:24–25. Lat. Iren. has *qui effusus est,* for which both the Greek and the Arm. Iren. have "He confessed." A scribe must have misread *confessus est as quem effusus est,* as the Clermont MS has, and that was corrected to *qui effusus est.* That an expression of affirming is needed is clear from the parallel in regard to the body (*confirmavit*).

9. In regard to the effects, both Lat. Iren. and Arm. Iren. have *auget* for the blood as well as for the body; but the Greek excerpt has "bedews" for the blood. SC follows the Lat. and Arm. version. I found it difficult to make a decision. Since these two translations agree, maybe the Greek was changed by the excerpter. In Greek *auxei* (give growth) could be intransitive, with "our blood" and "our bodies" as subjects, as SC translated. But they can also be transitive, with Christ as subject, just as he is subject of *confessus est* and *confirmavit,* as I translated.

10. Cf. A.H. 1, chap. 13, nn5 and 6. "the cup mixed" is what has been prepared for the Eucharist, so "the bread made" should also be what was made by man, not indirectly by God through creation. See A.H. 5.28.4, where Irenaeus speaks of making bread.

11. "Receive the Word of God." At first sight one might be inclined to take "Word of God" of the second Person, but on comparing this with *percipientia verbum Dei Eucharistia fiunt* in the same paragraph later, and with

panis percipiens invocationem Dei iam non communis panis est sed Eucharistia of A.H. 4.18.5, it becomes clear that this is directly the prayer by which the Eucharist was effected. Yet, one cannot exclude the Word of God from this. It is through his creative power that the Word effects the Eucharist. And if the bread "receives" this word, it must be the Word Incarnate and glorious. See A.H. 1, chap. 13, n5 and A.H. 4, chap. 17, n28.

12. The Body and Blood of Christ in the form of bread and wine are called the Eucharist. See A.H. 5, chap. 2, n 3. The Greek has only "and body." Quite certainly "blood" fell out. Both are in apposition to Eucharist. The Latin has a genitive construction: *Eucharistia sanguinis et corporis.* These are genitives of apposition. To be noted is Irenaeus's stating, here and a little farther down, that the bread and wine "become" the body and blood; so there is a change into the body and blood. Besides, his entire mode of arguing demands that he takes the bread and wine as changed into the body and blood of Christ. The cause of this is our partaking of the body and blood of Christ in the Eucharist, which really nourish us and prepare us for this imperishability. Besides, he argues as from a parallel case; just as the wheat is really changed into bread, so our bodies are really changed into imperishable ones, because we nourish them with the Eucharist. The Eucharist is, then, as real as wheat and bread and our own bodies, and that Eucharist is the body and blood of Jesus. Here too the Eucharist is presented as a sacramental food that nourishes and gives growth. If the effect is ascribed to the blood and the body, that is because the glorious resurrection of the body is the visible and tangible effect of the Eucharist on the soul.

13. "The substance of our flesh" is our corporal nature. "Gets consistency," namely, that which really holds it together: *συνέστηκεν*. SC's "s'affermit" seems weak.

14. The Eucharist is the pledge of the resurrection, which is God's gift to the flesh.

15. Eph 5:30. "of his flesh and of his bones" is not in the critical text of the Bible, though it is in some Greek MSS and in the Vulgate.

16. Luke 24:39.

17. Cf. Ezek 15:2, 6; John 12:24; Wis 1:7.

18. "Of men," in the plural as in Greek and Arm. Iren. Lat. Iren. has the singular, but obviously with the same meaning. "Through wisdom" as in Lat. and Arm. Iren. The Greek excerpt has "God's wisdom." The Greek excerpter could have tampered with the text. The context is about three steps to the formation of the Eucharist. The third step is expressly ascribed to God; so the other two seem to be God's action, not man's. *Per sapientiam* seems to parallel *per Spiritum Dei.*

19. Cf. Phil 2:11.

20. 1 Cor 15:53.

21. 2 Cor 12:9. The Greek excerpt has the future tense for "is made perfect," which is according to the Latin. This present tense in Latin is correct because all through here the present tense is used.

22. "Knowledge" is *gloria* in Lat. Iren., a translation of the Greek *doxa.* But the meaning here, in context, must be opinion or knowledge, according to the primitive meaning of *doxa.* This is confirmed by Arm. Iren. See SC (39n2).

CHAPTER 3

1. 2 Cor 12:7–9.

2. The term *word* might be a synonym for Scripture; or it could be the Word, who speaks in Scripture.

3. The construction of this sentence is somewhat obscure. Editors and translators have suggested various changes. I think the translation given catches the meaning without having to change the Latin text.

4. A longer section of the Jena papyrus is available for A.H. 5.3.2 to 13.1.

5. Irenaeus makes an interesting distinction here between God's skill or art or craft on the one hand and God's power on the other.

6. Lat. Iren. has *universae fabricationis quae est secundum membra hominis,* which must be understood in the light of the Greek: [πάσης τῆς κατὰ τὸν ἄνθρωπον μελοποίας]. SC (49n2) observes the last Greek word is, according to dictionaries, used only for a musical composition, but that Irenaeus takes the *melos* in its primitive sense of part. I am not so sure. Irenaeus liked musical terms. He could have kept the musical connotation in the composition of the body, as something quite harmonious. See A.H. 4, chap. 14, n11.

7. Ps 103 (104):24.

8. Here and in the next sentence the word *art* was restored according to the Greek and Arm. Iren. But in the next paragraph the Greek has "artful wisdom." Joppich (125–38) gives a neat synthesis on the fact that resurrection and imperishability and immortality belong to the essence of salvation for the whole person.

9. Here Irenaeus draws on 2 Cor 12:9, echoing one of his favorite themes that God's power is manifested in the weakness of human flesh.

10. Because of the difference in the witnesses to the reading we are not sure whether Irenaeus's figure was that of a torch with fire, or of a lamp with light. Lat. Iren. has *facula* and *ignis* in both phrases; the Greek excerpt has lamplight in the first phrase, but lamp-fire in the second; the Jena MS has lamplight in the first phrase, but unfortunately the second phrase is missing because of a defective papyrus. Arm. Iren. has lamplight in both phrases.

11. "Boastingly" follows the Greek and Arm. Iren. Lat. Iren. has *exsultantes* (joyfully).

12. Cf. Rom 8:11.

13. "More efficient" is missing in Lat. Iren. It was taken from the Greek excerpt.

14. Lat. Iren. has "by the fact that it is living," as I translated. That makes good sense in the context; it lines up well with the clause that follows. Irenaeus's aim was to prove that the body can accept life, because it is a fact that it is now living. He adds: It will live just as much as God wills it to live. If now he wills it a temporal life, that is it; if later he wills it to have everlasting life, fine, that will be it. See A.H. 5.4.2 for the same idea. Arm. Iren. says: "by the very life it is living." See SC (55n1) on the Greek readings, which seem to agree with the Arm. Iren.

15. "Long" as in Lat. Iren., which supposes μάκρα, with which Arm. Iren. agrees. But the excerpt of the Greek has μακαρία (happy), seemingly a false reading. In A.H. 4.38.3 both adjectives are found in the same sentence.

Chapter 4

1. Cf. A.H. 1.27.2; 2.1.2 for the Marcionite tenet.

2. The Greek is not extant. Irenaeus describes his opponents' view of God the Father with adjectives in three places in this paragraph, but not with the same adjectives altogether or the same number. Besides, Lat. Iren. differs from Arm. Iren. For a better view of the problem, I print the cases in parallel columns.

Case 1		**Case 2**		**Case 3**	
Latin	**Armenian**	**Latin**	**Armenian**	**Latin**	**Armenian**
—	—	impotens	—	—	—
infirmus	infirmus	infirmus	infirmus	—	—
inutilis	otiosum	—	inefficax	—	—
negligens	negligens	—	negligens	—	negligens
invidus	invidus	invidus	invidus	invidus	invidus
lividus	—	lividus	—	—	—
—	—	—	—	malignus	—

When so lined up, one might be tempted to give the right of way to Arm. Iren., as SC did, and judge that *lividus* (f) is a doublet translation in Latin; that *impotens* (a) is a variant for "useless," with an inversion of the order; that *malignus* represents a false reading for *negligens* (making it agree with Arm. Iren.), or a variant of *lividus.* Thus there would be four adjectives in all: *infirmus, inutiles, negligens, invidus.* The first two would refer to physical powerlessness; the second two to moral defects. But the matter is not that simple if one studies the words in the context, and in their usage throughout A.H. Not only was Lat. Iren. given to variant translations, but so was Arm. Iren. Besides, Arm. Iren. at times translated two words of Irenaeus by one word. Again, Irenaeus himself was not so consistent; he would change words to bring out new nuances. And so I think in case 2 (a) *impotens* is original. It is the most devastating characterization Irenaeus knows: he simply has no power. Lat. Iren. uses this word often and paraphrases it with *non potens*: see 2.29.1; 4.37.6; 38.1; 4.35.1. Later in this very paragraph he seems to explain this: *Si autem cum possit praestare, non praestat, iam non bonus.* Note 2.29.3: *invalidum* (possibly *impotens*), *infirmum, informem, in efficacem* (representing possibly the same word as *inutilis*). Omitting *informem,* we have the three first adjectives of my lineup. *Infirmus* is certain because it occurs in both cases and in both translations. It means being weak, even powerless to act. *Inutilis* is used by Lat. Iren. in the sense of not-used, not-operative, not-effective; and so, purposeless: see

A.H. 2.30.3, 4; 3.6.3; 3.12.6; 5.26.1. From some of these passages it becomes clear that *inutilis* is practically synonymous with *otiosum* (cf. 2.30.4). That is the term Arm. Iren. chose for this third adjective in the first and second case. A thing is useless or idle in this Irenaean sense because it was never put to use; there are no effects to show its power. *Negligens* is certain. It probably fell out accidentally in Lat. Iren. for case two. This indicates a moral fault of being unconcerned and consequently not good. *Invidus* is also certain, being in all three cases and in both translations. As I noted already, SC thinks *lividus* is a doublet translation for *invidus*, because it is missing in Arm. Iren. Lat. Iren. does not use his customary *sive* or *id est*, but *et*. So I think *lividus* is original. If *invidus* represents the Greek φθονερός and *lividus* βάσκανος, then this latter has a nuance of being malicious. Possibly then *malignus* is just a variant translation for *lividus* in case 3. On the other hand, Irenaeus may have changed to *malignus* πονηρός, in order to stress this malicious mind, in opposition to being a good God. Πονηρός is the scriptural name for the devil: see A.H. 3.4.3; 4.41.1, 3. There is sharp irony here.

3. "Spirit and soul" as in Lat. Iren., namely, nominative singular. Arm. Iren. has nominative plural for both. Only *–che* is extant in the Jena papyrus, but that is enough to make certain that the Greek had the nominative singular, ψυχή. SC (57n2) thinks the grammatical construction demands the accusative here; Arm. Iren. has accusative *talia.* I fail to see how *perseverare* could be transitive. It would be tautological for Irenaeus to have said that God continues the spirit and the soul immortal, and then add "because they are given life by the Father." No, they continue immortal, because they are given life by the Father. See A.H. 5.5.1: *perseverabant corpora* where also Arm. Iren. has the intransitive. On the immortality of the soul, see chapter 3, note 8 above.

4. Lat. Iren. has the present here (*ostendit*) as also a little later (*ostenditur*). Arm. Iren. has the future in both places, and correctly. SC (57). Only in chap. 15 does he give arguments from the Prophets. And there he repeats the present passage almost verbatim. Compare them:

A.H. 5.4.1: Demiurgo enim et hic vivificante mortalia corpora nostra et resurrectionem eis per prophetas promittente, quemadmodum ostendemus

A.H. 5.15.1: Demiurgo itaque et hic vivificante mortua corpora nostra, quemadmodum videre adest, et resurrectionem eis promittente,

As SC (201n1) observes, if one were to read this in c. 15 in the light only of the immediate context, namely, the citation from Ezekiel, one would say the vivifying and the raising to life are the same thing. But that is not the case. Chap. 15 begins with: *Quoniam autem is qui ab initio condidit hominem post resolutionem eius in terram promisit ei secundam generationem.* Here we have two stages and two acts: Demiurge creates man, and so vivifies him; and he will bring him to life at the resurrection, as he promised. That is the clue to the interpretation of both passages quoted above. The vivifying of man is at creation, then there is a promise of resurrection too. One and the same God, the true Demiurge, effects both.

5. Irenaeus alleges that his opponents subject God to necessity. That is, God is not omnipotent, but necessity is more powerful than God in the same

way that Fate is more powerful than the Greek gods. See Orbe 1:223 for more on this with bibliography.

Chapter 5

1. Cf. Pss 22 (23):6; 90(91):16.
2. Gen 5:24; Heb 11:5–6.
3. 2 Kgs 2:11. Orbe has a long and helpful note on this sentence. See Orbe 1:231.
4. "Spiritual" as in Greek and Arm. Iren, in place of Lat. Iren. *partum.*
5. Gen 2:8.
6. For presbyters see A.H. 4, chap. 26, n12.
7. 2 Cor 12:4.
8. 2 Kgs 2:11.
9. 2 Kgs 2:11.
10. Jonah 1–2.
11. Dan 3:19ff.
12. Dan 3:24–25.
13. Luke 18:27.
14. Lat. Iren. has *dispositionem,* but Arm. Iren. has the plural. SC (71n1) argues for the plural, because it is a question of various instances mentioned as "economies." But it seems to me that it must be singular, referring to the one just mentioned, by which "all things are subject to God and serve his will." This one economy has within it many partial economies.
15. Pss 22 (23):6; 90(91):16.
16. Cf. Rom 3:3. "Faithfulness" as in Lat. Iren. Arm. Iren. has "gift."

Chapter 6

1. Cf. Isa 42:1; Matt 11:18. Lat. Iren. has *puero,* in the sense of servant; but Arm. Iren. has "Son," which seems correct because the verbs allude to Rom 8:29, unless "Son" would be an interpretation. Man is essentially composed of body and soul. See also A.H. 5.8.; 9.1; *Proof* 2; and the next note.
2. According to Irenaeus the whole person is composed of body and soul and spirit. The spirit in his theology is the Holy Spirit with his grace, which spiritualizes man, and so he becomes spirit. That is, of course, already St. Paul's thinking; cf. 1 Cor 15:42ff. SC (73n2) thinks that *animaet Spiritus,* should be translated "the soul united with the Holy Spirit." But see the next note of SC, too. The soul is in the natural order, while the "spirit" is in the supernatural order, spiritualizing the whole man, not merely being united with his soul. Thus also SC (73n3). *Pars hominis* is according to the MSS of Clermont and Vatican. The Voss and Arundel MSS have *paree,* which I should judge to be a corruption of *partes*; and that would agree with Arm. Iren. SC (73n3) accepts this. But *pars* is correct. It fits into the context well. He wishes to say that man, if made of body and soul, is still not the whole man, but only a part. He does not say that each of these is a part of man, and so the two together are parts of man. That the body of man was made according to the

image of God himself is theologically correct, because God is the ultimate exemplar of all things. Irenaeus, however, does not have that in mind. It is the incarnate Word of God who is the exemplar of man's body. As a consequence from this Irenaean thought, God had to intend the incarnation prior to intending Adam; see Unger, FS 9.

3. 1 Cor 2:6.

4. 1 Cor 2:15; 3.1.

5. In this area, obviously, Irenaeus takes flesh not of the whole person but of man's bodily nature, which Irenaeus's opponents said could not share in salvation. SC (77n1) argues correctly that "man's spirit" and "God's Spirit" are terms taken from 1 Cor 2:11. This illustrates how deeply Irenaeus's thought was rooted in Scripture.

6. The Holy Spirit's role in the sanctification of man is stressed here and passim in the following sections. See the fine article of A. d'Alés, "La doctrine de l'Esprit en Saint Irénée," RSR 14 (1924): 497–538. For the "spirit" in man see A.H. 5, chap. 6, n12. For salvation as possession of the Spirit see González 59–68. And for an excellent monograph on the role of the Holy Spirit in Irenaeus's work, see Anthony Briggman, *Irenaeus of Lyons and the Theology of the Holy Spirit* (Oxford: Oxford University Press, 2012).

7. Lat. Iren reads: *animalis, <est> vere qui est talis, et carnalis derelictus imperfectus erit,* which I followed in my translation, with *est* (in brackets) added. A man whose soul lacks the "spirit" is only ensouled, and so, being left carnal, is imperfect. Arm. Iren. has the same words without *est* after *animalis*, supposing, as SC (77n2), that *derelictus* governs *animalis* as well as *carnalis*, as if we should read: "Such a one, who is left truly ensouled and carnal, is imperfect." "To be left truly ensouled" makes little sense. But it makes sense to say: "to be truly ensouled," that is, without the Spirit, and so "to be left merely carnal" is good logic and Irenaean theology. The Latin has correctly caught that meaning. If the Greek suggested by SC is correct, that too can be read in this meaning by putting a comma after ψυχικὸς ὄντος ὁ τοιοῦτος καὶ σαρκικὸς καταλειφθεὶς.

8. The same idea about the complete man is found in Tertullian, *De carnis resurrectione mortuorum* 14, 10–11 (CCL 2.937).

9. 1 Thess 5:23. Lat. Iren. does not support the translation I have given of this Scripture, because the adjective *integer* can modify only *Spiritus*. In the Greek of Paul the adjective has a neuter ending and could modify πνεῦμα, but that would make little sense. The neuter seems to be an adjectival noun—meaning totality or "whole self." That is how Irenaeus interpreted it immediately after. That also fits his thought above about all three elements being needed for the whole man. Arm. Iren. changed the verb to the active voice: God keeps the whole spirit blamelessly.

10. "To be preserved as a whole" is literally "to be a whole preservation," but that is rather clumsy and unintelligible without an explanation. The meaning is that the three elements are the whole man and should be preserved together. Arm. Iren. has *integram totam*, which is obviously an allusion to the Scripture text just quoted, where *integer* is *holokleron*. Now this adjective can mean both "whole" and "complete." So there is no problem with *integer*. But *perfectum* in Irenaeus translates *holokleron* in 5.12.5, and *perfecte* represents *holokleros*. So both in Latin and in Armenian there seems to be a doublet. Thus SC (79n2).

11. My translation is according to the Latin, which fits the context. Paul knew, Irenaeus wishes to say, that all three elements of man had one and the same salvation, and that was the restoration and the union of all three, not merely of two. SC translated as if Irenaeus were saying that Paul knew two things: that all three elements had to be restored and reunited, and that they had one and the same salvation. That translation does not show the relation of the two things as Lat. Iren. puts it. "Restoration" is in Lat. Iren. *redintegratio,* which most likely translates ἀποκατάστᾰσις, as it does in 1.14.1, and as *reintegratio* does in 1.17.1, and as *restauratio* does in 1.21.3. In other words, Lat. Iren. used three words for the one Greek. He did the same with the verb ἀποκαθίστημι which is given by *redintegrare* in 1.2.5; 5.3.2. This Latin occurs also in 5.12.5, 6; 21.3 (where the Greek was most likely the same). In 5.32.1; 33.1 *reintegrare* obviously stands for the same Greek, and so does *restaurare* in 2.31.2; 3.5.3; 23.2; 5.2.1. Now in all these cases of the nouns and the verbs the meaning is the same, namely, to restore to a pristine state, according to a pristine design. So I cannot agree with P. Siniscalco, "apokatastasis e apokathistemi nella tradizione della Grande Chiesa fino ad Ireneo," *Studia Patristica* 3 (TU 78, 1961): 380–96, who claims that Origen was first to use them in the sense of a restoration to a primitive state, and that for others it meant a liberation. For Irenaeus liberation may be involved, but the restoration was to a primitive state that had been designed prior to the need of liberation.

12. See A.H. 5, chap. 6, nn11 and 12.Irenaeus does not teach the false notion of trichotomy. Elsewhere, such as in A.H. 2.29.3; 33.5, he holds clearly that the natural man is composed of two parts only. The spirit he speaks of is the supernatural principle in the supernatural life, which comes from the Holy Spirit and his grace. See also 5.12.2; *Proof* 11; and especially A.H. 8.2; 9.1. Cf. J. Bainvel, "Âme," DTC 1 (1930): 984–85; and A. Orbe, "La definición del hombre en la teología del siglo II," *Gregorianum* 48 (1967): 522–56. That Irenaeus's notion about man is based on Pauline thought is the contention of J. Bentivegna, "Pauline Elements in the Anthropology of St. Irenaeus," *Studia Evangelica* 5 (TU 103 [1968]): 229–33. The last sentence has a number of difficulties due mostly to variant readings in the different languages. Lat. Iren. reads: *Perfecti igitur qui et Spiritum in se /semper/ perseverantem habent Dei, et animas et corpora sine querela servaverint, hoc est, illum quae ad Deum est fidem servantes et eam quae ad proximum est iustitiam custodientes.* In the Jena Papyrus three letters are extent (-r-sm-o-) for the word that is represented by *perseverantem.* So that Greek had to be προσμένον and not παραμόνεν, which is found in 4.38.3. In place of *in se* Arm. Iren. has *semper.* There is some warrant for *semper* in 4.38.3: τὴν εἰς ἀεὶ παραμόνεν. SC (81n1) thinks *in se* is a corruption of *semper.* But it could just as well be the other way around. Really, in the whole paragraph it is a question of the Spirit being within the human being and spiritualizing it. *In se,* as "within themselves," fits excellently. The verb *servaverint* is active in Latin, governing *animas et corpora,* with *sine querela* as an adverbial phrase. That makes good sense in the context, and is according to the quotation from 1 Thess, where *amemptos* is an adverb and not a nominative adjective. But Arm. Iren. has it as a predicate adjective with the verb in the passive voice, namely, "they stay blameless" in regard to body and soul. The last expression is an accusative of limitation. The verb seems verified

by the Jena Papyrus, which has these letters *STOTES*, which must have been *estotes.* Thus SC. But that would have been translated differently by Lat. Iren., who made it active with the adverbial phrase modifying it, as in the Greek of 1 Thess, though in 1 Thess the verb is passive. Did Irenaeus find his reading in 1 Thess or did Lat. Iren. adjust his translation to the Bible? The first case is quite probable; Irenaeus could have changed to the active voice, because he so argued in the paragraph. Then Lat. Iren. would represent the original. SC discards *servaverint,* because there are too many verbs here that express the same idea. But the Greek verb for *custodientes* was most likely different, e.g., διαφυλάσσοντες, while the others came from τέρειν.

13. 1 Cor 3:16–17.
14. John 2:19–21.
15. 1 Cor 6:15.
16. 1 Cor 3:17.
17. 1 Cor 6:13–14.

Chapter 7

1. John 20:25, 27.
2. 1 Cor 6:14.
3. Rom 8:11.
4. Gen 2:7.
5. "Not even," according to Lat. Iren. In the context Irenaeus is showing that the mortal bodies are not souls, nor are they the spirit. Under the first point (they are not the souls) he subdivides: they are not the souls, because these are not bodies; nor are they mortal. Lat. Iren. agrees completely with this context. So *ne mortalem quidem* is correct. If it were *neque mortalem,* as Arm. Iren. has, with SC (87n1) accepting it, this would be the second member coordinate with *sed neque Spiritum* as a third member. But that is not the thought of Irenaeus here.
6. Ps 21 (22):31.
7. For more on "substance" and "immortality," see Orbe 1:333–34.
8. Cf. Rom 8:11.
9. 1 Cor 15:42, 36.
10. 1 Cor 15:43.
11. Cf. Gen 3:19.
12. 1 Cor 15:44.
13. 1 Cor 13:9, 12.
14. 1 Pet 1:8. SC (93n1) recalls its long note in Book 4 where it was "proved" that the Arm. Iren. is more faithful than Lat. Iren. in giving the original Irenaean text for Scripture quotations. Lat. Iren. is said to adjust to his current Bible. At present SC has a long justification of its restoration, mostly by conjecture, of the Jena Papyrus at this place. In both A.H. 4.9.2 and 5.7.2, Arm. Iren. omits the negative before the first *videntes,* and also *diligitis,* then joins the first *videntes* to the rest in this way: "When you will see him, whom you, without seeing now, believe, you will rejoice." As can be seen, that curtailing changes the construction considerably. Now in 4.9.2 it is certain that Irenaeus had the *diligitis* phrase in his text, because before quoting it he

indicates for what he is quoting it: *in quem credimus, quem et diligimus.* It seems certain that it was also in 5.7.2. Arm. Iren. either read a defective Greek MS of Irenaeus or tampered with the text, as in numerous other places. This passage is no proof that Lat. Iren. adjusted to his Bible, while Arm. Iren. gave the original text of Irenaeus.

Chapter 8

1. "Part of his Spirit." For Lat. Iren. the Clermont and Voss MSS have a prepositional phrase, *a Spiritu eius*; while the Arundel, the Vatican, and Erasmus MSS have *Spiritus*, a partitive genitive. The meaning is the same. In this life we have only a partial participation in the Spirit; only in the next will we have a full participation. See SC (93n2).

2. Lat. Iren. reads: *sumimus ad perfectionem et praeparationem incorruptelae.* One might be tempted to say these nouns should be inverted: preparation comes before perfection. SC (93n3) observes that Arm. Iren. demands that one retranslate into Greek: εἰς προκαταρισμόν τε καὶ, and that Lat. Iren., which must have read this same Greek, gave a poor rendition by *perfectionem.* SC used two verbs; "nous disposeret nous preparer." Maybe. But since Irenaeus has been talking very much about man's being perfect by receiving the Spirit (cf. especially 5.6.1; also 4.12.2; 5.1.3), which happens already in this life, though final perfection comes through imperishability (cf. 4.11.1; 4.37–38), I think he is here saying that through the reception of the Spirit we are "perfect" initially, and that very thing prepares us for the final perfection of imperishability. See 5.12.6: *sanum et integrum redintegravit hominem, perfectum eum sibi praeparans ad resurrectionem.* The Greek suggested by SC can mean perfection; or Irenaeus's regular word for perfection could have been used here. What Arm. Iren. read is not certain. This would be just one more case where Arm. Iren. did not follow the thought exactly.

3. Eph 1:13–14. Irenaeus's explanation of "pledge" is very good. It is a kind of down payment on eternal life, not a pawn.

4. Cf. 2 Cor 5:4.

5. Rom 8:9.

6. Rom 8:15.

7. Irenaeus's use of "pledge" here likely comes from Eph 1:14. For more see Orbe 1:374.

8. Cf. 1 Cor 13:12.

9. This is a beautiful picture of our resurrection and eternal life in the Holy Spirit. For the resurrection as the climax of salvation see González 256. The best treatment of Irenaeus's understanding of salvation is Ysabel de Andia, *Homo Vivens: Incorruptibilité et divinisation de l'homme selon Irenée de Lyons* (Paris: Etudes Augustiniennes, 1986).

10. The meaning of *complectens in se* is not clear. *In se* must refer to *pignus,* which stands for the Spirit. *Complectens* is used twice later in a similar context, but about becoming part of a harlot, by "embracing her" (5.6.2). The Greek there was most likely a compound of πλέκω, e.g. πομπλέκω, as in A.H. 1.4.1; 14.7. But that could not have been the verb in our passage, because the Jena papyrus has the last six letters, which demand a compound

of λαμβάνω. In 5.12.2 *circumdans* translates περιλαβόν, also in 5.35.1, in the sense of surrounding, e.g., with clothing. That verb and meaning could fit here. SC (95n2) prefers συμπεριλαμβάνων. However, since throughout this section of chaps. 6—12, the Bishop is speaking about the Spirit taking to himself and uniting with himself man, or man taking to himself and uniting with himself the Spirit, and since that is frequently expressed by *assumens*, for which at times προσλαμβάνων is the Greek; e.g. 5.12.2, 3, also 4.38.3; 5.13.3), I opt for this as the Greek. In any case the meaning is the same, and is certain: the Spirit, as a pledge, takes man to himself, unites him with himself and fairly surrounds him.

11. The image and likeness after which man was created will reach its final perfection only in glory, as Irenaeus states often. For salvation is likeness to God; see González 82–89. Cf. Gen 1:26–28. For an extended study on Irenaeus on this theme see Jacques Fantino, *L'homme, image de Dieu, chez Saint Irénée de Lyon* (Paris: Cerf, 1986).

12. Cf. 2 Cor 1:22.

13. Cf. Rom 8:9.

14. "Constitute" is *perfecit* in Lat. Iren., which can mean either "make complete" or "constitute." Either meaning is correct here. And so Arm. Iren. in the sense of "constitute" agrees with Lat. Iren. There is no point in rejecting *perfecit* as a broad translation or a corruption, as does SC (97n1).

15. Cf. 1 Cor 3:3.

16. Cf. Rom 8:5.

17. Jer 5:8.

18. Ps 48 (49):21.

19. Irenaeus shows how man who lives a carnal life is irrational like the animals. In his thesis (8.2) and in his conclusion (8.3) he calls them pigs and dogs. Then he adduces proof for this from the Prophets, who brand them as wild horses (Jer.) and *iumenta-beasts* (Ps. 48 [49]). In the summation of 8.3 he calls them *iumenta* (referring back to Ps 48) and *feras* (referring to Jer.). In this summation Arm. Iren. calls them *pecora et feras. Pecora* is not exact. Judging from Ps 48 the Greek would have been κτενώδεις; for *feras* the Greek is extant in the Jena Papyrus as θεριώδεις. We can brand these two classes as beasts and (wild) brutes. Again, in his proofs (8.2) he appeals to custom that brands such men as: *iumenta et pecora irrationabilia.* For this Arm. Iren. Has *pecus et castratum* (*pullum*). The second is simply wrong and the first is not exact. But the point is that there are only two groups. Now, also in the summation (8.3), custom speaks of only two groups: *pecora* and *irrationabiles.* So in 8.2, according to custom, there may be two irrational groups: *iumenta et pecora*; or *iumenta et pecora irrationabilia*; or *iumenta* should not be there (it slipped in from the preceding), and there would be *pecora et irrationabilia,* as in the summation. This last I accept. In the summation Arm. Iren. Has only one term for custom, namely, *castratum* (*pullum*), which does not match its own two in 8.2. The Arm. Iren. Is therefore less reliable here. So, I think, Irenaeus himself called them pigs and dogs; the Prophets called them beasts and (wild) brutes, custom called them cattle (or herds) and simply irrational; the law called them unclean (8.3); and the apostle calls them carnal and animal. SC (99n2) does not agree with all these points.

20. SC (101n1) observed that Clement of Alexandria must have used this passage about clean and unclean animals because of the great similarities to *Stromata* 7.8 (GCS 3.77–78). The parallel printed of SC makes it easy to see this.

21. See Orbe 1:388–90; Lev 11:1–17.

22. Lev 11:2ff.; Deut 14:3ff.

23. Ps 1:2.

24. Literally "they do not have the firmness of their root fixed in the Father and the Son."

25. "Nearly" comes from the Jena Papyrus and Arm. Iren. Lat. Iren. has *videlicet.*

26. Luke 6:46. "call me," in place of "say to me," as in the Lat. Iren., comes from the Jena Papyrus and Arm. Iren. See SC (105n1). Cf. also 4.37.3, where SC had agreed to "say to me," because of the agreement of Lat. And Arm. Iren. Now SC thinks it should even there be "call me." This reading is found in some NT MSS and could very well have been in Irenaeus's Bible.

27. Cf. 1 Cor 3:3 and 1 Cor 2:14.

Chapter 9

1. 1 Cor 15:50.

2. Cf. A.H. 5.6.1, and A.H. 5, chap. 6, n2.

3. I followed Lat. Iren., which has *elevatur ab eo.* That supposes the Greek ἀντστιαμένης. Arm. Iren. has "flies upward," which supposes ἀνιπταμένης. SC (109n1) defends Arm. Iren. On the score that such a misreading occurred elsewhere. True, the idea of flying upward was correct when speaking of his opponent's understanding of Christ. But in our context the question is about the resurrection; so flying upward is out of context, and being raised up is alone correct. Further, *elevatur ab eo* is in contrast to *decidit in terrenas.* "Fly from" could be in contrast to "fall to" the earth. But "fall *into* the earth" is more naturally contrasted with "be raised up."

4. Luke 9:60.

5. Cf. Matt 5:8; 1 Cor 2:15; 3:1; Rom 6:11.

6. This is a wonderful idea on living God's own life through the grace of the Spirit. Cf. A.H. 4, chap. 20, n6.

7. Matt 26:41.

8. "Willing to do" is according to *in promptu habere* of Lat. Iren. This is according to the context, and the Greek verb, most likely προθύμειται as SC suggests (111n1), must be taken in the light of Christ's saying about "being willing and able" to do. So SC's translation: "avoir a sa disposition," or "avoir sou la main" is not acceptable.

9. "As an impetus" follows ἐγκεντρίδος δικὴν. *Stimulus* would represent ἐγκεντρίδος. Arm. Iren. read "insertion" or "graft." Since much of chap. 10 is about the graft of a wild olive on a domestic one, one could think that Irenaeus anticipated that idea here, which Arm. Iren. translated correctly. SC (111n2) remarks that Robinson and Lundström took that meaning. SC stays with the Latin. I do too, hesitatingly. "Willingness of the Spirit" is something active and calls for an active impetus. Yet, one could argue in the whole context there is question of the resurrection due to "a communion" with the Spirit, that is, a graft.

10. "On account of" as in Lat. Iren. (*propter*), which supposes διὰ with the accusative in Greek. A.H. 5.11.1. has the same reading. Arm. Iren. read "through," namely, διὰ with the genitive. In the context it is "through communion with" that the flesh will be raised up, and so even if "on account of" was written, it means not merely "because of" as final cause, but as efficient cause. The error could have occurred in various ways: either a Latin scribe could have changed *per* to *propter*, the Latin translator could have misread a genitive as an accusative, or Arm. Iren. could have misread an accusative as a genitive.

11. It is difficult to overestimate the importance of martyrdom in Irenaeus's thinking. On this see John Behr, *Irenaeus of Lyons: Identifying Christianity* (Oxford: Oxford University Press, 2013), 198–203.

12. Irenaeus clearly teaches that the Holy Spirit makes man a spirit, and so he does not teach tricotomy for the natural man. He rightly stresses the operation of the Spirit in the soul. For this he leans heavily on St. Paul, as was pointed out earlier; cf. A.H. 5, chap. 6, n5. In this matter Wingren (23–24) says beautifully: "There is hardly any passage in Irenaeus of greater importance than the one in which he describes in detail how it is only the man who receives the Spirit that is truly man." On this, see Ysabel de Andia, *Homo Vivens : Incorruptibilité et divinisation de l'homme selon Irénée de Lyons* (Paris: Etudes Augustiniennes, 1986).

13. Ps 21 (22):5.

14. 1 Cor 15:48.

15. Cf. Rev 6:10; 19:2.

16. 1 Cor 15:49.

17. Cf. Rom 6:4.

18. The Greek excerpt has: "Flesh by itself in the blood cannot inherit." That is scarcely correct. Arm. Iren. has "with the blood," which SC accepts and even corrects the Greek excerpt to "with." Lat. Iren. has as I translated, which is the most natural in the context. Irenaeus had written this correctly so often that he can scarcely be accused of adjusting to Scripture.

19. Matt 5:5.

20. "The servants" belong to Christ. See the same in A.H. 4.13.3. The opening of the NT is ascribed to the Holy Spirit also in 3.17.2.

21. We call attention to this beautiful doctrine on the indwelling of the Son and the Spirit. See Col 3:16; 1 Cor 6:9; 15:33; Gal 6:7.

Chapter 10

1. "The graft on to the Spirit" is in Lat. Iren. *insertionem Spiritus.* In the context it becomes clear that man is being grafted to the Spirit; so this is an objective genitive. Both the Latin *insertionem* and the Greek ἐνγκεντρίσμον can be the act of grafting, or the passive reception of a graft.

2. Cf. Rom 11:17, 24.

3. Matt 7:19.

4. "Produced" is according to the Jena Papyrus. As SC (125n1) notes, Lat. Iren. may have chosen *germinaverint* to avoid the clumsy *fructificationem fecerint.*

5. For this sentence and the one before, see Orbe 1:470–72.

6. Matt 13:25.
7. Matt 24:42; 25:13; Mark 13:3ff.
8. Gen 1:26.
9. 1 Cor 15:50.
10. 1 Cor 15:50.
11. Rom 8:8.
12. 1 Cor 15:53.
13. Rom 8:9.
14. Rom 8:10–11.
15. Rom 8:13.
16. Rom 8:13–14.
17. On flesh and spirit here, see Orbe 1:496–97.

Chapter 11

1. Gal 5:19–20.
2. Cf. Rom 8:4; 2 Cor 10:2; Rom 6:10.
3. Gal 5:22–23. I did not translate *animositates* and *irritationes* because there are simply doublet translations.
4. 1 Cor 6:9–11.
5. Cf. Rom 8:13.
6. 1 Cor 15:49–50.
7. 1 Cor 6:11.
8. Cf. A.H. 5.6.1 in regard to the handiwork as the image.

Chapter 12

1. "Ceases" for *interit.* That present is backed by Arm. Iren. and the Greek excerpt (ἀμαιρεῖται). But the Jena Papyrus read the perfect ἀνῄρηται. SC (141n1) argues hesitatingly for this perfect. The scribe of the Papyrus could have changed because he found the present odd, as did SC.
2. Cf. Rom 6:10–11; A.H. 5.12.6; 5.17.1; Orbe 1:530–31.
3. Isa 25:8 LXX.
4. Cf. Gen 2:7 and 1 Cor 15:45. Orbe 1:537–39.
5. Isa 42:5.
6. Isa 57:16.
7. Acts 2:17.
8. 1 Cor 15:46.
9. 1 Cor 15:45.
10. Luke 15:1–7.
11. Col 3:5.
12. Col 3:9.
13. Cf. Gal 1:15.
14. Phil 1:22; cf. 1:11.
15. Phil 1:22.
16. Col 3:9.
17. Col 3:10.

18. Gal 1:15–16.
19. Acts 9:4; Gal 1:13.
20. A.H. 3.12.7; 15.1.
21. Luke 6:6ff.

Chapter 13

1. Mark 5:22. Lat. Iren. has "daughter of the High Priest," but "servant of the ruler of the synagogue" is correct, as in Arm. Iren. SC (163n1) follows the Latin. But then one cannot find an episode in the Gospels to fit. Reference must be to Matt 9:18; Mark 5:22; Luke 8:41, where the *daughter* of Jairus is sick. So Arm. Iren. has "servant" incorrectly. But the father is a ruler of the synagogue, which can be written as one word, and was so written by Mark: ἀρχισυναγώγος. Now, either Irenaeus wrote correctly here, as he did in A.H. 1.8.2, and a scribe misread it as ἀρχιερέως, or Irenaeus himself made the mistake.

2. Luke 7:12.

3. John 11:39.

4. Mark 5:41, 43; Matt 9:25; Luke 7:14–15, which Irenaeus conflated in a such a way that it is an unsolvable puzzle, because at the beginning of this paragraph Irenaeus had distinguished the two cases (daughter of Jairus and son of the widow of Naim) and now he so confuses them and the gender of the people involved. See SC (165n1).

5. John 11:43–44.

6. John 11:44.

7. 1 Cor 15:52.

8. John 5:28.

9. Sophocles, *Oedipus the King* (Loeb 1, lines 1265ff.).

10. According to Orbe, this analogy requires no explanation. See his bibliography Orbe 1:617.

11. 1 Cor 15:50.

12. 1 Cor 15:53–55.

13. Phil 3:20–21.

14. "As he is able" is in Greek of the Bible: *τοῦ δυνάσθαι αὐτόν*. Latin Iren. translated that twice by *virtutis suae* and *ut possit.* Arm. Iren. has it only once.

15. Phil 3:21; 1 Cor 15:53. Orbe 1:631–32.

16. 2 Cor 5:4. This title to the letter is not in the Greek fragment. Harvey judged it to be an interpolation in Lat. Iren., and he infers that this is a clue that the "greater number of such references have come from the margin." That is too sweeping a statement. In fact, in this very place the fragment of *Sacra Parallela* could easily have omitted it as useless for its purpose. It is also in Arm. Iren. and so was in the Greek copies prior to Lat. Iren. and Arm. Iren. We should note Irenaeus's explicit remark that the soul, not only the spirit, is immortal; cf. chapter 3, note 8 above. Noteworthy, too, is the expression of redemption as victory over death which held man captive; cf. A. Orbe, *Antrop.* 361–87.

17. This is a nice expression of man's ultimate purpose, namely, to praise God. Jossa (196–98) wrongly claims that Irenaeus stresses the actual

possession in the Church and obscures the future kingdom, and in so doing does not follow Paul. No, one must use all of Irenaeus to understand any given passage. We do possess salvation now, but we will do so fully only in vision.

18. 1 Cor 6:20.

19. 2 Cor 4:10. "if" (εἰ) is in Lat. Iren., except for Erasmus, who has *semper*, and in Arm. Iren., though in NT it is "always" (ἀεὶ). How to explain this? SC (177n1) thinks since both Lat. and Arm. have "if," it comes from Irenaeus himself. Maybe. Irenaeus could have written εἰ, and some scribe changed it before either translation was made. Yet Irenaeus could have written "if" since it is already in such early Greek MSS of the Bible as P46, G, 489, syro.pesch. The Latin *si* is also in D and in a few minor MSS, and in Tertullian. The conditional sentence would, of course, be incomplete, without a protasis.

20. 2 Cor 3:3.

21. Phil 3:11. "Likened." The Lat. Iren. MSS are confused. Clermont has *cui honoratus*; Arundel and Vatican have *cooperatus*; Voss has *commemoratus*; and Erasmus has *conformis*. This last agrees with Arm. Iren. *conformatus*, and that fits the NT συμμορφιζόμενος. Arm. Iren. could have adapted to the NT. Lat. Iren. supposes συμφορτιζόμενος (burdened together). This reading, too, is found in some NT MSS. With the data we have it is difficult to say which word Irenaeus had written.

22. 1 Cor 15:32; 13–21.

23. 1 Cor 15:50.

24. 1 Cor 15:53.

25. 2 Cor 4:11.

CHAPTER 14

1. 1 Cor 15:50.

2. "His human nature" is *hominem eius*. This expression occurs in three other places in Book 5 (14.4; 21.2, 3) and without *eius* in two places (21.2 twice). SC (183n2) thinks a good translation is "humanity," namely, of Jesus. I think the *eius* could connote the fact that it belongs to him already by creation.

3. In this paragraph Lat. Iren. uses *habere* with a complementary infinitive five times. Such a construction was standard in Greek and was used even in Latin. Lat. Iren. is here most likely following his Greek copy. When so used *habere* can have three meanings: "must or should," "would" or "was to," or "can." Because of the context (Irenaeus is proving the possibility of a resurrection and salvation for the body), the idea of necessity is excluded here for all five; and it is also excluded for the three negative phrases by the fact that when *habere* is negated, somehow it consistently expresses an impossibility. So it is a toss-up between "would" and "can." The Greek is not extant. Arm. Iren. translates all five cases by *handerzem*, which would normally represent the Greek μέλλω, and express a determined future, "would." Yet the Arm. is no convincing proof that the Greek had μέλλω, especially in all five cases. True, the Arm. Iren. translated *habere* in the sense of possibility (impossibility) a number of times (cf. 4.9.2; 33.9; 35.3; 5.33.1) with the corresponding *ounim*. Yet in 5.12.6 (*non habebant salvari*) was translated by *handerzem*, although this is definitely

a case of impossibility. So, also in our paragraph Arm. Iren. could have used *handerzem* for impossibility; or it might have misinterpreted the mind of Irenaeus and thought he was speaking of determined future actions. In any case, the Arm. Iren. is here not decisive. Lat. Iren. often translated μέλλω by *incipio,* and if here he uses *habere* consistently, it is scarcely probable that the Greek had μέλλω in all the cases or in any of them.

The *habere* plus infinitive construction occurs in A.H. 34 times. Only once in a positive sense of necessity; ten times of a determined future, but always in a positive sense; 23 times of possibility, 19 of which are negative, and so, of impossibility. According to this pattern the three negatives in this paragraph would express impossibility, not a negative determined future act.

In Book 5 Irenaeus has as main objective to prove the possibility of the salvation of the flesh, that is, of its glorification or reception of imperishability. Since according to him the incarnation of God's Word was necessary for man's salvation, this also establishes the reality of Christ's human nature. The immediate aim of this paragraph is this: Irenaeus's opponents used 1 Cor 15:50 (that flesh and blood cannot inherit the kingdom of God) to prove that flesh *cannot* be saved. Irenaeus explains that this Pauline passage is not speaking of flesh as such, but only of a carnal, immoral way of living. In fact, Paul frequently speaks of flesh and blood for two purposes: to establish the reality of Jesus's human nature, and to affirm the salvation of our flesh. From the remote context it is certain that this means the possibility of salvation for the flesh. Irenaeus proves this by stating: *Si enim non haberet caro salvari, nequaquam Verbum Dei caro factum esset: et si non haberet sanguis iustorum inquiri, nequaquam sanguinem habuisset Dominus.* He adduces four Scripture texts to show that the blood of the just would (or could) be vindicated, namely, by salvation through Christ. To introduce some of those texts he states: *Et quoniam haberet exquiri sanguis ipsorum, dixit.* He tops these Scripture quotations by stating that Christ also spoke of this vindication of blood, which he introduces by: *Similiter autem et Dominus his qui habebant eius sanguinem effundere dicebat.* Then, after noting that Jesus thereby indicated he would recapitulate in himself all the blood of the just, he concludes: *Non autem exquireretur hoc nisi et salvari haberet.* Nor, he continues, would he have recapitulated them in himself if he had not become flesh and blood as Adam had.

Now in these uses of *habere,* it is my sense that the fourth certainly expresses future action ("would pour out"). And since this is similar to this fourth, it too possibly expresses a determined future action, although it seems possible that it might express a possible action. Those two cases were positive. The other three are negative in construction or in sense. As I noted above, according to Lat. Iren. pattern they would not express a negated future action, but impossibility. That is also in keeping with the context about the possibility of salvation for the flesh. The first and second case would be the thesis about the possibility of salvation; the fifth would be the conclusion also about the possibility. The third and fourth cases would be proofs taken from determined future actions (*Ab esse ad posse valet illatio*).

This paragraph has been a stronghold for those theologians who hold that the incarnation would not have taken place if man would not have sinned and had not been in need of redemption. They translated Irenaeus thus: If it had not been necessary for flesh to be saved, God's Word would never have become flesh. As I stated above, in the context *habere* can here not express necessity. Second, these theologians take the word *salvation* in a narrow sense of redemption from sin. In Irenaeus the word is broad. It means giving imperishability to the flesh. See Orbe, *Anthropo* 488. Neither were those correct who said flesh is here to be understood of passible flesh, which the Word would not have assumed if man had not sinned. Irenaeus is arguing against his opponents. They denied salvation as possible to all flesh, sinful or not. That is what Irenaeus is refuting. So whether one translates *habere* here with *would* or *could*, the passage is not against the theory that Christ was willed absolutely and from the beginning in our actual world plan. In fact, that view fits excellently into the thought of this paragraph. Flesh can be saved, glorified, and God always intended it to be glorified; but Irenaeus insists that the enfleshment of God's Word is necessary for such glorification of humanity. So the Incarnate Word was always intended to be part of this plan of salvation; and his human nature would be the first and most important recipient of that salvation.

4. Gen 4:10.

5. Gen 9:5.

6. Gen 9:6. The Arundel and Vatican MSS and Erasmus added *sanguis* as subject of "shall be shed," but it is only to be implied, since it is missing also in LXX.

7. Matt 23:35–36, with part from Luke 11:50.

8. On the role of recapitulation here, see Orbe 1:667–69.

9. Only what is related by real succession with the first man, Adam, is true flesh. In Lat. Iren. *successio* is predicate noun of *caro,* flesh *is* the lineage. In my translation I tried to make that clear. *Successio,* lineage, is an unbroken line by which the identical flesh of the first handiwork is passed on to others.

10. "Seeking out" is in Lat. Iren., *exquisitionem.* That supposes ζήτεσις; but Arm. Iren. supposes εὕρεσις for "acquisition." This is preferred by SC (187n2) because it is said to fit the sequence of thought better, namely, that the Word became flesh and so effected a communion with himself, and this communion effected the "acquisition." "Seeking out" would not fit so well for "acquisition." Yet, the relation between communion and *exquisitionem* is not so direct. *Et* joins the two, indicating that both the communion and the seeking out are effected by the Incarnate Word. Also in 3.20.1, *praeparans adinventionem salutis quae facta est a Verbo,* links the "method" of salvation to the Word. Note also 5.1.1: "By his coming, too, he gave us imperishability, securely and truly, through communion with himself."

11. True, the entire work of incarnation–redemption was accomplished for man's salvation; yet that does not militate against the idea that the incarnation as such was planned from the beginning. Irenaeus does not say that man's salvation was the primary or exclusive reason for the incarnation. Christ's own glory comes first, or is included as the primary object of the "salvation" of humankind. Cf. A.H. 4.33.1.

12. Col 1:21–22. Though Irenaeus had been speaking about salvation through recapitulation by the incarnation, he introduces a Pauline text that emphasizes the redemption through death. Irenaeus knows genuine

Paulinism, which Jossua (93–102) recognizes but Jossa (121ff.) misrepresents. See also A.H. 4, chap. 5, n22.

13. 1 Pet 2:22. Irenaeus clearly enough teaches that Jesus was without sin, and in that his flesh differs from ours. Cf. Tertullian, *De carne Christi* 16. (CCL 2.902). In the quotation from Peter, Lat. Iren. has "in his soul," but Arm. Iren. has "in his mouth," as in the NT. SC chooses Arm. Iren., and notes that it sees no reason why Lat. Iren. would have taken "soul" since the whole context is about salvation of the flesh. Yet, it seems that the change to *anima* is so strange it had to be made deliberately. Why? Irenaeus could have had a very good reason. He is speaking about personal sins, which are not in the flesh, but in the soul. Here there is no question about saving the soul or body, but about the sinlessness of Christ, and that was primarily in his soul. Besides, by taking soul instead of mouth he is extending the sins to all, not merely to sins of the tongue. And so, Arm. Iren. again harmonized with Scripture, something Irenaeus had changed deliberately.

14. "The word about reconciliation" follows more exactly Arm. Iren. than Lat. Iren., which has a genitive *reconciliationis sermo.* Since Irenaeus quoted Col 1:22–23. at the end of the preceding paragraph and is writing a kind of commentary on it here, he is most likely alluding to those verses here, with the idea both of enmity and reconciliation, though he could still have had a genitive phrase, taken from 2 Cor 5:19, which could then refer more generally to the entire teaching about reconciliation. SC (191n2) sides more with Arm. Iren.

15. Cf. Col 1:22.

16. Eph 1:7.

17. Eph 2:13.

18. Eph 2:14–15.

19. 1 Cor 15:50.

20. Rom 6:12–13.

21. Cf. Rom 6:21–22; 7:5.

22. Irenaeus uses this construction in the prologue of Books 3, 4, and 5 and just after the prologue in Book 2. See Orbe 1:700.

23. Col 2:19.

24. "Human nature" is *hominem eius* in Lat. Iren. See A.H. 5, chap. 14, n2 on this expression. That emphasizes the reality of Christ's human nature, which is a theme throughout Book 5. We "accept" that by faith. *Excipiens* means that here, as *recipientibus adventum Filii* does in 5.17.2. It does not refer to awaiting the human nature of Christ at the second coming as Harvey and ANF suggest.

Chapter 15

1. Isa 26 (27):19 LXX.

2. Isa 66:13–14.

3. Ezek 37:1–10.

4. This clause is in both Lat. and Arm. Iren., but LXX has only: "Lord, thou knowest them." SC (199n1) says he has not found the quotation in any early Christian writer as it is in Irenaeus; yet the Bishop certainly favored it,

because it shows up the identity of the God who created and the God who will effect the resurrection.

5. Ezek 37:12–14. For a discussion of the reading and meaning of Irenaeus's comment after this citation, see A.H. 5 chap. 4, n4.

6. Isa 65:22 LXX.

7. "Who each is." The reading is not certain. Lat. Iren. MSS favor *qui est,* in place of *quid est,* as does Arm. Iren. Yet I think the meaning would be practically the same in either. From the whole passage and from A.H. 4.6.3–4, it is certain that *qui* refers to both the Son and the Father. I tried to bring that out by using "each" instead of "he."

8. John 5:14. I inserted "and so" (in keeping with SC 203n4). That clarifies the Latin, which is somewhat obscure.

9. John 9:3. For a full treatment of Irenaeus's thoughts on original sin see Orbe, *Antropo.* 277–314. G. Leroux wrote a dissertation on this subject for the Institut d'Etudes Médiévales de Montréal in 1967 entitled *Mythe et Mystère du péché originel au IIième siècle. Contribution a l'étude des origines du dogme du péché originel chez saint Irénée de Lyon,* 198 pp. He treats the concept of man in Irenaeus in the first chapter; in the second he deals with the concept of man and of "antecedent" sin according to Irenaeus's opponents; in the third chapter he details the teaching of Irenaeus on original sin, in contrast to his opponents' aberrations.

10. Gen 2:7.

11. John 9:6.

12. Cf. also A.H. 5.12.5; 5.24.4, for the Word as Artificer. In *Proof* 38 he is called the "creative Word."

13. Cf. Luke 15:1–17.

14. Jer 1:5.

15. Gal 1:15–16.

16. For this addition, see Orbe 2:52.

17. "Re-formed" refers to a second formation. The context calls for such an idea. Arm. Iren. has this word, but Lat. Iren. has the simple "formed."

18. Titus 3:5.

19. John 9:7.

20. "Gave." SC (211n1) argues that, though Lat. Iren. and Arm. Iren. have a simple "gave" (*donavit*), the parallel here between "handiwork, regeneration" of the previous clause and "know the Fashioner, the Lord who restored" calls for "re-stored" and not merely "gave." That is not certain. Irenaeus is not always so precise in parallels. The agreement of the Latin and Armenian is a strong argument in favor of the simple giving of life at creation. The man who had received his sight (a presage of the resurrection) should recognize the God who created him and gave him the breath of life at creation.

21. Cf. A.H. 1.5.4. Irenaeus uses the very expressions that his opponents used.

22. Gen 1.26. For the reference here to the Trinity see *Proof* 55 and A.H. 4, Preface, n16.

23. Lat. Iren. reads: *ei qui ao Adam caecus erat formavit visionem.* Arm. Iren. has *caecus natus,* and *replasmavit oculos.* This last point is good. SC (213n1)

accepts *natus*, but still refers this man to man in general, read *ab Adam* as "since Adam" because man has been spiritually blind since then. However, *ab Adam* quite certainly means "descended from Adam," because at the end of the paragraph the whole human race is mentioned; it was to all that Christ manifested himself. So, I think it refers directly to the one man of John 9, who is a symbol of all men spiritually blind. *Natus* does not seem authentic in Irenaeus. Arm. Iren. introduced it, possibly because that was stressed in John 9:1, 3, 19, 20, 32. See also A.H. 5.15.2, 3; and later 5.16.2.

24. Gen 3:9.

25. "Voice" is correct according to Lat. and Arm. Iren. This is the "voice" that Adam heard in the Garden (Gen 3:8, 10), which Irenaeus identifies with the Word. Except for "Voice" in place of "Word" he repeats almost verbatim a line given shortly before. Also in A.H. 5.16.1 and 17.2 the Voice is God's Son. Thus SC (213n4).

Chapter 16

1. Gen 3:19.

2. "Very clearly" is *vere liquido* in Lat. Iren. Arm. Iren. has both words but in inverse order. SC (215n1) thinks that is a doublet translation, which in Greek was ακριβός, because in 4.26.1, *certus et liquidus* of Lat. Iren. represents the one term in Greek, ακριβεστάτος, for which Arm. Iren. also has only one term. On hands, see Orbe 2:82.

3. Gen 1:26.

4. John 1:14.

5. Both in the natural and the supernatural orders man was made according to the image and likeness of God. Irenaeus refers image to the natural in man, namely, to his body and soul, but likeness to the supernatural to the "spirit" in man. Christ restored this likeness, which Adam had lost.

6. Phil 2:8. Irenaeus has in this paragraph various elements about original sin. Not only Adam sinned, but we all become debtors to God and his Word because of Adam's sin. Cf. A.H. 5, chap. 14, n3.

Chapter 17

1. On "Maker and Fashioner," see Orbe 2:12–135.

2. 1 Tim 2:5. "In the last times" begins, according to Irenaeus, with the incarnation and lasts till the second coming. See also A.H. 5.18.3 and W. C. van Unnik, "Der Ausdruck 'in den letzten Zeiten' bei Irenaeus," *Novum Testamentum Supplementum* 6 (1962): 293–304; and Jossa 130–47. Other scholars, like Werner, had denied this.

3. "Came to the aid of" is *consolatus* in Lat. Iren. ANF took this to mean "cancelled," which seems a mere guess because of the contrast between disobedience and obedience. BKV has "machte wieder gut"; that catches the idea at least in general. *Consolare* is used elsewhere: in A.H. 3.9.3, in a quotation from Isa. 41, where the Greek has *parakaleo,* Lat. Iren. interprets it as *advocare,* "come to the aid of." See 5.19.1 on *advocata.*

4. Matt 6:12.

5. "Unknowable," though Lat. Iren. has *incognitus*. In the context of his opponents' "system" and because the Greek ἀγνώστος, which was used for this in his opponents' "system," the meaning is not merely "unknown." Irenaeus treated this problem *ex professo* in A.H. 4.6.1–4.

6. Lat. Iren. has "by Scripture," but Arm. Iren. has "by the Prophets." The meaning is the same, because for Irenaeus the Prophets could refer to the whole OT. *Praedicare* is used regularly of the Prophets (about thirty-five times), but rarely of Scripture. In A.H. 2.27.2 we read: *universae scripturae et prophetae et evangelia praedicent*; in 2.35.4; *ipsis scripturis praedicentibus*. See the longer Note in SC (223n2).

7. Gen 3:8, 10.

8. Matt 9:2; Luke 5:20.

9. Cf. Luke 1:79.

10. Matt 9:8.

11. Matt 9:6.

12. "On earth" is from Arm. Iren. It is also in NT. SC (229n1) follows Arm. reading but notes a variety of difficulties in explaining how they dropped from the Latin, here and in the comment later; but there are also difficulties in explaining how they were added to Arm. if not original in Irenaeus. A theological reason for their presence might be that they stress that this earth belongs to Jesus—a point Irenaeus's opponents did not accept.

13. Cf. Luke 5:21. Lat. Iren. has the plural "men." Arm. Iren. has the singular, referring to the individual cured, spoken of in #1. SC accepts this. But *curabat*, the imperfect of continued action, involving more than one case, might indicate that the plural is correct.

14. Cf. Matt 28:18; John 20:22–23.

15. SC (229n3) observes that there are several discrepancies between the Lat. and the Arm. Iren. And, of course, SC thinks only Arm. Iren. gives a satisfactory sense. As I translated the Latin, it makes excellent sense. The Armenian translator was not so precise in watching the thought of Irenaeus. Rightly did Irenaeus say Jesus suffered with us (past tense), but that as God he now has mercy on us and forgives our sins, using the present tense here, because that continues as Irenaeus is writing. There is much Christology condensed here. It is interesting that at this early date in Christianity Christ's divinity was defended explicitly on the grounds that he forgave sins in his own name.

16. Ps 31 (32):1–2.

17. Col 2:14.

18. *Per lignum* is not in Greek or Arm. Iren., only in Lat. Iren., and yet it must be original because it is needed for the parallel. The axe is a symbol of the cross, as also of the plow in A.H. 4.34.4 because it consists of some wood and iron, joined together to make a whole instrument. It is also a symbol of Christ as Word united with human nature, and in the effect of retrieving God's word, which men had lost through sin. This symbolism is found already in Justin, *Dialogus* 86.6 (MG 6.681), from whom Irenaeus could have borrowed it.

19. Matt 3:10.

20. Jer 23:20.

21. Lat. and Arm. Iren. do not have the fourth dimension (depth) but the Greek fragment does. SC (235n1) argues for its omission.

22. "Stretching out the arms" is according to Lat. Iren. The Greek has "divine arms"; however, reference is not to Christ himself but to the cross. If so, Irenaeus is describing a Latin cross, with the projection above the crossbar. Cf. *Proof* 34 for a very similar note.

23. Cf. Eph 4.6.

Chapter 18

1. Cf. A.H. 4.35.2. Orbe 2:202–3.

2. "Hidden" is for *absconsus* of Lat. Iren., while Arm. Iren. has "separated." SC (237n1) adopts the Arm. version, on the score that the idea of a created world "hidden" from the Father was foreign to Irenaeus's opponents, but not that it was "separated" from him. And if *absconsus* is a false reading for *abcissus*, then the Latin originally agreed with Arm. Iren. Further, since *absconsus* represents ἀποκεκρυμέμη, this could have been the false reading of the original αποκεκομμένος (cf. 1.22.1; 3.11.1), or of κεχοπρισμένος (cf. 1.26.1; 2.11.1). Yet if *absconsa* should be *abscissa* as in Arm. Iren., then there were two terms to express the same idea. That is highly improbable. Besides, since Irenaeus's opponents claimed Demiurge made the world out of ignorance, it is quite in keeping with their idea that the world was hidden from him and from Father.

3. John 14:11.

4. "Bears" is in Arm. Iren. a present participle (*portans*), with the Father as subject. That way the Father bears the Word, and the Word is borne, but the Word so borne together with the Father would be subject of the finite verb (*praestat*), and both would bestow the Spirit. SC (239n1) follow that. But I followed the Latin, where *portat* has the Father as subject, but then the subject of *praestat* is the *Verbum portatum* alone. "Spirit" in the context of the Father and the Word is the Holy Spirit, rather than the spirit in man.

5. This passage reads in Lat. Iren. thus: *Verbum...praestat Spiritum omnibus quemadmodum vult Pater. quibusdam secundum conditionem, quod est conditionis, quod est factum; quibusdam autem secundum adoptionem, quod est ex Deo, quod est generatio.* It is easier to understand the construction if one remembers that the Latin was handicapped in not having a definite article. Lat. Iren. used the relative pronouns profusely for this. So the six relatives here most probably stand for definite articles. *Quod est conditionis* was omitted by the Clermont and Voss MSS, but it is demanded by the parallel structure and is guaranteed by Arm. Iren. For *Deo* Arm. Iren. has *Patre*, which is probably correct. The antecedent of the *quod* is πνεῦμα—spirit of the introductory clause. In the first case he is the type that pertains to creation, and he is made; in the second case he is the type that belongs to supernatural adoption, and he is not made, but is a generation, an offspring. From this one cannot argue that Irenaeus thinks of the Spirit as being generated just as the Son is. He simply chooses a word that distinguishes this Spirit from the created spirit. On all this see the long and competent note of SC (241n1).

6. Cf. Eph 4:6.

7. 1 Cor 11:3.

8. Col 1:18; Eph 5:23.

9. Cf. John 7:38–39, and A.H. 3, chap. 17, n13.

10. Eph 4:6.

11. John 1:1–3.

12. John 1:10–12.

13. John 1:14. "in human nature" is *secundum hominem* in both Lat. and Arm. Iren., and with *secundum* it has, here as elsewhere, adjectival force, simply "human nature"; but to make this clear it is better to translate "the economy in human nature." Compare "coming in human nature" of A.H. 4.38.1; and "a generation in human nature" of 3.11.8; and "economy in human nature" of 3.17.4.

14. Cf. A.H. 1.28.4. "Prounikos" is in Lat. Iren. "Power of Prounikos," a genitive of apposition: the power is Prounikos. She was also known as Mother.

15. That the Word was invisibly present in his creation from the beginning is also in *Proof* 34. "Inscribed in the form of a cross" is from Arm. Iren. In a long note SC (245n2) cautions against making the mistake of reading the Armenian as *xacéceal*, an aorist participle from *xacém* (to crucify). It should be *xacaceal*, aor. part. from *xacanam* (to take the form of a cross). SC, with the aid of a better translation of *Proof* 34, justified in a long note, thinks the Greek word was *kechiasmenos*. *Xiazein* means to mark with two lines crossing as an x, or to make a cruciform incision. Lat. Iren. would have gotten only the general idea from the verb, to inscribe, without indicating the special form. So one cannot speak of the Word's having been crucified. Irenaeus sees in the symbol of the cross (made of iron and wood) the unicity of the Word creating all things and then saving as the Incarnate Word. Cf. Houssiau 107–9. On the cross symbol see above A.H. 5, chap. 17, n18.

16. "Visible manner." Both Lat. and Arm. Iren. have *invisibiliter*, supposing ἀορατος. But the context clearly and certainly demands *visibiliter*. The Greek text had been tampered with before either translation was made.

17. Cf. Gal. 3:13; Acts 5:30; 10:39.

18. Eph 1:10.

19. John 1:11.

20. Deut 28:66.

21. John 1:12.

22. Cf. Matt 28:18.

23. "Ruling over" is for *principans*, according to all the MSS and Arm. Iren. It is accepted by SC and Jossua (90n138). It fits the thought very well. *Participans*, which Massuet and Harvey read, does not fit at all. Cf. also Houssiau 109. "Rational manner" and "intelligent manner" are for *rationabiliter* and *sensuabiliter* of Lat. Iren. *Rationabiliter* supposes λογικός, which was a play on Λόγος. Literally it would mean in a manner befitting the Word. *Sensuabiliter* has nothing to do with sensually. It supposes the Greek νοήτος which comes from *νοῦς*, the mind, often translated in Latin by *sensus*.

24. Ps 49 (50):3a.

25. Ps 49 (50):3b–4.

Chapter 19

1. "Was brought the good news." Lat. Iren. has Mary as subject of *evangelisata est,* and this is the independent clause of the first parallel about Eve and Mary. Arm. Iren. has a relative *qua* before, which SC accepts without explanation.

2. "Was loosed" is according to Arm. Iren., which fits the context of being loosed after having been held bound. The Latin MSS are divided: Clermont and Voss have *salvatur,* but Arundel and Vatican MSS and Erasmus have *solvatur.* For "through the virginal disobedience" I followed the Latin, which has it in the nominative case; Arm. Iren has it in the ablative. This is the famous passage of Irenaeus on the antithesis between Eve and Mary, but, as is obvious, it is set within the antithesis between Adam and Christ, or, in other words, in the recapitulation of all things by Christ, as the very first sentence indicates. Mary is introduced here in order to explain how Christ, God's Son, could have recapitulated and given salvation to Adam. The answer is: he took his human nature—the same human nature that Adam had—from the virgin mother Mary. He states this first in a general way and then develops it in more detail. The general statement is that Eve, though wedded, was yet a virgin and was deceived by an angel (namely, into being disobedient); Mary, also wedded but a virgin, was brought good news by an angel, which she accepted by obedience, and thus undid the evil the first virgin had wrought. This he then explains by steps, contrasting Eve and Mary. Eve was deceived by the angel's word and was guilty of a transgression of disobedience, with the result that she fled from God: Mary, in contrast, was brought good news, also by an angel; she obeyed this word of God, with the result that she became the bearer of God. This obedience of Mary's resulted in her becoming the "advocate" of Eve. Again, the virgin Eve's action resulted in the whole race being put in bondage to death: the virgin Mary loosed those bonds, thus by her virginal obedience counterbalancing the virginal disobedience. Having stated this about Eve and Mary, he returns to his topic about Christ and Adam.

This paragraph has been treated in detail in Unger, *ME,* 82–89. To the bibliography given there we can now add Aldama 278–93; L. Begnault, *DS* p. 7.2 (1971), 1952–55. There is a close parallel to this in *Proof* 33; see also A.H. 3.22.4; 4.33.4. Mary's role in relation to Christ is clear and certain: she is the virgin mother of the Incarnate Word; he thereby has the human nature of Adam and is able to recapitulate and save all people.

Irenaeus also states an effect of Mary's being the virgin mother of Christ on Eve and on all the race. That must be analyzed more. Mary became the "advocate" of Eve. This word is taken from the Latin *advocare.* The Greek is not extant. Arm. Iren. helps us immensely here, because it gives not merely one word but three interrelated words. That does not mean that the Greek had three words. In *Proof* 34 the Armenian has only one word too. The three Armenian words mean Mary is comforter—consoler, adviser, and defender-advocate. In the detailed analysis of *advocatus* in A.H. offered in Unger, *ME* 82–99, Fr. Unger found that for Lat. Iren. *advocatus* meant a defender, e.g., against accusers (see A.H. 3.18.7; 23.8; 4.34.4); a consoler (A.H. 3.9.3; 17.2; 5.15.1; 16.3). Because of the Greek *parakalein* and *parakletos* involved in some of these passages, through scriptural quotations, it is fairly certain that the Greek word Irenaeus used here is παρακλέτος. The ending is masculine only apparently, because for such participles the same ending is used for masculine and feminine genders. This conclusion is strengthened by the fact that in the Letter of the Churches of Vienne and Lyons (which Irenaeus most likely wrote), Christ is called the παρακλέτος of the martyr Epagathos, and this martyr was called the παρακλέτος of the Christians, because he defended them against false accusers.

That much is said of Eve expressly. Now Irenaeus says that Mary by her action released men from the bondage of death, for which Eve had been responsible. That means that Mary was the cause of salvation for the race, as the Bishop states in A.H. 3.22.4. But I believe that what is said of Eve holds also for her race, and what is said of her race holds for her. So the complete statement would be that Mary became the advocate of, and so released from the bondage of death, Eve and her entire race.

Factually, by becoming Mother of the Savior, Mary defended Eve and us against Satan, and in that sense she interceded for us. But since her action was not merely physical, but was accompanied by acts of faith and obedience, these could not have been without a prayerful attitude on her part that "God's will be done"; and so I think the notion of Mary's being Eve's intercessor, and ours too, in a general way is included in the mind of Irenaeus; consequently, in kernel we have here the later, more developed notion of Mary our advocate. Aldama (*María,* 289) rejects my notion of intercession here; but as I explained it, it seems impossible to exclude it. M. Jourjon, "Aux origínes de la priére d'intercession de Marie," *Bulletin de Société Franc. des Etudes Mariales* 23 (1966): 38–42, argues convincingly for the inclusion of intercession in *advocate,* especially in view of its use for the martyrs of Lyons.

Scholars have discussed the origin of Irenaeus's teaching about Eve and Mary. He might have got it from Justin, *Dialogus* 100 (MG 6.709, 712). If he did, he certainly developed it far beyond Justin. Whether Justin had treated the matter more at length in his longer work, *Syntagma* (now not extant), is simply unknown to us.

3. Cf. Matt 10:16.

4. Cf. A.H. 1.6.1.

5. Cf. A.H. 1.31.4; 2.P.2. Orbe 2:293–94.

Chapter 20

1. There are various churches, scattered over the world; but all are united in one faith and government and worship, as described in the following lines. Compare also A.H. 3.2.2, to which he refers here; and 4.26.2, 4, 5.

2. For more on harmony and order here, see Orbe 2:298.

3. Notice here how Irenaeus links the Father, Son, and Spirit with the economy of salvation.

4. "Structure"—Lat. Iren. has *figura ordinationis. Figura* is shape or structure; *ordinatio* is order. So this is structure that results from order. Grabe rightly held that there is in this an allusion to the ordained ministry because the order in the Church is due to bishops and presbyters. Harvey wants to

refer it to the constitution of the Church in general and suggests the Greek was καταστάσις. But in the seven other places where *originatio* occurs in Books 3 to 5, it is always used of an ordering of things in succession or sequence, except in 4.36.6, in the quotation from Rom 8, where it refers to God's command and the Greek is διαταγή. In three of the other places the Greek is extant as τάξις. So in the present passage it certainly refers to the ordered succession in the hierarchy.

5. This last sentence is a clever summary of the main tenets of the Church, practically a creed.

6. Prov 1:20–21.

7. Cf. Exod 25:37; Rev 1:20. This is a beautiful figure of Christ's truth as his light.

8. Cf. A.H. 2.27.1; 3.11.7. Orbe 2:321.

9. Matt 15:25; cf. Matt 15:14; Luke 6:39.

10. 2 Tim 3:7.

11. Though there are many churches scattered over the world, as described in # 1, they are all united into one Church, which is unerring in its tradition, to which all people must have recourse. Cf. A.H. 3.3.2.

12. Gen 2:16.

13. Cf. Rom 12:3; A.H. 5.21.2; 3.25.7; 4.19.1. Orbe 2:332.

14. Gen 2:17.

15. On this point, see Orbe 2:334–35.

16. Rom 12:3. "Prudence" is *prudentiam* where the Vulgate has *sobrietas*.

17. Eph 1:10.

Chapter 21

1. For more on these key chapters, see Scott D. Moringiello, *The Rhetoric of Faith: Irenaeus and the Structure of the Adversus Haereses* (Washington, DC: Catholic University of America Press, 2019), 164–69.

2. In the past some have read *provocans* with *bellum*, but it is certain that this belongs with *elidens* and governs *eum*. *Provocans* means to "call to" something; e.g., to evangelize, as in 3.14.1, in a quotation from Acts 16:6 (Greek has προσκάλειν); or "calls for," in the sense of demands (3.25.3); or invited to (3.20.3; 5.17.2). So in the context of war it is a challenging. Arm. Iren is somewhat redundant in words here, but it seems this word is translated as "inciting to battle." *Elidens* fits in with the idea of defeating the enemy and *trampling* on him. But Arm. Iren. has *vincens* here, which SC (263n1) prefers, as more in keeping with the context of victory and in contrast to taking captive. It is interesting to note that the only other place where Lat. Iren. uses *elidere*, it is used in combination with *vincere*: in 5.17.2 the Devil is presented as having "conquered man and dashed him to pieces." In our present passage this kind of defeat is attributed to Christ over Satan. Irenaeus likes to present salvation as Christ's victory over Satan. Nearly all of A.H. 5.21–30 is on this theme. Cf. Lawson 176–96.

3. Gen. 3:15. In this paragraph Irenaeus teaches four things in regard to Gen 3:15. (1) The first Gospel speaks prophetically of Christ and the Virgin; (2) St. Paul clearly understood this in Gal 3:19 and 4:4 and practically gave

an interpretation to that effect; (3) the woman of Gen 3:15 is Mary, because it was through her mediation that we all receive life, just as we all inherited death through Eve; (4) the woman is a virgin mother, because her child is the offspring of her alone, as is clear from Paul, whom he quotes. See Unger, *ME* 120–29. A. Orbe, *Greg.* 1971, 237–38, correctly observes that God, even before Adam fell, thought of his Son as Head of the human race, with a divine headship, as the principle of human salvation. Already since Gen 1:26, Christ, in his glorious flesh, was the one and only efficacious principle of salvation for the human race. God positively chose him, in the flesh, and predestined him for that purpose.

4. Gal 4:19.

5. Gal 4:4.

6. "Justly" on Christ's part, not as if the devil had any rights over man—Irenaeus denies that emphatically over and over again—but precisely because he had no rights.

7. This is another classic passage from the ancient Church on the antithesis between Adam and Christ, and between Eve and Mary.

8. Gen 1:26.

9. Matt 4:1ff.; Exod 24:18; 2 Kgs 19:8.

10. "Fasts" is for *ieiunantem* of Lat. Iren. Arm. Iren. spelled that out more clearly by *inedia utentem,* which SC (267n1) accepts and translates: "while he abstains from food."

11. Matt 4:3.

12. Matt 4:4; Deut 8:3.

13. "Satiety" is *repletio,* which makes good sense. Harvey suggested that *repletio* represents *anaplerosis,* which was a misreading for *anaperosis,* a visitation. But that would seem to make little sense here.

14. Matt 4:6; Ps 90 (91):11.

15. Here Irenaeus explicitly links his opponents with Satan. Their interpretation takes its inspiration from him.

16. Matt 4:7; Deut 4:16.

17. Lat. Iren. reads: *ostendens (Christus) id [quantum] quidem quod est secundum hominem, quoniam non debet homo tentare Deum; quantum autem ad illum, quoniam in eo homine qui videbatur, non tentaret Dominum Deum suum.* I inserted *quantum* to indicate that the Greek construction was most likely more parallel than the Latin indicates. It is clear that there is an introductory clause of limitation to each of the prohibitions. The first clause is clear enough: According to the Law of Deuteronomy that the Devil quoted, man in general is not to tempt God. The difficulty is in the second clause. Who is antecedent of *illum,* and who, consequently, is subject of the second *temptaret*? Two opinions have been held. The one takes *illum* to refer to the Devil, and he is the subject of *temptaret*: As far as he (the Devil) is concerned, (Christ showed) that he may not tempt the Lord his God in the man here visible before him. This opinion takes *illum,* supposing *auton,* in its normal meaning, and it reads the phrase *in eo homine qui videbatur* quite naturally. However, Arm. Iren. has for *quantum... illum: id autem quod ad ipsum est,* which seems to refer to Christ speaking, and SC (271n2) defends that. Αὑτόν can mean "himself," and so it can mean: as far as the man Christ is concerned, neither he, in the man here visible, may tempt

God. It would be against the mind of Irenaeus to think Christ is telling the Devil that he may not tempt God. In fact, Christ reproved the Devil for suggesting that he tempt God. Yet, Christ could have turned tables on the Devil and refuted him by quoting the Law at him directly: You may not tempt God either in the person of myself whom you see here. It seems to me this is still the better interpretation. It was defended by M. Steiner, *La Tentation de Jésus dans l'interprétation patristique de Saint Justin á Origéne* (Paris: Etudes Bibliques, 1962), 55.

18. Matt 4:9.

19. Luke 4:6–7.

20. Matt 4:10.

21. For the same explanation of the Devil's name see *Proof* 16.

22. Matt 12:29.

23. Lat. Iren. is somewhat obscure in its cryptic style, and Arm. Iren. does not help much. My translation follows the Latin as closely as possible. *Contraria in sermone* (Arm. *sermoni*) refers back to the discussion about the Devil's trying to give Christ false advice that is contrary to the Scriptures.

24. *Homo eius* quite certainly refers to Christ, precisely in his human nature, or inasmuch as he was in visible form. *Eius* refers back to *Dominus.* See long note of SC (277n2).

25. The devil was fugitive from Christ by refusing him homage in the very first of his apostasies, namely, at his original trial in "heaven." Ever after, he tried to get people to apostatize from Christ and to have himself worshipped, to arrogate to himself the rights of Christ. See below #4, and 28.2. See also Unger, FS 124–28.

26. "Thereafter" is *postea iam* in Lat. Iren.; Arm. Iren. is "for the rest," supposing the Greek τὸ λοιπόν.

Chapter 22

1. "Commands us to praise." Lat. Iren. has an infinitive, *laudare,* which is then, together with *servire,* controlled by *iubet.* Arm. Iren. has *laudat,* and so only *servire* is subject to *iubet.* SC (279n2) defends this. However, in the sequel Irenaeus quotes Deut 6, in which there is a command to love, adore, and serve God. That *love* and *adore* refers, I believe, to the present *laudare* and *serve* to *servire.* So two things are commanded.

2. Rom 3:20.

3. Irenaeus refers to the theory that the Law was supposed to be from Demiurge, and he from Achamoth, and she from Wisdom, who erred through ignorance and degeneracy.

4. Deut 6:4, 5, 13.

5. Matt 4:7; Deut 6:16.

6. "Adversary": Lat. Iren. has *Satanam,* which means the Adversary, as Irenaeus explained earlier. Arm. Iren. has Apostasy, which SC (281n1) thinks might have corrupted to *Satanam.*

7. Rom 12:16.

8. Luke 4:6.

9. Matt 10:29.

10. Luke 4:6.
11. John 8:44.

Chapter 23

1. Gen 2:16–17.
2. Gen 3:1.
3. Gen 3:2–3.
4. Gen 3:4.
5. Cf. Gen 1:5. From the subsequent explanation it is clear that Irenaeus is taking *unus* to mean one, not first, as actually in Genesis.
6. Gen 2:17.
7. Irenaeus is extending his idea of recapitulation to unwarranted extremes in this chronological calculation.
8. 2 Pet 3:6.
9. "Day of preparation" is *caena pura.* In A.H. 1.14.6, this same Latin expression is used, but the Greek text has *παρασκευή*. *Caena pura* must be a Latin gloss since it is missing in Arm. Iren.
10. John 8:44.

Chapter 24

1. Matt 4:9; Luke 6:6.
2. Prov 21:1.
3. Prov 8:15–16 LXX.
4. Rom 13:1.
5. Rom 13:4.
6. Rom 13:6.
7. Matt 17:27.
8. Rom 13:4.
9. Rom 13:6. Since Irenaeus a little later alludes to 2 Thess 2:4, it seems likely that he does here too, in the sense that the laws are the restraining power mentioned in 2 Thess 2:7.
10. "Devour each other like fish." Cf. W. Parsons, "Lest men, like fish," *Tradition* 3 (1945): 380–88, who explains that this figure of people devouring each other like fish is in here in a political context. In Athenagoras, *Legatio pro christianis* 34 (ACW 23.75), it is in a socio-moral context. This metaphor is to have a long history in Christian literature.
11. I followed Arm. Iren., as indicated by the additions in angular brackets, which parts are omitted in Lat. Iren., possibly because a scribe did not duplicate an identical phrase as he should have. The Latin beginning with *Quae* from a quotation is abrupt. It could possibly be taken as a causal clause and then the rest would follow. But Arm. Iren. reads well. Besides, though the Greek excerpt is itself not in line with either Latin or Armenian, it does have an "and," suggesting that the Armenian is correct in the rest too. For the last phrase quoted see Rom 13:1.
12. Luke 4:6.

13. Cf A.H. 5.22.2; 5.24.1.

14. Lat. Iren. and Arm. agree, as I translated. The Greek excerpt has "not" in place of "whose," which is difficult to explain. See SC (303n3).

15. 2 Thess 2:4. "Begin to serve him" is according to Lat. Iren., for which Arm. Iren. has "they obeyed." SC (305n1) finds it difficult to see what the Latin translator read in his Greek copy, if that is the original Latin. But the Latin seems to give the correct meaning. If they begin to serve him, he can blind their hearts; if they do not, he can't. The Armenian might be saying the same thing with "if they listen."

16. Eph 2:2. Paul actually speaks of "the prince of the power of the air," and "the prince of the spirit which now works on the unbeliever." Irenaeus condensed this into the phrase "the spirit of the air."

17. Irenaeus stresses the envy of Satan against man, which was ultimately against the God-Man, whom he not only refused to worship, but whose worship he bought for himself. See Unger, FS 124–28. In the beginning he showed that envy against Adam, but gradually he revealed the real object of his envy, the God-Man. And so man became the *test* of his sentiments. Lat. Iren. has *examinatio sententiae,* for which SC gives a too paraphrastic translation: "la pierre de touche de se dispositions intimes," and justifies the Armenian as better than the Latin (307n1). Arm. Iren. is supposed to have read δοκιμεῖνον. This can have two meanings. The one, simply the testing of something for knowing its value. This material sense was taken by Lat. Iren., which is not too intelligible. Arm. Iren. took the second meaning: a means for testing. I think *examinatio* can mean that too. It is not merely the action of testing. Besides, to guess that δοκιμεῖνον is the Greek and then argue from it as if it were certain is not scholarly. Lat. Iren. uses *examinatio* once more in A.H. 1.11.1 for expressing a purpose for the emission of Spirit. It was to test the Aeons and also to make them fruitful. Here the Greek is *ἀνακρίσις*. I think there is great probability that this was the word Irenaeus wrote in our place. Man is the means against which or by which Satan disclosed his sentiments.

18. Luke 10:19.

Chapter 25

1. "Impious and lawless" is three terms in Lat. Iren, *impius et iniustus et sine lege.* Arm. Iren. has only two terms; and in a parallel case in A.H. 5.24.2, there are only two terms: *impie et contra legem.* So in our present passage *iniustus* and *sine lege* may translate one Greek term, possibly *anomos* (lawless) (cf. 2 Thess 2:8; 2 Pet 2:8). *Contra legem* may be the same as *sine lege,* given the penchant of Lat. Iren. to vary his terms. But it could also stand for ἀθέσμος, against the law, unlawful (see 2 Pet 7).

2. 2 Thess 2:3–4. "As God" is from Arm. Iren., which is not in the NT nor in Lat. Iren. It is superfluous because of the ending to this sentence "to be God." Yet it could have been in Irenaeus's Bible because it is in some minor MSS of the NT, e.g., in the Syriac Bible, but there it was in place of "of God." SC (313n2) thinks it easier to explain its addition in Arm. than its omission in Lat. Iren. I kept it hesitantly.

3. Satan betrays his original intention of refusing worship to the God-Man.

4. "Order" is *dispositio* in Lat. Iren.; and Arm. Iren. seems to represent *diatage*, which means order, more clearly than *dispositio* does. *Dispositio* could also suppose διαταγή in Greek. It need not suppose some more general word for arrangement. In A.H. 5.22.2 *ordinatio* is explained by *disponuntur*, but in 4.36.6, in a quotation from Rom 13:2, *ordinationi* represents *diatage*, the only place where this Greek word is extant in Irenaeus. So there is very little difference between Lat. Iren. and Arm. Iren., and both must have read the same Greek word, which seems to have been διαταγή. It should be noted that in the further explanation of *dispositio* Lat. Iren. uses *iussu*, in the very similar phrase: *cuius iussu hoc quodfactum est templum*; above it was *templum per dispositionem veri Dei est.* That makes *dispositio* practically a synonym of *iussus.*

5. Cf. A.H. 3.6–8.

6. Matt 24:15–17, 21.

7. Dan 7:8, 20–22.

8. Dan 7:23–25.

9. 2 Thess 2:8–12.

10. John 5:43.

11. Luke 18:6, and 2–3.

12. Dan 8:12 (Theodotion).

13. Dan 8:23–26 (Theodotion).

14. Dan 9:27.

15. Matt 24:15.

16. Luke 1:26–38.

17. "Sent" is from Arm. Iren., for which Lat. Iren. has the compound *praemisit*, which seems to be a slavish rendition of even the prefix in *ἀποστέλλω*. In A.H. 4.23.1 we have the same; but in 4.36.2 we read the simple *misit: qui prophetas misit, qui Filium suum misit.*

Chapter 26

1. Rev 17:12–14.

2. Matt 12:25.

3. Dan 2:33–34 (Theodotion).

4. Dan 2:41–42.

5. *Sive* in Lat. Iren. seems to indicate that *efficaces* was originally a marginal note explaining *agiles*, or it is a doublet translation.

6. Dan. 2:42–43. "Partly" translates the Latin *ab ipsa pars*, which is a slavish translation of Theodotion's version ἀπ' αὐτῆς ἔσται. LXX has the regular construction of μέρος τι here and also in vs. 33, where even Theodotion's version has this normal construction. So above *ab ipsa* means partly.

7. Dan 2:44–45.

8. Dan 2:44. Prior to this quotation, the expression "resurrection of the just" may allude to Luke 14:14.

9. "Economies relative to the human race." I followed Lat. Iren., which has: *secundum humanum genus dispositiones.* The prepositional phrase is, in Irenaeus's style, an adjectival modifier for *dispositiones*, meaning

"human economies." But to bring out the meaning more clearly I translated as above. "Human race" is correct. Lat. Iren. has the expression forty-three times. In seven of those cases the Greek is extant, and it is always ἀνυρωπότης. So it is quite certain that that was the term here. Lat. Iren. has the plural for *dispositiones*. This plural, indicating the various smaller economies, is found often; e.g., A.H. 3.11.8; 12.13; 4.20.7; 28.2; 33.7, 15. And so even though he also uses the singular for the one overall economy, and though the Arm. Iren. has the singular, and though the singular occurs in a similar case in A.H. 3.22.4, there is no reason to change the Latin. SC (333n2) followed Arm. Iren.

10. "Twisting the thought" gives the Latin: *secundum eversionem sententiae*. That agrees in thought with Arm. Iren. See A.H. 3.12.2, where he gives a longer explanation of this policy of his opponents.

11. Matt 25:41.

12. "As if being hidden" is *quasi latens Deum*. Arm. Iren. has either the infinitive *latere* or the gerund *ad latendum*. That is an attempt to bring out the meaning of the Greek, most likely λανθάνον.

13. The work of Justin referred to is not extant. Eusebius, *Hist. Eccl.* 4.18.9 (GCS 2.1.366), repeats the account, which was used often by the Greek writers of the Middle Ages.

14. Matt 25:41; Mark 9:42; 2 Thess 1:8.

15. "To his own free choice" is according to the Greek excerpt, with which Lat. Iren. agrees in a similar case in A.H. 5.27.2. However, at this place it reads: *suae voluntati et sententiae*.

Chapter 27

1. Matt 10:35.
2. Cf. Luke 17:34–35.
3. Cf. Matt 13:30.
4. Matt 25:32, 33, 34, 41.
5. Luke 2:34.
6. Luke 10:12.
7. Matt 7:21.
8. Matt 5:45.

9. In this paragraph the expression "good things with (or from) God" occurs three times, and twice in A.H. 4.39.4. It is not certain whether Irenaeus said they are *with* God or *from* him. In Greek the preposition would be the same, but for *with* the case would be dative, while for *from* it would be genitive. The Greek is extant in in our present passage, but not in 4.39. Lat. Iren. has *apud* (with) in the first two cases of the present passage and in the first case of 4.39, but *erga* in the second case (which is the same as *apud*); but it has *a* (from) in the third case of Book 5. Arm. Iren. has "with" in the first case of the present passage and in the two cases of Book 4; it has "from" in the second and third case of Book 5. SC translated all three with "from" according to the Greek (343n1). I think one could see a difference in the cases. In the first case it is a question of the good things enjoyed in beatitude, and that should be "with" God (as Lat. and Arm.). In the second case they are the good things

of which the bad have deprived themselves; this should be "from" (as in Arm. and Greek). The third case is a general principle: all good things come "from" God (as in Lat. and Arm. and Greek).

10. This is certainly a clear description of hell as fashioned by the sinner himself; see also 5.28.1. But heaven, too, is eternal and is given because of one's free choice, as he noted above.

11. John 3:18.

12. *Loc. cit.*

13. John 3:19–21.

Chapter 28

1. Cf. Matt 25:34, 41.
2. 2 Thess 2:10–12.
3. Rev 19:20.
4. 2 Thess 2:11.
5. Rev 13:2–10.
6. Rev 13:11–14.
7. Rev 13:14–18, with some omissions.
8. Gen 2:1–2.
9. 2 Pet 3:18.

10. Gen 1:26. "Hands" are certainly the Word and the Spirit, and so Lat. Iren. genitives (*Filii et Spiritus*) are in apposition to *Dei.* Lat. Iren. did not give a "contresens" here, as SC remarks (361n1). On creation through the hands of God see A.H. 4, chap. 20, n6. To the bibliography on this we can add Lawson 119–39, who correctly notes that this figure of the hands lends itself well to emphasizing equality of persons, with no semblance of modalism, and at the same time the unicity of God (129–32).

11. Cf. Matt 3:12; Luke 3:17.

12. I followed Lat. Iren. and Arm. Iren., which have two words (with slightly different meanings), where the Greek has only one λεπτονθέντες. This Greek has a varied meaning from threshing and husking, to grinding and thinning out. Now in this process of making bread that Irenaeus describes, he mentioned first the threshing (*paleis abiectis*), then putting the grain into the granary (*in horreum*), next comes this grinding (the one Greek word), then the kneading (*conspersi,* in Greek one word), and finally the baking (*igniti*). So, even though λεπτονθέντες could mean threshing, in our set up that is not possible, because that was expressed by a previous word as the first step. It is something done between taking the grain from the granary to kneading it. This can scarcely be thinning out. So it seems Lat. and Arm. Iren. gave a doublet translation to bring out the full meaning of grinding and grinding fine. SC (361n2) suggests that Lat. Iren. brought out the two meanings, which are "broyer" and "aminicir," but, as I noted, threshing is not part of that concept, and neither is to thin out, which would follow the kneading.

13. Ignatius, *Ad Romanos* 4.1 (ACW 1.81–82). According to this, Ignatius spoke of God's wheat and Christ's bread, which seems quite logical. Our Lat. Iren. and Arm. have Christ's wheat and God's bread, while the Greek excerpt has God's wheat and God's bread. SC took Lat. and Arm. Iren. with

no comment. Maybe this text was used often and quoted from memory. The Greek would favor God's wheat, but none of the other witnesses would favor "Christ's bread." On this, see Scott D. Moringiello, "Sacrifice, Eucharist, and Love in Ignatius of Antioch." *Studia Patristica* 109 (2021): 109–118.

Chapter 29

1. Isa 40:15, 17. Creation is for man, and man is the central figure in all creation, so he should have been grateful to God. See Orbe, *Antrop.* 39–40.

2. Matt 24:21.

3. As noted in the Introduction, recapitulation is a major theme in the *Adversus Haereses.* Here we see that Irenaeus discusses not only Christ's recapitulation but also the recapitulation of the Devil. See Orbe 3:222.

4. Cf. Rev 19:20.

5. Cf. Gen 6:1ff. For the numerical name 666 see Rev 13:8.

6. "Living being" cf. Gen 7:23, from which this whole phrase comes. Since it is in the context of the flood, the Greek fragment clearly took ἐχαλέοφων ἀνάστημα from there. In Gen this means every being, or every living being that had *arisen* on the earth. It is explained there as including men, beasts, reptiles, birds. Arm. Iren. has *resurrectionem*; since the idea of a resurrection is such nonsense in the context of the flood, one wonders if Arm. Iren. understood the Greek correctly but had no word to express it. This I believe is truer of Lat. Iren., who wrote *insurrectionem.* This is one of those attempts at a very literal rendition: since *resurrectionem* would be misleading, the translator added *in,* which also gave him the effect of the Greek prefix *ana-*, though that was already in the *re-* of *resurrectionem,* but in a different sense. Some Latin scribes had a problem with *inresurrectionem,* since some MSS (V and A and Erasmus) wrote *in resurrectionem*: See SC (367n1).

7. Cf. Dan 3:1.

8. Cf. Dan 3:20.

Chapter 30

1. "Trustworthy and ancient" follows the Greek fragment. For "ancient" both Lat. and Arm. Iren. have a doublet: *antiquis et probatissimis et veteribus* (Lat.); *veteribus-antiquis* (Arm.). Since Greek and Arm. agree in putting "trustworthy" ahead, I think in Lat. Iren. *antiquis* crept in as a marginal note.

2. This whole paragraph shows how Irenaeus's information reaches back to St. John through the disciples. Irenaeus was concerned to have the correct reading of the Scriptures on the number 666. He rejects 616, which is found in some MSS of Rev. Orbe, *Greg.* 1952, 259–62, notes that Hippolytus, *De Antichristo,* does not mention 616, so both may be relying on a common source.

3. "Reason" stands for *logos,* which is verified by the Greek, Lat. and Arm. Iren. But *logos* can have different meanings. As SC (371n1) ably shows, Irenaeus had proved that this number comes from the unimpeachable source of Scripture; it agrees with the testimony of the presbyters; and it also fits into

the whole theory of recapitulation, that is, it is according to "reason." That is what he will now show. The number 666 symbolizes the totality of evil that the Antichrist is, which Christ will recapitulate by overcoming it.

4. "Beginning" is for *inciperent*, which supposes the Greek idiomatic construction with μελλόντων. That fits into the sentence well. He is contrasting the beginning for correcting the affairs with the strengthening of the kingdom. Arm. Iren. has "imagine," which supposes δοκούτων, which is a misreading.

5. Matt 24:15.

6. 1 Thess 5:3.

7. Jer 8:16.

8. Cf. Rev 7:5–7.

9. Orbe notes that Euthanus means "very flowery" and by extension, "various colors." Euthanus is also one of the children of Dionysius and Ariadne. Orbe 3:267.

10. According to Overbeck, the name "Teitan" (Titan) is connected with the idea of a vengeful and punitive authority. See Overbeck 452–53.

11. Irenaeus refers to Roman mythology. This Titan, the grandson of the great Titan, was son of Hyperion, the Sun-god, Sol. Of him, according to Massuet, Cicero speaks in *Aratus* 60, and Ovid in *Metamorphoses* 1.10.

12. Domitian's regime was AD 81–96, which agrees with the authorities of early Christianity that Rev was written in the last years of Domitian. To be noted is that Irenaeus says John had his vision at this time. He does not say that is when John died. This, then, does not contradict what he says in A.H. 2.225, that John stayed on till the times of Trajan (A.D. 98–117), which is verified if he died in the early years of Trajan. True, as noted by B. Newman, "The Fallacy of the Domitian Hypothesis. Critique of the Irenaeus Source as a Witness for the Contemporary Historical Approach to the Interpretation of the Apocalypse," *New Testament Studies* 10 (1962/3): 133–39, this latter remark about the Trajan times is not relevant to the date of Revelation. Newman also notes correctly that Irenaeus does not, by his remark on Domitian, suggest that Revelation alludes to the persecution by Domitian, as if Rev were an account of contemporary history. Irenaeus takes it allegorically about all apostasies since the beginning of time, but with special emphasis on his own times.

13. Rev 17:8.

14. 2 Thess 2:4.

15. Matt 16:27; 24:64; from Dan 7:13; Luke 23:69.

16. Cf. Matt 8:11. There is here an allusion to his notion about the millennium, which he will describe at length later.

Chapter 31

1. "Pass over" is in Latin Iren. *supergredientes*, which is very exact for the idea that these people want to disregard and jump over the various steps upward toward eternal life that God has established. SC translates that with "negligent," which misses the nuance. For Irenaeus there are two points involved in the process of advancement: order and harmony. These are paired in A.H. 4.38.3; 5.31.1; 36.2. Both *ordo* (5.31.1) and *ordination* (4.38.3; 5.36.2) stand for the Greek τάξις. "Harmony" stands for the Greek ῥύθμος

which Lat. Iren. rendered variously by *convenientiam* (4.38.3), *modos* (5.31.1), and *dispositio* (5.36.2). Lat. Iren. was not embarrassed by this concept, as SC (389n2) thinks. He merely indulged in his elegant variations.

2. Cf. Tertullian, *De anima* 55, 1 (CCL 2.862).

3. On this apocryphal quotation see A.H. 3.20.4, and A.H. 3, chap. 20, n21.

4. Matt 12:40.

5. Eph 4:9.

6. Ps 85 (86):13.

7. John 20:17.

8. Col 1:18.

9. John 20:20, 27.

10. Ps 22 (23):4.

11. Of course, this is the major theme of Irenaeus's understanding of salvation. See de Andia 321–336, Overbeck 478–492, Moringiello, *The Rhetoric of Faith*, 176–80.

12. Luke 6:40.

Chapter 32

1. "Beginning" is *principium* in Lat. Iren. SC, guessing that the Greek was προοίμιον (see A.H. 5.1.1), translates it as "prelude." Arm. Iren. has a kind of doublet using a noun with an adjective: *arrhabo praevius*. SC (397n1) thinks that means a preamble or a prelude. But that is arguing too strongly from a Greek word that was merely a guess. Arm. Iren. *arhauatacem* means *pignus*. Since the genitive that follows (*incorruptelae*) is a synonym of *haereditatis* used with *pignus* (*arrhabo*) in Eph 2:14, and since Arm. Iren. would scarcely have used this odd word, which needed an explanation, unless it was in his Greek copy, I believe that was the Greek word Irenaeus wrote. So, this resurrection is a pledge of the imperishable life that will follow.

2. "All men" is from Arm. Iren.; it is missing in Lat. Iren., but SC (397n3) defends it fairly.

3. Rom 8:19–21. This paragraph, as all the last chapters, is on millenarianism. See G. Bardy, "Millenarisme," DTC 6, no. 2 (1929): 1760–63; E. Buonaiuti, "Il millenarismo d'Ireneo," *Revista storico delle scienze teologiche* 2 (1906): 903–18; Wingren 181–213. V. Cremers, "Het millenarisme van Irenaeus," *Bijdragen* 1 (1938): 28–80, attempted to prove by intrinsic reasons, such as the scriptural citations and theological concepts, that the Bishop did not write these millenaristic paragraphs. As Houssiau (130n2) remarks, the literary complexity of A.H. takes the force out of Cremers's reasoning. M. O'Rourke Boyle, "Irenaeus's Millennial Hope. A Polemical Weapon," *Recherches de théologie ancienne et médiévale* 36 (1969): 5–16, admits the genuineness of these sections but tones down the imputability of Irenaeus on the score that he had the good motive of defending the unity and goodness of God in salvation history and of all things created, matter included. Irenaeus had the good intention of refuting his opponents' theory that man should have been perfected immediately and completely in the beginning and unconditionally. In God's plan man is perfected gradually. However, because of this polemic purpose,

Irenaeus interpreted some of the metaphorical passages of Scripture too literally; besides, he did not sift the matter from tradition carefully on this point; further, he pushed his principle of gradually achieving perfection beyond due limits. All this made him fall into the error of millenarianism. He held that at the end of time the just will rise and enjoy themselves with Christ for one thousand years in an earthly kingdom. In consequence, he taught that the souls of the just will not enjoy beatitude in heaven till after the last judgment: see A.H. 2.28.3; 4.37.7; 5.31.1; 32.1; 5.10.1; 20.2. He did, however, make an exception for the martyrs (4.23.9; 31.3), among whom are the Holy Innocents (3.66.4). See also Vernet, "Irénée," DTC 7, no. 2 (1927): 24–99. Irenaeus's teaching on this did not involve any of the crass and even immoral practices propounded in some systems. See also *Proof* 61, where he appeals to the presbyters' authority for the peaceful era at the second coming of Christ. But here he definitely allows that this is already true in the Church, through the conversion of the barbarian peoples. The same is true in A.H. 5.35. Hence, he seems to have held the metaphorical interpretation of these passages for the Christian era on earth, but still held that these passages would be verified literally after the resurrection in a millenarian age. See another interpretation by Smith, *Proof*, Note 207.

4. Gen 13:14–15.
5. Gen 13:17.
6. Acts 7:5; Heb 11:13.
7. Gen 23:11ff.
8. Gen 15:18.
9. The last line is from Arm. Iren.; cf. Gen 15:19–21. It is missing in Lat. Iren. but seems genuine. See SC, n.1 to p. 401.
10. "Relative to him," that is, Abraham, as Arm. Iren. reads it; and correctly, since Christians are spiritual descendants of Abraham. The context and the quotation from Matt 3:9 make it clear that the reference is to Abraham. Some Latin scribe thought the adoption should refer to God, and so Lat. Iren. has *deum* in place of *eum*. The Church is called the offspring of Christ by adoption. She forms one whole with him.
11. Luke 3:8; Matt 3:9.
12. Gal 4:28.
13. Gal 3:16. The offspring is here interpreted to be the historical Christ, not the Mystical Christ, the whole Church.
14. Gal 5:6–9.
15. "In all things" is missing from Lat. Iren., but it is in Arm. Iren. SC (405n1) refers to A.H. 5.32.1 and 33.4, as similar cases, but there it is a question of how rich God is, and it is natural to add "in all things." Here it is a question of being true and reliable. So from the similarity one cannot argue very much.
16. Matt 5:5.

Chapter 33

1. Matt. 26:27–29. The reading of this quotation as given by Irenaeus is not certain in all parts. Lat. Iren. and Arm. Iren. do not agree. Lat. Iren. has

"new" with Testament, as in some codices of the NT, but Arm. Iren. omits it, as in the accepted text of the NT. Lat. Iren. has "this" modify vine, as in some codices of the NT, but Arm. Iren. has it modify "fruit," as in most codices of the NT. Maybe Lat. Iren. represents the Greek as Irenaeus had written it, while Arm. Iren. touched up the text to make it harmonize with the Bible.

2. Ps 103 (104): 30.

3. A too literal interpretation, together with his utter trust in the tradition of the presbyters, led Irenaeus astray into an intermediate realm of the millennium.

4. Luke 14:12–14.

5. A conflation of Matt 19:29 and Luke 18:29.

6. Cf. Gen. 2:2–3. The Bishop has here and in A.H. 5.36.3 (n14) a special view of the seventh day of the week, which is the symbol of the rest in the millennium before that of eternal life. The six days before symbolize the world history of six thousand years prior to the millennium. See J. Daniélou, "La typologie millenariste de la semaine dans le christianisme primitif," *VC* 2 (1948): 1–16, who thinks this opinion, which became the Western tradition till Augustine broke with it, started in Pharisaic apocalypses from which it came to the presbyters, from whom Papias picked it up. Because of his authority Irenaeus sponsored it too, and after him Hippolytus and Tertullian. The Eastern tradition was that the seven days were the symbol of the world's history, but the eighth day was the day of eternal rest.

7. "Wearisome" is adjusted according to "laborious" in Arm. Iren. Lat. Iren. has *terrenum* (earthly), which does not fit the picture.

8. Gen 27:27.

9. Matt 13:38.

10. Gen 27:28–29.

11. Gen 31:41.

12. Gen 32:33.

13. Gen 46–47; Exod 1ff.

14. This clause is according to Arm. Iren., and it seems quite genuine, though it is missing in Lat. Iren.

15. Here is a case where Irenaeus did not sift carefully the tradition of the presbyters from the truly apostolic tradition. This presbyter was most likely Papias, who is mentioned in the next paragraph.

16. Papias's work was known as *The Interpretation of the Lord's Words.* See Eusebius, *Hist. eccl.* 3.39 (GCS 2.1.284). This is a precious testimony about the relation of the earliest fathers with the apostle John and Irenaeus's relation to them.

17. Isa 11:6–9.

18. Isa 65:25.

19. Rom 10:12.

Chapter 34

1. Isa 26:19. I did not follow RSV here because it differed too much.

2. Ezek 37:12–14; the second quotation in Ezek 28:25–26.

3. The Latin text is here not extant in the Clermont or Arundel MSS.

What we have reads thus: *Et propter hoc, ut sciamus, quoniam in novo testamento ac veteri <unus sit Deus>, qui ex omnibus gentibus colliget eos, qui salvabuntur, ex lapidibus suscitans filios Abrahae, Jeremias ait.* I inserted in angular brackets what I think fell out of the text. The Latin MSS have *a veteri or ac veteri* (Voss). The first makes no sense, whatever one might think of supplying. The second does make sense. Arm. Iren. does not have this at all. Now let us work backward. *Suscitans* has as subject God, not the Church of the preceding sentence. That is certain. But the subject of *colliget,* on which *suscitans* depends, must be the same God. That justifies the relative *qui* of the Latin and disqualifies *quae* of Arm. Iren. Arm. Iren., having omitted *ac veteri,* tried to patch the matter, very poorly, by inserting *haec erunt quae.* Since God is nowhere in sight here, but is needed as subject, that word must have fallen out. If we insert it, as I did, we have the simple oft-repeated teaching of Irenaeus that there is one God in the New and the Old Testament.

4. Jer 23:7–8; 16:14–15. LXX, but not the last phrase. Lat. Iren had dropped a line, restored here in angular brackets from Arm. Iren., a simple scribal error of skipping from one word to its similar lower down.

5. Irenaeus distinguishes here between salvation from Egypt and salvation from Babylon. Orbe 3:453.

6. Isa 30:25–26.

7. Gen 9:27. This is missing in Lat. Iren. It was restored from Arm. Iren. See SC (427n1).

8. Isa 58:1. "upon the whole earth" follows Lat. Iren. That gets closer to the Hebrew and Vulgate: *sustollam te super altitudines terrae.* Arm. Iren. has "I will lead you to the goods of the earth," which agrees with LXX. Since Irenaeus did not use the Hebrew Bible but LXX, it is difficult to decide which is the original in Irenaeus. The fact that Arm. Iren. agrees with LXX is not enough reason to say that is what Irenaeus had written. Yet SC (427n4) favors the Armenian.

9. Luke 12:37–38.

10. Rev 20:6.

11. Isa 6:11–12. LXX.

12. Dan 7:27. "Of the kings" is restored from Theodotion's version, as SC (429n2) suggests. Lat. Iren. has in its place *eorum quae* (the things that); Arm. Iren. is no help with its *eorum qui sub regibus caeli,* which is a kind of conflation.

13. Dan 12:13.

14. "The height" is according to Lat. Iren. I retained that because it seems clear that Irenaeus wishes to contrast this with the "Profundity of error"; and so I think "of Truth" was at least implied if it actually did not fall out. Certainly, I see no reason for translating this with "truth" alone, as did SC (431n1). The contrast would not be obvious or complete.

15. Jer 31 (38):10–14. "On the islands" is an attempt to interpret. Arm. Iren. has a larger lacuna here. Lat. Iren. has the dative *insulis.* Maybe the translator read νήσους (as in LXX) with εἰς in the meaning of ἔν, as it often does and translated *in insulis,* but the *in* fell out; or he read εἰς (LXX) indicating to whom the announcement was to be made and translated it with the dative. See SC (341n1).

16. See A.H. 4.8.3. Cf. Matt 13:5, which he uses almost verbatim. Lat. Iren. has *profanabant* (past tense). NT has present tense. SC (433n2) thinks it should be present in Irenaeus. I see no reason why he could not have put the verb in the past, since he was not quoting and was referring to a past event.

17. Isa 31:9ff.; Isa 32:1.

18. Isa 54:11–13 LXX.

19. Isa 65:18–23 LXX. Arm. Iren., which differs from Lat. Iren., seems better in some points. "My people" in place of "of the people in you" of Lat. Iren.; "make use of" in place of Lat. Iren. "shall grow old." But "They shall drink wine" (omitted in Arm. Iren.) is retained as in Lat. Iren.

Chapter 35

1. Isa 6:11.
2. Isa 13:9.
3. Isa 26:10 LXX.
4. Isa 6:12.
5. Isa 65:21.
6. This is really from Bar 4:36–5:9, which was thought to be part of the Book of Jeremiah.
7. Bar 5:3.
8. Isa 49:16 LXX.
9. Gal 4:26.
10. Rev 20:11.
11. Rev 20:12–14.
12. Matt 25:41.
13. Rev 20:15.
14. Rev 21:1–4.
15. Isa 65:17–18.
16. 1 Cor 7:31.
17. Matt 26:35.
18. Cf. Exod 25:40.
19. Rev 21:56 [*sic.* Probably Rev 21:5 intended].

Chapter 36

1. Cf. A.H. 5.5.1. Rev 19:11–16. Orbe 3:556.
2. 1 Cor 7:21.
3. Isa 66:22.
4. Cf. Matt 13:8; Mark 4:8.
5. John 14:2.
6. It is hard to determine the passage to which Irenaeus refers. Grabe thinks it is from the tradition of the presbyters. Massuet holds that he is referring to the parable of the talents. Feuardentius, incorrectly, states the reference is to Matt 20:23. That Irenaeus is referring to one of the parables about an invitation seems indicated by some references here to those parables. But since immediately in the next sentence he definitely alludes to the parable of

the royal banquet (Matt 22:1ff.), and since there is talk in it of those invited who were "not worthy," I believe the reference is to this parable.

7. Matt 22:2.

8. "Method" is *dispositio,* which here most likely translates ῥυθμός, namely, a harmonious plan.

9. 1 Cor 15:25–26.

10. 1 Cor 15:27–28.

11. Cf. Matt 26:29.

12. Lat. Iren. omitted a whole paragraph, which was restored from Arm. Iren., because it seems genuine. It runs from here to the end of the paragraph.

13. John 5:25, 28, 27, 29.

14. Gen 1:31; 2.1.

15. On the equation of a thousand years and a day see above A.H. 5.23.2; 28.3.

16. Pss 131 (132):14; 117 (118):20.

17. Rom 8:19–21.

18. 1 Cor 2:9, from Isa 64:4.

19. 1 Pet 1:12. God's will to glorify humanity completely by union with himself through the Incarnate Word is the reason for the incarnation. This mystery is the admiration of the angels themselves.

20. Gen 1:26. This last passage is a fitting ending to the work of the great Bishop of Lyons: The Son of God Incarnate is the Mediator for the glorification of humanity, and so for the supreme glory of God. The *Doctor Catholicus* could not have ended on a more optimistic note, against the pessimistic tenet of his opponents, which excludes the whole man from salvation that is imperishability also for the body. Man was made to the image and likeness of God, in glory with the God-Man. Here the key passage from Scripture (Gen 1:26) in Irenaean anthropology reaches its climatic fulfillment. See the fine summation in Wingren (xiv).

BIBLIOGRAPHY

Aland, Barbara. “Fides und Subiectio: zur Anthropologie des Irenäus.” In *Kerygma und Logos*, 9–28. Göttingen: Vandenhoeck & Ruprecht, 1979.

Aldama, A. J. de. *Maria en la patrística siglos I y II.* Madrid, 1970.

———. “Polypousios dans le Protoévangile de Jacques et l’A.H. de s. Irénée.” *RSR* 50 (1962): 86–89.

Ales, A d’. “La Doctrine de l’Esprit en Saint Irénée.” *RSR* 14 (1924): 497–538.

Alfonsi, B. “Su un passo di Ireneo (Adv. Haer. 4.13.4).” *VC* 12 (1958): 225–26.

Andia, Ysabel de. *Homo Vivens : Incorruptibilité et divinisation de l’homme selon Irénée de Lyons.* Paris: Études augustiniennes, 1986.

Bacq, Philippe. *De l’ancienne à la nouvelle alliance selon S. Irénée : Unité du Livre IV de l’Adversus Haereses.* Paris: Lethielleux, 1978.

Bainvel, J. “Âme.” In *DTC*, 984. 1, 1930.

Bardy, G. “Millénarisme.” In *DTC*, 2:1760–63. 6, 1929.

Behr, John. *Irenaeus of Lyons: Identifying Christianity.* Oxford: Oxford University Press, 2013.

Bengsch, A. *Heilsgeschichte und Heilswissen. Eine Untersuchung zur Struktur und Entfaltung des theologischen Denkens im Werk Adversus Haereses des hl. Irenaeus von Lyon.* Leipzig: St. Benno-Verlag, 1957.

Benoît, André. “Irénée Adv. Haereses IV, 1–5 et les Testimonia.” *Studia patristica* 4 (1961): 20–27.

———. *Saint Irénée; Introduction à l’étude de sa théologie.* Paris: Presses universitaires de France, 1960.

Bentivegna, J. “Pauline Elements in the Anthropology of St. Irenaeus.” *Studia evangelica* 5 (1968): 229–33.

Berrouard, M.-F. “Servitude de la loi et liberté de l’evangile selon Saint Irénée.” *Lumière et vie* 61 (1963): 41–60.

Bousset, Wilhelm. *Jüdisch-Christlicher Schulbetrieb in Alexandria und Rom: Literarische Untersuchungen zu Philo und Clemens von Alexandria,*

Justin und Irenäus. Göttingen: Vandenhoeck & Ruprecht, 1915.

———. *Kyrios Christos: A History of the Belief in Christ from the Beginnings of Christianity to Irenaeus.* Nashville: Abingdon Press, 1970.

Boyle, M. O'Rourke. "Irenaeus' Millennial Hope: A Polemical Weapon." *R.T.A.M.* 36 (1969): 5–16.

Brakke, David. *The Gnostics: Myth, Ritual, and Diversity in Early Christianity.* Cambridge, MA: Harvard University Press, 2010.

Briggman, Anthony. *Irenaeus of Lyons and the Theology of the Holy Spirit.* Oxford; New York: Oxford University Press, 2012.

Brown, Raymond Edward, Joseph A. Fitzmyer, and Roland E. Murphy. *The New Jerome Bible Handbook.* Collegeville, MN: Liturgical Press, 1993.

Brox, Norbert. "Irenaeus and the Bible." In *Handbook of Patristic Exegesis: The Bible in Ancient Christianity,* edited by Charles Kannengiesser, 483–506. Boston: Brill, 2004.

Buonaiuti, E. "Il millenarismo d'Ireneo." *Revista storico delle scienze teologiche* 2 (1906): 903–18.

Charles, R. H. (Robert Henry). *The Book of Enoch, Translated from Professor Dillmann's Ethiopic Text; Emended and Revised in Accordance with Hitherto Uncollated Ethiopic Mss. and with the Gizeh and Other Greek and Latin Fragments Which Are Here Published in Full; Edited with Introduction, Notes, Appendices, and Indices.* Oxford: Clarendon Press, 1893.

Cremers, V. "Het millenarisme van Irenaeus." *Bijdragen* 1 (1938): 28–80.

Daniélou, Jean. "La typologie millenariste de la semaine dans le Christianisme primitif." *VC* 2 (1948).

———. "Rahab, figure de l'Eglise." *Irenikon* 22 (1940): 26–45.

Donovan, Mary Ann. "Irenaeus: At the Heart of Life, Glory." In *Spiritualities of the Heart,* 11–22. Mahwah, NJ: Paulist Press, 1990.

———. *One Right Reading? A Guide to Irenaeus.* Collegeville, MN: Liturgical Press, 1997.

Doutreleau, Louis. "À Propos d'Irénée, Adversus Haereses, Livre IV." *Recherches de science religieuse* 53, no. 4 (O-D 1965): 589–99.

Ebneter, Albert. "Die 'Glaubensregel' des Irenaeus als oekumenisches Regulativ." In *Unterwegs zur Einheit,* 588–608. Freiburg, Schweiz: Universitätsverlag, 1980.

Elfers, H. *Die Kirchenordnung Hippolyts von Rom.* Paderborn, 1938.

Fantino, Jacques. *La Théologie d'Irénée: Lecture des écritures en réponse à l'exégèse gnostique : Une approche trinitaire.* Paris: Cerf, 1994.

———. *L'homme, image de Dieu, chez Saint Irénée de Lyon.* Paris: Cerf, 1986.

Farmer, William Reuben. "Galatians and the 2nd Century Development of the Regula Fidei." *Second Century: A Journal of Early Christian Studies* 4, no. 3 (1985): 143–70.

Ford, John T. "St. Irenaeus and Revelation: A Theological Perspective." Rome: Pontifical Gregorian University, 1962.

González Faus, J. I. *Carne di Dios. Significado salvador de la Encarnación en la teología de san Ireneo.* Barcelona: Herder, 1969.

Grant, Robert M. *Irenaeus of Lyons.* New York: Routledge, 1997.

Harnack, Adolf von. *Der Presbyter-Prediger des Irenäus: IV, 27,1–32,1; Bruchstücke und Nachklänge der ältesten exegetisch-polemischen Homilieen.* Berlin: Trowitzsch, 1907.

———. *History of Dogma.* New York: Russell & Russell, 1958.

Hefner, Philip J. "Saint Irenaeus and the Hypothesis of Faith." *Dialog* 2, no. 4 (1963): 300–306.

Hemmerdinger, Bertrand. "Observations critiques sur Irénée, IV (Sources Chrétiennes 100) ou Les mésaventures d'un philologue." *JTS* 17 (n.d.): 308–26.

Hill, Charles E. *From the Lost Teaching of Polycarp: Identifying Irenaeus' Apostolic Presbyter and the Author of Ad Diognetum.* Wissenschaftliche Untersuchungen zum Neuen Testament. Tübingen: Mohr Siebeck, 2006.

Hitchcock, F. R. Montgomery. "The Doctrine of the Holy Communion in Irenaeus." *Church Quarterly Review* 129 (40 1939): 206–25.

Irenaeus. *Contre les hérésies.* Ed. critique d'après les versions arménienne et latine. Sources chrétiennes, no 100, 152–53, 210–11, 263–64, 293–94. Paris: Cerf, 1969.

———. *Proof of the Apostolic Preaching.* Translated by J. P. Smith. Ancient Christian Writers 16. Westminster, MD: Newman Press, 1952.

Irenaeus, and W. Wigan (William Wigan) Harvey. *Sancti Irenaei Episcopi Lugdunensis libros quinque Adversus Haereses.* Adversus Haereses. London: [Gregg Press], 1965.

Irenaeus, and René Massuet. *Tou en hagiois Patros hēmōn Eirēnaiou Episkopou Lougdounou kai Martyros Elenchou kai Anatropēs tēs Pseudōnymou Gnōseōs Biblia Pente = Sancti Irenaei Episcopi Lugdunensis et Martyris Detectionis et Eversionis Falso Cognominatae Agnitionis Seu Contra Haereses Libri Quinque: Post Francisci

Feuardentii et Joannis Ernesti Grabii Recensionem Castigati Denuo Ad Mss. Cod. Romanos, Gallicanos et Anglicanos, Necnon Ad Antiquores Editiones, et a Multis, Quibus Scatebant, Mendis Expurgati : Aucti Novis Fragmentis : Observationibus Ac Notis Copiosissimisque Glossariis et Indicibus Illustrati et Locupletati : Quibus Omnibus Praemittuntur Tres Dissertationes in Quibus Haereses Ab Irenaeo Memoratae et Loci Difficiles Explicantur, Ejusque Vitae Ac Ges.Orum [Sic!] Historia Discuitur. Réimpr. Patrologiae Graecae ; T. 7 et 7bis. Turnhout: Brepols, 1966.

Irenaeus, Dominic J. Unger, and Irenaeus M. C Steenberg. *Against the Heresies.* Ancient Christian Writers 65. Mahwah, NJ: Paulist Press, 2012.

Jenott, Lance. "The Gnostics: Myth, Ritual, and Diversity in Early Christianity." *Catholic Biblical Quarterly* 74, no. 3 (2012): 589–91.

Jong, J. P. de. "Der ursprüngliche Sinn von Epiklese und Mischungsritus nach der Eucharistielehre des Hl. Irenäus." *Archiv für Liturgiewissenschaft* 9 (1965): 28–47.

———. "Epiklese." *LTK* 3, no. 1959 (n.d.): 935–37.

Joppich, Godehard. *Salus Carnis: Eine Untersuchung in der Theologie des hl. Irenäus von Lyon.* Münsterschwarzach: Vier-Türme-Verlag, 1965.

Jossa, Giorgio. *Regno di Dio e Chiesa: Ricerche sulla concezione escatologica ed ecclesiologica dell'Adversus Haereses di Ireneo di Lione.* Historia Salutis. Serie Storica 002. Naples: D'Auria, 1970.

Jossua, J. P. *Le Salut. Incarnation ou Mystére Pascal chez les Péres de l'Eglise, de S. Irénée á S. Leon le Grand.* Paris: Cerf, 1968.

Jourjon, Maurice. "Aux Origínes de la prière d'intercession de Marie." *Bulletin de Société Française des Etudes Mariales* 23 (1966): 38–42.

Jugie, M. "La forme du sacrament de l'Eucharistie d'aprés Saint Irénée." *Mémoriale Chaine (Bibliothéque de la Faculté Catholique de Théologie de Lyon)* 5 (1950): 22–33.

King, Karen L. *What Is Gnosticism?* Cambridge, MA: Belknap Press of Harvard University Press, 2003.

Lanne, Emmanuel. "La Vision de Dieu dans l'oeuvre de Saint Irénée." *Irénikon* 33, no. 1 (1960): 311–20.

———. "La Xeniteia d'Abraham dans l'oeuvre d'Irénée : Aux origines du thìme monastique de la 'Peregrinatio.'" *Irénikon* 47, no. 2 (1974): 163–87.

Luckhardt, R. "Matthew 11:27 in the Contra Haereses of St. Irenaeus." *Revue d'Université d'Ottawa* 23 (1953): 65–79.

Maria et Ecclesia. Acta Congressus Mariologici-Mariani in Civitate Lourdes Anno 1958 Celebrati. Rome: 1959, n.d.

Moringiello, Scott D. "Allegory and Typology in Irenaeus of Lyon," *Studia Patristica* 93 (Leuven: Peeters, 2017): 255–64.

———. "The Pneumatikos as Scriptural Interpreter: Irenaeus on 1 Cor 2:15," *Studia Patristica* 65 (Leuven: Peeters, 2013): 105–18.

———. *The Rhetoric of Faith: Irenaeus and the Structure of the Adversus Haereses.* Washington, DC: Catholic University of America Press, 2019.

———. "Sacrifice, Eucharist, and Love in Ignatius of Antioch." *Studia Patristica* 109 (Leuven:Petters, 2021), 109–118.

Müller, A. *Ecclesia-Maria. Die Einheit Marias und der Kirche.* 2nd ed. Vol. 5. Paradosis. Freiburg: Universitätsverlag Freiburg Schweiz, 1955.

Newman, B. "The Fallacy of the Domitian Hypothesis. Critique of the Irenaeus Source as a Witness for the Contemporary Historical Approach to the Interpretation of the Apocalypse." *New Testament Studies* 10 (March 1962): 133–39.

Ochagavía, Juan. *Visibile Patris Filius: A Study of Irenaeus' Teaching on Revelation and Tradition.* Rome: Pont. Institutum Orientalium Studiorum, 1964.

Orbe, Antonio. *Antropología de San Irenaeo.* Madrid: Biblioteca de Autores Cristianos, 1969.

———. "Ecclesia, Sal Terrae según San Ireneo." *Recherches de science religieuse* 60, no. 2 (Ap–Je 1972): 219–40.

———. "El Hombre ideal en la teología de S Ireneo." *Gregorianum* 43, no. 3 (1962): 449–91.

———. "Ipse tuum calcabit caput (S. Ireneo y Gen. 3.15)." *Gregorianum* 52 (1971): 95–149; 215–69.

———. "La Definicíon del hombre en la teología del siglo II." *Gregorianum* 48 (1967): 522–56.

———. *Teología de San Ireneo, V 1: Comentario al libro 5 del Adversus Haereses.* Biblioteca de Autores Cristianos. Madrid: Editorial Católica, 1985.

———. *Teología de San Ireneo, V 2: Comentario al libro 5 del Adversus Haereses.* Madrid: Editorial Católica S A, 1987.

———. *Teología de San Ireneo, V 3: Comentario al libro 5 del Adversus Haereses.* Madrid: Editorial Católica, 1988.

Osborn, Eric Francis. *Irenaeus of Lyons.* Cambridge: Cambridge University Press, ca. 2001.

Overbeck, Winfried. *Menschwerdung: Eine Untersuchung zur literarischen und theologischen Einheit des fünften Buches "Adversus Haereses" des Irenäus von Lyon.* New York: P. Lang, 1995.

Parsons, W. "Lest Men, like Fish." *Tradition* 3 (1945): 380–88.

Radopoulos, P. "Irenaeus on the Consecration of the Eucharistic Gifts." In *Kyriakon: Festschrift Johannes Quasten,* edited by Patrick Granfield and Josef Jungman. Münster: Aschendorff, 1970.

Regnault, Laurence. "St. Irénée de Lyon." *Dictionnaire de la spiritualité* 7, no. 2 (1971): 1938–69.

Ricciotti, Giuseppe. *Life of Christ.* Catholic Home Library ed. The Catholic Home Library, 1. Nashville: Catholic Publishers, 1967.

Robinson, J. T. "On a Quotation of Justin Martyr in Irenaeus." *JTS* 21 (1930): 374–78.

Scharl, Emmeran. "Der Rekapitulationsbegriff des Heiligen Irenäus." *Orientalia Christiana Periodica* 6, nos. 3–4 (1940): 376–416.

Scheiwiler, A. "Die Elemente der Eucharistie in der ersten drei Jahrhunderten." In *Die Elemente der Eucharistie in der ersten drei Jahrhunderten,* 17–26, 43–56. Mainz, 1903.

Schermann, Th. "Eucharistia und Eucharistein in ihrem Bedeutungswandel bis 200 nach Christus." *Philologus* 69 (1910): 375–410.

Scherrer, Thierry. *La Gloire de Dieu dans l'oeuvre de Saint Irénée.* Tesi gregoriana. Rome: Pontifical Gregorian University, 1997.

Siniscalco, Paolo. "Apokatastasis e apokathistemi nella tradizione della grande chiesa fino ad Ireneo." *Studia Patristica* 3 (1961): 380–96.

Steiner, M. *La Tentation de Jésus dans l'interprétation patristique de Saint Justin á Origéne.* Paris: Etudes Bibliques, 1962.

Unger, Dominic J. "Christ's Role in the Universe according to St. Irenaeus." *FS* 5 (1945): 3–20; 114–37.

———. "The Divine and Eternal Sonship of the Word According to St Irenaeus of Lyon." *Laurentianum* 14 (1973): 357–408.

———. "Sancti Irenaei, Lugdunensis Episcopi, doctrina de Maria Virgine Matre, socia Iesu Christi Filii sui ad opus recapitulationis." *ME* 4 (1959): 67–140.

Unnik, Willem Cornelis van. "Der Ausdruck 'in den letzten Zeiten' bei Irenaeus." In *Neotestamentica et patristica,* 293–304. Leiden: Brill, 1962.

Vernet, François. "Irénée (Saint)." In *Dictionaire de theologie catholique,* 2:2476–78. 7. Paris: Letouzey, 1927.

Williams, Michael A. *Rethinking "Gnosticism": An Argument for Dismantling a Dubious Category.* Princeton: Princeton University Press, 1996.

Wingren, Gustaf. *Man and the Incarnation: A Study in the Biblical Theology of Irenaeus.* Philadelphia: Muhlenberg Press, 1959.

Ziegler, A. W. "Das Brot von unseren Feldern: Ein Beitrag zur Eucharistielehre des Hl. Irenäus." In *Pro Mundi Vita, Festschrift zum Eucharistischen Weltkongress,* 21–43. Munich: Max Hueber Verlag, 1960.

SCRIPTURE INDEX

SUBJECT INDEX